WRITING: PROCESS AND STRUCTURE

WRITING: PROCESS AND STRUCTURE

• JIM PINNELLS •

University of Maryland
European Division

Harper & Row, Publishers
London

Cambridge
Mexico City
New York
Philadelphia

San Francisco
São Paulo
Singapore
Sydney

Series Editor: Dr Martha S. Shull, University of Maryland,
          European Division.

Designer: Geri Davis, Quadrata Inc.

Project Editor: Byron O. Bush.

First published 1988

Harper & Row Ltd
Middlesex House
34–42 Cleveland Street
LONDON
W1P 5FB

Library of Congress Cataloging-in-Publication Data
Pinnells, James, 1939–
    Writing: process and structure.
    (The University of Maryland series on good English
writing)
    1. English language—Rhetoric.   I. Title   II. Series.
PE1408.P5357   1988   808'.042   87–35154
ISBN 0-06-317500-2

British Library Cataloguing in Publication Data
Pinnells, Jim
    Writing process and structure.
    1. English language—Composition and
    exercises
    I. Title
    808'.042   PE1413

    ISBN 0-06-317500-2

Typeset by Rowland Phototypesetting Limited, Bury St Edmunds, Suffolk.
Printed and bound by Richard Clay Limited, Chichester.

Thanks

Writing is never a simple activity. From its conception, this textbook has been an elaborate team project involving a startling number of people—so many that most of their names are unknown to me. A book such as this is written in many drafts. At each stage it is closely read by the publisher's staff, by professional readers and by colleagues. The final manuscript is copyedited, the book is designed, printed and bound. Dozens of people have done their best to ensure that the book you are now reading is as good as it can be. My thanks to all of them.

To a number of people I owe special thanks. Joan Breen shared with me her years of experience in helping students with library research; Louis Mazzotta gave my remarks on statistics a hard read and suggested numerous improvements; Tobe Levin, who has pioneered the "mainstreaming" of Women's Studies, read the book critically from that perspective and alerted me to a number of opportunities I would otherwise have missed. The book has been illustrated by Brian Minney; his creative understanding helped me turn several awkward corners. Two colleagues and one student, Karen Olsen, Aimée Doyle and Leslie Stoller-Reeds, offered many tactfully worded but nevertheless incisive comments on ideas that weren't working; in most cases, they were right. Field-testing and development involved a number of people: Johnnie Aldrich, Denise Cali, Steven Kaplan, Lillian Klein, Maria Newkirk, Patrick Quinn and Richard Shumaker —my thanks to them for their time and trouble.

In addition to such direct help, I have needed, and received, a great deal of more general support. Martha Shull, editor of the University of Maryland English textbook series, has given me unfailing encouragement, administrative backup, and that rarest of commodities, her time. Without her, this book would not have appeared. Developmental editor for the project has been Byron Bush; his mix of kindliness, shrewdness and publishing know-how has influenced every page, and probably every word, of the text. My family, too, has contributed—only they know how much. And finally, my students: what little I know about writing, I learned from them. I hope they learned something from me.

In gathering examples of writing, I have tapped many sources, some by professional writers, some by students. The students: Phil Alire, Susan Anderson, Anke Bridges, Pat Cunliffe, Robert Di Michiel, Will Hampshire, Mitzi Horner, Maria Jiminez, Dena Knauer, Guy Mitchell, Chester Mowery, Brand Nicholas, Jeanne Stepanova, Chuck Taylor, Ron Tolley, Abel Townshend, Alan Whinery, John Williams, John Wilson and Eunice Valentine.

Jim Pinnells

Acknowledgments and Sources

pp. 2–3   Schneider, Arnold, John Whitcraft and Robert Rosenberg. *Understanding Business Law*: 4th ed. New York: McGraw Hill, 1967, pp. 94 and 278 (twice).

pp. 3–4   Lorenz, Konrad Z. *King Solomon's Ring*. London: Methuen, 1952, p. 47.

p. 4   Thomson, A. Landsborough. *A New Dictionary of Birds*. New York: McGraw Hill, 1964. (Extract from the entry on *Play*.)

p. 5   Tennyson, *The Princess*. 1847.
           Fleming, Ian. *Goldfinger*. London: Jonathan Cape, 1959, p. 105.

p. 6   Ericksen, S. *Motivation for Learning*. Ann Arbor: University of Michigan Publication, 1974.
           Fraser, Antonia. *Mary Queen of Scots*. New York: Dell, 1971, p. 622.
           Dickens, Charles. *Hard Times*. 1854.
           Kaye, Oski, and Barness. *Core Textbook of Pediatrics*. Philadelphia: Lippincott, 1978, p. 61.
           Hardy, Thomas. *The Hand of Ethelberta*. 1876.

p. 9   Valentine, C. W. *The Normal Child*. Harmondsworth: Penguin, 1956, p. 176.
           Stephens, Harold. *Asian Portraits*. Hong Kong: Travel Publishing, 1983, p. 14.
           Brogan, Denis. From "Professor Celebrates American Public School" in *America in Perspective*. New York: Mentor, 1948, p. 316.

ACKNOWLEDGMENTS AND SOURCES

Argyle, Michael. *The Psychology of Interpersonal Behavior*. Harmondsworth: Penguin, 1967, p. 23.

pp. 11–12   Capote, Truman. *In Cold Blood*. New York: Random House, 1965, pp. 30–31.

p. 14   Baldwin, James. *Go Tell it on the Mountain*. London: Michael Joseph, 1954, pp. 23–24.

p. 15   Trollope, Anthony. *Barchester Towers*. Oxford: Oxford University Press, 1980, p. 29.
Mead, Margaret. *Coming of Age in Samoa*. New York: Morrow, 1928, pp. 8–10.

pp. 16–17   Wolfenstein, Martha. "French Parents Take Their Children to the Park." *Childhood in Contemporary Cultures*. Ed. Margaret Mead and Martha Wolfenstein. Chicago: University Press of Chicago, 1955, pp. 111–12.

pp. 17–18   Packard, Vance. *The Hidden Persuaders*. David McKay, 1957, pp. 18–20.

pp. 22–23   O'Hara, John. *Hope of Heaven*. New York: Harcourt Brace, 1938, pp. 374–376.

p. 35   Gogol, Nicolai. *Dead Souls*. 1842.

p. 39   Heistand, Anita. From "The Kissinger Critique." *Writer's Digest*. December 1986, p. 9.

p. 41   Ellis, Malcolm. *The World of Birds*. New York: Hamlyn, 1971, p. 86.

p. 52   King, Martin Luther, Jr. Excerpt from "Letter from Birmingham Jail, April 16, 1963" from *Why We Can't Wait* by Martin Luther King, Jr. Copyright © 1963 by Martin Luther King, Jr. Reprinted by permission of Harper & Row, Publishers, Inc.

p. 53   Ceram, C. W. *Gods, Graves and Scholars*. Trans. E. B. Garside and S. Wilkins. New York: Knopf, 1967.

pp. 78–79   Collins, William Wilkie. *Basil*. 1852.

pp. 79–80   Freundlich, Naomi, J. "Play TV!" Reprinted from *Popular Science* with permission © 1986 Times Mirror Magazines, Inc. November 1986, pp. 74–75.

pp. 84–85   Leacock, Stephen. "The British and American Press" from *My Discovery of England*. New York: Dodd, Mead, 1922. Reprinted by permission of Dodd, Mead & Company, Inc. Copyright © 1922 by Dodd, Mead & Company, Inc. Copyright renewed 1949 by George Leacock.

p. 111   Cleaver, Eldridge. *Soul on Ice*. New York: McGraw-Hill, 1968.

pp. 131–33   Lee, Laurie. *Cider With Rosie*. Harmondsworth: Penguin, 1959, pp. 78–94. Reprinted by permission of The Hogarth Press.

p. 158   Bierce, Ambrose. *The Collected Writings of Ambrose Bierce*. New York: Citadel, 1946.

pp. 186–88   Syfers, Judy. "Why I Want a Wife." *Ms.* Spring 1972 Preview Issue.

pp. 213–14   Fuller, Margaret. "Americans in Europe" from *At Home and Abroad*. 1847.

p. 227 Shaw, Bernard. *Androcles and the Lion*. Harmondsworth, Penguin, 1975, pp. 80–82. Courtesy of The Society of Authors on behalf of the Bernard Shaw Estate.

p. 232 Tolstoy, Leo. *An Afterword to "The Kreutzer Sonata."* Trans. Jim Pinnells.

p. 233 Zola, Emile. Speech delivered to the *General Association of Students*, 1893. Trans. Jim Pinnells.

p. 234 "Polling the Unhappy Poles," *Time*. November 24, 1980.

p. 236 From the "Donald Regan Interview." *The Economist*. November 22, 1986, p. 39.

pp. 241–43 Heller, Joseph. *Catch 22*. New York: Simon & Schuster, 1961. © 1955, 1961 by Joseph Heller. Reprinted by permission of Simon & Schuster, Inc.

p. 259 Mitchell, Steve. *How to Speak Southern*. New York: Bantam, 1976.

p. 264 Potter, Beatrix. *The Story of a Fierce Bad Rabbit*. London: Warne, © 1906.

p. 265 Hutchinson, Lois. *Standard Handbook for Secretaries*. New York: Wittlesey House, 1939, p. 454.
Burgess, Anthony. *A Clockwork Orange*. Harmondsworth: Penguin, 1972, p. 119.

p. 270–1 Wolfe, Tom. *The Kandy-Kolored Tangerine-Flake Streamline Baby*. New York: Farrar, Straus Giroux/New York Herald Tribune, 1965.

p. 274 Mayle, Peter. *How to be a Pregnant Father*. London: Macmillan, 1980, p. 1.
From "Leeches find their niches." *The Economist*. November 8, 1986, pp. 90–91.

pp. 274–75 Malcolm X. *The Autobiography of Malcolm X*. New York: Grove, 1966, p. 162.

p. 321 Clarfield, Gerard H. *Nuclear America*. New York: Harper & Row, 1984.

p. 329 *Psychological Abstracts*. 1984 No. 25189 and 1985 No. 8894.

p. 354 Vitruvius. *The Ten Books of Architecture*. 1914. New York: Dover, 1960, p. 228.

pp. 355–56 Murphy, Cullen. "The Buster Experiment." *Atlantic*. August 1985, pp. 20–23.

p. 359 From "Prague's Sullen Winter." *Time*. January 10, 1983, pp. 21–22. Reprinted by permission of *Time*.

p. 360 Whiteside, Robert L. *Face Language*. New York: Pocket Book (Simon & Schuster), 1975, pp. 14, 56–7 and 110.

pp. 362–63 Vitruvius. *The Ten Books of Architecture*. 1914. New York: Dover, 1960, p. 227.

p. 363 Landels, J. G. *Engineering in the Ancient World*. Berkeley: University of California Press, 1978, pp. 35–36 passim.

p. 364 From "Faded Triumph." *The Economist*. August 13, 1983, p. 21.

p. 365 From "Letters to the Editor." *Time*. May 12, 1986. Reprinted by permission of *Time*.

ACKNOWLEDGMENTS AND SOURCES

pp. 375–76   Stephens, Alexander. Cited in Bertrand Russell. *Freedom and Organisation 1814–1914*. London: Allen, 1934, pp. 322–23.

p. 376   von Däniken, Erich. *Chariots of the Gods?: Unsolved Mysteries of the Past*. New York: Putnam, 1970.

p. 382   From *Time*. November 11, 1985.
              From *Time*. October 22, 1986.

p. 384   From *Time*. December 6, 1982.

p. 390   From *Time*. September 18, 1978.
              From UPI report. November 8, 1980.

pp. 393–94   Claudia Wallis. "Salt: A New Villain." *Time*. March 15, 1982, pp. 53–57. Reprinted by permission of *Time*.

pp. 396–97   Deutscher, Isaac. *Stalin*. Harmondsworth: Penguin, 1966, p. 371.
              Medvedev, Roy A. *Let History Judge*. Trans. Colleen Taylor. New York: Knopf, 1972, p. 187 and p. 129.
              Conquest, Robert. *The Great Terror*. Harmondsworth: Penguin, 1971, p. 197.

p. 397   Solzhenitsyn, Alexander. *The Gulag Archipelago*. Trans. Thomas Whitney. 3 vols. London: Collins, 1974. Vol. 1, p. 409.
              Deutscher, Isaac. *Stalin*. Harmondsworth: Penguin, 1966, p. 371.

p. 402   Bryan C. B. D. "Say Goodbye to the Kennedys." *Rolling Stone*. December 5, 1986, p. 41.
              Conant, Jennet. "The Star-Crossed Kennedys." *Newsweek*. October 14, 1985, p. 37.
              Summers, Anthony. *Goddess*. New York: Macmillan, 1985, p. 319.

p. 403   Pepitone, Lena. *Marilyn Monroe Confidential*. New York: Simon, 1979, p. 249.
              Steinem, Gloria. *Marilyn*. New York: Holt, 1986, p. 133.
              Hoyt, Edwin. *Marilyn: The Tragic Venus*. New York: Duell, 1965, pp. 15–16.
              "The Misfit." *Saturday Review*. November–December 1985, p. 68.

pp. 414–15   Allen, M. R. *From Judaic-Communism Versus Christian Americanism: A Pro-American Publication*. Salt Lake City, 1945.

pp. 417–18   Schopenhauer, Artur. From *On Women*. 1830.

p. 419   Gauch, Hermann. From *New Principles for the Study of Race*. c. 1935.

p. 421   Asimov, Isaac. Letter in *Writer's Digest*, January 1987. Courtesy of the author.

p. 423   Karvonen, Martti J. "Ergonomics: A Young Technology." *World Health*, July–August 1974, p. 30.

Table of Contents

To The Student

Imagine you have a free evening ahead of you, and you're wondering about the most relaxing way to spend these precious hours. Would writing be one of your choices? Possibly you might write a letter, but even such personal, intimate writing is often more of a chore than a pleasure. Worse still, some people find writing not merely a chore but a source of positive anguish. There are even cases of students dropping a course when they hear that a term paper is required.

And yet writing is an essential part of the practical day-to-day world of a university or college. This kind of bread-and-butter writing is what this book is about. A systematic, step-by-step study should banish any terrors writing holds for you. Further, when you know how to do the job efficiently and quickly, writing will be less of a chore. Although writing may never become one of the great pleasures of your life, the feeling of competence while you work, of a job well done when you've finished, and of pleasure in a good grade received, are no small rewards. Outside the classroom, too, your skill as a writer can affect your chances of landing a job or gaining promotion.

At what point in your studies does writing become important? A glance at a college catalog shows hundreds of courses numbered from 100 to 499; in general, the higher the number, the more demands the course makes on the student intellectually. Benjamin Bloom, a celebrated educational psychologist, has ranked these demands into a pyramid in which each layer depends upon all those below it.

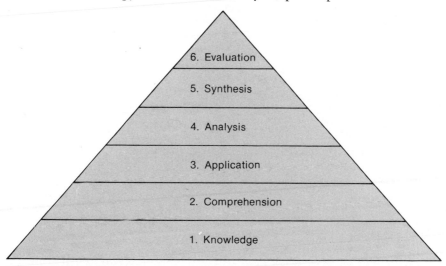

Bloom's Hierarchy of Learning Skills

At the end of any course you take, you'll expect to know something that you didn't know before. This is the bottom level of the pyramid: *knowledge*. To pass the simplest freshman courses, not much more is required than short-term retention of this knowledge. Writing won't help you much in a knowledge-oriented course—a quiz will effectively test your stock of facts. Rote memorization, something most students find tedious and unrewarding, is enough to pass this kind of course.

At the next level, *comprehension*, you have to understand how the facts fit together. For example, in an astronomy class working at Level 1, you might be asked to name in the correct order the planets in the solar system. Working at Level 2, however, you might be asked to explain how the solar system formed. At this higher level, instructors expect an *explanation* from you—in the form of either an examination essay or a term paper. Your grade in this type of course depends on two things: (1) your comprehension of the material (the solar system, or whatever) and (2) your ability to convey this comprehension to your instructor in writing. Both factors are equally important. A student who says, "I understand it, but I can't quite explain it," is merely saying, "I can't function at Level 2. All I'm good for is Level 1—rote memorization."

Higher levels make tougher demands, and writing becomes ever more important. Level 3, *application*, asks you to take what has been explained in one context and to apply it in another. *Analysis*, Level 4, requires you to draw valid conclusions from given facts; you are told where to start thinking, and the rest is up to you.

And so it continues. Level 5, *synthesis*, requires you to develop a theory and to validate it. The final level, *evaluation*, involves weighing theories and arguments and deciding which make the most sense.

As you can see, in all but the most basic courses the ability to write is crucial. Think of it like this: your instructor cannot know if you've mastered the course material unless you can express your ideas *in writing*.

To sum up with a practical example. Two students study hard and succeed in mastering the course material; one can write, the other cannot. The student who can write will make an A while the student who cannot will make a C at best. In down-to-earth terms, that's what this book is all about: the writing skills you need to make a success of your courses.

What are these skills? In this book, our concern is with straightforward *expository writing*. By studying it, you won't become a supersalesman or a thousand-dollar-a-page essayist, but you'll be able to write papers that "make the grade".

What is expository writing? It is simply writing that conveys your ideas with the minimum of fuss, in the minimum number of words, but with the maximum of impact. Such writing is seldom inspiring or witty or clever: it uses practical language for a practical goal—the clearest possible communication between student and instructor.

A good expository style is within the reach of most serious students. Such a style is simple; its sole aim is to establish clear relationships among ideas. Second, the expository style always lets the reader know where the paper is headed. Finally, the expository style is never a mere listing of facts; it always has something to *say*.

To write in this way is not a gift; it is a skill. Compare it with driving. Not everyone could drive a 200-mile-an-hour Indy-car. That kind of driving takes superfast reflexes and iron concentration; such things are gifts. On the other hand, nearly everyone can learn to drive at normal speeds on normal roads; this kind of driving is a skill—it can be learned. The same is true of the practical skill of expository writing.

Sumi-brush painting   Courtesy of the Japan Society, Inc. of New York

Think for a moment about skills. There's a story about a Japanese sumi-brush artist. He was an old man who sat in the window of his little studio effortlessly producing one masterpiece after another. A tourist watched him and asked the price of a picture. "A hundred dollars," replied the artist. The tourist was shocked: "A hundred dollars! But how long did it take you to paint that? Sixty seconds at most!" The artist nodded in agreement. "Sixty seconds yes . . . and sixty years," he said.

Skill is the habit of years. It is built by countless experiments, many only partly successful and many absolute failures. "It would have been better if . . . ," you think. "Perhaps I could have . . . ." In this way choices are mapped out, and slowly patterns of choice begin to crystallize. In fact, skill is probably choice that has become almost automatic. You won't reach the automatic phase during a single term, but as you progress through these assignments, you'll realize that straight-forward expository writing, the writing on which your success as a student depends, is a skill that you too can master.

Jim Pinnells
Heidenfahrt, 1988

Basic Materials— Basic Skills

Introduction

1 •

**The Problem:
What Do Writers *Use*?**

A carpenter gathering the materials to make a chair must select the right wood and then find whatever is needed to hold the pieces together—glue maybe, screws or nails. A dressmaker starting work on a blouse needs cloth and something to hold the cut-out pieces of cloth together—thread, buttons and so on. A writer embarking on a paper needs . . . ? The answer to this question is less obvious. What *are* the construction materials a writer uses?

Imagine picking up a book entitled *Understanding Business Law*—not an inviting subject at first glance. As you are thumbing through the book, however, some problems set off in boxes catch your eye:

> *Dick Abel needed money. It was three days until payday, and he had an important date. He offered to pay his friend Sam Mackey $1 in cash if Sam would lend him $10 until payday. Was there anything illegal in this transaction?*

> *When Ned Porter borrowed his neighbor's lawn mower, he was told that the handle was weak and that he should be careful. Ned was in a hurry, and pushed the mower too fast. The blades stuck; and, because Ned was pushing hard, the handle snapped. Ned says he is not liable because he was using ordinary care. Is he correct?*

These little puzzles are immediately interesting—they are real examples of things that could happen to anyone. When you scan the book for the answers, however, you find a string of legal abstractions that (at first glance) looks decidedly boring.

> *Gratuitous bailments* are those in which either the bailor lends the goods to the bailee for his use without charge; or the reverse, those in which the bailee takes possession of the goods for the bailor and keeps them safely without charge. When the bailor lends the goods without charge, the bailment is for the *sole benefit of the bailee*. When the bailee cares for the goods without charge, the bailment is for the *sole benefit of the bailor*.

The interesting/boring distinction is clearly superficial, so let's label these two kinds of material more formally as *specific cases* (the interesting parts) and *explanation* (the boring parts). Most writing contains material of both kinds: specific cases (or other hard fact) followed by explanation or analysis.

Turning this around gives you an idea of your task as a writer: to collect specific information and then to hold it in place with the necessary explanations and continuity material. Two skills are involved here: (1) presenting the information and (2) combining chunks of information. Obviously the chunks of information must be in good shape before you combine them. **Accordingly, Part 1 of this book (Chapters 1–3) shows you how to construct the basic building blocks of expository writing, descriptions, and then how to combine two descriptions into a simple structure. After that, you'll be ready to tackle the full essay assignments discussed in Part 2.**

2 •
Kinds of Information:
Concrete versus Abstract

Is all informative writing based on description? Certainly, a straightforward description offers easy access to an idea. In the following anecdote, for example, Konrad Lorenz shows that cockatoos can be playful by describing a remarkable trick performed by a single bird:

> One of the nicest cockatoo-tricks was one which, in fanciful inventiveness, equalled the experiments of monkey or human children. It arose from the ardent love of the bird for my mother, who, so long as she stayed in the garden in summertime, knitted without stopping. The cockatoo seemed to understand exactly how the soft skeins worked and what the wool was for. He always seized the free end of the wool with his beak and then flew lustily into the air, unraveling the ball behind him. Like a paper kite with a long tail, he climbed high and then flew in regular circles round the great lime tree which stood in front of our house. Once, when nobody was there to stop him he encircled the tree, right up to its summit, with brightly colored woolen strands which it was impossible to disentangle

from the wide-spreading foliage. Our visitors used to stand in mute astonishment before this tree, and were unable to understand how and why it had been thus decorated.

Konrad Z. Lorenz
From *King Solomon's Ring*

For the layman, this description is enough to show that cockatoos can be playful. A professional ornithologist, however, would expect less human interest and a more impressive number of cases. Professor Szent of Budapest Zoo fills the bill with a piece called "Playfulness Among Parrots".

In a study conducted at the zoo in 1983, five cockatoos (*Cacatua alba*) and five macaws (*Ara macao*) were offered two kinds of objects in otherwise bare, one-bird cages. One kind of object was denoted as "playthings" and the other as "objects of use". Playthings included small mirrors, pieces of colored wool, and so on. "Objects of use" were hinged to the sides of the cage; if agitated, the objects of use released a hazel nut (or other food) into the cage. Both kinds of birds quickly learned to manipulate the objects of use to obtain food, and they spent approximately the same amount of time on this activity. (See table.) After briefly toying with the playthings, the macaws apparently lost interest in them. The cockatoos, however, spent significantly more time manipulating the playthings. The data suggest that significant differences in "playfulness" exist among species of birds, although there is no apparent explanation of why this should be so.

	Time spent on objects of use	Time spent on playthings	Time spent on other activities
Cockatoos	25%	22%	53%
Macaws	27%	8%	67%

In *A New Dictionary of Birds* the whole subject is given a far more summary, or abstract, treatment:

PLAY: a form of activity much less apparent in birds than in many mammals, but nevertheless occurring—and not exclusively in the young. Playful behavior in young animals can commonly be identified as, so to speak, a "rehearsal" of adult activities; so it forms part of the learning process, whereby innate capabilities are educated for full performance. . . . Seemingly playful actions of adult birds, of which a few examples are known, cannot be so readily explained.

There is more, but the general tone of the dictionary is obviously a long way from Lorenz's mother sitting in the garden and a fair distance from Szent's experiment. The essential difference here lies in the degree of *concreteness*: Lorenz is extremely concrete, the dictionary extract is wholly abstract, while Szent lies somewhere in between.

Concrete versus abstract—how exactly can you tell the styles apart? Concrete writing appeals directly to the imagination. Look carefully at the word *imagination*. Its root is the word *image*, a picture. In the Lorenz passage there are many pictures: his mother knitting in a sunny garden; the cockatoo decorating the tree; the astonished visitors standing in dumb bewilderment. These images are all visual, but the reader has five senses, and the writer can construct images that appeal to any of the five. For example, in his poem, *The Princess*, Tennyson writes of:

> The moan of doves in immemorial elms
> And the murmuring of innumerable bees.

Say the lines aloud and listen to the cooing and humming noises Tennyson uses to create this vivid sound image. The senses of smell, taste, and touch can also be invoked, though this happens more rarely.

Good concrete writing, the kind of thing you'd find in a novel, is very appealing. On the other hand, the best professional writing is often abstract. What course is best for the beginning writer? The first assignments in this book will steer you toward concreteness for two reasons. For a start, abstract writing degenerates quickly into "hot air," a problem we'll meet again in the Introduction to Part 2. This is how it's done:

A safe automobile is always kept in good condition. Failing to maintain your car properly is dangerous for you and for other road users. Only cars that are regularly serviced and efficiently maintained can really be called safe.

Saying the same thing three times over will not captivate the reader. The second problem with abstract writing is that it demands great concentration from the reader. To generate such concentration, the writer must move faultlessly along a chain of argument: gaps or jerky transitions kill the reader's concentration. For the beginning writer, it makes more sense to work on concrete, imaginable material.

Concept Review

Abstract versus Concrete

How would you rate these passages on their degree of concreteness? Are they fully concrete, wholly abstract, or somewhere in between? If the piece is concrete, then it forces every reader to imagine a more or less identical picture. If there is no picture, or there is a wide range of pictures, then the piece is not fully concrete.

a. The Korean slowly pulled off his gloves and came and stood at arm's length from Bond and held out his hands palm upwards. Bond got up and looked at them. They were big and fat with muscle. The fingers all seemed to be the same length. They were very blunt at the tips and the tips glinted as if they were made of yellow bone.

Ian Fleming (1959)

PART ONE
Basic Materials—Basic Skills

b. Most students cannot afford the high cost of residential campus living.

S. Ericksen (1974)

c. Stripped of her black, she stood in her red petticoat and it was seen that above it she wore a red satin bodice, trimmed with lace, the neckline cut low at the back; one of the women handed her a pair of red sleeves, and it was thus wearing all red, the color of blood, and the liturgical color of martyrdom in the Catholic Church, that the queen of Scots died.

Antonia Fraser (1969)

d. There is nothing which has been contrived by man, by which so much happiness is produced as by a good tavern or inn.

Samuel Johnson (1776)

e. [The town] had a black canal in it, and a river that ran purple with ill-smelling dye, and vast piles of building full of windows where there was a rattling and a trembling all day long, and where the piston of the steam-engine worked monotonously up and down, like the head of an elephant in a state of melancholy madness.

Charles Dickens (1854)

f. Where the black theater in the United States is concerned, a new era was ushered in when black artists, not altogether freed of the minstrel tradition, set out consciously to alter what they considered to be its deleterious effects.

Clinton Oliver (1971)

g. Caloric deficiency, a form of starvation, is probably the leading cause of failure to thrive in young children.

Kaye, Oski and Barness (1978)

h. Ethelberta breathed a sort of exclamation, not right out, but stealthily, like a parson's damn.

Thomas Hardy (1876)

i. I lament that women are systematically degraded by receiving the trivial attentions, which men think it manly to pay to the sex, when, in fact, they are insultingly supporting their own superiority. It is not condescension to bow to an inferior. So ludicrous, in fact, do these ceremonies appear to me, that I scarcely am able to govern my muscles, when I see a man start with eager and serious solicitude to lift a handkerchief, or shut a door, when the *lady* could have done it herself, had she only moved a pace or two.

Mary Wollstonecraft (1791)

j. In nature there are neither rewards nor punishments—there are consequences.

Robert Ingersoll (1890)

3 •

The Process of Description: Static versus Dynamic

For wild animals, survival depends on observation. A baby monkey that cannot distinguish between a moving, predatory snake and a never-moving branch will not survive long enough to contribute its genes to the gene pool. For the descriptive writer too, the key distinction is between what is unchanging, still, *static* and what is changing, moving, *dynamic*. If a thing changes, you describe it in one way; if it moves, you describe it in another. Since this distinction is so vital, let's study an example.

Imagine that you are writing a piece on the (unlikely) subject of German winemaking. During your research you visit a wine cellar in Germany—in fact it's a bombproof bunker left over from World War II. You decide to include a description of this slightly sinister cellar in your piece as well as a description of how the wine is made. Two descriptions, then. Let's begin with the cellar. Study the picture. Where would you start your description? With the "sound of silence"? With the oppressive concrete vaulting? With the resinous, sappy smell of the maturing wine? With the history of the bunker? With the 40° chill that keeps the wine in such good condition? With the winery worker standing in the gangway? Probably there is no ideal way to begin—neither is there an ideal way to end, nor an ideal order for the intermediate details. Because many structures might produce an effective piece, the thoughtful writer would try several arrangements before deciding which structure had the best feel to it. A further point: how much detail would you include? The wattage of the light bulbs? The number of bottles in each bin? The kind of wood the bins are made of? Again, you'd include what felt right for the article and for your intended readership.

Your second description concerns the production of the wine itself. Let's ask the same questions. Where would you begin? Obviously with Step 1—obtaining the grapes. Where would you end? With the wine ready to be sold. What would be the order of the details in between? This time the "inner logic" of the material provides the answer: the details will follow the sequence of the production process. And finally, how much detail is required? Enough to form a continuous chain of events without gaps. If you leave gaps, if for example the wine mysteriously appears in the cellar without someone putting it there, then the reader will quickly lose track of the process.

Do you see the difference between these two descriptions? The cellar itself is static—nothing in it changes. The structure of this description and the amount of detail included are at the discretion of the writer. In writing a *static description* of this kind, the writer develops an effective-seeming structure out of whatever details are appropriate. (Chapter 1 will explain how to do this.) With the *dynamic description* the writer's task is different: to discover the sequence built into the material itself and then to develop this *predetermined* sequence with the necessary detail. (Chapter 2 explores the problems of dynamic description.)

Static versus dynamic—no other distinction is as basic or as important. So, if your task is to describe something, the first question is: does it change or does it stay the same? If it changes, you are locked into a step-by-step sequence that follows certain logical requirements; if it does not change, then more is at your discretion, and you'll have an array of choices. How this works out in practice we'll see in the upcoming chapters.

Cellar with maturing German wine   Courtesy of Deutsche Presse-Agentur GmbH

Concept Review

Static or Dynamic?

Decide for each of the descriptive subjects suggested below whether a static or a dynamic treatment is appropriate.

a. The bedroom of a small, untidy child

b. How this bedroom got this way on one particular occasion

c. A bride and bridegroom standing at the altar

d. How they came to be married

e. What a well laid dinner table for two looks like

f. How to lay it

g. How beer is made

h. The atmosphere in the stadium the moment after Pete Rose made his record-breaking hit

i. The moment of calm before the storm strikes

j. How to find out if a pot roast is cooked through

Review Assignment

Abstract into Concrete

Choose one of these four *abstract statements*. Write a short description that uses a specific case to make the same point. Your description can be either static (a collection of details) or dynamic (the story of something that happened).

1. *Children's attitudes to teachers*. A good number of enquiries have been made, especially in the U.S.A., as to what children liked or disliked most in teachers. . . . The main results are pretty much what one would expect. Friendliness and kindness, fairness in discipline, and a sense of humor are very prominent as reasons for liking. Important also are good temper, and with older pupils and especially girls, even appearance.

   C. W. Valentine, *The Normal Child*

2. Often we do not recognise exciting people when we meet them. In our fast moving world we hardly get to know our next door neighbor let alone a person sitting next to us on a jet liner. . . . It takes time to find someone out, to learn if they have truly led interesting lives. It takes time to separate the braggarts from the real. Today we don't have the time, or I should say, we don't take the time to do this.

   Harold Stephens, *Asian Portraits*

3. For nearly all immigrants, America is promotion, and this promotion is more clearly felt by their children. The old people may hanker after the old country, but the children—whatever sentimental feelings for their ancestral homes they may have, especially when provoked—are, above all else, anxious to be Americans.

   Denis Brogan, *The American Character*

4. Dependence, or submission, is closely related to its opposite, dominance, in that some people may show both types of behavior on different occasions. The so-called "authoritarian personality" is submissive to people of greater power or status, and dominant to those of less. He can be found displaying these alternating styles of behavior in hierarchical organizations like the army.

   Michael Argyle, *The Psychology of Interpersonal Behavior*

• Summary: The Flowchart

So far, a single key choice in the descriptive process has emerged: static treatment versus dynamic treatment. In the form of a flowchart, this part of the process looks like this:

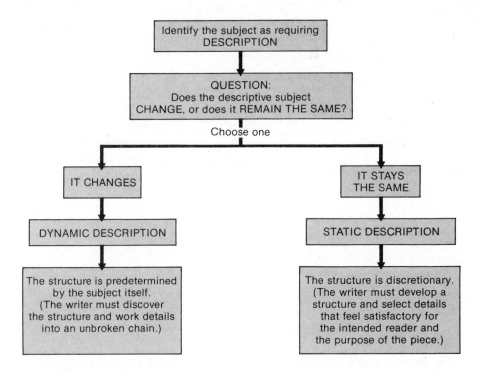

A word of caution about flowcharts.   A chart of this type is a *model*; it does not claim to represent what actually happens in a writer's brain during composition: nobody knows much about the psycho-mechanics of writing. Try to remember that what the chart shows as a step-by-step progression may work out very differently in practice, where second thoughts, revisions, and rearrangements play a major role in putting your piece together. The purpose of the chart is to review, not to dictate. So far, then, the chart is a simple fork with only a few steps in it. Later concepts will require more elaborate charting.

ONE

Static
Description

1 •
The Problem:
What Makes a Good Description?

• The Filter—Choosing the Right Detail

"A single picture is worth a thousand words." Sometimes this cliché is unquestionably true. No soldier carries into battle a thousand-word description of his wife and children: he carries a photograph. Does this mean that the written description is simply the poor relation of the picture? To answer this question, consider this description by Truman Capote:

> Dick stripped to his briefs was not quite the same as Dick fully clothed. In the latter state, he seemed a flimsy dingy-blond youth of medium height, fleshless and perhaps sunken-chested; disrobing revealed that he was nothing of the sort, but, rather, an athlete constructed on a welterweight scale. The tattooed face of a cat, blue and grinning, covered his right hand; on one shoulder a blue rose blossomed. More markings, self-designed and self-executed, ornamented his arms and torso: the head of a dragon with a human skull between its open jaws; bosomy nudes; a

gremlin brandishing a pitchfork; the word PEACE accompanied by a cross radiating, in the form of crude strokes, rays of holy light; and two sentimental concoctions—one a bouquet of flowers dedicated to MOTHER-DAD, the other a heart that celebrated the romance of DICK and CAROL, the girl whom he had married when he was nineteen, and from whom he had separated six years later in order to "do the right thing" by another young lady, the mother of his youngest child. . . .

But neither Dick's physique nor the inky gallery adorning it made as remarkable an impression as his face, which seemed composed of mismatching parts. It was as though his head had been halved like an apple, then put together a fraction off center. Something of the kind had happened; the imperfectly aligned features were the outcome of a car collision in 1950—an accident that left his long-jawed and narrow face tilted, the left side rather lower than the right, with the results that the lips were slightly aslant, the nose askew, and his eyes not only situated at uneven levels but of uneven size, the left eye being truly serpentine, with a venomous, sickly-blue squint that although it was involuntarily acquired, seemed nevertheless to warn of bitter sediment at the bottom of his nature.

Truman Capote
From In Cold Blood

What sort of person is Dick? In a word, *unbalanced*. His body stripped is startlingly different from his body clothed; his tattoos show an unbalanced mixture of brutality and sentimentality, almost a Jekyll-and-Hyde split in his personality; the unmatched halves of his face create the same unsettling effect. Would a photograph of Dick work with such sinister force? Probably not, for two reasons.

For a start, the photograph would necessarily show the body, the tattoos, and the face simultaneously while Capote presents his material in *sequence*. Look, for example, at the order of the tattoos: there's a brutal opening cluster including the skull-eating dragon; then some heavy sentimentality with Mother and Dad among flowers; finally comes Carol, long abandoned, but ironically still etched into his skin.

BRUTALITY → SENTIMENTALITY → FAILURE

No photograph could achieve this sense of order. Then, as soon as the tattoos have made their unbalanced impression, Capote shows us the twisted face. The order TATTOOS → FACE is again well judged: Dick's terrible left eye makes a strong climax. With a photograph, on the other hand, the face would have attracted our attention *first*—the exact reverse of Capote's effect. This is one aspect in which written description excels: its fingertip control of the flow of information.

The second plus for the description is that it is highly evaluative. Typically, a picture gives only raw fact, while a description explores the *significance* of the facts. The Carol tattoo, for example, is meaningless until Capote tells us why Dick pulled out on Carol. A photograph has no way of expressing that desertion. A writer can easily handle evaluation like that while a photographer cannot.

Probably, most readers form much the same picture of Dick and evaluate

CHAPTER ONE
Static Description

Dick's character in much the same way. If this is true, then good communication must be taking place. How is the trick worked?

Capote seems to work in two ways. First, he makes the picture easy to imagine by the concreteness of his style: Dick's tattoos are carefully described as are his facial features. *Concreteness* is one key to effective description, as we saw in the last chapter. The second point is Capote's *selectivity*. Capote doesn't tell us everything he noticed about Dick during their many interviews; a complete inventory of Dick's physical being might have been a hundred pages long. Capote selected what he thought was *significant* for the purpose in hand, and he rejected everything else. For a writer, selecting for significance is not an option; it is a *must*.

How does selection take place? Let's compare the way a writer separates usable from unusable detail with the way an auto mechanic separates water from gasoline. In fact, to separate the two liquids, a simple filter built into a funnel is enough. The mesh of the filter holds back water, while gasoline passes easily through it.

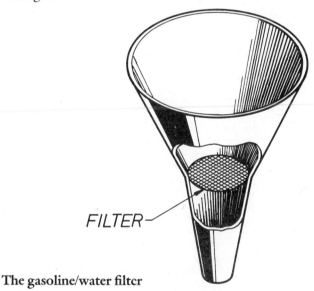

FILTER

The gasoline/water filter

What about the writer? For the writer, the *mixture* is the wealth of detail available for use—in Capote's case, the thousands of things he must have observed about Dick. The *filter* is the single idea that Capote wanted to put across in this description: Dick's unbalanced personality. To confirm that this is so, add back (imaginary) details that do not suggest a "split personality." If Capote told us that Dick had a mole on his chest, for example, the description would become suddenly incoherent. The mole would make us question what Capote was driving at. Or maybe Dick had an ingrown toenail. Such meaningless detail cannot be fitted into an overall reading; it disrupts communication.

There's another way of looking at "meaningless" detail. When you listen to a car radio, you hear two things, sounds and noise. The sounds are the signals you want to hear (the music, the newsreader's voice, or whatever). The noise is the background of rumbles, hisses, plops and clicks that plague most transmissions. The engineers who designed the radio used various *filters* to reduce this white noise, as it is called. How do you react to white noise? If it gets bad enough, you probably switch off or tune to another station. The same happens to the reader: if the white noise (random, meaningless detail) builds up beyond a certain threshold, then the reader "turns off."

This principle of filtering suggests one way of approaching descriptive writing: first choose an appropriate *controlling filter*, then use the filter to select significant *concrete detail*. In essence, if a detail goes through the filter, it can be used; if it doesn't, it can't.

Concept Review

The Controlling Filter

The following three descriptions are by professional writers. Bearing in mind the idea of the filter, read them through, and then answer the questions.

a. Does the description work? In other words, do you think most readers have much the same picture in mind and evaluate that picture in much the same way?

b. Can you formulate a controlling filter for the description—perhaps in a single, very specific word?

c. Can you find any "meaningless" details in the descriptions, details that do not pass through the controlling filter you chose?

d. If so, can you reword the filter so that the details pass through? Or is the writing in part white noise?

e. If there is white noise, is the level acceptable or not?

THE GRIMES' HOME

The room was narrow and dirty; nothing could alter its dimensions, no labor could ever make it clean. Dirt was in the walls and the floorboards, and triumphed beneath the sink where roaches spawned; was in the fine ridges of the pots and pans, scoured daily, burnt black on the bottom, hanging above the stove; was in the wall against which they hung, and revealed itself where the paint had cracked and leaned outward in stiff squares and fragments, the paper-thin underside webbed with black. Dirt was in every corner, angle, crevice of the monstrous stove, and lived behind it in delirious communion with the corrupted wall. Dirt was in the baseboard that John scrubbed every Saturday, and roughened the cupboard shelves that held the cracked and gleaming dishes. Under this dark weight the walls leaned, under it the ceiling, with a great crack like lightning in its center, sagged. The windows gleamed like beaten gold or silver, but now John saw, in the yellow light, how fine dust veiled their doubtful glory. Dirt crawled in the gray mop hung out of the windows to dry. John thought with shame and horror, yet in angry hardness of heart: *He who is filthy, let him be filthy still.*

James Baldwin
From *Go Tell it on the Mountain*

OBEDIAH SLOPE

Mr. Slope is tall, and not ill made. His feet and hands are large, as has ever been the case with all his family, but he has a broad chest and wide shoulders to carry off these excrescences, and on the whole his figure is good. His countenance, however, is not specially prepossessing. His hair is lank, and of a dull pale reddish hue. It is always formed into three straight lumpy masses, each brushed with admirable precision, and cemented with much grease; two of them adhere closely to the sides of his face, and the other lies at right angles above them. He wears no whiskers, and is always punctiliously shaven. His face is nearly of the same color as his hair, though perhaps a little redder: it is not unlike beef,—beef, however, one would say, of a bad quality. His forehead is capacious and high, but square and heavy, and unpleasantly shining. His mouth is large, though his lips are thin and bloodless; and his big, prominent, pale brown eyes inspire anything but confidence. His nose, however, is his redeeming feature: it is pronounced, straight, and well-formed; though I myself should have liked it better did it not possess a somewhat spongy, porous appearance, as though it had been cleverly formed out of a red colored cork.

I never could endure to shake hands with Mr. Slope. A cold, clammy perspiration always exudes from him, the small drops are ever to be seen standing on his brow, and his friendly grasp is unpleasant.

Anthony Trollope
From *Barchester Towers*

SUNRISE IN SAMOA

The life of the day begins at dawn, or if the moon has shown until daylight, the shouts of the young men may be heard before dawn from the hillside. Uneasy in the night, populous with ghosts, they shout lustily to one another as they hasten with their work. As the dawn begins to fall among the soft brown roofs and the slender palm trees stand out against a colorless, gleaming sea, lovers slip home from trysts beneath the palm trees or in the shadow of beached canoes, that the light may find each sleeper in his appointed place. Cocks crow, negligently, and a shrill-voiced bird cries from the breadfruit trees. The insistent roar of the reef seems muted to an undertone for the sounds of a waking village. Babies cry, a few short wails before sleepy mothers give them the breast. Restless little children roll out of their sheets and wander drowsily down to the beach to freshen their faces in the sea. Boys, bent upon an early fishing, start collecting their tackle and go to rouse their more laggard companions. Fires are lit, here and there, the white smoke hardly visible against the paleness of the dawn. The whole village, sheeted and frowsy, stirs, rubs its eyes, and stumbles towards the beach. "Talofa!" "Talofa!" "Will the journey start today?" "Is it bonito fishing your lordship is going?" Girls stop to giggle over some young ne'er-do-well who escaped during the night from an angry father's pursuit and to venture a shrewd guess that the daughter knew more about his presence than she told.

Margaret Mead
From *Coming of Age in Samoa*

• Narrative: Bringing a Description to Life

So far we've seen how a writer combines observed details into a meaningful cluster by filtering. There's another kind of detail, however, that really brings a description to life: the narrative.

Narrative is anything from epic movie to office gossip. Let's start with gossip. Imagine this scene: In a block of twelve apartments, two housewives are sitting over coffee discussing the new arrivals in Apartment 6, a family recently transferred from out of town. One of the women already knows the family. The conversation might go like this:

"Well, what are they like then? If you knew them before, what are they like?"

"They're pretty nice, matter of fact."

"Nice? I mean, what do you mean, nice? They won't stay nice too long in a dump like this."

"No, not that kind of nice."

"What kind of nice then? Come on, Louise, tell us!"

"Well, I don't really know how to say it. Look—I'll tell you what happened one time. My Fred was away on a job—I didn't even know where he was exactly. Well, I got this terrible pain in my stomach —appendicitis. Remember, I told you I had my appendix out. So I was in the hospital. Can you imagine, with my oldest only four! Well, this woman, Lena Turner I mean, said to me: 'Don't worry about the kids. I'll look after them.' And she did. Five days she fed the three of them, drove them to nursery school, put them to bed along with hers. And when I came out she wouldn't take a penny—nothing. Not even for their food. I mean, there aren't many people like that around."

This reads like simple gossip, but, really, it's a resourceful act of communication. Wisely the speaker does not attempt what psychologists call a personality inventory of Lena Turner. Instead she tells an anecdote. This anecdote works well: it lets her listener know exactly how Lena Turner is "nice."

Such anecdotes are not restricted to informal speech. As the two following extracts show, professional writers are also strong on anecdote.

A. CHILDREN AT PLAY

Social scientists specialize in description: it helps them avoid unnecessary value judgments. Martha Wolfenstein, as an anthropologist, developed a descriptive style based on watching, taking notes and reporting. Her work is, therefore, of special interest to the beginning writer. The subject in this case is French children taken to the park by their parents. Wolfenstein is showing that French parents see themselves as "above" the emotions of their children, although she does not say if this is good or bad.

On an occasion when a mother punished a little boy, she appeared quite unconcerned about his rage and grief and was amused when he later came to fling his arms around her. I did not see what it was that provoked the mother's punishment. My attention was attracted when I saw the boy, of about six or seven, running, with his mother, a sturdy, athletic-looking woman, hard at his heels. When she overtook him, she gave him several hard whacks on the behind, and the boy burst into tears. The mother then sat down on the bench beside her husband, who was holding the baby; for her the episode seemed finished. The boy, however, continued crying, his posture very tense, with an expression of raging protest. He stalked off, still crying, looking helplessly angry and hurt, and walked around the playground, where several other children and mothers turned to look at him. His own mother was not looking but after a while glanced in his direction, smiling, seemingly not at him but about him. The boy returned to the parents' bench, stood first in front of his father, then threw his arms around his mother and put his head in her lap. The mother put her arms

CHAPTER ONE
Static Description

around him and turned to a woman on the other side of the bench and laughed. The other woman laughed back. The boy remained for some time with his head buried in his mother's lap. The mother had apparently been unperturbed by the boy's stormy tears and by his gesture of walking away, while his return to her, as his love and longing overpowered his angry feelings, seemed to her humorous. In laughing with another adult about it, she seemed to express: that's the way children are; that's all that comes of their little scenes (Sévres-Babylone, July 24, 1953).

Martha Wolfenstein
From "French Parents Take Their Children to the Park"

B. WHY THE CONSUMER BUYS

Serious writing is often based on documented case studies. Vance Packard, in a book on the advertising industry, begins with a chapter explaining how unreliable people can be when explaining their reasons for buying a product. Packard uses a series of anecdotes (case studies) to make his point.

A brewery making two kinds of beer made a survey to find what kind of people drank each beer, as a guide to its merchandisers. It asked people known to favor its general brand name: "Do you drink the light or the regular?" To its astonishment it found people reporting they drank light over the regular by better than three to one. The truth of the matter was that for years the company, to meet consumer demand, had been brewing nine times as much regular beer as light beer. It decided that in asking people that question it was in effect asking: Do you drink the kind preferred by people of refinement and discriminating taste, or do you just drink the regular stuff?

Psychologists at the McCann-Erickson advertising agency asked a sampling of people why they didn't buy one client's product—kippered herring. The main reason the people gave under direct questioning was that they just didn't like the taste of kippers. More persistent probing however uncovered the fact that forty per cent of the people who said they didn't like the taste of kippers had never, in their entire lives, tasted kippers!

Finally, the marketers decided it is dangerous to assume that people can be trusted to behave in a rational way.

The Color Research Institute had what it felt was a startling encounter with this proneness to irrationality when it tested package designs for a new detergent. It was testing to see if a woman is influenced more than she realizes, in her opinion of a product, by the package. It gave the housewives three different boxes filled with detergent and requested that they try them all out for a few weeks and then report which was the best for delicate clothing. The wives were given the impression that they had been given three different types of detergent. Actually only the boxes were different; the detergents inside were identical.

The design for one was predominantly yellow. The yellow in the test was used because some merchandisers were convinced that yellow was the best color for store shelves because it has very strong visual impact. Another box was predominantly blue without any yellow in it; and the third box was blue but with splashes of yellow.

In their reports the housewives stated that the detergent in the brilliant yellow box was too strong; it even allegedly ruined their clothes in some cases. As for the detergent in the predominantly blue box, the wives complained in many cases that it left their clothes dirty looking. The third box, which contained what the institute felt was an ideal balance of colors in the package design, overwhelmingly received favorable responses. The women used such words as "fine" and "wonderful" in describing the effect the detergent in that box had on their clothes.

Vance Packard
From *The Hidden Persuaders*

Look back at these extracts as a pair. What they have in common tells us a lot about how the expository writer uses narrative. First, neither writer drags the story in for its own sake. In each case the story illustrates a point—and illustrates it in the best possible way. Second, each of the narratives is kept *lean*: a well-told story contains enough detail to make its point and no more: it's the problem of white noise again. If Wolfenstein had told us what the mother was wearing, what the weather was like in the park, or what trees grew there, the narrative would have lost intensity. Third, each of the narratives uses the age-old trick of keeping the reader guessing about the outcome. No barroom storyteller gives away the punch line of a joke until the last possible minute. The expository writer should follow suit.

Narrative, to sum up, has a wonderful way of involving the reader in the description. A well-told story can make your descriptive point for you and at the same time bring your description to life.

Concept Review

The Use of Narrative

Read this narrative by a writer who definitely hasn't mastered the art of telling a story. Then explain why the story is such a failure.

It can get very snowy in Maine. Let me tell you something that happened on one occasion. My father got home from work very late one night because the factory where he worked was on overtime. My mother usually cooked a hot meal in the evening, and we ate it in the kitchen where it was nice and warm. At the time my father had a Ford station wagon. It was blue with grey vinyl seats. It was these seats that were to freeze up in the night and crack up next morning when we sat on them! We heard him draw up. We certainly didn't realize then how frozen up we would be by the next morning. We all ate our hot stew, watched television, and went to bed. In the night the temperature dropped unbelievably low and the snowfall was a record. Next morning the radiator of the car was frozen solid and—would you believe it?—the vinyl seats of the car had become so cold that they shattered to pieces when we sat on them.

Review Assignment

Free Writing an Anecdote

The story about the snow in Maine started out on the right lines. In fact the first two sentences should give you a catapult start into an anecdote of your own. Think about some extreme of weather *you* have experienced: heavy snow, high winds, torrential rain, crippling heat, deadly cold, or whatever. Begin with the two "catapult" sentences below, and then write the story without pausing to polish your work—tell it on paper just as you would if you were talking to a friend. This kind of "free writing" may contain errors of spelling, and so on, but don't worry. The goal is a spontaneous piece of writing that tells a simple story in natural language. Your catapult:

> It can get very <weather condition> in <name of a place>. Let me tell you something that happened on one occasion. (Now tell it.)

• Structure: Putting Things in Order

We saw in the Introduction that a *dynamic description* follows a strict step-by-step structure while a *static description* has no such tailor-made organization. Nevertheless, order cannot be left to chance. Let's assume that you have a subject and that you know roughly what you want to say. (This is a big assumption. We'll go into more detail in the second part of this chapter.) What next?

At this point in the writing process, experts disagree. Some say: draw up a formal outline and follow it exactly. Others say: forget outlining, just go ahead and write—you can tidy up the mess afterwards. Most commentators seem to prefer a compromise position: think out a preliminary "game plan" and try to stick to it, but don't let the plan stifle your creative flow. In practice each approach has pros and cons. In fact the game plan for a single description involves nothing more than deciding on an *order* for the ideas you want to use. Before you can make a decision about order, you need to know your options. In essence you have three: order of occurrence, order of significance, and logical order.

OPTION 1: ORDER OF SIGNIFICANCE

Your first option is to arrange information in its order of significance. One example of this method is Truman Capote's description of Dick earlier in this chapter. If this description is worked back into a game plan, the result looks like this:

Body:	Clothed: unimpressive
	Unclothed: welterweight
Tattoos:	Aggressive
	Sentimental
Face:	The unrelated halves
	His unmatched eyes

The key point is Dick's eyes, the "mirror of his soul," and Capote put them *last*. This is a typical working method: the writer begins with lesser items and then works with growing intensity toward the key idea, building for a climax. Imagine if Capote had worked the other way, starting with the eyes and finishing with Dick's unimpressive clothed body: the description would have dried up like a river draining into a desert. The principle implied here is important: *what is most significant goes last*. (See *Close-Up*.)

Close-Up

Getting it in First

Rules change when the game changes. The normal rule for the expository writer is to keep the best for last. On the other hand, some writers, for example military clerks and newspaper reporters, are trained to put the key idea not last but *first*. Why is this? In the case of the clerk, military urgency is paramount—in battle a message must be transmitted with the key items first since lines of communication may be cut at any second or the clerk may not survive to complete the transmission. The journalist's reasons are different. Daily newspapers are printed in several editions. News stories are constantly breaking, and the later editions must find space on the news pages for the latest information. There is, however, no time to create more space by rewriting the early stories more briefly. The stories are shortened—with scissors. A subeditor who needs ten column inches of space for a new story simply snips the bottoms off existing stories. Maybe five stories lose two inches each. The subeditor knows that the tail end of the story contains the least significant facts because every journalist is trained to write that way—with everything up front. These two cases show us a major principle: *structure must be adjusted to the total communication situation*. If this situation includes bullets or deadlines, so be it.

OPTION 2: ORDER OF OCCURRENCE

Sometimes a description works best if you arrange the details in their order of occurrence: what happens first is discussed first. Maria Jiminez, a typical beginning student, chose this option in describing a military commissary (or grocery store) on payday. Recalling the stress of payday shopping, Maria quickly picked the word *frustrating* as a controlling filter. Taking a blank sheet of paper and "brainstorming" for frustrating details, Maria came up with:

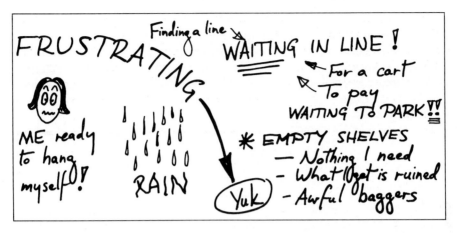

She then realized that everything from parking to bagging was on her list, and so she rearranged the items in order of occurrence. This gave her a list of seven steps, an easy-to-follow structure.

1. Parking
2. Finding a shopping cart
3. Selecting produce
4. Selecting a line
5. The line itself
6. Paying
7. The bagger

Maria's description is given in full in Section 2 of this chapter because it illustrates not only strong structure but also personal voice. As an example of how to use order of occurrence, you might like to read it right away.

OPTION 3: LOGICAL ORDER

No single logic applies to every kind of description. Two logical patterns are common: *hierarchical* patterns and *inductive* patterns. Mostly, however, it is the inner logic of the material that provides the pattern. Structures based on this inner logic can be called *tailor-made* patterns.

Option 3a: The Hierarchical Pattern.   A hierarchy is a ranking system, usually with a small number of chiefs at the top, a group of braves in the middle, and masses of just plain Indians at the bottom. What kind of description will be hierarchical? A good example is a description of a piece of equipment. Normally such a description starts at the top with the main parts and works downward; each main part is broken down into its subparts, and so on down to the smallest part. A case in point: the description of a stereo turntable would not begin with the anti-skating device on the tone-arm: it would begin at the top, with the three main parts (housing, tone arm, drive assembly) and work downward. Whenever the subject you are working on is organized as a hierarchy, you can take the hint and structure your description accordingly.

Option 3b: The Inductive Pattern. More often a description works in the other direction—that is, it begins with low-level descriptive detail and works upwards. Riddles work in this way. "What is black and white and red (read) all over?" A newspaper. "What is green, has four legs, and moves at 400 miles per hour over the water?" A jet-propelled frog. If you don't like such simple riddles, try this one by Dena Knauer. What is she describing?

> White with white
> Hot
> Dark blue with black
> Light blue
> Brown, green and yellow
> Warm
> Delicate, red and all the rest
> Cold

The pattern is clear: in a riddle the descriptive detail *must* precede the unifying concept. This pattern, working from scattered detail towards a general concept, is called *induction*. The inductive pattern recreates for the reader the process of discovery, leading the reader from observations through to a conclusion. The standard format for describing scientific experiments follows this inductive pattern. A memorandum suggesting an improvement also works inductively: it begins with a description of the facts as they are at present and concludes with a solution. Whenever you are describing something that is essentially a mystery with a solution, then the inductive pattern is what you are looking for.

Option 3c: The Tailor-Made Pattern. Often your ideas fit into no ready-made pattern. In such cases, you must look at the material to see if it contains some built-in logic of its own. A description by John O'Hara in his novel *Hope of Heaven* offers a clear example. The subject is Miller.

> He stood up. He was wearing an inexpensive Glen plaid jacket, cheap gray flannel slacks, imitation suède shoes, a dark brown polo shirt, and the conventional Hollywood neckerchief. . . .
>   He was a good six feet tall, with the kind of athletic build that is athletic, but one look at his face and you knew that this was no athlete. Probably he could do hand-stands on a beach. Possibly he could dive well. Maybe he had played high school basketball or had picked up some golf or tennis. He undoubtedly was strong, but in a way that I was not afraid of. He had long fingers, with long wide nails that had been buffed to a nice shine. I bet myself that he played the piano, a sort of fraternity-house piano; competent, unimaginative piano; improvising-sounding, but someone else's improvisation. I could all but hear him, playing something like "Easy To Love," which at that time was brand new. Slow, not in any steady tempo, and all chords. That's what those hands were for. . . .
>   He didn't like my Luckies. He had Camels, which he took out of his shirt pocket. He reached in, surrounded the pack with his hands, slapped

CHAPTER ONE
Static Description

two fingers of his left hand on the top of the pack (noisily, and much harder than was necessary) until two cigarettes popped up. He extracted one and put it in his mouth. He scratched a match and held it to the cigarette and cocked his head far over to one side and took a deep inhale. Enough smoke to fill a bicycle tire came out of his mouth and he blew out the match.

John O'Hara
From *Hope of Heaven*

O'Hara first lets us *see* Miller (his phony clothes, his sham athletic build); then he invites us to *watch* Miller in action. First we watch Miller play an (imaginary) piano, badly and showily. Finally, watching Miller smoke a cigarette macho style, we understand exactly what kind of person he is. There is a strong inner logic in this sequence: *seeing* logically precedes *watching*. Working back once more to the game plan, O'Hara's description looks like this:

> Appearance (seeing):
> Cheap, phony clothes
> Sham athletic build
>
> Behavior (watching):
> Imitative pianist
> Macho cigarette smoker

Concept Review

The Appropriate Structure

Imagine you are writing each of the descriptions below. What would be an appropriate structure in each case?

1. *Subject:* The personnel structure of Light Engineering, Inc.
   Included detail: The boss; below the boss, four main groups—production, marketing, research and administration; within the production group, manufacturing and quality control; within marketing, the sales force and the advertising department; within administration, bookkeeping and the front office.

2. *Subject:* The atmosphere of excitement under the Christmas tree just before the children open their presents.
   Included detail: Buying and ordering gifts; hiding them around the house; secret wrapping sessions; laying out the gifts; the children jostling and guessing under the tree.

3. *Subject:* Your mischievous son.
   Included detail: His kicked-out sneakers; his untidy hair; the chocolate and ice-cream stains on his clothes and around his mouth; his way of avoiding household chores; his idea of tidying his room; the time he got hold of a can of gold spray paint.

4. *Subject:* The exotic richness of the Temple of the Emerald Buddha in Bangkok.
   Included detail: The richly colored roof tiles; the golden doorways; the jewel-studded dragons guarding the doors; the monks dressed in vivid orange; the extraordinary statue of the Buddha smothered in jewels.

5. *Subject:* Your plan to solve quarrels about who makes coffee for whom.
Included detail: The quarrels in the office between junior male and female employees
about coffee-making; the dirty cups all over the office; time wasted looking for one's own
cup; your idea—a coin-operated coffee machine using disposable cups.

2 •
The Personal Voice

Sometimes the purpose of a writing course seems to be to throttle your individual, personal voice and to turn you into a clone of millions of other "competent" students. If you resent this, you're right. To escape from the clone-laboratory atmosphere, each chapter includes a piece by a writer who is using the technique discussed in the chapter, but in an unmistakably personal way. In this case the writer is Maria Jiminez; we met her earlier in the chapter. She's describing a military commissary (or grocery store) on payday. The voice in her piece expresses a kind of mock frustration and weariness of the world. The resulting deadpan humor gives her description a voice of its own.

The commissary on payday can be a frustrating place. Parking is my first problem. Usually it rains on payday, and all the parking spaces within a hundred yards of the commissary are taken. When I do find a spot, it is so far away that I am guaranteed a drenching from my hike in the rain and a two-dollar extortion smile from the bagger who will eventually wheel out my shopping.

Once inside the commissary, I tamely line up for a shopping cart; by the time I get one, my clothing is perfectly dry again, but my feet ache with standing. On payday even the most defective carts are pressed into use. I usually get one that steers violently to the right, has sharp plastic splinters where the handle should be, and is stained with dead lettuce leaves and decaying yogurt. I generally start shopping at the produce stands. Somehow my payday shopping list always includes exotic things that aren't the strong point of the commissary at the best of times. I start with kiwis—there are none. Avocados—none. Beansprouts—none. Tomatoes—a pulpy scarlet trough marks the place where earlier shoppers have rejected tomatoes in what must have been murderous fury. And so it goes on. Half an hour later I have a cart half full of the things I didn't really need, and it's time to check out.

My frustrations so far are nothing to what I am about to experience. Naturally all the lines stretch from the checkouts to the meat counter fifty yards away. Tortured by indecision, I join the most hopeful-looking line; three people fall in behind me so that for a second I feel smug—I beat them to it. Then ahead I dimly see that my checkout is no longer functioning. TEMPORARILY CLOSED reads the sign in worn red letters. The three people behind me disappear into other, happier lines. I decide to wait. Ahead of me I have observed three women with almost empty carts. Unfortunately I have not observed that these women are babysitters: they have brought with them a dozen children who are sent on elaborate missions to locate catfood, plastic spoons, pepper and frozen dinners. The empty carts ahead slowly fill up. They overflow. Other children arrive with extra carts, and the line ahead slowly lengthens. Forty minutes of acute boredom follow during which something compels me to read the instructions on the packages as I inch past them: strawberry cake mix, vanilla cake mix, chocolate cake mix. I shudder at what people consume imagining it to be food. The person in the line behind me is probably a frustrated surgeon since he is practicing a little-known medical procedure: removing a kidney (mine) with the corner of a shopping cart slammed forward at twenty miles an hour. I am nearing my goal when I hear the fatal words: "Price check." The children who have filled the line of carts ahead of me have also been experimenting: if they pull the price labels off the catfood and stick them on the frozen dinners, how long will it be before the checkout clerk guesses something is wrong? "Not long," is the answer. Silent, motionless waiting. I hear a slow splashing as my chocolate chip ice cream melts onto the washing powder. The washing powder pack, now damp, splits and discharges Tide into my sack of onions. A third checkout opens. I pay.

I am outside in the rain again with a bagger wheeling my groceries in soft brown bags behind me. From experience I know that these soaking bags will collapse as the bagger tosses them into my car. The melted ice cream will stain the expensive carpet in my trunk; the washing powder will corrode my paint. I check my purse and find only a single dime and a five-dollar bill. I try to pluck up courage to ask the drenched, bedraggled bagger for change, but I can't. Frustration—it's free with every order at your commissary on payday.

Maria Jiminez

Review Assignment

Controlling Tone of Voice

Think of an occasion when you ended up feeling like a drowned chicken. Some suggestions: a visit to the dentist, a bus tour with some overnights on the bus, a hitchhiking trip in bad weather, the day your car broke down, an arrest and questioning, a promotion party, an aerobics class that you weren't ready for, a children's outing, a date that didn't work out as planned, a mothers' day gift that backfired, a hunting trip from which you came back empty-handed. In each case you probably look back on this event with a rueful kind of amusement. Describe what happened in a *tone of voice* that conveys this feeling to a reader.

3 •
Writing Workshop:
The Process of Description

• Physical Considerations

Good writing demands concentration. If you've written nothing for a while, you'll need to set aside some *writing time* to make concentration possible. Why is writing time so special? When you're writing, you must concentrate on many problems simultaneously: the ideas you are struggling to express, good wording, sentence structure, the structure of the whole description, and so on. Any distraction (a search for a new pen, a snack, a trip to the store before it closes, changing the baby, or whatever) breaks your concentration at all these levels. It can be tough to pick up where you left off. For this reason, you should allocate a definite block of quality time, maybe two or three hours, for writing assignments. These two hours are *writing* time: planning and proofreading may well take place outside this special period—on a bus, in the cafeteria, even waiting in a checkout line. The ideal is an uninterrupted session at a time of day when you feel fresh and relaxed. Two hours of quality time can be worth a whole weekend of sporadic, incoherent struggle rising to panic as your deadline nears.

• Choosing a Subject and Developing a Game Plan

Invent something—something useful. And have it on my desk by next Monday! It's not easy to be inventive, especially to a deadline. In a sense, writing is also invention. Certainly it follows a similar track: deciding (or chancing upon) what you're going to invent and then inventing it. Of the two steps, deciding what to work on is often the trickier.

STEP 1: CHOOSING A SUBJECT

The first assignments in this book are intended to get you writing without too many roadblocks. For this reason, particular subjects are suggested; that way at least you'll know what you're supposed to invent. Subjects for static description are potentially endless; however, you need to practice *concrete writing* so the subject should be easy for you and your reader to picture; you need to practice *filtering* so you're looking for a subject on which you have overabundant information; the subject should offer a chance to use *narrative*, and it should pose some problems of *structure*. Only two subjects fill the bill readily: real people and real places known to you personally.

People.   Movie stars, famous singers, politicians, sporting personalities and so on do *not* make effective subjects. Why not? Because the information available to you has already been ruthlessly filtered by press agents, journalists and camera crews. It's more worthwhile to choose someone about whom you have abundant random information—that is, someone you know personally. The following are examples.

> A colleague at your place of work
> Your roommate
> Your boss (past or present)
> A colorful member of your family
> One of your children
> Someone well known in your local community (examples: a barkeeper, a cop, the local gossip, a storekeeper, a gang leader)
> Someone you respect (examples: a preacher, a doctor, a schoolteacher, a brilliant mechanic, a woman who is making it in the business world, someone who has been a role model for you)
> Someone who disgusts you (examples: a drunk, a drug addict, a "barracks rat," a village Romeo, a sadistic schoolchild, a selfish athlete, a flashy dresser, a mama's boy)
> Or anyone else

Places.   A suitable place for a short description is somewhere very restricted, somewhere you can take in from a single vantage point, somewhere that might prompt you to take a snapshot. Try to steer clear of subjects such as New York or the Atlantic Ocean: they are too big for a single paragraph. Some suggestions, complete with controlling filters to start your imagination working:

The Place	Possible Controlling Filters (pick one filter only)
A room in your home	Relaxing, full of memories
A bar or discotheque you frequent	Rowdy, quiet, threatening
Your place of work	Hectic, efficient, chaotic
A favorite beach or corner of the woods	Serene, free, restorative
A church, synagogue, mosque, or ashram	Inspiring, lively, silent
A gymnasium	Energetic, alive
A place where you have felt too alone	Sinister, frightening, eerie
A big store just before Christmas	Crowded, cheerful, suffocating
A kindergarten	Noisy, lively, mischievous
Or anywhere else	

Since a place changes its atmosphere from night to day, from winter to summer, from workday to weekend, think of a place *at a particular time*.

STEP 2: INVENTION AND THE CONTROLLING FILTER

Often a subject and a controlling filter spring to mind together: a vivid picture strikes your imagination—it's almost like turning on the television. This is what happened to Brand Nicholas, a beginning student, trying his first written assignment for many years. The place was the Irish Pub, the time was Friday night at 11:00 P.M., and the controlling filter was *rowdy*. Brand was ready to go.

What happens, though, if inspiration doesn't strike, or if you're reluctant to jump to conclusions? "I want to write about this old man I saw one time sitting outside a hut in Mexico, but I can't seem to get going on it." You have a picture in mind, but the words don't suggest themselves. This is not necessarily a bad thing; thinking over your material before you commit yourself to a controlling filter makes perfect sense. While you are thinking over the old Mexican, keep the "filter questions" in mind: *How* was this person? What exactly was he like? If you're dealing with a place: What was the *atmosphere* of this place? When you're ready, maybe after a day or two of casual, unstructured thinking, a strong filter word usually suggests itself.

And what if you're stuck—the mental logjam? There are two ways to break a logjam: increase the pressure of the water, or start shifting the logs around (with dynamite, if necessary). Increasing the water pressure, for a writer, means increasing the flow of ideas. How is it done? Where do these extra ideas come from?

A simple technique, appropriate to writing a description, is to use either "automatic" writing or "free" writing. *Automatic writing* is letting the ideas flow onto the paper almost as though you are in a trance; you exercise *no control whatever* over your writing beyond starting with the name of your subject. Your subconscious does the rest. The theory is that a free association of ideas produces unexpected but valuable material. (Of course, you won't know until afterwards if this has been the case.) It's worth trying automatic writing to see what it produces even if you are *not* stuck.

Free writing is more controlled. In the case of the old Mexican outside the hut, you'd try to write a description, completely unfiltered, letting your memory play across the scene to catch anything and everything you can recall. During writing you completely ignore such issues as spelling or sentence structure. If the flow of writing dries up for a second, you can keep writing the last word you used until the flow starts again. What you are seeing in your imagination is all-important; the words on the page simply blaze the trail for you to follow later. When you look back at your material, it often suggests just the filter word you're looking for. As with automatic writing, free writing is useful at this stage even if you already have the perfect filter word.

A logjam can also be broken by studying the logs: moving one log may release all the others. For a writer, this means taking a *systematic* look at the subject. In describing a room, for example, you might start at the door and list everything you can see (or remember) moving clockwise around the room. In describing the view from the top of a tower, you could compose your list from background to foreground. With a person, you could work from top to toe. If you have a photograph, you can simply list what you see. Studying such a list should highlight the crucial point, the key idea you need as a controlling filter for the whole description.

The end product of this step is a subject and a controlling filter. One way to keep things straight is to use a format of some sort. At the start of this step we mentioned Brand Nicholas's piece on the Irish Pub. In this case a suitable format would be:

Subject time and place	Controlling Filter *how* the place is	Materials and Structure
Place The Irish Pub **Time** Friday, 11:00 p.m.	Rowdy	

STEP 3: FILTERING AND BRAINSTORMING

If your subject and the controlling filter came to you instantly, you'll now have to brainstorm for details. Each idea you come up with must pass through the filter before you can use it. If, on the other hand, the filter word came late, you'll already have plenty of ideas to work with. As an example, let's look at how Anke Bridges, another beginning student, set about describing her grandmother.

Anke quickly decided that the word *kind* summed up her grandmother and would make a workable controlling filter. When she began to collect ideas, however, very little occurred to her. To jog her memory, she found a photograph of her grandmother. The photograph helped, and she noted down everything about her grandmother that she remembered as *kind*:

CHAPTER ONE
Static Description

When Anke studied these ideas, she realized that the word *kind* wasn't quite right, and she switched to the word *loving*. Love, in this special sense, became the keynote of the piece that Anke finally wrote.

In general, be ready at any stage to change an earlier decision. Writing is a creative process, not a mechanical procedure, and you must allow yourself the freedom to have many second thoughts.

STEP 4: STRUCTURE

With a supply of well-filtered detail to hand, your next step is to put your ideas in order. We discussed your options earlier in the chapter. Let's see, now, how Anke and Brand proceeded.

Anke decided to adopt the tailor-made structure that she'd studied in O'Hara's description of Miller:

APPEARANCE (Seeing) → BEHAVIOR (Watching)

Three of Anke's ideas let the reader *see* the old lady: her clothes, her plumpness, and her smile. That order seemed fine; the kindly smile was the key point so it went last. As to behavior, there were again three points: the excursion to Disneyland (which took place after Anke had received a dreadful report card); the fact that her grandmother cooked only what Anke liked to eat; and the apartment with the pictures of the family everywhere. The excursion story made a good wrapup, and the family pictures made an effective opening to the behavior section. Anke's game plan looked like this:

Subject	Controlling Filter *how* the person is	Materials and Structure

My grandmother	Loving	**Appearance**
		    Unkempt clothing
		    Comfortable plumpness
		    Her smile
		 Behavior
		    Her family pictures
		    Her cooking
		    Anecdote: excursion to
		       Disneyland

Brand remembered the Irish Pub as rowdy. This rowdy atmosphere had three sources: the noisy people, the raucous music, and the riot-torn barroom itself. Brand decided to use order of significance; this put the people, the key point, last—Brand liked the idea of using them as a climax. The room itself formed the background, so Brand put it first; the music fell into the middle spot. Brand's basic structure was now clear.

BARROOM → MUSIC → PEOPLE

Brand did not plan each of his three sections in detail: he let each segment of the description simply flow onto the page. This meant rearranging some of the details afterwards, but Brand, like many people, was a minimum planner. In its final form, Brand's game plan looked like this:

Subject time and place	Controlling Filter *how* the place is	Materials and Structure

Place
 The Irish Pub
 Time
 Friday, 11:00 p.m.
	Rowdy	**Barroom**
		    Guinness-stained walls
		      and floors
		    Decorations: pictures of
		      racehorses and pinups
		 Music
		    Irish punk-folk band
		 People
		    Heavy drinkers
		    Their amusements:
		      drinking contests,
		      singing, fights
		    Anecdote: the night
		    Kevin and Jane got
		      engaged

• Writing the First Draft

RECURSION AND THE GAME PLAN

Were you ever told at school to write an outline and then stick to it? If you tried to do this, you probably cheated a little, tidying up the outline from the writing. Let's get things straight: *you were not really cheating, you were being asked to do something impossible*. The writing process, as any experienced writer will tell you, is *circular*: you have an idea, a game plan; you put the idea into words, the first draft. Writing this draft usually changes your idea, so now you revise the game plan; this new game plan forces you to rewrite; this new draft. . . . And so it goes on until deadline time. This circular process is called *recursion*. If you push recursion to the extreme, you'll finalize your game plan at about the same time that you finalize the paper. The essence of the problem is summed up in two terms: *game plan* and *outline*. Let's look at the difference.

On the sports field, a game plan can be anything from a hazy "Just go in there and do your best" to a detailed scheme of plays and counterplays. The successful coach delivers a game plan adapted to the strength of the players, the strength of the opposing team, the weather, and so on. The game plan is an idea—an idea that seldom works out on the field of play. An *outline* is more like a videotape of the highlights of a game. Such a tape outlines the game for the viewer, breaking it into phases and showing exactly what happened in each phase. The game plan exists for the benefit of the players; it is flexible, and it changes as the game develops. The taped outline is for the benefit of the onlooker; it is fixed once and for all.

Back now to the practicalities of writing. As a writer you need a game plan; it may be sketchy—just a word or two on a scratch pad (or even in your head), or it may be an elaborate pre-analysis of your material. The game plan should suit the subject, your knowledge, your available time, and so on. During the writing process, the game plan tends to grow and become more refined. Let it happen. When the first draft is complete, only then should you consider writing an outline, an "edited tape" of your work. The outline offers the reader an overview of your piece: that is its only function. We shall say no more about the reader's outline until we need one to accompany a full-length essay. (See Chapters 4–8.) What concerns us here is the writer's game plan.

Recursion, then, is the circular process by which an idea acquires an ever more definite shape as you write about it. It is a basic principle of good writing. Some students know this instinctively: their problem is knowing when to stop fiddling with what they've written. How much recursion is enough? Writing experts disagree on this: some frown on any growth in the game plan, while others encourage seemingly endless recursion. Naturally, you'll want to try various possibilities and find what works best for you. (A word of caution: at one time there was a fashion for dispensing with game plans altogether; that can work well with short, creative pieces, but it makes longer, expository subjects tough to develop.)

GETTING STARTED: THE TRASH-BASKET SYNDROME

Not all writing gets off to a smooth start. A common scenario is this:

10:00 Domestic chores are completed; writing can begin.

10:15 A game plan on Uncle Joe has fallen nicely into place.

10:30 Five awkward, unsatisfactory sentences with many erasures cover half a page of scratch paper.

10:31 The five sentences are in the trash basket.

10:45 Three even more awkward and unsatisfactory sentences disfigure a new page.

10:46 These three sentences are in the trash basket.

10:47 The game plan on Uncle Joe is in the trash basket.

11:02 A new game plan on Preacher Sims has taken shape, but reluctantly.

11:15 One sentence on Preacher Sims stares at you from the page.

11:16 Preacher Sims is in the trash basket.

11:45 A game plan on the town drunk is half completed.

11:59 Nothing more has been written.

12:00 The game plan on Uncle Joe is retrieved from the trash basket, smoothed out, reread, recrumpled, and thrown back in the trash basket.

Your two hours of quality time have produced absolutely nothing. The problem is painfully common but luckily not insoluble. Two escape routes exist:

Route 1. Do not reread anything you have just written. Just roar ahead and write your way at top speed through the whole game plan. This is close to the technique of free writing mentioned earlier, except that you keep one eye on your game plan. At the end of this writing spurt, you'll often find that the opening sentences need rewriting while later sentences are markedly better; at some point you'll have hit your stride. Finishing a first draft (even with weaknesses) is a strong motivator to review and improve rather than to dump the whole thing in the trash basket.

Route 2. Since you have a game plan, find the easiest part to work on, and start there. Beginning writers often forget that a first draft can be pieced together in any order. If your anecdote looks easy to tell, tell it first. As segments of the description take shape, your motivation to attack the remaining, trickier parts increases. Nobody throws into the trash basket something that is developing nicely but has a few unresolved problems.

CONCRETENESS

Concreteness, as we said earlier, is a major goal for beginning writers. The point will stand repeating. While you are writing your first draft, form a mental picture of what you are describing, and try to get the picture down on the page. The goal of descriptive writing is to create for the reader the picture you see in your mind's eye.

• Revising

Planning, drafting, revising—the first two steps are creative. Revising is more down-to-earth—somehow, you must turn your plans and your first draft(s) into a presentable finished product. It's a little like washing your hair: after shampooing, your hair is clean enough, but it isn't *presentable* until it's been combed into shape. With many written assignments, combing (the process of revising) makes the difference between a C− and an A.

Step 1 in revising is to leave the draft to jell. The ideal period is about six months; normally, however, allow at least overnight. Then review. What is the reviewing process intended to achieve? The three C's: continuity, cost effectiveness (or economy), correctness. The best plan is to check over your draft three times, looking specifically at each problem. First then, continuity.

REVISION CHECK 1: CONTINUITY—AVOIDING THE GRASSHOPPER EFFECT

While you are writing, the connections between your ideas are clear in your mind, so clear that you may jump from one idea to the next without linking things up for the reader. A first draft by even a top-flight writer is liable to this weakness. Coming back to your work after a cooling-off period, you'll notice this "grasshopper effect" clearly. How should details be linked? Let us look at a case in point: a description of "My Uncle Ben" wholly lacking in continuity.

My Uncle Ben never married. His face was always flecked with dirt and his nose pitted with blackheads. His callused hands were deeply ingrained with grime, and his fingernails were black and broken from countless minor accidents. Every time he drilled a hole for a pipe, his greasy hair would collect thick plaster and brick dust. He wore a filthy blue coverall and a kicked-out pair of army boots. He put on a jacket to go to the bar, though he seldom bothered with a shirt. He was a keen fisherman and bought expensive tackle. His tackle had become hopelessly entangled in a closet with a defunct vacuum cleaner, old sections of lead pipe, coveralls that even he thought were too old to wear, and some horse harness he had found in a customer's attic. Often he ate just bread and cheese, not bothering with a plate or knife, but simply gnawing on a loaf and a hunk of cheese. His refrigerator was so disorganized that food rotted, and he was often home sick with food poisoning. I was staying with him once. Despite my mother's warnings, Uncle Ben had gone out for the evening, leaving me to put myself to bed. The front door banged. I heard Uncle Ben curse the doorstep. He had dropped his jacket on the doorstep and left the door wide open. He was sitting on the stairs, quietly singing. He took off his boots and threw them out into the yard; then he stood up, heaved himself up the stairs, and slept on the landing. He had rolled up one corner of the rug to make a pillow.

Each fact here is plain enough, but the way the writing jumps from one idea to the next is disconcerting. To improve continuity, the piece needs three things: (A) linking sentences, or *transitions*, (B) time and place markers, and (C) some brief words of explanation. In the next draft, the necessary continuity has been added.

PART ONE
Basic Materials—Basic Skills

Margin notes (left):
(1) Link marriage to appearance
(2) Link hygiene to grooming
(3) Explain *why* he drilled holes
(4) Link grooming to clothing
(5) Place marker
(6) Time marker
(7) Link appearance to environment
(8) Explain how the closet fits in

Margin notes (right):
(9) Time marker
(10) Time marker
(11) Link environment to behavior
(12) Explain how eating fits in
(13) Link description to anecdote
(14) Time marker
(15) Time marker
(16) Time marker
(17) Explain overall message

My uncle Ben never married. (1) *He lived on his own for many years, and his appearance went steadily downhill.* His face was always flecked with dirt and his nose pitted with blackheads. His callused hands were deeply ingrained with grime, and his fingernails were black and broken from countless minor accidents. (2) *His grooming was as primitive as his hygiene.* (3) *He was a plumber by trade, and,* every time he drilled a hole for a pipe, his greasy hair would collect thick plaster and brick dust. (4) *His clothes did nothing to improve his appearance.* (5) *At work* he wore a filthy blue coverall and a kicked-out pair of army boots. (6) *In the evenings* he put on a jacket to go to the bar, though he seldom bothered with a shirt. (7) *His environment was a direct extension of his personality.* (8) *One closet sums him up perfectly.* (9) *As a young man,* he'd been a keen fisherman and bought expensive tackle. (10) *By the time I knew him,* his tackle had become hopelessly entangled in a closet with a defunct vacuum cleaner, old sections of lead pipe, coveralls that even he thought were too old to wear, and some horse harness he had found in a customer's attic. (11) *His behavior mirrored the chaos around him.* (12) *Like many bachelors, he was uncritical about food.* Often he ate just bread and cheese, not bothering with a plate or knife, but simply gnawing on a loaf and a hunk of cheese. His refrigerator was so disorganized that food rotted, and he was often home sick with food poisoning. (13) *One episode sums up the man perfectly.* I was staying with him (14) *While my mother was in the hospital having my younger brother.* Despite my mother's warnings, Uncle Ben had gone out for the evening, leaving me to put myself to bed. (15) *Very late that night* the front door banged. I heard Uncle Ben curse the doorstep. He had dropped his jacket on the doorstep and left the door wide open. He was sitting on the stairs, quietly singing. He took off his boots and threw them out into the yard; then he stood up, heaved himself up the stairs, and slept on the landing. (16) *Next morning I found him still asleep.* He had rolled up one corner of the rug to make a pillow. (17) *He was without doubt the untidiest man I have ever known.*

The principle is clear: when you shift from one aspect of the subject to the next, (A) make the reader aware of the transition, (B) offer the necessary time and place clues, and (C) show how the new facts fit with what went before.

Your first proofreading should insure *continuity*. If in doubt, have a friend read the piece to see if it hangs together.

REVISION CHECK 2: COST-EFFECTIVENESS

Managers want ideas that are cost-effective: will a project repay the investment of time and money it requires? For a writer, the question is much the same: for an investment of x words, what return of meaning will I get? Three main faults hurt cost-effectiveness: unnecessary repetition (saying the same thing too often), colloquialism (using long-winded *spoken* English), and abstraction (becoming too general). Your second revision should look for these faults and aim at a ruthless tightening up of language. Don't slice out any hard facts—simply try for the *same content* in *fewer words*.

a. **Repetition.** Sometimes repetition gains emphasis; more often the writer is simply repeating things for no good reason. Unnecessary repetition has two forms. The first is "hot air." Two examples:

a. Mr. Smithers was never late for work; he was always either early or on time.

b. Melinda kept her house spotless, and it was always perfectly clean.

In each case cost-effectiveness is about half what it should be. The other form of repetitiveness is "overlapping"—two inches forward, one inch back:

The butcher was very skinny. This skinniness was commented on by many of his customers. His customers commented on it because it seemed so inappropriate in a butcher. What would be more appropriate in a butcher, they felt, was a sort of jovial chubbiness.

Review carefully. If you're saying the same thing twice, you can double your cost-effectiveness by saying it only once.

b. Colloquial (Spoken) English. Colloquial (spoken) English and written English are not distinct forms, but one common feature of speech is deadly in writing—its wordiness. For example:

Okay—so you go into the storeroom. Well, just as you get inside the door you'll see a kind of table on your left.

It is more than twice as cost effective to write:

To the right of the door is a table.

In academic papers, the student/writer does not have time to gossip with the instructor/reader; the emphasis is on hard-hitting communication. In the business world, of course, economy of language is even more valued.

c. Abstraction. We've already seen the value of concrete writing. When revising, develop the habit of dropping abstract, general words and substituting concrete or specific equivalents. Look at this description of a miser's hoard as it might be written by a beginning student:

There was so much stuff in his house, no one could begin to describe it. This guy had collected everything he could lay his hands on, and all of it was useless old junk. It was lying around everywhere in heaps. His house was the biggest mess imaginable. Heaven knows where he'd got all this garbage from. It was all just trash. He must have been collecting it for years.

Cost effectiveness is poor here. The writer uses seventy words to create nothing but a vague impression of a heap of rubbish. By way of contrast, here is how the Russian writer, Nicolai Gogol, describes the hoard of a miser named Plyushkin.

On the bureau, inlaid with a mosaic of mother-of-pearl, which had fallen out in places, leaving brown holes filled with glue, lay a great assortment of all kinds of things: a heap of closely written bits of paper held down by a marble paperweight with a little egg-shaped handle on top, all green with age, an ancient book in a leather binding with red chasing, a lemon shriveled to the size of a hazel nut, the broken-off arm of a chair, a wine glass with some liquid and three flies in it, covered with a letter, a piece of sealing wax, a bit of an old rag picked up somewhere, two ink-stained quills, all burnt out as though from consumption, and a tookpick grown so yellow with age that its owner had probably cleaned his teeth with it since before the French marched on Moscow.

Nicolai Gogol
From *Dead Souls*

No problem with concreteness here! Gogol's piece forces the reader to *see* exactly the hoard that Gogol has in mind; the student's description forces no one to see anything.

Feeble abstraction is easy to spot when it coagulates into large globs, but you'll find it too in the most innocent-looking sentences:

Annie was a great person with a fantastic personality.

That doesn't tell the reader much about Annie. Perhaps the writer means:

> Annie was a sensitive person with a responsive personality.
> Annie was a hilarious person with a dynamic personality.
> Annie was an affectionate person with a warm personality.
> Annie was a case-hardened person with a tough personality.

General, blanket words tell the reader next to nothing. Try to get closer to the facts; it's more cost effective.

REVISION CHECK 3: CORRECTNESS

After revision checks 1 and 2, you'll have a description that has good continuity and that doesn't waste words, but it still won't make the grade unless it is free of spelling, grammar, and punctuation errors, and similar problems.

Proofreading to spot these errors does not come naturally. Sometimes you let errors slip by even when you know the rules perfectly. The best technique for catching such slips is *print-shop proofreading*. In the print shop, a text is read *aloud* by a reader to a listener; both have a copy of the text in front of them. This catches most errors. You can achieve much the same effect by reading your work into a tape recorder. One trap is *screen proofreading*. If you work at a computer, don't try to proofread from the screen—you'll miss too much. Always proofread from a printout. Finally, a trick. If you often overlook misspellings, try reading the piece backwards: start with the last word and work towards the first; that way you'll look at each word separately—there is no train of thought to divert your mind from its task.

While you are proofreading, you'll obviously use a dictionary to check the spellings and meanings of words. Let's look at these two procedures.

When checking *spelling*, get into the habit of glancing at the definition, or you might get the correct spelling of the wrong word. To home in on the target word, you might find the *Bad Speller's Dictionary* useful. It lists common misspellings alphabetically and suggests alternative spellings for you to check out in a normal dictionary.

Checking *meanings* is a bigger problem. First, for serious work you'll need a good, fat dictionary. Why? Pocket dictionaries, though cheap, give amateurish definitions: for example, *brave* may be defined as *courageous*, and *courageous* may be defined as *brave*. You need a dictionary that explains the differences among the words in a word group; that means investing a few more dollars. The second problem is that most dictionaries are unselective in what they list. "There ain't too many dumb kids round here" is not a sentence most instructors would accept, for example. But if you check out the suspect words in *Webster's Ninth New Collegiate Dictionary* (1986 edition), you'll find *ain't* (in the sense of "are not"), *dumb* (in the sense of "stupid"), and *kids* (in the sense of "children"); there is no warning that these words should be shunned, although you'll learn that *ain't* "is disapproved by many." The trap is obvious: the fact that you find a word in a dictionary does not mean that it is appropriate in academic writing. Finally, dictionaries are written by fallible people. If you research a word in three dictionaries, you'll find three different opinions as to exactly what the word means or how it is used. Maybe they are all right or all wrong. Our language is alive; a dictionary, even a good one, is an attempt to deep-freeze words at some arbitrary stage in their development.

To check punctuation, capitalization, grammar and so on, you'll need a handbook. If you know you have a problem, then the index at the back of the handbook will help you track down the information you need. Of course, you won't know at first that the grammar error in the sentence "We was out of town that day" is indexed under *Subject-Verb Agreement*. By the end of the course, though, you'll know the errors you personally make and where to find the necessary information.

What happens, on the other hand, if the sentence looks good to you but is actually substandard? If you have this kind of problem, then you'll have to make a special effort to catch up; a freshman English course at a college or university seldom has time to review high school work. Experience shows that certain errors tend to occur when a writer is describing; others occur when contrasting; others when defining, and so on. As each writing method is covered, this book will flag for you the associated errors. *If any of the rules mentioned are unclear to you, or you are rusty in using them, then review them thoroughly in your handbook before you proofread.*

• Special Correctness Problems—Static Description

PROBLEM 1: CAPITAL LETTERS WITH NAMES

In describing a person or a place, you'll need to *name* your subject. This can present problems with capital letters. If the rules are shaky in your mind, check your handbook under *Capital Letters* or *Capitalization*.

PROBLEM 2: POSSESSIVES

Names attract possessions: *my grandmother's house, my sister's best dress, Aunt Eliza's idea of a good time*. The problem is the use of the apostrophe. Since the apostrophe is also used to show that a letter has been omitted, forms such as *its* and *it's* are easily confused. To remind yourself of the rules, check your handbook under *Possessives, Omission of Letters* or *Apostrophe*.

PROBLEM 3: YOU, THE READER

To make a description vivid, you'll often want to "grab the reader's elbow." Naturally, the word *you* is used for the reader. The danger is that you'll use the same word to mean *people in general*. For example, a female student might write "When you go out with your boyfriend you should pay for yourself." If the teacher is male, or is a married woman, this could be absurd or even insulting. The rule is: Unless you mean *you, the reader*, don't use *you* at all. If you need a review, check your handbook under *You* or *Indefinite Pronouns*.

PROBLEM 4: ADJECTIVES IN LISTS AND IN COMPOUNDS

Descriptive writing is rich in nouns; adjectives are used in descriptions to give these nouns greater concreteness. A list of adjectives is broken up by commas. Almost all two-word adjectives (as in *a gray-green coat*) require a hyphen. To review, check your handbook under *Coordinate Adjectives*, *Adjectives in a Series*, *Compound Adjectives*, or *Hyphen*.

PROBLEM 5: PLAIN-AND VERSUS COMMA-AND

When you're building descriptive detail, you'll often link ideas together with the word *and*. There are, in fact, two forms of the word *and*: one has a comma immediately in front of it, while the other does not. (The same is true of *but* and *or*.) The rule is: *comma-and* joins sentences; *plain-and* is used for virtually all other purposes. To review this concept, check your handbook under *Commas with Coordinate Clauses*, *Coordinate Main Clauses*, or *Superfluous Commas*.

PROBLEM 6: USING THE PAST TENSE

The past tense is the most appropriate for normal descriptive writing. Description in the present tense is found mostly in horror stories and other "breathless" fiction. To review, check your handbook under *Tense*, or *Sequence of Tenses*.

• The Final Draft

There is no standard layout for academic written work. Confirm with your instructor exactly how your work should be turned in. Completing the checklist below will give you a clear idea of what you are shooting for.

The Final Draft:
A Checklist

a. What information must be included on the title page?

b. Should the work be submitted in a folder of any kind?

c. Is the format loose-leaf, bound at the top, or bound at the side?

d. What margins are required? (Remember to allow for binding.)

e. If you have no typewriter, is handwriting acceptable?

f. Is single spacing or double spacing required?

g. Are last-minute, inked-in changes in a typescript acceptable?

> **h.** Is a dot-matrix printout acceptable?
>
> **i.** Are sourcenotes and bibliography required? If so, in what form? (These items are covered in later chapters.)
>
> **j.** Is an outline required? If so, in what form?
>
> **k.** Are there any special instructions?

Finally, don't forget to proofread the final draft. A shoddy typescript can ruin days of hard work. It's the end product that makes the grade, so make a super job of it. A letter in *Writer's Digest*, December 1986, sums up perfectly the art of the final draft:

THE KISSINGER CRITIQUE

A friend of my family was a graduate student under Dr. Henry Kissinger. When the friend produced his first piece of writing for Kissinger, he took it in and left it for a few days, expecting a critique. When he returned, Kissinger said, "Is this the *best* job you can do on this?"

"Maybe I could change a few things," the young man admitted. "I'll take it back and see what I can do with it."

He reworked it and brought it in again. When he returned after a few days, Kissinger asked, "Is this really your best work?"

"Probably I could improve it a little," the student said, retrieving it again. He spent hours poring over it, working word by word. Then he left it again at Kissinger's office.

Upon his return a few days later, Kissinger asked, "Are you going to tell me this is your best effort?"

"Yes, sir, this is the *best* job I can do," the young man said emphatically.

"All right, then," Kissinger said. "I'll read it."

Anita Heistand

•   Summary: The Flowchart

The purpose of this flowchart is to review what we've discussed. It is not a "writing program" that you are obliged (or expected) to follow.

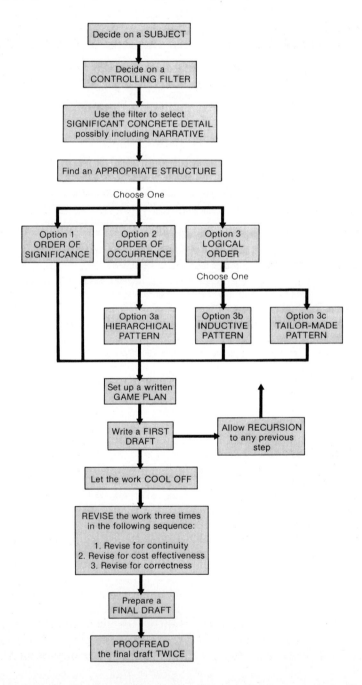

TWO

Dynamic Description: The Analysis of Process

1 •
The Problem: Moving Step by Step

• The Easy Case

> Most ingenious of all nests are those constructed by a small group of warblers which live in South East Asia. Aptly named tailorbirds, they have long straight bills and long tails, which they hold erect like a wren. They select two large leaves, and with their bills puncture holes around the edges of them. They then collect strands of cottony fluff, which they push through the holes of the two leaves, so that they are drawn together. In the little pocket which is formed, the tailorbird constructs its nest proper, composed of fine grasses and plant-down.
>
> Malcolm Ellis
> From *The World of Birds*

Descriptions like this are a pleasure to read. In such a description we are taken step by step through a chain of events, starting at the beginning and finishing at the end. The events are linked like that most systematic of all human creations, a string of beads. For his description of the tailorbirds, this is Ellis's "string of beads," or his *schema*, as we can call it. The birds:

| Select two large leaves | → | Puncture holes round the edges | → | Collect strands of "fluff" | → | Use the strands to sew the leaves together | → | Construct a nest on the leaves |

Whether or not Ellis actually used a formal schema like this, the description is evidently *planned*. How important is this planning? A glance at an unplanned piece immediately answers the question.

How to Pitch a Tent

The flysheet of a tent is an outer protective layer that completely covers the main tent. Spreading the flysheet over the main tent is the last step but one in pitching a tent. The last step of all is holding the flysheet in place with its own guy ropes and tent pegs. Let us say you have a two-pole tent with a ridgepole between the uprights. Normally, each end of the ridgepole has a hole in it: one upright pole fits into each of these holes. But not yet, of course—first you must peg out the groundsheet. Let's assume that the groundsheet is sewn in as the floor of the tent. Along the edges of the groundsheet will be little notches or rings. The idea is that you put skewers through these rings to "peg out" the groundsheet. But first, obviously, you must lay out the groundsheet on the grass, keeping it smooth and square. Before you lay it out, check which direction the door should point in. Then crawl inside the tent with the two upright poles. (You'll need to unzip the tent first.) The ridgepole will later fit between the upright poles <u>outside</u> the main tent. The main tent is held in place with guy ropes, but first (as we were saying a moment ago) you must get the poles in position and upright. Finally then, put on the flysheet, and you're in business. (The ridgepole, by the way, goes <u>under</u> the flysheet.)

Concept Review

Constructing a Schema

Describing a process is one of the most common short assignments; it seems simple enough, but the tent instructions show how easily a writer can go off the track. To find out what went wrong, try to draw up the "beads-on-a-string" schema that our camping expert should have followed. If you've never pitched a tent, the diagram should help.

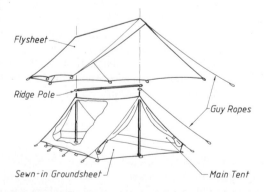

• Types of Process—Four Patterns

The general principle in describing a process is to make a step-by-step schema and to follow it. This is what Ellis did with his tailorbirds and what you have just done with the tent instructions. If processes were that simple, this chapter would be rather short. But anyone who has tried to draw up a schema knows that in practice there are problems. This is because there are so many *kinds* of process. One type (the nestmaking of the tailorbirds, for example) is simple: the chain of events runs smoothly from *A* to *B*; only one thing is happening at any one time; the process always follows the same course, and it follows a logical, step-by-step sequence. But what happens if you're describing a process that goes not from *A* to *B* but around in a circle instead? Or if a dozen things are happening at the same time? To learn how to handle such common but puzzling variations, you first need a clear sense of what the variations are.

VARIATION 1: STRAIGHT-LINE VERSUS CYCLIC PROCESSES

The simplest kind of process proceeds in a *straight line* from one state to another. For example:

How I planted a vegetable garden last summer
How I gave up smoking
How I built a log cabin

In each case, you start out in one state (not having a vegetable garden, being a smoker, and so on) and finish up in another state (having a garden, being a nonsmoker, and so on). The process is straight-line. There's another possibility, however; a *cyclic* process, for example the chicken-and-egg cycle, has no start and no finish. The cycle of the seasons is the same: each season follows the one before in a never-ending cycle. The recycling of such industrial raw materials as paper, glass, or aluminum is also an endless process. Two definitions, then: a process that goes from *A* to *B* is *straight-line*; a process that finishes where it started is *cyclic*.

Concept Review

Straight-Line and Cyclic Processes

To check that you've understood this distinction, label these processes either straight-line or cyclic:

a. The process by which the moon (apparently) changes shape

b. The process by which one passenger passes through an air terminal

c. The process by which the QE2 was built

d. The process by which a single bus provides a shuttle service

VARIATION 2: SIMPLE VERSUS COMPLEX PROCESSES

A second way of looking at processes asks how many activities are happening *simultaneously* while the process is under way. The straight-line processes given in Variation 1 (how I built a log cabin, and so on) all contain the word *I*. Since one person does one thing at a time, these processes are not only straight-line, they are also *simple*—that is, two or more activities never occur simultaneously. In discussing how "I" built a log cabin, for example, the chain of actions is a simple "string of beads":

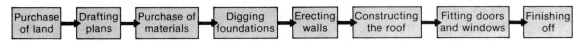

Let's increase the number of builders to three (dad, daughter, son). With several actions happening simultaneously, the process becomes *complex*, and this complexity is reflected in the schema:

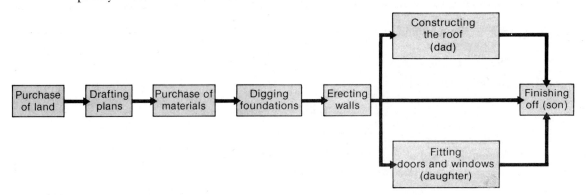

Imagine now a building site with workers in twenty different trades simultaneously sawing, mixing, wiring, laying pipes, plastering and so on. You can see that a description can become very complex and difficult to write. Some examples of inherently complex subjects:

The struggle of women for equal rights
The process by which President Nixon was forced to resign
The development of a piece of computer hardware

To summarize: in a *simple* process, only one thing happens at a time; in a *complex* process two or more things happen simultaneously.

Concept Review

Simple and Complex Processes

Label these examples *simple* or *complex*:

a. The process by which a cruise ship is prepared for a trip

b. The process by which you set the hands on a watch

c. The process of wrapping a parcel

d. The process of launching an infantry attack

VARIATION 3: UNIQUE VERSUS REPEATED PROCESSES

Some processes happen once and once only; others are repeated. If you pick up a promotional leaflet entitled *How Pinelog and Shingle, Inc., Builds a Log Cabin*, you'll anticipate that this company has built many log cabins. You, on the other hand, have built only one. Your building is an example of a *unique process*—the job was done once and once only. The building of a log cabin by Pinelog and Shingle is a *repeated process*, performed many times over. *Unique:* the process happened only once; *repeated:* it happened two or more times.

Concept Review

Unique and Repeated Processes

Again decide if these processes are *unique* or *repeated*.

a. The process by which the Empire State Building was constructed

b. The process by which skyscrapers are built

c. The process by which Edison invented the first light bulb

d. The process by which patents are registered

VARIATION 4: STEPPED VERSUS CONTINUOUS PROCESSES

When people set a process in motion (building a log cabin, or whatever), they plan in steps; this makes the development of a step-by-step analysis easy—the analysis closely reflects what originally happened. Planned processes are inherently *stepped*. On the other hand, nature (or history) does not work purposively, step by step. The classic example of a *continuous process* is the way wind and rain erode an outcrop of rock. Over millions of years, grain by grain, the rock is eroded through endless shapes. The process cannot easily be reduced to steps. Historical and natural processes—both common writing assignments—are usually continuous or unstepped in this way. For example:

Historical Processes
The destruction of tribal American Indian society
The rise of Japan as an industrial nation

Natural Processes
The process by which the Grand Canyon was formed
The formation of cirrus clouds

The distinction once more: a *stepped* process falls readily into steps, while a *continuous process* has no built-in step markers.

Concept Review

Stepped and Continuous Processes

A final group of processes: are these examples *stepped* or *continuous*?

a. The process by which the small farmer is disappearing

b. The process by which an acorn grows into an oak

c. The process by which the Brooklyn Bridge was built

d. The process by which a book is printed

THE FOUR VARIATIONS—SUMMARY

You will often be asked to describe a process. First you must find out what kind of process it is. You may spot immediately that the process is:

Straight line	(it goes from *A* to *B*)
Simple	(only one thing is happening at once)
Unique	(it has happened only once, or always happens in exactly the same way)
Stepped	(it falls easily into steps)

If so, your next move is clear: draw up a string-of-beads schema as the basis of a game plan. If you are less lucky and your subject turns out to be cyclic, complex, repeated, or continuous, then you'll need to go more deeply into the planning stage. In the following section you'll see the special problems associated with each variation, along with some ideas on how to solve them.

• Four Variations—Four Kinds of Problems

PROBLEM 1: CYCLIC PROCESSES

Let's say you are taking ECON 301, *Current Issues in American Economic Policy*. In class, the lecturer has presented the farm price support system, making it clear that this system is *cyclic*. She has explained that since the Great Depression this cycle has had no beginning and no ending. She stresses the problem by using the term "vicious circle," and she draws this picture on the chalkboard:

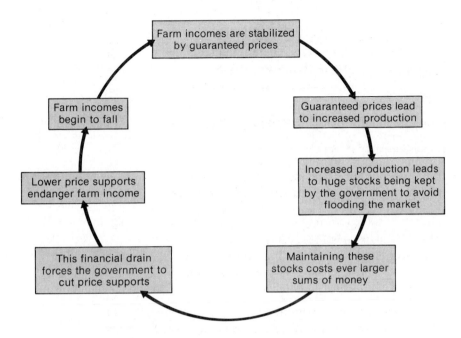

The lecturer then assigns the subject: "Describe the price support system for agricultural products." Let's look at the approaches of two students. One begins:

> Our system of farm price support is like a dog chasing its own tail—an endless circle without a beginning or an end. There is no obvious place to break into the cycle, so I'll begin with the moment when farm incomes are falling and the government must take action. This is a point the cycle will return to later; before then, however, a chain of six events must be repeated. As soon as the government decides . . .

As each new step in the process begins, this student stresses the idea of a *cycle*, using such phrases as:

> The next step in this cycle . . .
> At this stage, the real nastiness of this vicious circle is apparent.
> The final step, which takes us back where we began, is that . . .

The other student begins: "The price support system is triggered when farm incomes are falling rapidly." Each new step begins simply: "The next step is that . . ."

Who makes the better grade? Obviously, the student who knew and who explained that the system was a *cycle*. The other student may have the steps in the right order, but the description is unsatisfactory: it fails to reflect what the lecturer worked hard to put across. Is the mistake really so serious? Think of it this way: An instructor assigns an essay to test that students know the facts and that they understand how these facts fit together. Of the two, understanding is by far the more important. The first student has shown understanding; the second has not.

Review Assignment

Making the Cycle Go Round

Rewrite this short description, making it clear that the process discussed is *cyclic*:

When the mountain snow melts in spring, it turns into river water. Rivers flow down to the sea. Sea water evaporates because of the effects of sun and wind, forming clouds. These clouds precipitate their moisture partly as snow.

PROBLEM 2: REPEATED PROCESSES

The main problem with repeated processes is that they are seldom repeated in the same way. "How I respray a car," for example:

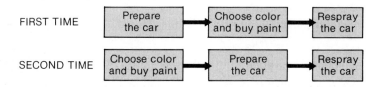

Which version would you use? Obviously neither—if you plan on telling the truth. The only way out is to *consolidate* the first steps into a single super-step:

The two-step process is true for *both* resprays. Unless a process is performed identically every time, then some steps will need *consolidation* in this way. If you have performed an action ten times, you'll have to draw up ten schemas and then find a way to reduce them to a "superschema."

The tense used to describe a repeated action may seem odd at first sight. Let's say you've bought five motorcycles, including the one you own now; if you were making the following comment, which tense would you use?

Whenever I buy/bought a motorbike, I always check/checked that the tires are/were good and that the brakes work/worked well.

Most writers instinctively (and correctly) choose the present tense, although the action is in the past. Strange.

A final hint: to keep your work alive and interesting, be ready to use examples of things that happened only once. The example goes in the past tense, of course. For instance:

CHAPTER TWO
Dynamic Description: The Analysis of Process

One thing I never do when I'm building the walls of a log cabin is to leave holes for the windows. (So far, present tense. Now switch to past for an anecdote.) I learned that the hard way one time in Castle Rock. On that occasion I tried to cut the logs so that the gaps for the windows occurred in the right places. The result was ragged, and the windows leaked. An old hunter told me how to do the job properly: build the log walls as a solid box and then cut out the window-gaps with a chain saw. (End of anecdote, end of past tense, back to the present.) Now I always do it his way.

Review Assignment

The Superschema

You are writing on the subject "How I Prepare for Examinations." You have taken four examinations. This is what happened in each case:

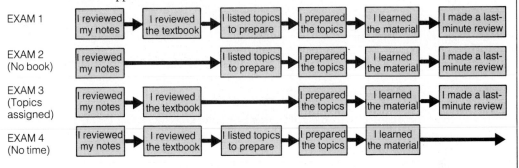

Draw up a superschema that is true for *all* these examinations.

PROBLEM 3: COMPLEX PROCESSES

Have you ever asked for directions, followed them carefully, and still become hopelessly lost? Probably you took a wrong turning. But why? Often because you saw a choice of roads, an alternative, that your informant, being familiar with the road, failed to clarify. Look at these two ways of giving directions to a stranger in town:

Version 1. You want to see the statue of Susan B Anthony. You want to walk. You go down this street to the big intersection and turn left. You see the station ahead of you. You go down the street and turn right. That road leads to the gasworks. You go straight ahead. You come to a big park. The statue is in the park. You don't want to walk at all. You'd better take a taxi.

Version 2. If you want to see the statue of Susan B Anthony, but you don't want to walk, then take a taxi. If you want to walk, then first you go down this street to the big intersection. There you have three roads to choose from. The road to the left leads only to the station, while the road to the right leads only to the gasworks. If you go straight ahead, however, you come to a big park. The statue is in the park.

The problem here is *branching*. Version 2 will get you to the statue because it labels all the branches and alternatives, explaining where they lead. A complex description often branches in a similar way. If the reader is not to get lost, very methodical "signposting," as in Version 2, is essential.

Where actions take place simultaneously, you have the same problem of complexity with much the same solution. Even a simple recipe can pose problems, for example:

1. Boil the brown rice in a covered skillet; it takes about thirty minutes.
2. Clean and chop the twelve vegetables, but not too finely.
3. Prepare the sauce (see recipe on previous page).
4. Stir the ingredients together immediately after the rice is fully cooked.

The danger here is all too apparent—if Steps 1, 2 and 3 are carried out in sequence, then Step 4 becomes impossible. To solve the problem, the reader must simply be "clued in":

1. Boil the brown rice in a covered skillet; it takes about thirty minutes. As soon as the rice is under way, begin Steps 2 and 3 below, since these must be completed before the rice has cooked.

Now there can be no mistake. The rule is simple: keep the reader in touch with the *structure* of your description. Every zig, every zag, every overlap, every choice must be carefully labeled.

Review Assignment

Spelling Out a Procedure

If you've ever wrested paperwork from an unwilling bureaucracy, you'll know the problem of discovering the correct procedure. On holiday in Ruritania, you ask the hotelkeeper about the local procedure for obtaining a fishing license. Because of his poor command of English, this is what you hear:

You want a fishing license. You want it for river fishing. You apply to the Department of Rivers. You want it for lake fishing. You apply to the Department of Lakes. You apply in duplicate. You hear nothing. You apply in triplicate. You enclose a check for 20 ruris. You hear nothing. You enclose a check for 20 ruris and a bribe of 10 ruris. You hear. You want both licenses. You apply to the Department of Rivers. You apply to the Department of Lakes.

Without the words *and*, *or* and *if*, these instructions are impossible to follow. Rewrite the piece to make the meaning unambiguous. (Where the original is unclear, make the most likely choice.)

PROBLEM 4: NATURAL PROCESSES

You are standing on a bridge, watching the flow of a river beneath you. How would you describe the process you are observing? It would be difficult: the water flows in an unbroken continuum, while the description of a process won't work unless it is broken into steps. Let's look at another case that's a little easier to deal with. A female frog lays her eggs in a pond as frog spawn. Slowly, each egg turns into a frog. The change does not occur step by step, but a writer will need to use steps to make the process understandable:

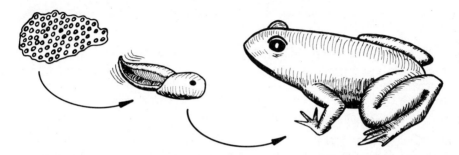

The infinitely gradual process is thus arranged in three brisk steps. The obvious problem now is to "draw the lines" between the steps: exactly when does spawn cease to be spawn and become a tadpole? Exactly when does a tadpole qualify as a frog? Every description of a continuous process will spend some time defining (and sometimes justifying) boundaries.

Review Assignment

The Continuum of Life

1. Draw up a step-by-step schema for human life, giving each step a clear label (*childhood*, *senility*, and so on). You'll probably have between four and ten "beads" on your string.

2. Define exactly the boundaries between each step. For example, what exactly separates *babyhood* from *childhood*, or *adolescence* from *maturity*, if you used those terms? Put another way, what "tests" must the individual pass to qualify for the next stage?

3. Try writing up two consecutive steps explaining (and perhaps justifying) the boundary you've established between them.

THE FOUR POTENTIAL PROBLEMS: SUMMARY

Working through these distinctions, seeing the problems that arise, and spotting possible solutions will help you with a dynamic description whenever you have to write one. More important, in doing this work you've probably begun to realize a major principle: planning a piece of writing is simply a matter of thinking a problem through. Thinking about the structure of your writing, once you understand how this kind of thinking works, will improve the quality of your work and save you an enormous amount of time. Eventually you'll forget the careful distinctions and the special terminology used in this book. But, if you've learned how to think through a writing problem, then you've learned the only lesson that really matters.

Concept Review

How Writers Use Dynamic Descriptions

Both of the following descriptions are "building blocks" from much longer works. Read the pieces, and then:

1. Draw up the "beads-on-a-string" schema that lies behind them.

2. Critique the pieces purely as examples of dynamic description. Do you find them perfectly coherent and easy to follow? Are any steps omitted? Is the transition from each step to the next absolutely clear? Is each step covered in the same way and in the same amount of detail?

3. Suggest ways of righting anything that you found troublesome.

> NONVIOLENT PROTEST
>
> In any nonviolent campaign there are four basic steps: collection of the facts to determine whether injustices exist; negotiation; self-purification; and direct action. We have gone through all these steps in Birmingham. There can be no gainsaying the fact that racial injustice engulfs this community. Birmingham is probably the most thoroughly segregated city in the United States. Its ugly record of brutality is widely known. Negroes have experienced grossly unjust treatment in the courts. There have been more unsolved bombings of Negro homes and churches in Birmingham than in any other city in the nation. These are the hard, brutal facts of the case. On the basis of these conditions, Negro leaders sought to negotiate with the city fathers. But the latter consistently refused to engage in good-faith negotiation.
>
> Then, last September, came the opportunity to talk with leaders of Birmingham's economic community. In the course of the negotiations, certain promises were made by the merchants—for example, to remove the stores' humiliating racial signs. On the basis of these promises, the Reverend Fred Shuttlesworth and the leaders of the Alabama Christian Movement for Human Rights agreed to a moratorium on all demonstrations. As the weeks and months went by, we realized that we were the victims of a broken promise. A few signs, briefly removed, returned; the others remained.
>
> As in so many past experiences, our hopes had been blasted, and the shadow of deep disappointment settled upon us. We had no alternative except to prepare for direct action, whereby we would present our very bodies as a means of laying our case before the conscience of the local and the national community. Mindful of the difficulties involved, we decided to undertake a process of self-purification. We began a series of workshops on nonviolence, and we repeatedly asked ourselves: "Are you able to accept blows without retaliating?" "Are you able to endure the ordeal of jail?" . . . [After waiting out Birmingham's mayoralty election] we felt that our direct-action program could be delayed no longer.
>
> You may well ask: "Why direct action? Why sit-ins, marches and so forth? Isn't negotiation a better path?" You are quite right in calling for negotiation. Indeed, this is the very purpose of direct action. Nonviolent direct action seeks to create such a crisis and foster such a tension that a community which has constantly refused to negotiate is forced to confront the issue. It seeks so to dramatize the issue that it can no longer be ignored. My citing the creation of tension as part of the work of the nonviolent-resister may sound rather shocking. But I must confess that I am not afraid of the word "tension." I have earnestly opposed violent tension, but there is a type of constructive, nonviolent tension which is necessary for growth. Just as Socrates felt that it was necessary to create a tension in the mind so that individuals could rise from the bondage of myths and half-truths to the unfettered realm of creative analysis and objective appraisal, so must we see the need for nonviolent gadflies to create the kind of tension in society that will help men rise from the dark depths of prejudice and racism to the majestic heights of understanding and brotherhood.
>
> Martin Luther King, Jr.
> From *Why We Can't Wait*

CHAPTER TWO
Dynamic Description: The Analysis of Process

MUMMIFICATION

Corpses were usually handled in the following manner: The brain was first pulled out through the nostrils with a metal hook. The visceral cavity was then laid open with a stone knife, and the soft guts removed. An alternative method was to drag the viscera out through the anal aperture. In either method they were preserved in the so-called "canopic jars," or large vases. The heart was removed and replaced by a stone scarab. After this the remains were thoroughly washed and soaked for more than a month in brine. Finally the cadaver was dried out—a process that, some sources say, lasted for seventy days.

The pickled corpse was then interred in several nested wooden coffins, of human shape, and the coffins deposited in a stone sarcophagus. The body was placed in the innermost coffin in a reclining position. The hands were arranged in a crossed position over the chest or lap or even allowed to hang by the sides. The hair was usually cut short, though with female cadavers it was often allowed to remain at full length, after being beautifully waved. The hair about the genitals was shaved off.

To protect the cadaver from the entrance of destructive agents, the orifices of the body were plugged with lime, sand, resin, sawdust, balls of linen, and the like, with aromatic substances sometimes being added to the plugs. Sometimes, oddly enough, onions were used to perfume the stoppers. The breasts of the women were padded out. Thereafter came the tedious process of swaddling the body in linen winding cloths and bandages. These, with the passage of time, became so thoroughly impregnated with the sticky bituminous material poured over them in great quantity that the archaeologist frequently has had trouble unwinding them.

C. W. Ceram
From *Gods, Graves and Scholars*

• Summary: The Flowchart

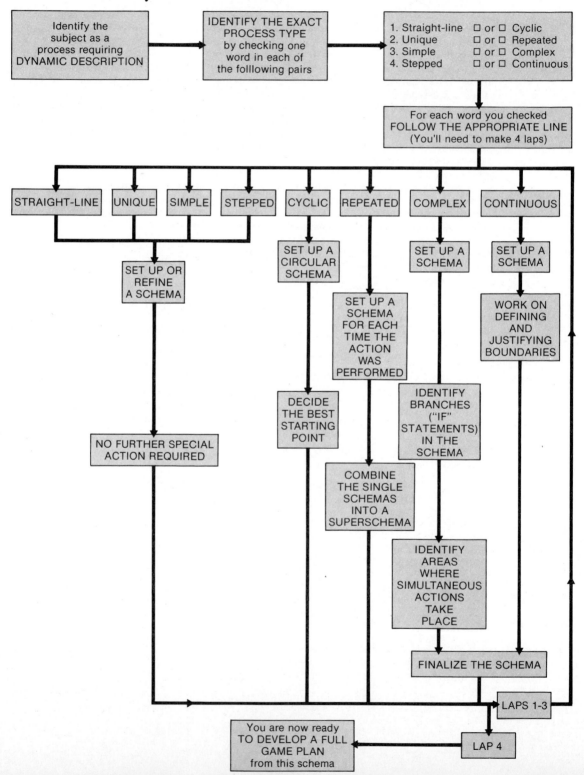

2 ·

The Personal Voice

In describing his struggle with the Demon Gum, Timothy Thompson does not use his own voice: he mimics the voice of those who urge us to give things up: to give up eggs, bacon, cigars, butter, rare steak, well-done steak, alcohol, salt, snuff, aerobics—the list is endless. What Tim catches here is the *voice* of the do-gooders: their preachy style and bossy self-righteousness. The piece is a step-by-step dynamic description, but its "claim to fame" is its skillful use of voice.

My Struggle with the Demon Gum

Whenever it wasn't full of something else, there was something I used to put in my mouth—a piece of chewing gum. I was lucky: not even my parents accused me of "substance abuse," but I was in the grip of a habit I knew I had to break.

One day I was just about to pop another piece in my mouth when I saw the light. I have always been contemptuous of those unfortunate individuals who are hopelessly addicted to alcohol, drugs or chocolate-covered ants, not because of their addiction, but because they'd allowed themselves to reach the point of addiction with no thought for where the downhill track would end. As I stared at that piece of gum, I realized that I too, sinner that I was, was on the primrose path to hell. As yet I was not addicted—I didn't crave gum-juice, nor would I become a social pariah if I continued chewing—but I was allowing a habit to control my actions. I knew I had to kick the habit immediately.

I searched my conscience about gum-chewing, seeking to learn the good and the bad. I found one solitary benefit: chewing gum strengthens the jaws. I wasn't fool enough to fall for that trap; I knew other ways to develop my bite. The bad simply overwhelmed me. First, chewing made my jaws sore and gave me a headache. Then there were the academic sanctions: chewing gum during school hours was frowned on; if caught, one could be detained after classes. It was also disgusting to watch someone else chew gum. Finally, the financial drain could not be ignored. Too much of my allowance was going towards supporting my habit, and I knew it wasn't worth it. I was mentally prepared to start the long uphill struggle toward sugar-free blood.

My first step was to allow myself gum only after school hours. This reduced the risk of detention, but it did not decrease the aches in my head and jaws. I decided on more drastic measures: I would chew only on weekends. The problem here was casual temptation: friends still unthinkingly pressed bubble gum on me in unguarded moments. But when the weekend finally came, my desire for bubble gum had almost evaporated. I was ready for the final phase.

On the following Monday, having watched an otherwise attractive girl lewdly suck and masticate her gum, I vowed to abstain from all gum for three months. Luckily, I hardly missed the stuff at all. I was cured.

I am now what is called in chewing circles a "social chewer." This means that I occasionally chew to avoid embarrassing chewers who lack my iron determination. I feel it would be unfair in me to stigmatize others for the sin that I myself once committed.

Review Assignment

There are probably styles that irritate you. Some examples: the hard-nosed, factual tone in which medical operations on the famous are reported in the media; the no-nonsense approach the agony columnists sometimes take to grave personal problems; the sensuous, overheated language in which advertisers describe such machines as cars, motorbikes, stereos, cameras or computers; the almost worshipful tone in which the latest pop idol is described, regardless of the truth; the language used to hype quite trivial sporting events to the point where they become "world-stoppers"; the way in which real estate agents overdescribe properties; the sarcastic tone in which teachers sometimes analyze student writing; and so on. Try writing a short piece in one of these descriptive styles. The goal is to catch the exact *tone of voice* you are mimicking.

3 •
Writing Workshop:
The Process of Describing Change

• Choosing a Subject

Early on, most students prefer to invest their time in planning and writing and to avoid the added problem of research. For this reason, when you decide what you'll be writing about, you'll probably steer clear of subjects that take you to the library. In fact library research might prove counterproductive: the task is to set up a step-by-step analysis; finding one ready-made is not very instructive.

a. Continuous Processes.   Let's begin with some general problems—things that have happened over a number of years. Usually these subjects are *continuous processes*. Changes that have occurred in a specific community often feature here:

1. How unemployment grew in a community
2. How crime destroyed the quality of life in a community
3. How military attitudes to women or to minorities have changed over the years
4. How hard drugs disappeared from (or took over) a school or workplace
5. How a community expanded (or died) over a period of years

Many things in our society change. Styles, crazes, preoccupations, machines are born, and some of them die. Some sample subjects:

6. How a craze was born and died, as *you* saw it (mini-skirts, skateboarding, break dancing, punk hair styles—there are many examples)
7. How an activity, a preoccupation, or a social pattern has grown (examples: jogging, rejection of tobacco use, promotion of women to management positions)
8. How the style of something changed over the years (examples: cars, dirt bikes, surfboards, swimwear, furniture)
9. How the design of a product or a piece of equipment developed over a period of time (helicopters, aircraft engines, the personal computer, firearms, cameras, pianos—the specific choices are endless)

If you prefer writing about people, think of those unplanned processes that slowly change our lives:

10. How a family fell apart
11. How someone became an alcoholic or a drug addict
12. How someone became a juvenile delinquent

b. Repeated or Repeatable Processes. If you write about a repeated procedure, then obviously you must have performed that action many times. A word of warning here: you are *not* writing instructions for someone else to follow—this is not a how-to paper. Most often the subject is "How I . . ." It is never "How to . . ." Some examples:

13. How I prepare for end-of-term examinations
14. How I develop a roll of film
15. How I prepare my skis before the season begins

Problems of complexity arise if, each time you performed the procedure, you did it a different way. For example:

16. How I throw a surprise party
17. How my family celebrates Christmas (or some other festival)
18. How I watch the Big Game on television
19. How I prepare for a hunting/camping/cycling trip (pick one)

Some subjects produce phony steps that will not form a *sequence*. Be wary. Use only genuinely sequenced steps.

20. How I get back into training after a lay-off
21. How I lose weight

c. Cyclic Processes. Examples of cyclic processes include:

22. How a particular waste item is recycled (paper, glass, aluminum are the best examples)
23. How substances are cycled through an ecosystem (rainwater and usable nitrogen are the classic examples)
24. How a particular economic cycle functions (the boom-and-bust cycle, the inflationary cycle, the employment cycle are worth examining)

d. Unique Processes. Simplest of all to write about are unique processes, especially those that involve only one person. The keyword here is *once*. The list below contains only a handful of suggestions: your own experience should quickly suggest others. The subjects have been clustered: the first group is people oriented, the second job oriented, the third is more mechanical.

25. How the life of a patient was saved in difficult circumstances

26. How my team achieved success during one season

27. How a couple saved a marriage on the brink of collapse

28. How I once abandoned a bad habit

29. How a family adopted a child

30. How I once trained a difficult or uncooperative animal.

31. How my military unit or office once prepared for an inspection

32. How my work in a particular job was reorganized

33. How I once made a suggestion that was implemented

34. How an employee once achieved an unfair promotion

35. How an office or unit in which I worked relocated on one occasion

36. How I once found an unusual malfunction in a piece of equipment and corrected it

37. How I got the "great photograph" (enclose the picture if you wish)

38. How I once developed a usable computer program

39. How I once built (or rebuilt) a piece of equipment or a piece of furniture

40. How I once planted a garden

• Invention: Developing a Schema and a Game Plan

Having chosen your subject, the next steps are to create a schema and a game plan. To see how it's done in practice, let's take an example. Abigail Tree is a keen cyclist. For four successive summers, she's taken a camping vacation with her bicycle. The fourth trip was the best, and Abby attributes this success to her careful preparation. Her first problem: should she write about preparing for all four trips, or just about the successful one? If she writes about all four, she'll face the problems of repeated processes. On the other hand, if she cuts back to the one successful trip, the problems disappear: the process of preparing is then unique (that is, she prepared for this trip once only); the process is also linear (that is, Abby begins unprepared and ends ready to go); then it is a simple process (that is, she did only one thing at a time); and finally the process is stepped (that is, she prepared systematically, step by step). This is the simplest form of all, so Abby decides to use it. She is now ready to work out a schema.

The first and last points in preparing for this cycling trip are clear: the process begins with planning the trip and ends with Abby on her bike ready to start. What happens in between is a simple matter of history: she bought supplies and equipment, she overhauled her bicycle, she packed, and that was it. The schema:

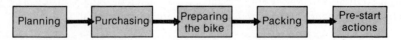

Planning → Purchasing → Preparing the bike → Packing → Pre-start actions

CHAPTER TWO
Dynamic Description: The Analysis of Process

At this stage, Abby has invested very little effort in this idea. Since a mistake here could waste time later, she should check the schema for shortcomings. A checklist helps:

Schema Checklist

(With *Yes* answers, proceed: with *No* answers, review.)

1. What exactly is the subject? ....

2. Is the first step the true starting point of the process? (With a cyclic process: is it the best place to start?)   Yes   No

3. With the last point, does the schema reach the exact end of the process named as the subject? Has it avoided falling short? And going too far?   Yes   No

4. Is the sequence free of gaps?   Yes   No

5. Are the points in the correct order? (With a repeated process: is this order true for *every* occasion on which the action was repeated?)   Yes   No

---

The general point is this: *if you go any further than this with an unsatisfactory schema, you're simply wasting time.*

    With a workable schema, the next step is to *brainstorm* for the details that belong in each step. Because she knew her subject well (she was the world's leading authority on it), Abby had no trouble expanding the schema into a functional game plan:

STEPS

① Planning — Time Frame / Route / Cost

② What I bought — New Waterproof Tent / Tires

③ Preparing the bike — Reserve Food Supply (the night I went hungry) / Cleaning / Oiling / Changing Tires / Adjusting Saddle

④ Packing — Clothing / Camping Equipment / Food and Water

⑤ Before I set off — Dressed / Ate breakfast / Checked my checklist

---

The steps that Abby listed on the left are simply the "beads on a string" from the schema. Getting the details together for each step can be trickier than it looks.

There can be two distinct difficulties: (a) grouping ministeps and (b) clustering overlapping actions.

A. GROUPING MINISTEPS

Look again at Abby's Step 3. It includes three "details": Cleaning and Oiling, Changing Tires, Adjusting the Saddle. Since Abby performed these actions in exactly this order, why did she not list them as full-blown steps in the chain? In fact, she could have, but only at the cost of some disproportion. Adjusting the Saddle takes only a few seconds, while other full steps (Planning, for example, or Packing) take a great deal longer and are relatively weightier matters. To equate Planning with Adjusting the Saddle by making them both steps implies that they have equal importance. Unequal steps, as we all know, can lead to trouble.

The principle is this: main steps should have *roughly the same importance* in the overall process. If you have too many trivial ministeps, then cluster them into one big step, exactly as Abby grouped Cleaning and Oiling, Changing Tires and Adjusting the Saddle into Preparing the Bike.

B. CLUSTERING OVERLAPPING ACTIONS

Look now at Abby's Step 4, Packing. She must pack three groups of items: clothing, camping equipment, and provisions. A typical mistake is to treat each kind of packing as a separate step when in fact it is not. Why not? Because the three kinds of equipment—the cooker, the tent, a sweater, wet-weather gear, emergency food—are inextricably mixed during packing. Describing each kind of packing separately is close to impossible. Packing is a typical *complex process*: you must cluster the components into a single step, because they do not form a sequence.

• Writing the First Draft

Developing a completed game plan into a description means turning notes into text. Chapter 1 suggested some ideas about writing first drafts, particularly about the need for *recursion*. (Review Chapter 1, Section 3, if you're rusty on *recursion*.) All these ideas still apply, of course. With a dynamic description, two new angles must be considered: *openings* and *headings*.

A. OPENINGS

In journalism school, reporters are taught about one way to begin news stories: with the four *W*s—Who, What, Where, and When. (The fifth *W*, Why, is not part of the opening; it's the body of the story.) For most dynamic descriptions, the four-*W* technique, coupled with a lead-in sentence, makes a neat and necessary introduction. Some examples:

> In May 1988 (when) I (who) made a four-hundred-mile bicycle trip (what you did) around Idaho (where). Preparing for the trip fell into five distinct phases (lead-in).

> Since my family (who) moved to Newglade, Florida (where), in 1979 (when), the community has grown to nearly five times its original size (what has happened). Although continuous, this expansion can be broken down into three main steps (lead-in).

> In 1969 (when), Pope Paul VI (who) became the first pope to visit the continent of Africa (what and where). His trip marked the dawn of full acceptance for "third-world" Christianity (lead-in).

After such an opening, Step 1 of your analysis can begin. With repeated processes, a four-W opening is seldom possible, but at least the What and the lead-in sentence should be in place.

> Each year (when) my family (who) celebrates Christmas (what) in much the same way. The festivities fall into seven steps (lead-in).

> Developing a film (what) is most easily understood if the procedure is divided into three clear steps (lead-in).

B. HEADINGS

A trick that will make your process descriptions easier to read is the use of *section titles*. A section title is simply a numbered label inserted at the start of each main section. In a very short piece (a single page perhaps) such titles get in the way, but in a longer description they offer a quick visual clue about the structure of the material. This book is broken up all through with section headings; imagine how difficult it would be to keep track of the argument if it were not. (If you glance at the example of a final draft at the end of this chapter, you'll see how section headings break up and highlight the material.)

One word of caution: the section titles are not an integral part of the description itself. The description should make perfect sense *even without the titles*. The general principle is this: *section titles help the reader to see at a glance where the description is going and recapitulate where it has just been.*

Look back now at the extracts by Martin Luther King and C. W. Ceram at the end of Section 1. Would either of them have been easier to follow with section titles?

• Revising

Everything that was said earlier about revising naturally still applies. First, let your piece "cool off" before attempting to revise it. Once the piece is cold, it helps to read it several times looking for specific problems—your "search mechanism" works better if it concentrates on one quarry rather than if it scans broadly for several. The first reading should examine continuity, the second cost-effectiveness, and the third correctness.

REVISION CHECK 1: CONTINUITY

In a dynamic description it is obvious where the breaks occur: between the steps. For this reason continuity is largely a matter of easing the reader across each gap as it occurs. This can be done, perhaps rather mechanically, by two kinds of sentences. At the *beginning* of each section, you can introduce the new step briefly with a formula such as:

> The third step was to prepare the bicycle itself.
> The final phase in this process is polishing.
> Next I had to leave the rushes to soak for three weeks.

Similarly, at the *end* of each section you can use a link sentence, a transition, to prepare the reader for the next step.

> We were now ready for the next step—varnishing.
> With speakers in place, it was time to wire them up.
> The photograph was now developed; the next step was to dry it.

With sections held in place like this, continuity is guaranteed. If such opening and closing phrases seem wooden, you can refine them and blend them in more subtly, although there may not be much point: continuity material is like signposting a road—bold and unmistakable is usually better than picturesque and discreet.

REVISION CHECK 2: COST-EFFECTIVENESS

Your goal is still the greatest quantity of accessible information in the smallest possible package. Beware, though! You can go too far in cutting back language: your description should not read like an international telegram where every word costs $1.25. For academic papers, the appropriate style achieves the maximum economy possible without sounding tight-lipped or bad-tempered.

REVISION CHECK 3: CORRECTNESS

Again a two-part check is necessary. First you must look for the errors that you personally tend to make. Then you must look for the errors that occur most frequently in dynamic description; you'll find them listed in the next section.

• Special Correctness Problems—Dynamic Description

Two problems commonly occur in handling time sequences: tenses, and the overuse of *and then*. These problems are briefly described here. If you feel you should know more, review the handbook material *before* you proofread.

PROBLEM 1: THE SEQUENCE OF TENSES

English has a special tense that uses the word "had": *I have gone* as against *I had gone*. The *had* form goes back from the past to the "superpast," as in the sentence:

In 1986 I moved to Florida; before that I had lived in Georgia.

To review, check your handbook under *Sequence of Tenses*, *Pluperfect* or *Past Perfect*.

PROBLEM 2: "AND THEN . . .": TIDYING UP TIME SEQUENCES

A small child relating an adventure often strings episodes together with ". . . and then . . ." An example:

We were walking beside the river, and then we saw a boat, and then we got in it, and then we pushed off, and then we tried to row across the river, and then we were about half way across, and then the current caught us, and then we tried to row for the bank, and then one of the oars snapped, and then we were getting dangerously near the rapids. . . .

This is improved by *subordinating* background ideas and putting the main ideas in *main clauses*:

As we were walking beside the river (subordinate), we saw a boat (main). After we'd got in and pushed off (subordinate), we tried to row across the river (main). When we were half way across (subordinate), the current caught us (main). Before we could reach the bank again (subordinate), one of the oars snapped (main). We were getting dangerously near the rapids (main) . . .

To review, check your handbook under *Subordination, Subordinate Clauses,* or *Adverbial Clauses*.

• The Final Draft

Once you've checked your first draft for the three *Cs*—continuity, cost-effectiveness, and correctness—you are ready for the final draft. If you like to use someone else's paper as a model, the following paper by Alan Whinery may help you. Alan is a pool enthusiast and describes in a simple, down-to-earth piece the steps he went through in buying a made-to-measure pool cue. Alan makes no claims to being a brilliant stylist; he is simply trying to "tell it like it is."

How I Purchased my Custom Cue

Steps	Details
1. Deciding what I wanted	Cue length must fit the body
	Shaft must fit the hand
	Tip must fit the cue ball
	Weight must inspire rhythm
	Balance must be in front of the hand
2. Selecting a cue-maker	Collecting brochures
	Evaluating waiting time, price, reputation and location
3. Selecting style and price	Cost and decoration
4. Ordering the cue	Specifications and payment
5. Picking up the cue	Anecdote: the big test

Who, What, Where, and When opening Lead-in sentence

In January 1984, I finally took possession of my custom-made pool cue in Linn, Missouri. That was the last step in a process that had taken almost a year and fell into five distinct steps.

Section heading

1. Deciding What I Wanted

Concrete information

I am 6 feet 3 inches tall. I soon discovered that the average pool cue, 57 inches long, is too short for me since it is made for an "average" man. I started to look for a longer cue. A search of the yellow pages turned up the A. E. Schmidt Billiard Manufacturing Company in St. Louis. In their showroom I found a 60-inch cue, the longest normally available. After I'd used it for a month, my game improved, but I found the tip too small for regular pool balls. The shaft was too small for my large hands and long fingers, and this made it hard to control the english. I returned to Schmidt's and found a cue with a tapered shaft and a bigger tip. The thicker shaft fitted my hand well. A week later I was controlling the ball better, but the stick was too light for me to get a good rhythm.

CHAPTER TWO
Dynamic Description: The Analysis of Process

To establish the correct balance, I went to the local hardware store and bought some lead tape. I wrapped tape around the butt of the cue until it weighed 20 ounces. This improved my rhythm, but for jump shots the balance was wrong. I moved the tape closer to the joint until I was happy with both rhythm and balance. I now had a cue that looked like hell, but played like an angel. I was ready for the next step: finding a cue-maker.

Continuity to next step

2. Selecting a Cue-Maker

Section heading

To locate a cue-maker, I simply took out the latest copies of National Billiard News and Billiard Digest and called every custom cue-maker listed. I asked each one to send me a brochure and a delivery date. Once I had all the information, I began the process of elimination. Anyone who offered a delivery date more than a year away, I eliminated immediately. I then asked pool-playing friends if any of the cue-makers had a bad reputation. That eliminated a few more. Since all the rest quoted roughly the same price, I chose the one nearest to my home, Paul Hubler of Hubler Industries, Linn, Missouri. I was now ready to choose the cue itself.

Continuity from previous step
Concrete information
Continuity to next step

3. Selecting Style and Price

Hubler's brochure listed cues priced at between $80 and $300. I decided to pick the one I liked best, regardless of price. Naturally, it was the $300 model, the Renaissance Custom Three. What I especially liked was its checkerboard decoration of wood inlaid in wood. The next step was to order the cue from Hubler.

4. Ordering the Cue

It was November when I called Paul Hubler and told him what I wanted. We talked for a long time, and he told me to put the exact specifications in writing and send them to him. He also said that the cue would cost an extra $50 because of its length. I accepted this on condition that I could use my Master Card to pay. We reached agreement, and I sat back and waited for the final step.

5. Picking up the Cue

Paul called in late January and told me that my cue was ready. I drove to Linn and checked out the cue on one of Paul's tables. It was everything I had dreamed it would be. On my way back home, I stopped at a place I knew in St. Louis to try out my new cue in earnest. I won about $400—enough to pay for the cue, the trip and most of the phone calls.

• Summary: The Flowchart

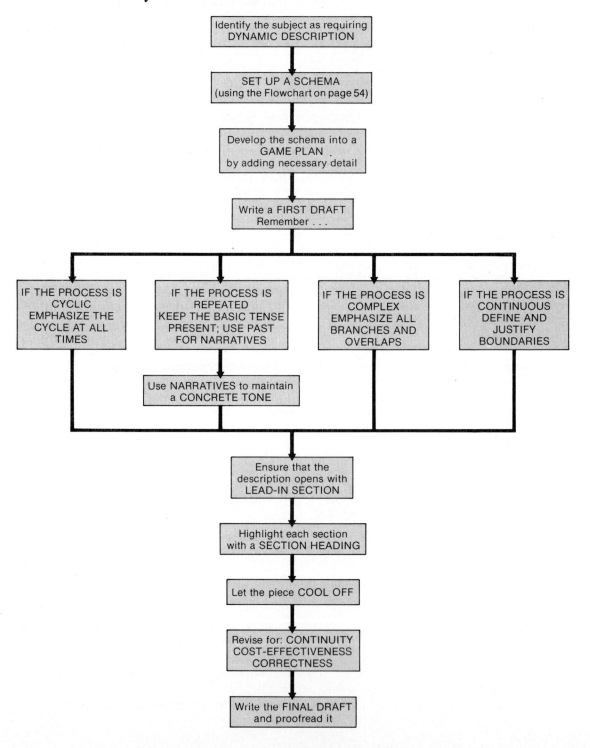

THREE

Combining: The Art of Structure

1 •
The Problem: Putting Things Together

In a bricklaying course, you'd first study the properties of bricks, and then you'd learn how bricks are mortared together into walls. In a way, a writing course is similar: having studied the basic materials (static and dynamic description), the next step is to construct something from them. This chapter looks at the simplest kind of construction: setting up two descriptions side by side. By studying what happens, you'll learn the guiding principles of combination.

• Structure and Meaning

At first glance, the structure of a piece of writing seems a mere empty scaffolding, in itself meaningless. The *meaning* of a piece, you might think, lies exclusively in the ideas you want to express. This viewpoint is profoundly wrong: the secret of *combining*, of developing papers that have something to say, is to understand how a structure conveys meaning—or destroys it.

As a starting point, let's take an example from photojournalism. Imagine you're a cub photographer on a newspaper in Washington, D.C. It's an exciting time: Washington is buzzing with rumors of a tremendous scandal, with at least fifty senators and congressmen implicated. Your boss calls you in: he needs a picture of Washington "as it is today." Since it's a beautiful day, you mingle with the tourists along the Mall and return with a sunny picture of the Capitol and children playing under the Lombardy poplars. But your boss is not happy. He glances at your picture. "What's it about?" he asks. "It's not about anything," you reply. "It's a picture. That's how Washington looks today." Moments later you are out in the street, searching again for your assigned picture. This time you wander through the less attractive part of town. The debris all round looks the way you feel, and you take a thoroughly depressing picture. Again your boss is unhappy. "You got great composition," he says, "and a lovely range of grays, but the picture doesn't *mean* anything." Having lost your first job, you see in the next morning's paper the picture you should have taken. Look at this picture closely. Something odd has happened.

Your boss rejected a picture of the Capitol, and he rejected a picture of

"Image of Government," photo John Melius.

debris—but he accepted a picture that was simply a combination of the two: Capitol + debris. Why? What *meaning* did he find in the combination of the two images? In fact, remembering the rumors of a government scandal, the meaning of the picture is clear enough: "If they heap any more garbage round the government, we won't be able to see it at all." The source of the meaning is also clear: it comes from the *contrast* between the two elements. The Capitol is an image of government, hopeful, historic, beautiful; on it is superimposed an image of decay and hopelessness. Look again at what has happened: an idea that *is not* present in either of the component parts *is* present when the parts are combined. In other words, the structure itself has generated the meaning. An old saying expresses this idea exactly: The whole is greater than the sum of the parts. This example gives us a first guiding principle: *structures create meanings*.

Concept Review

Combining for Meaning

Study the pictures labeled *A* and *B*. Each picture contains two main elements. What are these elements? Taken individually, do these elements convey a meaning? What new meaning does the picture achieve by *combining* the two elements?

A   "At the Time of the Louisville Flood," by Margaret Bourke-White. From *Life Magazine*. Copyright © 1937, TIME.

PART ONE
Basic Materials—Basic Skills

B   A Keystone Photo. Courtesy of the Frankfurter Rundschau

Review Assignment

Sketch a picture of your own in which you combine two elements to produce a message. Probably the two elements you choose will be in some way contrasted, for example: a whiskey bottle (pleasure) and a car wreck (misery); a computer (mechanical) and a human brain (natural); a mustang (rare now) and a Mustang (more common). Try to avoid words. Just use images, however badly drawn.

• How the Reader's Mind Works

For a moment, let's think about a piece of writing exclusively from the *reader's* point of view. A reader is confronted by a string of facts and ideas. Somehow the reader must spot a pattern in this data—its structure—or nothing will add up. The reader's intelligence scans the material for this pattern. (See the Close-Up below.) Once spotted, the pattern allows the reader to form a theory, a hypothesis, about the overall meaning of the piece. As each new fact arrives, it either confirms the theory, or it fails to confirm it. If the theory is not confirmed, then the reader must come up with a new theory that includes *all* the information given so far. For example:

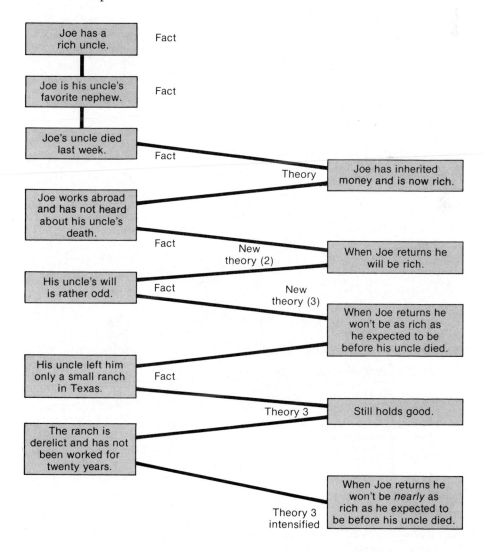

Close-Up

Meaning, Structure and Gestalt Psychology

The expression "the whole is greater than the sum of the parts" is a key principle of the Gestalt school of psychology. The Gestaltists see the most characteristic activity of the mind as grouping random fragments into meaningful wholes. In fact the German word *Gestalt* means, roughly, *whole*. Three Gestaltist principles (at least) are involved in a reader's discovering the meaning of a piece of writing: *closure*, *clustering*, and *simplification*.

1. **Closure:** What is incomplete is completed by the brain to form a whole.

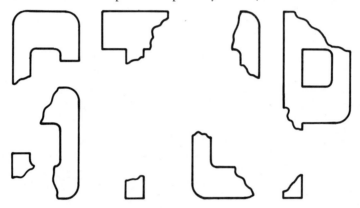

Example: If you saw these fragments of white paint on the road at an intersection, what "whole" would you assume?

2. **Clustering:** The brain clusters similar items into meaningful groups.

Example: Using the levels as a clue, you probably see these six figures as three "teams" of two, although what connection the figures might have is difficult to say. From the heights you probably infer a 1-2-3 ranking, even though there is no clear reason for the figures to be ranked at all.

3. Simplification: The brain seeks a simple explanation rather than a complicated one.

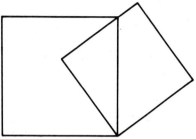

Example: Most people see these figures as *two* squares rather than as an arrangement of *three* irregular shapes.

This is how one might read a story. Your reader, an instructor or professor, works on your paper in exactly the same way, picking up each new fact and developing a theory about your overall meaning. Let's call this the *reader's theory*. In an academic paper the writer's overall meaning is usually stated in a single sentence either at the beginning or at the end of the paper. This we can call the *writer's stated thesis*. Now we have not one but *two* versions of the overall meaning of the piece:

The reader's final theory	The writer's stated thesis

Probably you can see where this is leading: to the danger that *theory* and *thesis* are not identical. In fact there are four possibilities here:

Possibility 1: The reader's theory and the writer's thesis are identical.
　　　　　　　Result—clear communication
Possibility 2: The reader's theory and the writer's thesis are both present but are not identical (or even contradictory).
　　　　　　　Result—confusion
Possibility 3: There is no clearly expressed writer's thesis.
　　　　　　　Result—uncertainty
Possibility 4: The facts are too confused for the reader to form a reader's theory.
　　　　　　　Result—disaster

Your opportunity and your danger are now clear. *Opportunity:* If you skillfully control the structure, then you mobilize the reader's intelligence to confirm or anticipate your thesis; the explicit wording of your thesis simply bears out what the reader must conclude from reading your piece. *Danger:* If the facts suggest an incorrect reader's theory, or no reader's theory at all, then the result is at best confusion, at worst disaster.

　　The guiding principle: *The writer must harmonize the meaning created by the structure and the meaning expressed in the text.*

Concept Review

The Reader's Theory

Read the following narrative. After the first sentence, you'll be prompted to put into words your initial reader's theory as to where the story is leading. As things develop, respond to each prompt by refining or reformulating your reader's theory.

Two weeks ago I saw a group of workmen measuring the cafeteria.

State your initial theory

Next day I saw the building manager in the cafeteria looking at paint colors and floor coverings with a salesman.

New theory	Same theory	Modified theory

When I asked the manager of the cafeteria if it was going to be redecorated he said, "Definitely not."

New theory	Same theory	Modified theory

Then I saw an article in the paper about an extension to the computer room.

New theory	Same theory	Modified theory

The computer room is next door to the cafeteria.

New theory	Same theory	Modified theory

When I next went to the cafeteria, there were posters up everywhere: BITES NOT BYTES, BEANS NOT SCREENS, and FRENCH FRIES NOT CHIPS.

New theory	Same theory	Modified theory

Then an official notice went up: "Because of lack of space, the computer room is being relocated in the basement of Building 3741 downtown."

New theory	Same theory	Modified theory

Finally the truth emerged: we lost our cafeteria to a day-care center for toddlers.

New theory	Same theory	Modified theory

• Controlling the Structure

Controlling the structure of one simple narrative is not difficult; things begin to get interesting when you try to make two elements work together. Exactly how do more complex structures operate? Two cases will establish the guiding principles.

A. THE LADY AND THE MAMMOTH: THE PRINCIPLE OF ORDER

Look at the picture of the woman and the mammoth skeleton. To combine a description of the woman and a description of the mammoth into a single piece, a

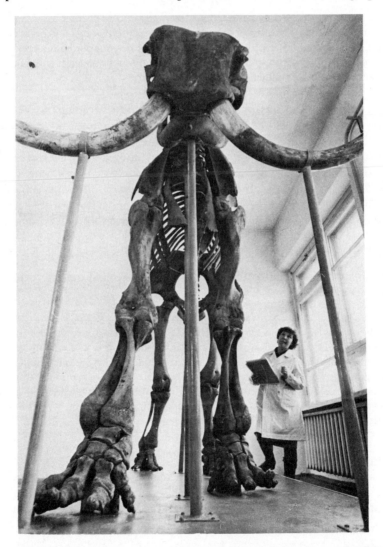

"Out of the Depths of Centuries," photo A. Polyakov. TASS from SOVFOTO.

writer must make a choice: the woman last? Or the mammoth last? (*Simultaneous* description is obviously impossible.) Let's try it both ways:

VERSION 1

> In the center of a large room stands the enormous skeleton of a mammoth supported on iron posts painted white. In the corner of the room stands someone gazing in fascination: it's a woman dressed in a blue coverall. She has a notebook in her hand. Is she taking notes, or is she drawing?

VERSION 2

> A smiling woman is standing in the corner of a large room with a notebook in her hand, drawing or perhaps taking notes. In front of her, supported on iron posts painted white, is an extraordinary object: it is an enormous skeleton with gigantic legs, a huge skull, and immense tusks—a mammoth.

In each case, what was in your mind when you finished reading? In Version 1, probably the woman; in Version 2, probably the mammoth. So, even though these descriptions are only four lines long, they take control of the reader's imagination and produce a clear sense of priority: in Version 1 the real subject is the woman; in Version 2 the real subject is the mammoth. This confirms what was said in Chapter 1 about the order of significance: *the most important point goes last*. As a guideline for developing larger structures, the principle of order stands: *the reader usually feels that the last point is the key to the piece, its most important idea.*

B. MY TWO DOGS: THE PRINCIPLE OF PARALLELISM

In the following attempt to contrast two dogs, a second guiding principle is conspicuous by its absence.

> I once owned two dogs. One was called Bill. He was mostly a fox terrier and the other was called Fido. Bill was mostly a hunting dog and would eat only rabbit, though I fooled him occasionally with stewed cat. He was easy to train. Fido loved children. Bill, on the other hand, was intelligent. He drank water straight from the faucet. Once Fido tore up a term paper I had just finished writing, while Bill's bluish ears were often remarked on. In fact, Fido came from a litter of seven, while Bill slept under the old boathouse.

As you perhaps felt while reading this, unbalanced facts within a framework of contrast are strictly *meaningless*. In an academic context, a contrast is written to "score points"; you can score points only when exactly balanced facts are presented. Unattached facts score nothing. If you doubt it, look at this scorecard:

SCORECARD FOR CONTRAST BETWEEN TWO DOGS			
Contrasted Area	*Dog 1 (Bill)*	*Dog 2 (Fido)*	*Score*
Type of dog	Yes	No	0
Preferred food	Yes	No	0
Drinking habits	Yes	No	0
Sleeping habits	Yes	No	0
Attitude to children	No	Yes	0
Discipline	No	Yes	0
Siblings	No	Yes	0
Intelligence/trainability	Yes	No	0
		TOTAL	0

Most instructors have seen academic papers constructed in this style: routinely, they assign them the grade of F. The proper way of doing the job is to balance fact with fact all the way through.

> I once owned two dogs. Bill was more or less a fox terrier, and Fido was a poodle. Bill was a hunting dog and ate only rabbit, though I fooled him occasionally with stewed cat. He drank water straight from the faucet and slept under the old boathouse. In contrast, Fido was highly fastidious. His favourite food was canned salmon; tunafish he despised. He never drank water, only milk. As to sleeping, he had a soft cushion at the foot of my bed. Bill was faithful, intelligent, and easy to train. He knew at least twenty words of command and obeyed them all. Fido, on the other hand, was easily excited and undisciplined. He chased sheep, cats, and children. Once he tore up a term paper I had just finished typing. To sum up, Bill was a useful, lovable animal, although his bluish ears betrayed some kinks in his bloodline. Fido was a spoiled "brat," a pure-bred nuisance from a litter of seven nasty little aristocrats.

For this version, the score sheet registers the maximum: 8 points. The principle of parallelism then: *when combining two descriptions, the information about each side must be presented in close parallel.*

Review Assignment

Eating Out

The following informal paragraph contrasts the service in two restaurants. Rewrite it so that it "scores points" and so that the concluding sentence ("So that's why I prefer Rigoletto's") is supported by the structure.

If you want to eat out in Smallville, you have two choices: Farm Fried Chicken or Rigoletto's. Farm Fried Chicken offers cafeteria-style self-service and a row of tall stands on which to perch your food. Rigoletto's has a broad menu with typical Italian dishes such as spaghetti and pizza in a hundred combinations. Rigoletto's is next to the bus shelter, so its customers include anyone with a long wait for a bus. Farm Fried Chicken is not particularly clean—in fact the Department of Public Hygiene threatened to close it down twice last year. As to cost, you can eat your fill at Farm Fried Chicken for $7. So that's why I prefer Rigoletto's.

• The Contrast Module: A Building Block for Bigger Structures

Professional writers often use simple two-element "modules" when they're developing larger, more complex ideas—usually, to show a contrast. You'll be doing the same when you begin to write full-fledged essays. These contrasts, embedded in complete, often very elaborate structures, can be called *contrast modules*. In the two cases below, William Wilkie Collins, the inventor of the detective novel, and Naomi Freundlich, a technical journalist, use a *contrast module* to make their very different points. First, Collins.

A. In his novel *Basil,* Collins describes two rooms. The first room belongs to Mr. Sherwin, a rich store-owner; the second belongs to one of his clerks, Mannion. The descriptions occur almost sixty pages apart in the novel, yet the reader, as in all detective fiction, is expected to put two and two together and reach a valid conclusion. Read this contrast, and then ask the question: what do the contrasted facts tell you about the relationship between the rich Sherwin and the poor clerk, Mannion?

NORTH VILLA: THE SHERWIN HOUSE
On my arrival at North Villa, I was shown into what I presumed was the drawing-room.
Everything was oppressively new. The brilliantly-varnished door cracked with a report like a pistol when it was opened; the paper on the walls, with its gaudy pattern of birds, trellis-work, and flowers, in gold, red, and green on a white ground, looked hardly dry yet; the showy window-curtains of white and sky-blue, and the still showier carpet of red and yellow, seemed as if they had come out of the shop yesterday; the round rosewood table was in a painfully high state of polish; the morocco-bound picture books that lay on it, looked as if they had never been moved or opened since they had been bought; not one leaf even of the music on the piano was dogs-eared or worn. Never was a richly furnished room more thoroughly comfortless than this—the eye ached at looking round it. There was no repose anywhere. The print of the Queen, hanging lonely on the wall, in its heavy gilt frame, with a large crown at the top, glared on you: the paper, the curtains, the carpet glared on you: the books, the wax-flowers in glass-cases, the chairs in flaring chintz-covers, the china plates on the door, the blue and pink glass vases and cups ranged on the chimney-piece, the over-ornamented chiffoniers with Tonbridge toys and long-necked smelling bottles on their upper shelves—all glared on you. There was no look of shadow, shelter, secrecy, or retirement in any one nook or corner of those four gaudy walls. All surrounding objects seemed

startlingly near to the eye; much nearer than they really were. The room would have given a nervous man the headache, before he had been in it a quarter of an hour.

MANNION'S LIVING ROOM

The fire was blazing in the grate; an arm-chair, with a reading easel attached, was placed by it; the lamp was ready lit; the tea-things were placed on the table; the dark, thick curtains were drawn close over the window; and, as if to complete the picture of comfort before me, a large black cat lay on the rug, basking luxuriously in the heat of the fire. While Mr. Mannion went out to give some directions, as he said, to his servant, I had an opportunity of examining the apartment more in detail. To study the appearance of a man's dwelling-room, is very often nearly equivalent to studying his own character.

The personal contrast between Mr. Sherwin and his clerk was remarkable enough, but the contrast between the dimensions and furnishing of the rooms they lived in, was to the full as extraordinary. The apartment I now surveyed was less than half the size of the sitting-room at North Villa. The paper on the walls was of a dark red; the curtains were of the same color; the carpet was brown, and if it bore any pattern, that pattern was too quiet and unpretending to be visible by candlelight. One wall was entirely occupied by rows of dark mahogany shelves, completely filled with books, most of them cheap editions of the classical works of ancient and modern literature. The opposite wall was thickly hung with engravings in maple-wood frames from the works of modern painters, English and French. All the minor articles of furniture were of the plainest and neatest order—even the white china tea-pot and tea-cup on the table, had neither pattern nor coloring of any kind. What a contrast was this room to the drawing-room at North Villa!

William Wilkie Collins
From *Basil*

B. The same structure is used by Naomi Freundlich in describing two versions of the latest electronic gadget, the tiny TV. The style, the subject matter, and the purpose of her article are totally different from those of the novel; yet the structure of her ideas is exactly the same. Structures are the *invariables* of writing.

Basically, two ways are now used to make TVs small: redesign the conventional cathode-ray tube (CRT) or use a liquid-crystal-display (LCD) screen. In Sanyo's new 2¼-inch-deep hand-held color TV, the clunky CRT has been scaled down to a flat three-inch version with the electron gun dropped below the phosphor screen rather than behind or perpendicular to it. Instead of using three electron beams and a metallic shadow mask, Sanyo uses a digital technique called beam indexing to create a color image with only one electron beam. "Had we used a standard picture tube, we should have come up with a set about six to seven inches deep," says Chuck Davis, sales promotion manager at Sanyo.

The smallest TVs—pocket-sized—use LCD screens. Epson, Seiko, and, this month, Panasonic have introduced tiny TVs that are the size of an audio cassette. They use an advanced LCD technology called active-matrix LCD. In these sets each pixel, or picture element, is driven directly by a thin-film transistor. "With the active matrix you can get varying shades of color, depending on how hard you drive the transistor," says Jerry Surprise, TV product manager for Panasonic. "This gives the display more precise color value." To step up resolution, the Panasonic Pocket Watch has almost 90,000 pixels. Its contrast ratio (the ratio of black to white) is 30:1, almost six times greater than earlier LCD sets. . . .

Although LCD advancements hold the most promise for building ultra-thin TVs and other displays, the CRT sets at this point still have better picture resolution. But with CRT sets you do give up compactness, and they use up batteries about twice as fast as LCD models.

Naomi J. Freundlich
From "Home Electronics"

• Invention: Developing a Contrast Module

Dan Lee is a Korean-American. He is a junior executive with an import-export company in San Francisco, and he is taking a degree in business management. During BMGT 464, *Organizational Behavior*, Dan decides to write a term paper on the differences he's seen between the Japanese and American ways of doing business. In particular he's been favorably impressed by the cool, unemotional style of the Japanese in contrast with the confrontational, heavyweight style of many Americans. He also finds the American attitude to contracts too legalistic, too ready to insist on the exact *wording* of the contract while ignoring its *spirit*. On the other hand, he is a young man, and he likes the way American companies let young people, especially women, take important decisions. As part of his paper, Dan intends to contrast the American and the Japanese way of handling a contract. Since a contract involves three consecutive steps, Dan sketches out a three-step dynamic Schema:

That looks good: first one negotiates a contract; then one signs it; then one carries it out. Next, since Dan has *two* subjects (the Japanese and the American), he needs a double game plan:

JAPANESE	AMERICAN
A. Negotiating	A. Negotiating
B. Signing	B. Signing
C. Performing	C. Performing

Putting the two game plans side by side makes them look rather like a *balance sheet*. Developing material as a balance sheet helps greatly: it ensures that parallel ideas stay exactly balanced and in exactly the same order. Next, Dan brainstorms for details just as he would for a single dynamic description—but there's a new problem: the principle of parallelism requires that a detail on one side must be balanced by a corresponding detail on the other. For everything Dan spontaneously invents, he must carefully craft a balancing point. Tidied up, Dan's thoughts look like this:

JAPANESE	AMERICAN
A/1. Negotiation of the contract	A/2. Negotiation of the contract
a. Negotiation takes as much time as necessary.	a. Negotiation may be rushed to meet a deadline.
b. The goal is harmony and mutual satisfaction.	b. The goal is a watertight legal contract.
c. Very little overt emotion is shown during the negotiation.	c. A combative, confrontational atmosphere is normal.
B/1. Signing the contract	B/2. Signing the contract
Merely a formality	The "moment of truth"
C/1. Performance of the contract	C/2. Performance of the contract
If a problem occurs, the contract is rethought along "fair" lines.	If a problem occurs, the parties stick to the letter of the contract or sue each other.

Three-step dynamic sequence

Main steps are balanced

Details are balanced

Dan studies this game plan: somehow, despite its clarity, it isn't what he wants—it doesn't highlight what he thinks is important. Look for example at the last point, Performance: that isn't his key idea at all. What *are* the points he wants to make? He notes them down:

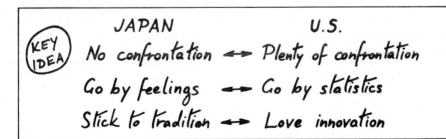

Dan decides to scrap the dynamic game plan and to try a second version, this time based on static description. Jumping ahead to the finished balance sheet, this is how it looks:

JAPANESE	AMERICAN	Three features in order of significa
A/1. Tradition and innovation	A/2. Tradition and innovation	Main steps are balanced
a. Older people and those in senior positions make most decisions.	a. Young people and those lower in rank are often "given their heads."	
b. Women have few senior positions.	b. Senior women are no rarity.	Details are balanced
B/1. Feelings and statistics	B/2. Feelings and statistics	
A good feeling about the project or the people outweighs statistics or computer predictions.	Data, especially statistics generated by computers, are sacred.	
C/1. Negotiating style	C/2. Negotiating style	Key point goes last
a. Emotions are concealed.	a. Emotions are allowed full play.	
b. Loss of face is a serious matter.	b. The loser plans to win the next round.	
c. Confrontation is avoided at all costs.	c. The players are ready to "play rough" if necessary.	Key detail goes last of all

As you can see, the balance sheet arrangement once more ensures that every piece of information has an exact counterpart—that everything Dan includes will "score a point."

Dan now studies the structure of the balance sheet carefully. In fact, a balance sheet has two structures: a *horizontal*, left-to-right structure and a *vertical*, top-to-bottom structure. In both cases the principle of order applies: horizontally, what is on the right is more important than what is on the left (we read left to right); vertically, what is at the bottom is more important than what is at the top (we read top to bottom). To check if the structure of his game plan is correct, Dan must decide what he is trying to say: in essence, "American-style confrontation, playing it rough, is no way to do business." That would put *America* on the right, and *confrontation* at the bottom. That's exactly where Dan has it.

Concept Review

The Balance Sheet

Reread the two pieces by William Wilkie Collins and Naomi Freundlich in the previous section. Draw up a balance sheet for one of these pieces.

• Presenting a Contrast Module

With a strong game plan like Dan's, most of your thinking is done. But one problem remains: presentation. There are only two options here: what can be called *block presentation* and *switch presentation*. Let's see how this works out for Dan's paper. One way of presenting his material is in the form of two *blocks*: hence the term *block presentation*. Restructuring the game plan into two blocks (and leaving out the details) it looks like this:

Dan's other choice is to *switch* from side to side: hence the term *switch presentation*. The restructured version follows this sequence:

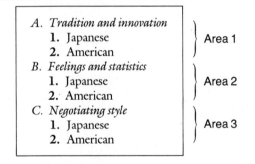

What decides the presentation method? In essence, length and complexity. In a very short contrast module (up to about 500 words), the two methods work equally well. However, if the module becomes longer than about 500 words, or if it contains many tiny details that the reader must closely compare, then block presentation begins to collapse. In a long or detailed piece, the pattern of the first block of information becomes hazy in the reader's mind; the balancing facts when they appear in the second block are not easily interrelated. If that is a danger, then switch presentation is preferable.

Concept Review

Problem Presentations

Study these game plans. What problems do you foresee in developing them?

Two
cassette
recorders
(block
presentation)

Pioneer CT–2070R:	Frequency response
	Wow and flutter
	Bias setting
	Special features
	Price
Pioneer CT–3070R:	Frequency response
	Wow and flutter
	Bias setting
	Special features
	Price

Two
hunting
trips
(switch
presentation)

A. *Setting out*
Lion hunt: afternoon
Bear hunt: before dawn
B. *On the trail*
We followed the lion's tracks.
We followed a trail of blood left by the bear.
C. *Closing in*
The lion was at a watering hole.
The bear was brought to bay in the woods.
D. *The kill*
The lion was running away.
The bear nearly killed us.

2 •
The Personal Voice

Stephen Leacock, the great Canadian writer, had many voices. In this piece we hear at least two of them: the roar of the American newspaper-lion and the bleatings of the English newspaper-lamb. Leacock doesn't merely describe differences, he acts them out for us. (Note: The English newspapers Leacock satirizes do still exist, although they are no longer quite so "stuffy.")

With us in America the great thing is to get the news and shout it at the reader; in England they get the news and then break it to him as gently as possible. Hence the big headings, the bold type, and the double columns of the American paper, and the small headings and the general air of quiet and respectability of the English press. . . . Thus, suppose that a leading member of the United States Congress has committed suicide. This is the way in which the American reporter deals with it:

CHAPTER THREE
Combining The Art of Structure

"Seated in his room at the Grand Hotel with his carpet slippers on his feet and his body wrapped in a blue dressing-gown with pink insertions, after writing a letter of farewell to his wife and emptying a bottle of Scotch whisky in which he exonerated her from all culpability in his death, Congressman Ahasuerus P. Tigg was found by night-watchman Henry T. Smith, while making his rounds as usual, with four bullets in his stomach."

Now, let us suppose that a leading member of the House of Commons in England had done the same thing. Here is the way it would be written up in a first-class London newspaper. The heading would be HOME AND GENERAL INTELLIGENCE. That is inserted so as to keep the reader soothed and quiet, and is no doubt thought better than the American heading, BUGHOUSE CONGRESSMAN BLOWS OUT BRAINS IN HOTEL. After the heading "Home and General Intelligence" the English paper runs the subheading, INCIDENT AT THE GRAND HOTEL. The reader still doesn't know what happened: he isn't meant to. Then the article begins like this:

"The Grand Hotel, which is situated at the corner of Millbank and Victoria Streets, was the scene last night of a distressing incident."

"What is it?" thinks the reader.

"The hotel itself, which is an old Georgian structure dating probably from about 1750, is a quiet establishment, its clientele mainly drawn from business men in the cattle-droving and distillery business from South Wales."

"What happened?" thinks the reader.

"Its cuisine has long been famous for the excellence of its boiled shrimps."

"What happened?"

"While the hotel itself is also known as the meeting-place of the Surbiton Harmonic Society and other associations."

"What happened?"

"Among the more permanent of the guests of the hotel has been numbered during the present Parliamentary session Mr. Llewyllyn Ap Jones, M.P. for South Llanfydd. Mr. Jones apparently came to his room last night at about ten p.m., and put on his carpet slippers and his blue dressing-gown. He then seems to have gone to the cupboard and taken from it a whisky bottle which, however, proved to be empty. The unhappy gentleman then apparently went to bed. . . ."

At that point the American reader probably stops reading, thinking that he has heard it all. The unhappy man found that the bottle was empty and went to bed—very natural; and the affair very properly called a "distressing incident": quite right. But the trained English reader would know that there was more to come and that the air of quiet was only assumed, and he would read on and on until at last the tragic interest heightened, the four shots were fired, with a good long pause after each for discussion of the path of the bullet through Mr. Ap Jones.

I am not saying that either the American way or the British way is the better. They are just two different ways, that's all.

Stephen Leacock
From "The British and American Press"

Review Assignment

Following Leacock's hint, try to develop a single idea in two different voices. For example: contrast the preacher putting an idea across in church with Mom re-explaining it to her children on the way home; contrast an officer giving orders to his sergeant with the sergeant passing them on to the troops; contrast a history teacher and a history student explaining a historical event; contrast the way a teenager who has wrecked his dad's car explains the smash to his friends with the way he explains it to his father; contrast the way a student complains about a grade to a fellow student and to the teacher who gave the grade; contrast what a secretary says to her boss with what she simultaneously thinks. In each case, find the right *voice* to act out the contrast for the reader.

3 •
Writing Workshop:
Combining for Contrast

• Choosing a Subject

The simplest construction is a contrast, so writing a contrast module makes a valuable first exercise in combining. Since you've already written a static description and a dynamic description, you could, of course, reuse this material as one half of a contrast module. In describing a place, for example, the *time* was a crucial factor. If you change the time, you immediately create a contrast: a disco at 11 o'clock on a Saturday night may be *lively*, while at 6 o'clock on a Monday evening it may be agonizingly *boring*. If you described one of your colleagues as *super-efficient*, you may have another colleague who is *chaotic*. If you wrote on "How I watch the Big Game on television," one contrast springs to mind immediately: "How I watch the Big Game at the stadium." Such contrasts would work well. On the other hand, you may be weary of your earlier subjects and ready to try something new.

If you prefer people-oriented subjects, two kinds of contrast suggest themselves: a contrast within one person and a contrast between two people. An inner contrast is based on some change of status that creates a change in appearance and behavior. For example:

1. Contrast the same person when drunk and sober.
2. Contrast a woman's personality before and during a pregnancy (or during and after, or before and after).
3. Take someone who has experienced a religious conversion and contrast his or her personality before and after conversion.
4. Contrast the way you did a job before and after specialized training.
5. Select someone who has been given a promotion; show how the promotion affected his or her personality.

In choosing two people to contrast, you'll often have some simple "thesis" in mind: I prefer *A*'s way of behaving to *B*'s. Topics include:

6. Think of two next-door neighbors you have had (or two roommates). Contrast their concepts of neighborliness.

7. Pick two coaches; contrast their approach to their job.

8. Contrast the sportsmanship of two athletes (amateur or professional) in a particular sport.

9. Contrast two clerks who have served you recently.

10. Contrast the personalities of two animals you have owned.

Anybody who travels comes into contact (if not conflict) with contrasting institutions and ways of doing things. Your experience can provide the basis for a unique and interesting contrast module.

11. Contrast two schools you have attended. They might be in different parts of the country; one might be a religious foundation, the other secular; one might be military, the other civilian.

12. Contrast the atmosphere of a high-school classroom with that of a university classroom.

13. Contrast Christmas in the northern and southern hemispheres.

14. Contrast driving in two different countries (or at two different seasons).

15. Contrast the night life in two cities.

16. Contrast eating out in two different countries.

17. Contrast a no-frills transatlantic flight with a normal commercial flight.

18. Contrast the attitudes of people in two countries toward American tourists.

19. Contrast daily life in a hot climate with daily life in a cold climate.

20. Contrast the way children are brought up in two parts of the world.

Job experience also provides a wealth of contrasts.

21. If you have served in the military, contrast your daily life when your unit was in barracks with your daily life in the field.

22. Take a job with which you are familiar and show how a man and a woman tackle it differently.

23. Contrast working a day shift with working a night shift.

24. Describe two jobs you have done; contrast the job satisfaction they offered.

25. Select two fellow workers and contrast their attitudes to their jobs.

26. Contrast the way in which two supervisors under whom you have worked tried to accomplish a specific job or mission.

27. Contrast an indoor job with an outdoor job.

28. Contrast the way you did your job before and after computerization.

29. Contrast the working atmosphere in a successful company that you worked for with that in an unsuccessful company.

30. Contrast two ways of getting promoted.

If you prefer writing about machines, again many contrasts would work:

31. Take two machines of broadly the same type (for example, two motorcycles) and show how they are adapted for contrasting uses (for example, city roads as against cross-country).

32. Contrast two broadly similar musical instruments (for example, two guitars).

33. Contrast a typewriter with a word processor.

34. Contrast some specific piece of machinery in use today (for example, a power drill, a tractor, the ignition system of a gasoline engine) with the comparable item in use fifty years ago (or ten years or any other time period).

35. Contrast two broadly similar computer programs you have used.

Finally, hobbies, interests, life in general—the sources are endless.

36. Contrast two live concerts you have attended.

37. Contrast two styles of furnishing a home.

38. Contrast having a baby at home with having one in the hospital.

39. Contrast mail-order shopping with shopping at a store.

40. Contrast driving your own vehicle with using public transport.

• Coming Up with a Game Plan

You already have some experience of brainstorming for descriptive material, of filtering, and so on. The new problem is combining two descriptions into a single piece. Let's assume you have a subject you're interested in and some promising ideas for developing it. The next task, as we saw with Dan's paper on business styles, is to decide if the contrast works best statically or dynamically. The subject you chose may be essentially static, for example Topic 1: "Contrast the same person when drunk and sober." Obviously this subject requires you to contrast two *states*. Other subjects suggest a dynamic approach, for example Topic 30: "Contrast two ways of getting promoted"—a step-by-step analysis of the two cases looks best here. Most subjects, however, can be handled either way—it's your decision. If both methods are possible, you might first try sketching out the schema for a dynamic description and seeing what occurs in the *final* position. If the last step is not the most important, then a static description might be preferable. To be clear on this, let's take an example, Topic 17: "Contrast a no-frills transatlantic flight with a normal commercial flight." The dynamic schema might contain five steps:

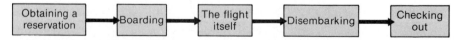

If you decide that *checking out* is not the key point and would make a poor ending, then try again using the static model. Working statically, you might discuss four subtopics: cost (the key point), safety, comfort, and convenience. There is no problem now in ending with your key point:

> 1. Convenience
> 2. Comfort
> 3. Safety
> 4. Cost (key point)

Probably, in this case, you'll prefer the static model. If both methods seem equally effective, use whichever looks easier.

With a basic pattern established, it's a good idea to draw up a skeleton balance sheet; you can then flesh it out with details. Remember, of course, to use a "double entry" system: if you add a detail to one side, you must add the balancing detail on the other.

The next steps involve deciding rather than inventing: (1) structure the piece horizontally (with the more important element on the right); (2) structure the piece vertically, with the last step in the sequence (in dynamic description) or the main point you are making (in static description) at the end; (3) finally, decide whether to use block presentation or switch presentation. Your grounds for making these decisions were discussed in the first part of the chapter. That done, your game plan is finished, and you are ready to write.

• Writing the First Draft

A. THE OPENING

A module requires only a short, functional introduction. A Who-What-Where-and-When sentence, or some shorter variant, is appropriate. For example:

> In July 1986 I was transferred from Ice Falls, Maine, to Cairo, Egypt; living for the first time in a hot climate radically changed my daily routine.

Or:

> Having used a typewriter for more than ten years, I bought a word processor three months ago after a single demonstration in the store. It has revolutionized my working methods.

Openings are difficult. If you have trouble with yours, leave writing it until later. In fact, some professional writers routinely skip the opening in a first draft, picking it up later—an idea you might try.

B. WRITING: BLOCK PRESENTATION OR SWITCH PRESENTATION?

A major trap yawns open for you at this stage: indecisiveness. Your piece should be written using *either* block presentation *or* switch presentation: if you try to change horses in midstream, you may radically confuse the reader.

If you decide to use *block presentation*, your first goal is to create two "chunks" of description. As with earlier descriptive assignments, this means following your game plan and refining it as new ideas occur. But be specially careful now! A contrast module is in two parts, and you can't change one without changing the other. This is a general principle: as a game plan becomes more elaborate, changing one detail often means making a whole chain of interrelated changes.

If you decide on *switch presentation*, you'll be "crossing the line" from side to side (from Japan to America, for example) fairly often. As a signal to warn the reader of each border crossing, you'll need a phrase such as:

On the other hand . . .
Looking at the American side of the coin . . .
Turning to America . . .

With switch presentation, try not to "cross the line" too often. Glance ahead at Susan Anderson's essay at the end of this chapter. She discusses four main ideas; in presenting each idea, she "crosses the line" only once; if she'd skipped backwards and forwards for each detail, the piece would have degenerated into a confusion of *on the other hands*.

C. THE CLOSING

A contrast module is not an essay. If it has a message, it's unlikely to be more than a simple *statement of preference* or a *question*. Such a message makes a neat ending for the module. For example:

Statement of Preference

a. Without doubt, Joe is nicer sober than he is drunk.
b. Overall, a university classroom is more conducive to study than a classroom in a high school.

Question

a. This contrast raises a question: is it possible for Americans to learn business techniques from their Japanese counterparts?
b. The question is this: when flying the Atlantic, do you put cost or comfort first?

• Revising

REVISION CHECK 1: CONTINUITY

A. Transitions.
If the contrasted descriptions are the bricks, then the *continuity material* is the mortar. Changing to a geological comparison: when you combine two descrip-

tions, you create gaps or "fault-lines" in the material. If you are using block presentation, there is necessarily a gap between the two halves. The gap is valuable because it breaks up the material into accessible segments, but it must not become a yawning gulf that your reader cannot cross. What is called a *transition* is necessary both to point out the gap and to bridge it.

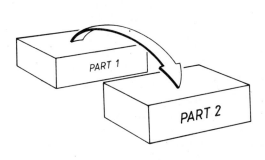 

The formula for such a transition is:

So far I have discussed ⟨A⟩; now I will discuss ⟨B⟩.

For example:

So far I have discussed how the Japanese negotiate; now I will discuss American negotiating style.

If you use switch presentation, you may have quite a number of sections. Each one should begin with a clear label so that the reader knows what territory you are now entering. The underlying formula for such a label is:

The ⟨ordinal⟩ area of contrast is ⟨X⟩.

For example:

The third area of contrast is negotiating styles.

You may want to rephrase these formulas more elegantly; if you do, work sparingly: transitions must be short and hard-hitting, like roadsigns on the freeway.

B. Headings.

In writing the dynamic description, you probably used section headings. If you did, you saw how these headings improve the readability of your work. In a contrast module, the headings depend on the mode of presentation. If you use block presentation, each block needs a heading; if you use switch presentation, each section needs a heading.

REVISION CHECK 2: COST EFFECTIVENESS

The goal has not changed—tight, clear expression. One new problem arises, however, when you combine descriptions: *balance*. As we've seen, an isolated fact without a balancing counter-fact is meaningless. Does this mean that the two sides of the contrast should come out to the same length? In fact, if both sides are unfamiliar to the reader, then both sides do need roughly equal exposure. But often the reader is already familiar with one side, while the other is a complete novelty. Let's say, for example, that you're contrasting buying a sweater from Macy's in New York with buying one from GUM in Moscow. The reader can master the New York side of things with just a sentence or two for each major step. On the other hand, the reader will expect, and enjoy, more detail about the unfamiliar Moscow scene. (For a Russian reader, it's the other way round, of course.) In general, if you find yourself covering familiar ground in too much detail, then prune back—though not to the point where the parallels become lost.

REVISION CHECK 3: CORRECTNESS

By now you should have become aware of the writing mistakes to which you personally are prone. Search for them carefully and correct them. Errors that commonly occur in contrast modules are listed in the next section.

• Special Correctness Problems—Contrast

Just as before, read through the material in this section so that you know what problems to look for.

PROBLEM AREA 1: TENSE—THEN AND NOW

Many contrasts depend on the before-and-after syndrome. This often seems to require a shift in tense—for example, your description of Lucille *before* she became a Christian belongs in the past tense; the way she is *now* seems to require the present tense. If you find, however, that the piece shifts tense too often, then write it all in the past.

PROBLEM AREA 2: THE CASE IN COMPARISON CLAUSES

A contrast module tends to be rich in "comparison clauses." These two comparison sentences contain an error of *case*:

> Orientals show their emotions less *than us*.
> Russians do not eat as much meat *as us*.

If you can't spot and explain the error, review the concept in your handbook under *Comparison Clauses* or *Case with "than" or "as."*

PROBLEM 3: ILLOGICAL CONTRASTS

A common short circuit in contrast papers results in an apparent contrast of two dissimilar things. For example:

My father's punishments were not as tough as my mother.

Another short circuit occurs when you apparently contrast a thing with itself. For example:

Alaska is bigger than any state in the United States.

If you don't see the problem, then review the conception in your handbook under *Faulty Comparisons* or *Illogical Comparisons*.

• The Final Draft

As an example of the way your final draft might look, consider this contrast by Susan Anderson on a current controversy, breast-feeding versus bottle-feeding a baby. Susan is a beginning student, and so she's wisely chosen a subject she knows at first hand.

Bottle-Feeding or Breast-Feeding: Is it a Real Choice?

Bottle-fed Baby	Breast-fed Baby

A. Convenience
    a. Bottles, nipples and formula must be used.
    b. Warming a bottle is a chore, especially when half-asleep.
	A. Convenience
	    a. No supplies are needed.
	    b. Night-time and early morning feeds require no preparation.

B. Social acceptance
    Bottle-feeding is socially acceptable.
	B. Social acceptance
	    Breast-feeding in public can cause raised eyebrows.

C. Effect on the baby
    a. Nutritionally this is second-best
    b. The mother must leave the baby to prepare food.
	C. Effect on the baby
	    a. Nutritionally this is ideal.
	    b. The mother feeds the baby immediately.

D. Bond
    a. The bond is weaker.
    b. The mother feels replaceable.
	D. Bond
	    a. The bond is absolute.
	    b. The mother is irreplaceable.

Balance Sheet Game Plan

Presentation Method: Switch

I have two children. The first I bottle-fed, and I breast-fed the younger. The two experiences were radically different.

A. Convenience

The first difference between bottle-feeding and breast-feeding is convenience. When I bottle-fed my baby, I somehow accumulated at least thirty-five bottles, all of which had to be scrubbed and sterilized. The kitchen sink was constantly full of them. Keeping a supply of formula in the house was an even bigger problem. More than once I ran out of formula—going out on a cold night with a hungry baby to a 24-hour "convenience" store was no fun. Night-time and early morning feedings are

Simple opening

Section heading

Sentence to clarify topic

Concrete material (including anecdote)

another unpleasant memory. I would stumble into the kitchen half asleep, mix the formula, warm it in a pan, and then pour most of it on the counter, giving me the extra task of clearing up the mess.

With my second, breast-fed baby, I never had to buy bottle-feeding equipment or formula. I already had everything I needed—and there were no messy bottles to wash. Late night and early morning feeds required no special preparation. Clearly breast-feeding is more convenient than bottle-feeding.

B. Social Acceptance

Feeding the baby in public is the next contrast. Bottle-feeding in public is socially acceptable. In shopping centers, restaurants, even on buses I was never ashamed to produce the bottle and feed the baby. People would smile at us, evidently thinking how "right" we looked.

On the other hand, breast-feeding in public is not nearly so acceptable, and I often felt ill at ease. On one embarrassing occasion, I was nursing my baby in an overcrowded restaurant. For the sake of discretion, I covered the baby completely under a light blanket. An old man came up to my table smiling and said: "You must have a baby under that blanket!" He jerked the blanket away to reveal the baby. I am not sure whose face was redder, his or mine. Although breast-feeding in public is not socially accepted, a good mother can learn to cope with the problem.

C. Effect on the Baby

Babies need careful nutrition. Bottle-feeding is without doubt second-best in nutrition. Cow's milk, on which formula is based, is not ideal for babies. It has a high electrolyte content and a poor calcium/phosphorus ratio. Cases of allergy to a particular formula are common and very distressing for mother and baby. Infection due to poorly sterilized bottles is also a serious drawback. Preparation time, too, has an effect on the baby. If the baby wakes up hungry, the mother may have to "abandon" it for several minutes to prepare the formula. A baby can scream itself into a rage in that short time—something that is unpleasant for everyone.

Breast milk, on the other hand, contains important antibodies which protect the baby against common viruses, its balance of vitamins and minerals is perfect, and babies seldom have allergies to human milk. Further, risks of infection are slight if the mother practices normal hygiene. As to preparation, there is none. If the baby awakes hungry, it can be fed instantly. Breast-feeding tends to produce happy and well-fed babies.

D. Bond

Bonding between mother and baby is vital during the first few months of the baby's life. With bottle-feeding, this bond can arise, but it is not automatic. The baby may be given to babysitters or to older siblings to feed; the mother may prop up the bottle so that no one at all is feeding the baby. Such things lessen the chance of a strong bond forming. Further, the mother is led to believe that she is replaceable—that her baby will do just as well with her or without her.

With breast-feeding the situation is the opposite. The nursing couple feel an irresistible bond that nothing can replace. The mother knows that the baby's welfare depends uniquely on her. Nothing else I have experienced creates a comparable feeling of being needed.

From this account of my experiences of bottle-feeding and breast-feeding, I think it is clear which I prefer.

Margin notes:

Switch to
other side
Balancing
information
Wrapup
sentence

The
established
pattern is
repeated in
all the
following
sections

CHAPTER THREE
Combining The Art of Structure

• Summary: The Flowchart

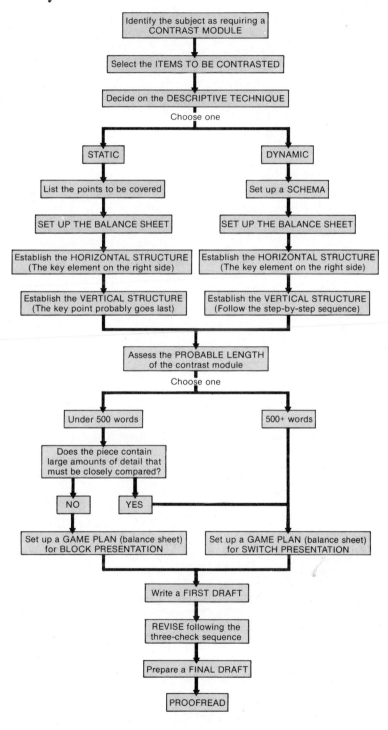

· PART TWO ·

The Essay

Introduction

1 •

The Problem:
Meeting Expectations—What Is an Essay?

This introduction is a hub; the five chapters that follow are spokes. After you've read this chapter, you can proceed directly to *any* of the next chapters. The reading plan you follow should be determined by your immediate needs as a writer or by the study plan developed for your class.

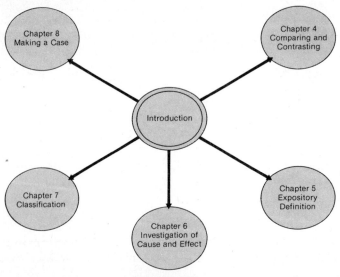

INTRODUCTION

Academic writing demands two specialized skills, *organization* and *research*; neither is much use without the other. *Organization* means putting your ideas into the best possible shape; *research* means finding the information you want to use. In fact these two processes, resourceful searching and coherent organizing, cannot be separated in practice: you know where to dig for facts because you know what idea you are developing, and you know what idea you are developing because you have a fair idea of the facts. To break out of this variation of catch-22, Part 2 of this book (the next five chapters) highlights *effective organization*; you probably know enough already to tackle most of the suggested assignments. Part 3 deals with techniques of *research*.

Courtesy of Jefferson Communications, Inc

Is it true? Like many students, what Skyler needs from a writing course is a "survival kit" for the academic jungle ahead. Taking survival as our priority, we must ask what teachers *expect* when they assign written work. What characterizes *essays* or *term papers* for the people who assign and grade them?

• Expectation 1: Literacy

Obviously an essay must be *literate*—or is it so obvious? Sometimes teachers are asked: "Do you take off points for English?" (This happens to English teachers, too.) Even if the answer is "No, I don't," be careful. It is hard to imagine "correct" ideas expressed in "incorrect" English: if the language is not right, how does your reader know what you are talking about?

• Expectation 2: Professional Presentation

I once passed an incoming batch of twenty-two essays around a class and asked the students to guess the grade of each essay *without reading one word of it*. In eighteen of the twenty-two cases, the average guess correctly predicted the grade. In this instance, presentation and the quality of thought went more or less hand in hand. Whether or not that is generally so, a teacher expects from you a professionally presented paper.

• Expectation 3: Well-Researched Content

A teacher also expects you to know what you are talking about. Occasionally you may be asked to write from personal experience; usually, however, the facts, figures, theories and ideas you use will not be your own. They will be the result of *research*, the subject of Part 3 of this book.

• Expectation 4: Strong Organization

Organization is not a goal in itself, it is a way of achieving a goal. You probably know people who keep their belongings in strictly regimented places, from the spare towels in the bathroom to the reserve can of gasoline in the car. For such fanatics, organization has become a goal in itself. Most of us organize our belongings with a *purpose* in mind: to make life simpler. What is the purpose of organization in an essay?

An essay has something to say, a point to put across; that is its reason for existence. The point of a description, as we saw in Chapter 1, can often be summed up in one phrase: its controlling filter. The point of an essay is more elaborate: usually it takes the form of a single sentence, the so-called *thesis statement*. (This will be explained below.) As we saw earlier, a description without a filter is just a random heap of glittering detail. Without a thesis statement, an essay is much the same—except that it may not glitter. The expectation: an essay organized so that its point, its *thesis*, is perfectly clear to the reader.

2 •
The Process of Writing an Essay

To meet these expectations, you'll need to develop the skills associated with the four stages of essay writing. The first stage is *investigation*. Investigation requires the skill of formulating a problem and then searching until you have the material for an answer. Stage 2 is *organization*; this means finding an effective way of handling the material you have discovered. The end product of the organizing stage is the game plan. Stage 3, *presentation*, is turning your idea into words that a reader finds convincing. Finally comes *revising*, a series of checks to ensure that the end product is as good as it can be. Bearing always in mind that most writers "circle back" during the writing process, let's now look at each of these four stages more closely.

• Investigation

INVESTIGATION
ORGANIZATION
PRESENTATION
REVISION

A. INVESTIGATIVE TECHNIQUE: THE PROBLEM FORMS

"Hello! Officer Green, here. Can I help you?"

"Oh officer! Something terrible has happened. Please come quickly."

"I'm afraid you'll have to be a little more specific, sir. I mean, what exactly is it that's happened? And where are you calling from? Could you start with your name please?"

The police are powerless to help until they have a clear idea of the problem that confronts them. A student writing an essay is in much the same position: to kick off the writing process, you must be confronted by a problem. In academic practice, problems take two forms: *ready-made* and *do-it-yourself*. The ready-made problem is assigned by the professor; the do-it-yourself problem is invented by the student.

Let's take the easy case first: the ready-made, teacher-assigned problem. At first glance you may see no limit to such assignments. Although there are indeed an infinity of subjects, luckily there are only a handful of *forms* in which problems can be assigned. Implied in each of these problem forms is the technique you need to deal with it; therefore, by studying the problem forms and their associated answer techniques, you'll learn to handle virtually any question that can be thrown at you.

Problem Form 1: Describing. The simplest assignment of all is to *describe* something. Here you have only *one element* to deal with. (In this case, you've already studied how to proceed.)

Problem Form 2: Comparing and Contrasting. Next comes the *two-element* assignment. Whatever the wording, if you're asked to handle two items, your approach is the same: to find out (a) what links the items together, (b) what distinguishes them from each other, and (c) to work from there. The traditional label for the two-element assignment is *Comparison-Contrast*. Some specimen questions:

a. Compare the American and the Soviet attitudes to spying.

b. Discuss the tactics of the NAACP and those of the Black Panthers.

c. Contrast the women's rights movement of the 1870s–1880s with that of the 1970s–1980s.

Problem Form 3: Defining. Defining means pinning down a concept with great exactness—saying what characteristics it has and what characteristics it lacks. The number of elements you introduce here is up to you. Examples:

a. Define schizophrenia.

b. What characterizes the abusive parent?

c. Discuss what is meant by "democracy."

Problem Form 4: Investigating Causes. This is the classic investigation technique. It takes a given situation and asks "*How come?*" Again, the number of elements you discuss is at your discretion. Some examples:

a. Explain the popular appeal of President Reagan.

b. Why are parts of America running short of water?

c. How do you account for the swing back to "traditional" values?

Problem Form 5: Classifying. After one-element, two-element, and cluster-of-element structures, there is one more possibility: some subjects treat an endless array of elements—nobody knows how many—and yet you must discuss them all. How can that be? Think of a subject such as "The techniques of treating cancer." How many techniques are involved here? Probably as many as there are doctors. Tackling an indefinite number of elements encounters the problem of *classification*. Again some examples:

a. Discuss the tactics that have been used against terrorists.

b. Categorize social attitudes to "house-husbands."

c. Analyze the reasons for jogging.

Problem Form 6: Making a Case. Finally, you might be asked to argue for or against a certain point of view, to make a case. *Making a case* is not simply a matter of stating your opinion, take it or leave it: there's no difficulty in doing that. You'll be expected, rather, to convince the reader, perhaps even to change the reader's mind. Some examples:

a. "White supremacy in South Africa is a danger to the rest of the world." Do you agree?

b. "America will never have a woman president." Discuss.

c. "Make love, not war." Is it time to return to the old hippie slogan?

These six problem forms recur endlessly in lists of "assigned subjects." The trick is obvious: you study the question and identify the problem form (definition, classification, or whatever); you then invoke the appropriate answer technique. (In particular, a good examination technique depends on doing this quickly and

INTRODUCTION

efficiently.) Naturally, nothing is quite so simple in practice—but you'll be surprised how much it helps to know the "tricks of the trade."

A word now about do-it-yourself problems, the ones you have to invent yourself. Here again a strong sense of the problem forms is valuable. Once you know your subject area, you must decide exactly what problem you want to tackle. You can maximize your options by trying a question that uses each of the problem forms: you ask, "How might my subject work as a definition, as a classification, as a case, or whatever?" Before you can do that, however, you must explore the problem forms and their associated answer techniques. That is the purpose of the next chapters.

Concept Review

Problem Forms

We have briefly described six problem forms:

a. Problem Form 1: *Describing*—describing **one** element using static or dynamic description

b. Problem Form 2: *Comparing and contrasting*—discussing **two** elements in relationship with one another

c. Problem Form 3: *Defining*—listing in full the characteristics of a target word or concept

d. Problem Form 4: *Investigating causes*—taking a given situation and asking, "How come?"

e. Problem Form 5: *Classifying*—discussing **all** the elements in a series of unknown size

f. Problem Form 6: *Making a case*—arguing for a point of view in the hope of convincing the reader

Look at the essay subjects below. Decide which of the six problem forms is implied by the exact wording of the question.

1. Compare downhill skiing and cross-country skiing.

2. What constitutes "sociopathic behavior"?

3. Discuss the available methods of birth control.

4. Describe the operation of tonsillectomy (removal of tonsils).

5. Why did Custer lose the Battle of Little Big Horn?

6. Discuss Martin Luther King, Jr., and Malcolm X as leaders.

7. "America should return to Prohibition." Discuss.

8. What was Prohibition?

9. Why was Prohibition a failure?

10. Should prostitution be legalized and taxed in the United States (as it is in much of Europe)?

B. INVESTIGATIVE TECHNIQUE: KINDS OF INFORMATION

So far, most of what you have written has been based on personal observation. As you get closer to the mainstream of academic writing, the personal element fades out as a source while formal research figures more prominently. Our concern in the next chapters, however, is not with research but with techniques of organization. In mastering these techniques, it scarcely matters whether you use personal observation or formal research as your raw material; the organizing skill is much the same. For this reason you may prefer to write on low-key, personal subjects. Thus, when the following chapters talk about *information*, they mean either information based on your own direct observation or information from a research source such as a book, a magazine, an interview or a lecture.

• Organization

INVESTIGATION
ORGANIZATION
PRESENTATION
REVISION

Good organization does not occur by chance. In the next chapters, you'll be studying the game plans associated with different problem forms. One feature is common to all the game plans, however: the thesis statement is always the foremost consideration. Yet coming up with a thesis statement is not always easy and seldom follows the same track twice. Let's see how four students arrived at a thesis statement: their experience will show us four shapes that a thesis statement can take, regardless of the subject.

A. THE COMMAND AS THESIS STATEMENT

Joe Tyler had a knee-jerk reaction to the subject "Two ways of training an animal." He knew immediately what he wanted to say. Joe had worked in a stable and had successfully broken in horses, using patience and consistency as his guidelines. Not everyone works that way. At the stable Joe had a fistfight with an owner who was using a whip to break the spirit of a rebellious filly. To Joe there was a right way and a wrong way to break in a horse. Joe's thesis statement, instantly formulated, gave the reader a direct command: *Break in a horse with patience, not with brutality.* In certain writing situations, a command like that makes a strong thesis statement.

B. THE PLAIN STATEMENT AS THESIS STATEMENT

Leigh Melrose was writing on a painful subject: "Two ways of treating an elderly member of the family." Leigh had put her own mother into an old people's home while a friend of hers, faced with the same problem, had kept a senile mother at home for many years. Leigh compared the two cases: if she wrote about them, what was she going to *say*? Then she jotted down: "It's better to keep old people home with the family." And underneath the opposite idea: "They have to go where they can be properly cared for." Two contradictory thesis statements —what next? Leigh rejected both versions as simply untrue. Then she talked to her husband. In his view *both* families were right—everything depends on the circumstances. This gave Leigh a third statement, the one she actually chose: *Both families did what was right in their own circumstances.* A plain statement like this is the most common thesis of all. What happened to Leigh is normal: a thesis statement goes through several transformations before it reaches an acceptable shape. In the next two cases, you'll see what happens when *no* acceptable form suggests itself.

C. THE CHOICE AS THESIS STATEMENT

Lincoln Hill was a computer fanatic. He decided to write on "Two personal computers: the Macintosh and the Apple IIe." Lincoln drew up two lists, one headed *Similarities*, the other *Differences*. The detail on these lists was amazing —Lincoln knew what he was talking about. But he still had no thesis: he was stuck. When he brought the lists to me for help, I couldn't understand all the technical details, and I asked him who the essay was *for*.

"You," he said.
"Why?" I replied.
"I don't know. Maybe you want to buy one of them."
"So which one would you recommend?"
"It depends what you want to do with it."
"What is there to do with it? I mean, what are my choices?"
"Well, if you're a hacker like me, you couldn't stand the Macintosh. It just hands you everything on a plate."
"I'm a teacher. I don't have time for that stuff."
"Macintosh be fine, I guess."
"That's your thesis statement then."
"What is?"
"*For quick results, buy a Macintosh, but to learn about computers, buy a IIe.*"

Offering the reader a choice is a resourceful way of returning a "split decision" on your material.

D. THE QUESTION AS THESIS STATEMENT

Holly Virbon had a talent for asking questions but none for answering them. "Compare and contrast a child from a disciplined home with a child from an undisciplined home" was a subject she really wanted to write about. But again, what should she *say*? Holly remembered babysitting Dennis: he'd been a dreadful brat who had later turned into a rather boring "model citizen." She'd also looked after his brother, Albee. Albee had been his parents' pride and joy until he'd dropped out of college and disappeared in San Francisco. Apparently the strict discipline in the family had turned the rebel into the conformist and the conformist into the rebel. Then Holly thought of her own sister, Jennie; they'd both grown up in an easygoing family, yet Holly herself had grown up chaotic and dissatisfied, while sister Jennie had become self-disciplined and successful. The more Holly thought about it, the harder the question became: *Does discipline in the home have any predictable effect on children*? Holly's thesis statement never progressed beyond this question. The general principle: if your evidence does not produce a clear conclusion, then your thesis statement may well take the form of an open question.

Concept Review

Formulating a Thesis Statement

The thesis statement, the innermost core of an essay, can take four forms:

TYPE	EXAMPLE
A. The order (imperative):	"Break in a horse with patience, not with brutality."
B. The statement (declarative):	"Both families did what was right in their own circumstances."
C. The choice (alternative):	"For results, buy a Macintosh, but to learn about computers, buy a IIe."
D. The question (interrogative):	"Does discipline in the home have any predictable effect on children?"

It often helps to formulate a thesis statement in different ways to see which comes closest to your real idea. In the cases below, you're given the subject and the first formulation of your thesis statement. Try reformulating each thesis statement in the other three available forms.

1. You are writing a comparison-contrast on Dobermans and German shepherds as watchdogs. Your first formulation is the command: "Never trust a Doberman."

2. You are writing a definition essay on the subject, "What is patriotism?" Your first formulation is the choice: "For some people, patriotism is a blind, irrational prejudice; for others it is a critical, reasoned preference. What is the *true* form, I have not been able to discover."

3. You are writing an investigation into the causes of Hitler's rise to power. Your first formulation is the question: "What attracted a civilized, scientific nation toward a murderous cult of unreason?"

4. You are writing a classification of the reasons young men avoided the draft during the Vietnam era. Your first formulation is the statement: "Not all draft dodgers were cowards."

• Presentation: Writing the Essay

INVESTIGATION
ORGANIZATION
PRESENTATION
REVISION

A strong thesis statement and a tidy game plan do not automatically produce a good essay: clear presentation is a must. An essay is an attempt to present a thesis to the reader: there are essentially two methods of presentation, and it helps if you decide early on which you are using. The two methods can be labeled *theorem* and *inquiry*.

A. THEOREM AND INQUIRY AS PRESENTATION METHODS

In the theoretical sciences such as mathematics, many presentations are *proofs*: "Prove that in a right-angle triangle, the square on the hypotenuse equals the sum of the squares on the other two sides." The proof itself takes the form of a *theorem*. A theorem begins with a clear statement of what is to be proved (the "hypothesis"); it offers a faultlessly logical argument, concluding with the words: "Therefore, it follows that . . ."; the hypothesis is then restated as a proven principle.

An essay might use this form. For example, imagine an essay beginning with a statement like one of the following:

This essay will show that America should normalize relations with Cuba.

In this essay I shall explain why the Yellowstone National Park should belong to the grizzlies, not to the tourists.

This paper will make it clear that the production of asbestos should be stopped immediately.

After such a strong start, the reader anticipates strong evidence, scientific proof almost, that the hypothesis is a "fact of life." If you have such a proof, then there is nothing against presenting your thesis statement as a theorem. In this case, your thesis statement would belong at the beginning of the essay as "to be proved" and at the end as "what I have just proved." Unfortunately such unarguable proof is rare outside the pure sciences; usually you must work with more controversial arguments. When this happens, you cannot present your ideas in the form of a proof: the appropriate form is an inquiry.

An *inquiry* begins with a problem. It evaluates the available evidence and reaches a conclusion—often an "open verdict." The three subjects just given would probably be more convincing as inquiries, since none of them is really provable. The essay might then begin:

Should America normalize relations with Cuba? That is the question this essay will try to answer.

There is a conflict of interest in the Yellowstone National Park between the grizzlies and the tourists. This conflict is the subject of this essay.

That asbestos dust causes cancer is known. Does this mean that production of asbestos should be stopped immediately?

The reader now anticipates not a proof but a balanced argument leading to a conclusion. The conclusion might well have reservations, or it might leave the question completely open. The thesis statment in this kind of presentation belongs *at the end*.

Let's compare the two presentations side by side:

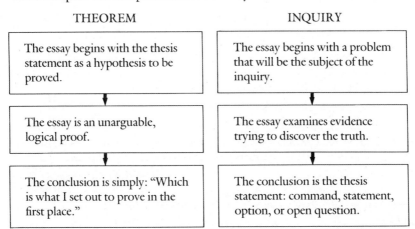

THEOREM	INQUIRY
The essay begins with the thesis statement as a hypothesis to be proved.	The essay begins with a problem that will be the subject of the inquiry.
The essay is an unarguable, logical proof.	The essay examines evidence trying to discover the truth.
The conclusion is simply: "Which is what I set out to prove in the first place."	The conclusion is the thesis statement: command, statement, option, or open question.

A decision between these two options should be made before you begin writing; obviously the language of a hard-and-fast proof is different from the language of a thoughtful evaluation of evidence. Every word you write is influenced by this choice.

Concept Review 1

Theorem or Inquiry

a. One of the approaches below presents an idea as a *theorem*; the other presents an *inquiry*. Which is which?

b. Which of the two approaches is more likely to *convince* a reader who is trying to decide the truth of the matter?

Approach A.   I will now show that jogging is good for you. It is good for you because it stimulates the heart, because it improves muscle tone, and because it takes your mind off your worries. Now you know why jogging is good for you.

Approach B.   Have you wondered if jogging really does any good? Maybe you have heard stories of stress fractures and heart attacks that were actually caused by jogging. Such things happen but usually as the result of excessive jogging. Normal jogging stimulates the heart, improves muscle tone, and takes your mind off your worries. Does anyone doubt that? Moderate jogging does seem to be good, at least for most people.

Concept Review 2

Method of Presentation

How would you present the thesis in each of the following situations? As a *theorem* or as an *inquiry*? Give your reasons.

a. The health regulations for Broadville state that household water may not contain more than 50 milligrams of nitrate per liter of water. You have measurements showing that 120 milligrams is the current figure. Your thesis is that the figure must be lowered.

b. You have observed that many students are not well prepared for college-level courses. Your thesis is that the public school system is largely to blame.

c. You have investigated "copycat crimes." Your thesis is that if the media gave fewer details about exactly how crimes are committed, there would probably be fewer copycats.

d. A statute in your state dated 1923 grants one tribe of Indians the rights to their lands "in perpetuity." Following the discovery of mineral deposits, an attempt is being made to shift the Indians to other land. Your thesis: any attempt to move the Indians is illegal.

B. OPENINGS

An academic essay should let the reader know early on what it is *about*. Don't rely on the title of the essay to do this; you must spell it out in the essay itself. In an inquiry essay, the "formula" for doing this is obvious:

> This paper will ask:
> if kindness or brutality is the better way to break in a horse.
>
> what exactly is meant by the word *schizophrenia*.
>
> what caused the shuttle *Challenger* to explode.
>
> what treatment offers the best hope for heroin addicts.

The formula opening for a theorem essay uses the word *prove* instead of the word *ask*.

Even in polished form, such an opening may seem too abrupt. In fact an opening usually does more than state the subject: it tries to *hook* the reader's interest, to suggest that the essay is worth reading. Let's look at four classic ways of doing this. There are other ways, but experiment will help you more with openings than will guidelines.

Starting Concretely, The Who-What-Where-When Opening. A Who-What-Where-When opening plus a lead-in sentence often gets an essay up and running. For example:

> When I lived in Detroit I worked as babysitter for a one-parent family, the Dwyers, and a two-parent family, the Earles. (Who, What, Where and When) Pauline Dwyer felt that her children were deprived because they had only a mother; somehow she envied the Earles. The Dwyers and the Earles: which family really gave its children a better start in life? (lead-in sentences setting up the problem)

Starting with a Quotation. Countless books of quotations indexed by subject are available. A check in the index often produces the opening you are looking for: witty and to the point. For example:

> "If an animal does something, we call it instinct; if we do the same thing for the same reason, we call it intelligence," Will Cuppy once said. (quotation and source) What exactly is this intelligence on which we pride ourselves? That is the question this essay will try to answer. (lead-in sentences setting up the problem)

Starting with an Anecdote. This technique is the favorite of public speakers. A writer can use it too, provided the story has some bearing on the subject and the context is not very formal. For example:

> The story has it that Edison's home was full of ingenious labor-saving devices—except at the main gate, where a very heavy turnstile kept cattle out of his garden. One day a frail guest who'd had trouble with the turnstile asked him why he didn't invent a better one. "No, indeed, ma'am," said Edison.

"Everybody who pushes through that turnstile pumps eight gallons of water into the tank on my roof." (anecdote) This story tells us a lot about a dying species: the inventor. Today we are spending billions of dollars replacing the inventor with the research worker. The question I want to raise is—why? (lead-in sentences setting up the problem)

Starting with a Question.   The so-called rhetorical question does not require an answer. It is simply a trick for sweeping readers off their feet. For example:

How many kinds of love can a man and a woman enjoy? This is a curious and intricate question to which I have devoted much thought and some enjoyable experimentation.

Concept Review

Openings

a. Look at some of the essays in this book. Read only the openings. In which cases do you want to read on? In which cases are you definitely put off further reading? Explain what it is in the *writing* (not so much in the subject matter) that creates your positive or negative reaction.

b. Of the essays you scanned, decide which had the *least* inviting opening. Draft an opening for that essay that would have appealed to you more.

C. WRITING: PARAGRAPH STRUCTURE

Paragraphing is an art, not a science. In academic papers, the best clue to paragraphing is usually contained in the game plan or outline. Look back at Susan Anderson's discussion of feeding a baby in Chapter 3. Her outline contains *eight* main "chunks," four on bottle-feeding and four on breast-feeding. Accordingly, the piece itself contains *eight* main paragraphs. A rough-and-ready definition of *paragraph* might therefore be: a self-contained "chunk" of a game plan turned into writing.

For most students, in fact, the problem is not *when* to paragraph, but *how* to structure paragraphs. There are no rules—but there are certain common sense guidelines. First, the reader should usually be told fairly early in the paragraph what it is about. (The sentence announcing the topic is traditionally called the *topic sentence*.) The paragraph usually contains information or argumentation that go well beyond this opening statement. Finally, on completing the paragraph, the reader should know how it fits the overall structure of the essay; clarifying the *point* of a paragraph is called *pointing*. These three "requirements" can be breached for many good reasons, but, taken as they stand, they offer a classic three-part paragraph:

INTRODUCTION

What the paragraph is about	Topic sentence
What the paragraph has to say about this subject	Information or argumentation
How the paragraph fits in	Pointing

In writing the assignments in Part 1 of this book, you learned how to state the subject of a paragraph and how to develop this subject with concrete information. In these short assignments, *pointing* was not a major concern. In an essay, however, many paragraphs must be crafted to fit a master plan. Without *pointing*, you may create a string of paragraphs, but it won't be an essay.

To understand *pointing*, it's necessary to delve once more into "reader psychology." To do this, let's begin with an anecdote clean out of context. All you need to know is that the writer is black and in jail:

> In the process of enduring my confinement, I decided to get myself a pin-up girl to paste on the wall of my cell. I would fall in love with her and lavish my affections upon her. She, a symbolic representative of the forbidden tribe of women, would sustain me until I was free. Out of the center of *Esquire*, I married a voluptuous bride. Our marriage went along swell for a time: no quarrels, no complaints. And then, one evening when I came in from school, I was shocked and enraged to find that the guard had entered my cell, ripped my sugar from the wall, torn her into little pieces, and left the pieces floating in the commode: it was like seeing a dead body floating in a lake. Giving her a proper burial, I flushed the commode. As the saying goes, I sent her to Long Beach. But I was genuinely beside myself with anger: almost every cell, excepting those of the homosexuals, had a pin-up girl on the wall and the guards didn't bother them. Why, I asked the guard the next day, had he singled me out for special treatment?
>
> "Don't you know we have a rule against pasting up pictures on the walls?" he asked me.
>
> "Later for the rules," I said. "You know as well as I do that that rule is not enforced."
>
> "Tell you what," he said, smiling at me (the smile put me on my guard), "I'll compromise with you: get yourself a colored girl for a pinup—no white women—and I'll let it stay up. Is that a deal?"

What is the *point* of this anecdote? At first reading, it seems to have many. Which of the following do you personally see as the *main* point?

a. A black prisoner is not allowed to have a white pinup.
b. Blacks are unfairly treated in jail.
c. Jails enforce the same prejudices as society in general.
d. Sexual deprivation torments prisoners.
e. Prisons break their own rules to help "morale."
f. Fear and suspicion are (were) dominant in relationships between races.

In fact, all six answers are legitimate: the anecdote makes *all* these points; however, the correct answer is actually "none of the above." In Eldridge Cleaver's own words: "The disturbing part about the whole incident was that a terrible feeling of guilt came over me as I realized I had chosen the picture of the white girl over the available pictures of black girls. I tried to rationalize it away, but I was fascinated by the truth involved. Why hadn't I thought about it in this light before?" Did you as reader spot Cleaver's key point? Probably not. Do you see the writing problem implied here? Imagine an "essay" consisting of just two illustrative anecdotes. It blocks out like this:

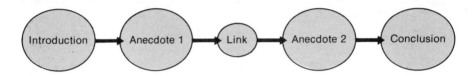

Let's take Cleaver's anecdote (exactly as it stands) as *Anecdote 1*. The *link* is simply the words, "A second incident confirmed what I had just learned." Now, we earlier listed six legitimate ways of understanding *Anecdote 1*, *none of which was Cleaver's actual point*. Let's say the reader "exits" from the anecdote with one of these wrong ideas in mind and then reads the link words "A second incident confirmed what I had just learned." Serious problems are at hand. The reader will obviously strain *Anecdote 2* so that it makes the same point as *Anecdote 1*. If this works, then the reader is on absolutely the wrong track. If, even under strain, *Anecdote 2* will not produce the same point as *Anecdote 1*, then the reader becomes confused: what *is* this writer trying to say? (Cleaver's string of anecdotes in *Soul on Ice* is, in fact, a model of clarity.)

The moral of the story is clear: never offer an anecdote—or any other kind of evidence—without clearly *pointing* it. Without pointing, the reader will lose track of the direction and structure of your piece. Good writing is rich in suggestion; it creates all sorts of ideas and lines of thought in a reader's mind. *You must ensure that the point the reader carries away from each paragraph is the one you want to make.*

Review Assignment

You are writing on the subject: "What makes a boss pleasant to work for?" Your thesis statement is: "A boss who is pleasant to work for usually has a well-motivated work force." You have listed eight defining characteristics of the *pleasant* boss.

1. A boss must give praise where it is due.

2. A boss must have a sense of humor.

3. A boss must listen to suggestions from below.

4. A boss must correct mistakes tactfully and gently.

5. A boss must show interest in what the staff does *outside* work time.

6. A boss must allow reasonable time off for personal problems.

7. A boss must help workers reach their full potential.

8. A boss must know when to relax the pressure on the workers.

Write a classic three-part paragraph on any one of these eight characteristics. The *topic sentence* should be close to the sentence given above. The *information* may well be an anecdote ("Let me tell you something that happened on one occasion . . .") If you use an anecdote, it might concern a boss who *had* a particular quality and was, therefore, pleasant, or a boss who *lacked* this quality and was, therefore, unpleasant. The *pointing* will be at least one sentence beginning, perhaps: "What this incident shows is that . . ." Remember, *pointing* shows how specific items of information relate to the overall "message" of the essay.

D. VARIETY

An essay is, inescapably, a chain of paragraphs. The danger is that you (and your reader) may fall into a repetitive rut. Let's say you're writing on "What makes the Ideal Husband?" For you, the ideal husband has seven main characteristics. If you develop all seven by referring to just one case, Simon Superhusband, the reader's interest will flag; a single case will not sustain the seven paragraphs of your essay. There's another problem too: a narrow range of reference suggests that your knowledge is limited, making your piece unconvincing. Ideally you should go for *variety*. If the Ideal Husband essay is based on case studies, then choose them from a *range* of marital situations: history (Dr. Crippen and the Brides in the Bath, Henry VIII with his six wives), fiction (the downtrodden Walter Mitty, James Bond and his bride of one day), the contemporary scene (President Carter and Rosalind, Humphrey Bogart and Lauren Bacall)—many sources beyond your direct experience can be tapped for cases.

The exclusive use of cases is not, of course, ideal: it is a source of predictability and, therefore, of potential boredom. You can vary your rhythm with findings from sociological studies, with professional opinions or relevant statistics. An interview with a "marriage guidance counselor" might produce quotable ideas. By coming at your reader from a variety of angles, you sustain interest and make your piece authoritative and convincing.

Concept Review

A Variety of Presidents

You are writing on the subject "What makes an effective president?" You decide that five qualities are necessary: charisma, the ability to make the right decisions, skill at working with Congress, skill at choosing a good team, and personal integrity. You decide to work with a contrast module in each case: one president who lacked the quality and lost effectiveness as a result; one president who gained effectiveness by having the quality. Staying close to home, you decide to use the postwar presidents: Truman, Eisenhower, Kennedy, Johnson, Nixon, Ford, Carter, Reagan. How would you couple the presidents to get the most variety into these five contrasts?

1. Charisma
   a. President_____lacked it.
   b. President_____had it.
2. Ability to make the right decisions
   a. President_____lacked it.
   b. President_____had it.
3. Skill at working with Congress
   a. President_____lacked it.
   b. President_____had it.
4. Skill at choosing a good team
   a. President_____lacked it.
   b. President_____had it.
5. Personal integrity
   a. President_____lacked it.
   b. President_____had it.

E. THE CLOSING

A clever lawyer does not sum up a case simply by repeating the established facts. Instead, the lawyer hammers home the conclusion to be drawn from the facts: the unquestionable guilt (or innocence) of the accused. Try to think of your closing in the same way. Look again at the Concept Review above. It would be inept to close an essay on this subject with:

> To be absolutely effective a president needs five qualities: charisma, the ability to make the right decisions, skill at working with Congress, skill at choosing a good team, and personal integrity.

The closing, especially in an inquiry essay, is the obvious place for the thesis statement, the point you've been shooting for all along:

> Each of these five qualities is essential if a president is to be absolutely effective; unfortunately, however, no president since the war has possessed all five in equal measure. Two conclusions are, therefore, possible: either the electoral system does not choose the right person for the job, or the demands of the job are too great for any one person to fulfill.

F. THE SENTENCE OUTLINE AS OVERVIEW

A lengthy essay is easier to follow if it includes some kind of "overview." This overview may be a summary or *abstract*. An *abstract* is a single paragraph of about 100 words, spelling out the line of argument taken by the essay. It precedes the essay itself. The most common kind of overview in traditional academic practice is the outline.

The difference between a game plan and a reader's outline has already been clarified. The essence of a good outline is its *transparency*: the qualities of clarity and accessibility that enable the reader to view the essay "at a glance." Compare these two outlines:

A Game Plan: Of Value Only to the Writer

SUBJECT: MOTORCYCLES	
Bike 1:	Different uses
	Power
	Overall cost
Bike 2:	Different uses
	Power
	Overall cost

A one-word subject is far too vague

"Bike 1" (and "Bike 2") convey nothing precise

Identical headings give no clue about the actual differences

A Reader's Outline: The Outline is Transparent to the Reader

SUBJECT: THE CONTRAST BETWEEN TWO MOTORCYCLES I HAVE OWNED
Bike 1:   Harley-Davidson 1000
The bike could be used only on roads.
It was powerful only when perfectly tuned-up.
The bike was expensive to buy, maintain and repair.
Bike 2:   Kawasaki 850
The bike was good on roads, tracks, or even dirt.
A very occasional tune-up kept it at peak power.
It was a good bargain in the showroom and later in the workshop.

The exact subject is specified

Bike 1 (and Bike 2) are named

Balanced information is spelled out in sentences

In practical terms, a Reader's Outline has a second use. Many instructors offer (or agree) to "look at an outline" if you submit one early enough. This is an enormous bonus. *If the outline is clear and easy to follow*, the instructor can tell you at once what is missing, what is in the wrong place, and what looks good. Feedback like that can turn a good paper into an excellent one. (It should also rule out unpleasant surprises.) But notice the *if*—it's a big *if.*

• Flowchart for Writing the Essay

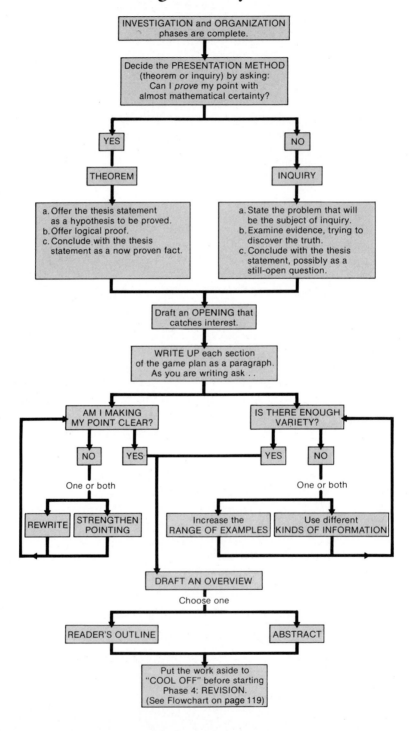

• Revision and the Final Draft

INVESTIGATION
ORGANIZATION
PRESENTATION
REVISION

Since the next five chapters refer you to this section, you may prefer to postpone reading it until you have a newly completed essay to revise.

Revising an essay falls into five steps.

REVISION STEP 1: ALLOW COOLING OFF

Set yourself *two* deadlines: (a) a deadline for your first draft and (b) a deadline for your clean, final copy. Leave as much as a week between the two deadlines if you can. To revise a piece, you must read it objectively. If you've just finished writing it, it's still a subjective part of you, and making changes can feel like self-mutilation.

REVISION STEP 2: CHECK COMMUNICATION—ARE YOU GETTING YOUR POINT ACROSS?

A first draft is often a long way from an end product. Why? Because an essay must convince the reader that the thesis statement makes sense in the light of the evidence. When you wrote the piece, it made sense to you—but will it make sense to your reader? You could run a test by letting a friend read your work *with the thesis statement omitted*. Ask your friend to explain in one sentence what the essay is saying. If you get the wrong answer, don't argue—just revise.

An academic essay is more than just a way of airing a personal opinion: it should *convince* the reader. If the assignment is to show that the tall-grass prairie needs protection, then the reader must be driven to this conclusion by strong, detailed evidence. That you happen to hold this opinion is of very little interest to the reader. After your first draft has cooled off, read it and see how it would strike a stranger. Rephrase your ideas, search for new material, and if necessary rethink your game plan, until no stranger could doubt that you have a strong case.

REVISION STEP 3: CHECK CONTINUITY—LABELS, TRANSITIONS AND POINTING

A. Labels.   The reader of an essay must cope with an elaborate chain of ideas. It helps if each new idea is labeled as soon as it is introduced and if its place in the overall plan is clear. For example, in defining the qualities that characterize an effective president, each of the five characteristics could probably be labeled right away:

Paragraph 1: To be elected in the first place, a president needs charisma.

Paragraph 5: The most important quality in a president is personal integrity.

Check the opening of each of your paragraphs and of each section to ensure that the reader will not become lost.

B. Transitions. Check the transitions next. These occur whenever there is an important change of approach in the essay. If, for example, you have discussed the ways in which reptiles and amphibians are similar and you want to shift to their differences, then a *transition* is necessary. You'll find key transitions noted in each chapter.

C. Pointing. With the labels and transitions in place, look next at the pointing. Pointing, as we saw in the previous section, ensures that the essay is firmly on track at the end of each paragraph. Accordingly, review each paragraph by asking: "Is it absolutely clear how the information in this paragraph fits into the essay as a whole?" If not, strengthen the pointing.

D. Section Headings. If you and your reader find section headings an aid to clarity, then use them—but not as a substitute for text. Headings are an extra, visual clue about the structure; the essay should remain perfectly intact if you delete them.

REVISION STEP 4: CHECK COST-EFFECTIVENESS

An essay contains more abstract material than a description. The pointing sections and the buildup to the thesis statement are often analytical and abstract. Check these parts for wordiness with especial care.

REVISION STEP 5: CHECK CORRECTNESS

In the next five chapters, as in Part 1 of the book, there are notes on the grammatical problems associated with each technique. Study these notes and the relevant entries in your handbook; then try to identify these problems in your essay.

Techniques of proofreading were discussed in Chapter 1. Nothing has changed.

STEP 6: COMPLETE THE FINAL DRAFT

Always make sure *before* you begin the final draft that you know exactly how it is supposed to look. The Checklist in Chapter 1 still applies.

Finally, don't forget to give the final draft a "hard read." Your goal is a final draft with no errors in it.

INTRODUCTION

• Flowchart for Revising and Completing An Essay

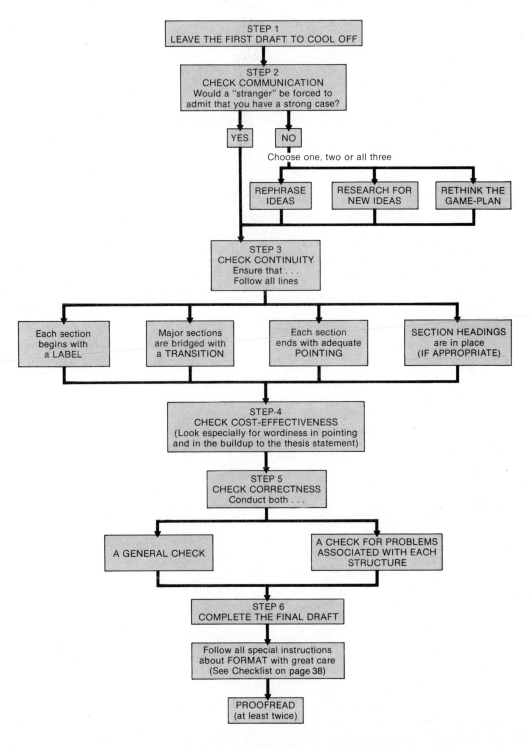

3 •
The Personal Voice:
The Art of Saying Nothing at All

Let's go back to Skyler, wrestling with his essay. If only he'd known it, he could have used *The Pinnells Patent Hot Air Program* to generate his paper for him.

THE PINNELLS PATENT HOT AIR PROGRAM

How to say "I don't know" in 300 words

Step 1—Create a simple subject-verb-object sentence that fulfills two requirements:

Requirement 1: The sentence must be completely abstract.

Requirement 2: The sentence must be positively worded.

Example: The Industrial Revolution changed many people's lives.

Step 2—Perform the following ten operations on the sentence:

Operation 1: Substitute synonyms for all key words.
Result: This great *technological upheaval altered* the way that much of *society* functioned.

Operation 2: Negate the subject and verb of the original sentence.
Result: *Without* the Industrial Revolution there would *not* have been change in people's lives.

Operation 3: Negate the verb and object of the original sentence.
Result: The Industrial Revolution left *un*touched the life of *no one*.

Operation 4: Powerfully emphasize subject, verb and object.
Result: This staggering volcanic eruption in technology, science, and manufacturing techniques of every kind (= The Industrial Revolution) caused the most far-reaching and astounding reversals (= changed) in the life, the existence, the day-to-day habits and the most profound beliefs (= the lives) of almost every soul on this planet (= of many people).

Operation 5: To create a new sentence to work on, simply reverse the subject and object of the original sentence. (Provide a new verb if necessary.)
Result: The lives of many people changed during the Industrial Revolution.

Operation 6: Repeat Operation 2 on the new sentence.
Result: *No* life was *un*changed during the Industrial Revolution.

Operation 7: Repeat Operation 3 on the new sentence.
Result: People's lives had *not* changed so much in the whole *pre*-industrial period.

Operation 8: Offer some pseudo-examples.
Result: Many cities and villages, countless families large and small saw the familiar old way of life that they loved and knew so well slipping away from them as the new ways took over.

Operation 9: Cite some pseudo-authorities.
Result: No subject has attracted more research or more detailed and scholarly

> comment; we know more about this period than perhaps about any period before or since.
>
> *Operation 10:* Summarize.
> Result: What all this evidence shows is that the Industrial Revolution did indeed affect the lives of many people.

Each operation generates the kind of sentence you might hear at the average political press conference or on the evening when the professor forgot to prepare any lecture notes. But all of them? With a little polishing, Skyler has his essay:

> This paper will attempt to document the way in which the Industrial Revolution changed the lives of so many people. The great technological upheaval known to us as the Industrial Revolution altered the way in which almost all levels of the society of the time functioned. Without this extraordinary Revolution, none of the changes that have made our lives what they are today would have occurred. Probably this period left untouched the life of no one who lived through it. What we are confronted with here is a staggering volcanic eruption in technology, science and manufacturing techniques of every kind that caused the most far-reaching reversals in the life, the existence, the day-to-day habits and the most profound beliefs of almost every soul on this planet. Yes, our society in all its ramifications was destined never to be the same again. No life, however high or however humble, passed through the Industrial Revolution unscathed. In the whole previous history of the world nothing had wrought such an unforeseen, such a revolutionary effect. Let's take some examples. How many cities and villages, how many families large and small saw the familiar old way of life that they loved and knew so well slipping away from them as the new ways took over? No subject has attracted more research or more detailed scholarly comment than this; we know more about this period than perhaps about any period before or since. In conclusion, what this mass of evidence points to is the extent to which the Industrial Revolution did indeed inexpressibly affect the hard but rewarding lives of so many of our American forebears.

There is a serious point to all this, although a negative one. This kind of hot air is disastrously common in student essays. Probably, it is mistaken for argumentation, but the fact that it is "programmable" shows that it is just mindless words. At all costs avoid this kind of mindlessness.

Review Assignment

If you enjoy playing with language, and if you'd like to hear what your voice sounds like when you have nothing to say, try running a sentence of your own through the program, or try one of these:

Americans admire courage.

This political party rejects all bribes.

Our department accepts your proposal.

Mutual affection makes a successful marriage.

Proven criminals have earned punishment.

Pollution threatens our way of life.

FOUR

The Two-Element Paper: Comparison and Contrast

1 •
The Problem:
Working to a Thesis

• Comparing and Contrasting: The Ground Rules

Study this row of shapes for at least sixty seconds.

Although you were given no specific instructions about *how* to study the shapes, you probably checked to see if any of the shapes were identical; you realized at some stage that the solid black shape fits one of the cutouts exactly. The urge to match things in this way is almost irresistible. If you did match the shapes, how did you do it? Probably you scrutinized the black shape in conjunction with each of the cutouts in turn, looking for significant differences (round lobes as against square ones, for example); when you'd found the most likely match, you probably compared the two shapes to ensure that they were in all respects similar.

This simple experiment highlights two general principles: (a) our minds have a built-in tendency to work with *pairs* (you paired the black shape against each cutout in turn), and (b) in pairing two elements, we search for both differences and similarities. These two principles govern one of the most common of all writing structures, comparison and contrast.

Pairing things, comparing and contrasting them, comes naturally to the skillful writer. For example, a journalist might make the rapid growth of Newtown, Alaska, vivid to the reader in this way:

Five years ago the site of Newtown was an icy desert in winter and a mosquito-infested swamp in summer. Today it is a bustling, noisy city, with the fastest growth rate in the United States.

Or, to create a sense of third-world poverty:

Before I left New York, I fed my dog half a can of dog food, fortified, of course, with minerals and vitamins. There are children in the slums of South America who do not eat that much meat in a month.

The writer's instinct to heighten ideas by comparing and contrasting creates powerful images; the same device can be used to structure a whole essay. How might such an essay structure work?

Whenever two things are discussed side by side, inevitably they will be *similar* in certain ways, and inevitably they will be *different*. (In fact, without similarities and differences, no discussion is possible. How, for example, would you tackle the subject "Compare Mice and Honesty"? There is no underlying similarity. How would you handle the subject "Compare two atoms of oxygen"? There are no differences.) An essay that discussed two elements in terms of their *links* (similarities) and *differences* would fall naturally into two parts: a links section and a differences section. In essence, a comparison-contrast essay is no more than that.

One major question faces the essay-writer, however: which goes first, links or differences? There are only two choices:

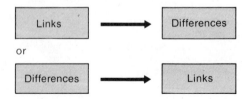

How do you decide? The principle of order places the more important idea last, but which is the more important? To answer that question, we must look at an example.

Jack Cooper was taking a class on The History of Civilization. He was struck by the role played by women in ancient Roman society, and he decided to write on the question of whether women today are better off than they were two thousand years ago. Women then: women now. After investigation, Jack concluded that the differences were mostly superficial—at a deeper level, he found surprisingly little change in the role of women. The principle of order was now easy to invoke: the differences could be dismissed as superficial, so they went first; the links were at a deeper level and were more important, so they went last. Accordingly Jack's game plan looked like this:

Differences:			Superficial level
Arranged marriages	versus	"Free" choice of husband	
Women had no vote	versus	Women can vote	
Women could not hold office	versus	Women can stand for office	
Links:			Deep level
Very few women actually held/hold important positions.			
Women's most accepted role was/is as wives and mothers.			
Women had/have no financial power.			
Thesis Statement:			The thesis comes from the deep level.
Despite some changes, women today are still assigned much the same role as their Roman counterparts 2,000 years ago.			

To confirm the validity of this SUPERFICIAL → DEEP structure, let's take an upside-down piece and see how it reads:

As a lover of sports cars, I've owned both a Porsche and a Corvette. Two different design philosophies created these two cars. The Porsche goes all out for efficiency, while the Corvette goes all out for looks. The Porsche may not look like much but it rides like a dream. The Corvette, on the other hand, takes a lot of handling: it's not a car for the novice. But, let's face it, there's tremendous pleasure in handling both cars. There's the feeling of power as the acceleration forces you back into your seat. There's the superb instrumentation, which every engineer will love. The finish on both cars is elegant and luxurious. But above all, there's the thrill of driving a car that seems to know what you're thinking before you do. Thesis statement: Overall, as you can see, I much prefer the Porsche.

"No," you reply. "I *don't* see. I'd formed the idea that the two cars were fun to drive despite their different design philosophies." The piece is upside down: the structure generates one idea (the *reader's theory*), but the explicit statement at the end (the *writer's thesis*) contains another. To make it look good, the structure must be turned the right way up.

PART TWO
The Essay

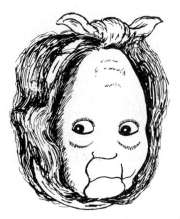

In this case, the appropriate structure would be:

What the cars had in common	Dismissed as superficial
What made the cars so different	Taken at the deeper level
Thesis: I prefer the Porsche	

Concept Review 1

Identifying Upside-Down Structures

Using the principle of order, decide which of the following mini-game plans are the right way up and which are upside down.

1. Link: Both Stevie and Al started life in the ghetto.
2. Difference: Stevie lost hope and finished up in jail; Al struggled hard and made it as a businessman.
3. Thesis: The ghetto is not sealed; there are ways to escape.

1. Difference: The piano and the guitar require very different techniques.
2. Link: Both techniques demand years of study and practice.
3. Thesis: No matter what the instrument, mastery comes from hard work.

1. Link: These two schools both produced outstanding scholars.
2. Difference: One was a school for the rich, the other for the poor.
3. Thesis: Social background is unimportant; a good school produces good students.

1. Difference: Larksville had full employment and was a happy, bustling place; unemployment in Graytown had soared to 45 percent, and it was a town close to despair.
2. Link: Larksville and Graytown were both attractive factory towns of about 250,000 inhabitants.
3. Thesis: Unemployment changes the atmosphere of a city.

Concept Review 2

Deciding on the Structure

Look at the following thesis statements. Which structure does each of them most obviously imply? (Note: In practice it might be possible to choose two elements that would reverse the obvious order.)

a. Whether amateur or professional, the athlete must strive for perfection.

b. Atomic power can be harnessed for peace or war; in both cases it is extremely dangerous.

c. Do not confuse patriotism and nationalism. One is a source of much that is good in our society; the other is a source of evil.

d. While politicians try to draw a fine line between totalitarian and authoritarian regimes, for most people this is a distinction without a difference.

e. In the end, we felt as much love in our hearts for our adopted child, Nguyen, as we did for our natural daughter, Mary.

f. The external differences in the rites of Catholics and Protestants do not matter as much as the inner reality of faith.

• Thesis-Oriented Thinking

Once you've thoroughly investigated a two-element subject, it's easy enough to develop lists of the links and the differences between the two elements—the major components of a game plan. If a thesis statement comes readily to mind, then structure is no problem, either. Unfortunately formulating a thesis statement is sometimes easier said than done. Occasionally, in fact, it is tempting to write the paper first and to discover afterwards what it chanced to say, grafting a thesis onto an already existing paper. That can't be right. The thesis statement works as a *filter*; without this filter, the paper will be infested with foreign bodies in the form of meaningless facts, stray ideas and directionless explanations. The thesis, at least in a provisional form, comes early in the writing process. (Naturally you should be ready to change your thesis as your ideas develop, but, if the thesis changes, be ready for heavy rewriting.) To study thesis-oriented thinking, let's use pictures to provide the cues.

Look at the pictures labeled *A* and *B*. There is a single, strong link between these pictures: they both show people with dogs of some sort. What are the

PART TWO
The Essay

differences? A man on holiday versus men at work; a relationship between friends versus a relationship between enemies; a tame dog versus a wild wolf; a pampered life versus a cruel death. Does some thesis statement come to mind when you look at the two pictures? Command? Statement? Choice? Question? Perhaps the statement: "The traditional policy of pampering pets while exterminating wild life is a terrible mistake; *all* animals have rights." If you accept this thesis statement, then the Principle of Order pins down the structure for you: first you'd present the superficial view that a cuddly pet and a wild wolf are plainly different. Then you'd move to the deeper, more ecology-minded view, that humanity has an equal duty to all the forms of life that share "spaceship Earth"—wolf and dachshund alike. In general terms, since the thesis statement comes from the links, the *links go last*. (On the other hand, a thesis statement such as "We love those that love us" would place the *differences last*.) After this planning phase, you could begin a coherent discussion of these two pictures. If you follow the same steps in thinking through essay materials, you'll be ready to *write*.

A

Courtesy of Deutsche Presse-Agentur GmbH

B

Courtesy of Deutsche Presse-Agentur GmbH

CHAPTER FOUR
The Two-Element Paper: Comparison and Contrast

Concept Review

Formulating and Using a Thesis Statement

Study these pairs of pictures. Then (a) list the links between them; (b) list the differences; (c) formulate a thesis statement; (d) on the basis of this thesis statement, decide the structure of a possible essay.

Links _____
_____
_____

Differences _____
_____
_____

Thesis _____

Structure: | Links | → | Differences |

or | Differences | → | Links |

Courtesy of Deutsche
Presse-Agentur GmbH

Courtesy of
Deutsche Presse-
Agentur GmbH

PART TWO
The Essay

Courtesy of Deutsche Presse-
Agentur GmbH

Courtesy of Deutsche Presse-
Agentur GmbH

Links _____

_____

_____

Differences _____

_____

_____

Thesis _____

Structure: | Links | → | Differences | or | Differences | → | Links |

2 •

The Personal Voice

In Laurie Lee's autobiography, *Cider with Rosie*, he describes the villagers he knew in his childhood. In the extracts below he's describing two old countrywomen who share a cottage, one living upstairs and one downstairs. At first the reader has the impression that the women are in perfect contrast. Then, in the final paragraphs, we see that they actually lived for each other. This is the classic comparison-contrast "formula," but in Lee's hands the structure takes on a vivid life. What is Lee's secret? In part it lies in an extreme concern for concrete detail; he also uses many comparisons, all of them earthy, country-style comparisons, appropriate to his subject. Finally, he uses the dialect of his characters to let us hear them in action.

> Granny Trill and Granny Wallon were rival ancients and lived on each other's nerves, and their perpetual enmity was like mice in the walls and absorbed much of my early days. . . . In all their time as such close neighbors they never exchanged a word. They communicated instead by means of boots and brooms—jumping on floors and knocking on ceilings. They referred to each other as "'Er-Down-Under" and "'Er-Up-Atop, the Varmint"; for each to the other was an airy nothing, a local habitation not fit to be named.
>
> 'Er-Down-Under, who lived on our level, was perhaps the smaller of the two, a tiny white shrew who came nibbling through her garden, who clawed squeaking with gossip at our kitchen window, or sat sucking bread in the sun; always mysterious and self-contained and feather-soft in her movements. She had two names, which she changed at will according to the mood of her day. Granny Wallon was her best, and stemmed, we were told, from some distinguished alliance of the past. Behind this crisp and trotting body were certainly rumors of noble blood. But she never spoke of them herself. She was known to have raised a score of children. And she was known to be very poor. She lived on cabbage, bread, and potatoes—but she also made excellent wines. . . .
>
> Whatever the small indulgences with which Granny Wallon warmed up her old life, her neighbor, Granny Trill, had none of them. For 'Er-Up-

PART TWO
The Essay

Atop was as frugal as a sparrow and as simple in her ways as a grub. She could sit in her chair for hours without moving, a veil of blackness over her eyes, a suspension like frost on her brittle limbs, with little to show that she lived at all save the gentle motion of her jaws. One of the first things I noticed about old Granny Trill was that she always seemed to be chewing, sliding her folded gums together in a daylong ruminative cud. I took this to be one of the tricks of age, a kind of slowed-up but protracted feasting. . . . The old lady sat and watched us mildly, taking very little notice, while her dry yellow arm swept up and down, and the black-toothed comb, as it slid through her hair, seemed to be raking the last ash of a fire.

"You going bald, Gran?"

"I still got me bits."

"It's coming out."

"No, it ain't."

"Look at that dead stuff dropping out of yer comb."

"That's healthy. It makes room for more."

We didn't think it mattered; it was merely conversation, any subject at all would do. But suddenly the old lady skipped out of her seat and began to leap up and down on the floor.

"'Er down there! I got more than 'er! Er's bald as a tater root! Wicked old lump, I'll see 'er gone. 'Er's failing, you mark my words". . . .

They arranged things therefore so that they never met. They used separate paths when they climbed the bank, they shopped on different days, they relieved themselves in different areas, and staggered their church-going hours. But each one knew always what the other was up to, and passionately disapproved. . . .

Then one day, as Granny Trill was clambering out of her wood, she stumbled and broke her hip. She went to bed then for ever. She lay patient and yellow in a calico coat, her combed hair fine as a girl's.

The little church was packed for her funeral, for the old lady had been a landmark. They carried her coffin along the edge of the wood and then drew it on a cart through the village. Granny Wallon, dressed in a shower of jets, followed some distance behind; and during the service she kept to the back of the church and everybody admired her.

All went well till the lowering of the coffin, when there was a sudden and distressing commotion. Granny Wallon, ribbons flying, her bonnet awry, fought her way to the side of the grave.

"It's a lie!" she screeched, pointing down at the coffin. "That baggage were younger'n me! Ninety-five she says!—ain't more'n ninety, an' I gone on ninety-two! It's a crime you letting 'er go to 'er Maker got up in such brazen lies! Dig up the old devil! Get 'er brass plate off! It's insulting the living church! . . ."

Granny Wallon had triumphed, she had buried her rival; and now there was no more to do. From then on she faded and diminished daily, kept to her house and would not be seen. Sometimes we heard mysterious knocks in the night, rousing and summoning sounds. But the days were silent, no one walked in the garden, or came skipping to claw at our window. The wine fires sank and died in the kitchen, as did the sweet fires of obsession.

About two weeks later, of no special disease, Granny Wallon gave up in her sleep. She was found on her bed, dressed in bonnet and shawl, with her signalling broom in her hand. Her open eyes were fixed on the ceiling in a listening stare of death. There was nothing in fact to keep her alive; no cause, no bite, no fury. 'Er-Down-Under had joined 'Er-Up-Atop, having lived closer than anyone knew.

Laurie Lee
From *Cider With Rosie*

Review Assignment 1

Dialect as Voice

America is rich in local dialects. It's a useful experiment to take a dialect you know well and to try to reproduce it on paper. For example, turn back to a paragraph you wrote earlier in this course, and reword it in dialect. When the piece is complete, read it aloud to an audience and ask the audience what kind of writer they perceive behind the words: not only the writer's region, but also age, sex, educational level, income, attitude to life, and general character. The answers should show you how strong an image the voice of a writer creates.

Review Assignment 2

Voice and Comparisons

Read Laurie Lee's passage again and underline all the *comparisons* Lee makes. You'll find that they all refer to the sights and sounds of the countryside. You could experiment with the same technique. For example, you could write a physical description of a car fanatic using comparisons from the automotive world. ("She had a chromium-plated smile and hair the color of 10-40 oil. . . .") Or you could describe a computer buff using comparisons from the world of computers. ("When Mac woke up each morning, he cold-booted himself and prepared to interface with the day. . . .") The same would go for a bookworm, an experimental scientist, a sailing enthusiast, a history buff, or a video fanatic. Your imagination will suggest other possibilities. When the piece is finished, study the effect of the accumulated comparisons; they will give the piece a strongly characteristic voice.

3 •
Writing Workshop—
The Process of Comparing and Contrasting

• Choosing a Subject

Any subject that brings two elements into play against each other automatically implies comparing and contrasting. In choosing a subject, it helps to think ahead a little: is there something you want to *say* about the subject? If there is, then thesis-oriented writing becomes much easier.

Subjects based on the behavior of two individuals

1. Think of two superiors under whom you have worked. Compare and contrast their powers of leadership.
2. Compare and contrast the attitudes of a mother and of a father toward a family crisis. (Some suggestions: an unwanted pregnancy, a drug charge, a car smash, a runaway marriage, a serious financial loss.)
3. Looking back on your training or schooling, compare and contrast two of your teachers.
4. Compare and contrast two women in the light of their attitudes toward the women's rights movement.
5. Dating is a learning experience. Explain some of the things *you* learned by comparing and contrasting two people you have dated.
6. Compare and contrast two ways of training a particular kind of animal (horse, dog, and so on).
7. How important are one's high school years? Compare and contrast the attitudes of two high-school students in the light of what happened to them later in life.
8. Compare and contrast the driving styles of two people you know.
9. Compare and contrast the way two people play a particular musical instrument (piano, guitar, and so on).

Subjects based on the behavior of two groups

10. Compare and contrast the attitudes and approaches of two civil rights groups in America.
11. If you have played on the same team in two consecutive seasons, you may have found the team spirit very different. Compare and contrast the two seasons.
12. Have you ever been given medical treatment for the same complaint in two different wards or hospitals? If so, compare and contrast them.
13. If you attended two schools, you may have thought a lot about the attitudes of the teachers and students. Compare and contrast the two schools.
14. The transition from a high school to a university or college can be interesting. Compare and contrast your experience of these two institutions.

Subjects involving broad social issues

15. Compare and contrast a family living on welfare with a family (of about the same size and income) in which at least one parent has a job. (Discuss two specific families.)

16. Compare and contrast a child from a disciplined home with a child from an undisciplined home. (Discuss two specific children.)

17. Compare and contrast the life of a family with a working mother with the life of a family whose mother does not work outside the home. (Discuss two specific families.)

18. Compare and contrast the life of a one-parent family with the life of a two-parent family. (Discuss two specific families.)

Subjects based on situations

19. If you have attended a college or university as a full-time day student and as a part-time evening student, compare and contrast the two experiences.

20. Compare and contrast the conditions in two roughly equivalent military and civilian jobs.

21. Have you ever had a job in which you spent part of your time in an office and part on the road or in the field? If so, compare and contrast these two aspects of your work.

22. Take two roughly comparable sports in which you have participated. Compare and contrast them.

23. Amateur versus professional—compare and contrast these two versions of a single sport.

24. Compare and contrast life in a highrise building (or other high-density housing) with life in "your own four walls."

25. If you have both worked for someone else and been your own boss, compare and contrast the two experiences.

Subjects based on events

26. Think of two women who reacted differently to having an abortion. Compare and contrast them.

27. Select two people who have escaped from the ghetto. Compare and contrast their methods of escape and their later success in life.

28. Choose two people discharged from their jobs. Compare and contrast the circumstances.

29. Pick two people who have made it (or are making it) to the top. Compare and contrast their methods of achieving their goals.

30. If you know someone who has been married twice, compare and contrast the two marriages.

Subjects based on the before-and-after syndrome

31. Sometimes you have to make an important decision that cuts you off from a familiar, known world: to move to another city, to join the military, to leave the country for the town. Compare and contrast yourself as you are today with someone who "stayed behind."

32. If you have changed fields, you may have found that the new job had more similarities with the old job than you expected. Compare and contrast the two jobs.

33. After a divorce, people expect radical change in their lives. Compare and contrast the life of a divorcee known to you before and after.

Subjects based on systems, mechanisms or institutions

34. Compare and contrast two personal computers.

35. Compare and contrast two magazines aimed at much the same readership.

36. Compare and contrast two farming techniques—for example, raising chickens in a battery or in a free-ranging environment.

37. If you have lived in a country that has experienced a change in its system of government, compare and contrast the two systems as they affected your life.

38. Welfare and workfare: compare and contrast the two systems.

39. Compare and contrast two pieces of equipment designed to do a comparable job, for example a reel-to-reel and a cassette recorder, a phonograph and a laser disc player.

40. Compare and contrast two ways of treating a particular illness.

• Developing a Game Plan

A. GATHERING LINKS AND DIFFERENCES

At an early stage, you'll have to brainstorm to create two lists: a list of links and a list of differences. The list of differences is, of course, the contrast module we studied in Chapter 3. For a specimen list of links, you can look at Jack Cooper's game plan at the start of this chapter or at Jeanne Stepanova's list on page 139.

One problem commonly arises at this stage: the list of links may seem inadequate. In writing on the NAACP and the Black Panthers, for example, you might find only one link: that both are dedicated to the cause of the black American. Can that one link balance a list of twenty differences in tradition, methods, success and so on? The answer is—yes it can; this single link might easily outweigh the manifold differences. There are no rules of thumb about the number of points you should make; everything depends on the subject and on what you are doing with it.

B. FORMULATING THE THESIS STATEMENT

Once you have thought about your subject, you'll need to formulate a thesis statement: command, statement, choice or question. As we saw earlier in the chapter, the thesis statement decides the structure of the essay. Another way of putting this is to say that the essay can be reduced to one of two formulas:

a. Although these two elements appear *similar* on the surface, in reality, and at a deeper level, they are really very *different*—which leads to the conclusion that ⟨thesis statement⟩.

or

b. Although these two elements appear *different* on the surface, in reality and at a deeper level they are really very *similar*—which leads to the conclusion that ⟨thesis statement⟩.

The thesis statement has a second vital function: it acts as a *filter*. We saw in Chapter 1 how the controlling filter works in a description. The thesis statement has exactly the same function in the essay: if an idea strengthens the thesis statement, then it goes *in*; if it does not, then it stays *out*. At this stage it helps if you filter your two lists in this way. You may find you have a number of interesting but irrelevant points on your lists. Delete them.

C. QUESTIONS OF ORDER

With the two lists and a thesis statement in hand, you must take three decisions about *order*:

a. The overall structure: do the differences or the similarities go last?

b. The order within each main section: which item on each list goes last?

c. The order of presentation: will you use block or switch presentation?

a. The Overall Structure.   The two available structures have already been discussed:

Differences (Superficial) → Similarities (Deep) → Thesis Statement

Similarities (Superficial) → Differences (Deep) → Thesis Statement

b. The Order Within Each Main Section.   In general, the most important link goes at the end of the links section; the most important difference goes at the end of the differences section. But remember, this is a principle, not a regulation. The *correct* order is the one that best suits your current purposes.

c. Order of Presentation.   As you remember from Chapter 3, you can present parallel material either in two big blocks (block presentation) or by switching from side to side at each main heading (switch presentation). The same choice confronts you here, especially in discussing differences. (If this principle is rusty, you should review Chapter 3 right away.)

D. THE BIG TRANSITION

As we have seen, a comparison-contrast essay necessarily falls into two main segments: links and differences. Such an important division requires a strong transition: if the reader misses the changeover, confusion will result. To avoid this danger, some writers set off the transition as a separate paragraph. (Jeanne Stepanova's essay on ballet teachers at the end of this chapter does this.) If you think of the big transition as the waist of an hour glass, it may help you keep the overall structure clear in your mind.

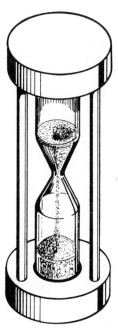

The "formula" for the big transition:

> Now that I've finished with differences, which are superficial, I'd like to look at the similarities, which are in fact more important.

or

> Now that I've finished with similarities, which are superficial, I'd like to look at the differences, which are in fact more important.

E. A CASE STUDY

Let's see then how one student, Jeanne Stepanova, developed a usable game plan. Jeanne trained as a ballerina. Later, to work her way through college, she took a job teaching beginners to dance. Like any new teacher, Jeanne tried to remember her own teachers and what she'd learned from them. Two great influences on her dancing career had been Felicia Ramirez and Jaime Santos. They had both taught her a great deal about dancing, but even so they had startlingly different *attitudes* to their dancers; Jeanne remembered one with cold admiration and the other with warm affection. How important was attitude? Jeanne wondered. And what attitude is most helpful to beginning dancers? During her first weeks as a dancing teacher, Jeanne was also a student—of writing. When the comparison-contrast assignment came up, her subject was ready at hand: "Compare and contrast two dance instructors." Jeanne's first notes were two simple lists:

<u>Links: Jaime and Felicia</u>

Both: in their 40's
 of Cuban descent
 trained in Cuba under the same teachers
 arrived in the United States in the early 1950's with their parents
 had successful careers in dancing before they became teachers
 kept up contact with dance experts in Cuba
 dedicated their lives to dancing
 gave technically difficult but dancy and enjoyable classes
 were respected by their dancers
 could instill dedication and enthusiasm
 produced outstanding career dancers

Differences:

 Felicia chose favorites and spent the class and rehearsal time on them. Jaime paid attention to anyone who worked hard.

 Felicia forbade us to have interests outside the studio. Jaime was tolerant, as long as outside activities didn't interfere with our performance.

 Felicia never allowed a dancer to miss a class, regardless of injuries or illness. Many became anorexic or broke down physically or mentally. Jaime put health above everything.

Jeanne came to me with this material a little perplexed: what next? Talking her ideas through, we found that she had two options. She could say:

Although on the surface one instructor was a strict authoritarian and the other was more relaxed, at a deeper level they both produced excellent results. Teaching style is superficial: results are what count, and "casualties" don't matter.

or:

Both methods produced good dancers; that was what the public saw on the surface. Behind the scenes, however, Felicia's dancers paid too high a price. The harassment, the hysteria, and the breakdowns were unnecessary. Jaime's attitude was preferable.

This is the familiar problem: do the similarities or the differences go last? While Jeanne was trying to decide, something happened during one of her dancing classes—nothing serious, but it was the first emotional casualty among her own students. That decided her: Jaime was right.

In drawing up her game plan, Jeanne filtered out a number of items from the list of links—they had nothing to do with the thesis statement. The game plan then:

Similarities

> Background:
>> Mid-forties/Cuban/successful dancers
>
> Teaching Styles:
>> Russian technique/rewarding classes/produced many career dancers/put on successful shows

Differences

> Favorites versus no favorites
>
> Forbade outside interests versus encouraged outside interests
>
> Drove dancers until many cracked versus helped and sympathized

Thesis:

Dancers are people not machines—Jaime was right.

• Writing the First Draft

With a strong game plan, turning your ideas into words is often surprisingly easy. To review the various steps, reread the section on *presentation*. (Pages 106–116.)

• Revising

A general scheme for revising your first draft has already been presented. (Pages 117–119.) Reread this material carefully. To revise a comparison-contrast essay, you'll need two additional items: a checklist for continuity and a hint about special grammar problems.

A. A SPECIAL CHECK FOR CONTINUITY

To ensure continuity in a comparison-contrast essay:

a. Check that the links and differences sections are introduced as such. The formula:

> At the superficial level there are a number of links (differences) between (A) and (B).
> At the deeper level there are a number of differences (links) between (A) and (B).

b. Check that each section is introduced by a short label or "flagword." The formula:

> The first (second, and so on) difference/link between (A) and (B) is their. . . .

c. Check that the big transition, the waist of the hourglass, is in place. (The formula was given earlier.)

d. Check that there is a transition each time you switch from (*A*) to (*B*). The formula:

Turning from (A) to (B), . . .

e. Check that each section ends with an appropriate *pointing statement*.

B. A SPECIAL CHECK FOR CORRECTNESS

a. Agreement of Double Subjects. In a comparison, you'll often use a double subject. Are you certain of the correct verb form in each of the following cases?

  i. Dickens and Thackeray was/were both married to unbalanced women.

 ii. Dickens as well as Thackeray was/were married to an unbalanced woman.

iii. Either Dad or Uncle Marvin was/were always there to help.

 iv. Neither President Reagan nor his men is/are taking responsibility.

  v. Neither the president's men nor the president himself is/are taking responsibility.

If you have any doubts, review what your handbook says about *Subject-Verb Agreement*.

b. Comparison of Adjectives. Comparisons invite the use of the *-er* and *-est* forms of adjectives (fat, fatter, fattest). Can you identify *and explain* the errors in these sentences?

  i. It's the beautifullest mountain in Oregon.

 ii. In a football game, one team is usually quickest on its feet.

iii. What could be delightfuller than a day by the sea?

 iv. Dogs are more greedier than cats.

If you don't know what's wrong, review your handbook under *Comparison of Adjectives*, *Comparative forms of Adjectives*, or *Superlative Forms of Adjectives*.

· The Final Draft

As an example of a "finished product," study Jeanne Stepanova's essay on two ballet instructors. Notice how the outline (prepared for the reader) differs from the game plan (used by the writer) we saw earlier in the chapter. In particular, notice how the thesis statement has "firmed up."

SUBJECT: TWO BALLET INSTRUCTORS, FELICIA RAMIREZ AND JAIME SANTOS

Similarities

    Background:
        Both were Cubans in their forties who had trained in Cuba and been successful dancers.
    Teaching Styles:
        Both were dedicated.
        Both taught the Russian technique.
        Both trained successful performers and produced excellent shows.

Transition

Despite their similarities, Felicia and Jaime were radically different people.

Differences

    Attitudes to Their Dancers:
        Felicia played favorites; Jaime encouraged anyone who worked hard.
    Attitudes to Outside Interests:
        Felicia forbade interests outside the studio; Jaime encouraged them.
    Attitudes to Mental and Physical Health:
        Felicia drove many of her dancers into anorexia, and into physical and mental collapse; Jaime stressed health above everything else.

Thesis Statement

If an art form is to mean anything in the modern world, it must be based on cooperation and respect for the individual, not on authoritarianism and the exercise of personal power.

Who, What, and When Lead-in to problem	My training as a dancer goes back over fifteen years. The two instructors who influenced my career the most were Felicia Ramirez and Jaime Santos. Which was the better teacher? I often wonder.
Main heading	## Similarities
Subheading	### Background
List of similarities of background	In many ways, Felicia and Jaime were strikingly similar. They were both in their early forties and of Cuban descent. They had trained in Cuba under the same teachers and had enjoyed successful dancing careers before they took up teaching.
Subheading	### Teaching Styles
List of similarities in teaching style Superficial similarity stressed	Both Felicia and Jaime were dedicated teachers. Their classes taught the Russian technique and were, therefore, difficult, but at the same time they were dancy and rewarding. Both teachers had lists of outstanding dancers to their credit, and their shows were well received by the public and the critics. To the outsider, they must have looked very similar.
Main heading	## Transition
Formal transition paragraph	Yet, despite their similarities, Felicia and Jaime were radically different people.

Differences

Attitudes to their Dancers

The first difference between Felicia and Jaime was their attitudes to their dancers. Felicia made favorites of the most talented and spent much of the class and rehearsal time on the chosen few. They occupied the best places at the barre and the front line during practices. She showered her "little ones," as she called them, with corrections and compliments. Those who were excluded from this little aristocracy led a miserable, belittling existence.

It was a different story with Jaime. He snubbed no one. Of course he gave the talented the most attention, but he helped and encouraged anyone who worked hard. Most of us had a place in the front line at different times. Jaime also had a sense of humor, and he set us all laughing, even when things went wrong.

Looking back, I can see that Jaime taught me more than just dancing. From him I learned how to work with other dancers rather than against them, and I learned how to laugh about the inevitable setbacks a dancer suffers.

Attitudes to Outside Interests

Felicia and Jaime thought differently about interests outside the studio. Felicia was ruthless: no friends, no romantic relationships, no vacations, and in some cases no school. Sometimes we were expected to skip high school in order to come to extra classes or rehearsals. Many of the dancers finished high school by correspondence.

Jaime, on the other hand, felt that without outside interests, a dancer would have difficulty coping with the tensions of a dancing career. Jaime never encouraged us to skimp on our studies.

Jaime understood something that Felicia ought to have known: an artist is more than a machine. A well-rounded human being will ultimately dance better than a well-drilled robot. Technically Felicia's dancers were phenomenal; they could perform four pirouettes and 128 fouettés on pointe, but few of them could touch the emotions of an audience. How could they when all they knew was the closed world of the dance studio? Musicality and artistic sense—those qualities I learned only from Jaime.

Attitudes to Mental and Physical Health

And finally, health. Felicia expected us to dance regardless of injury or illness. She kept us skinny—below the healthy level for young adults. The punishment for gaining weight was demotion away from the front line and ever further towards the back. Some of the dancers cracked. They became anorexic; some became physically and mentally ill. It was the survival of the fittest.

Jaime was different. If a dancer was sick or injured, she was encouraged to observe class but not to perform. Although he wanted his dancers thin, Jaime stressed a healthy diet. Dangerously thin dancers were told to gain weight or quit the class. For him, health was all-important.

In this respect, Felicia's methods were not merely strict but actually harmful. In her studio I saw talented people go to pieces—and it hurt. Jaime shamed and degraded no one, not even his failures. That's how it should be.

Conclusion

What made Felicia and Jaime the way they were? Felicia was one of the Old School. She grew up in a world where dancers were underpaid and treated like dancing machines. She saw no reason to change. Jaime also knew this world, but he wanted to change it. He believed that dancers, like other workers, should form labor unions and defend their rights. A few years ago he supported the strike by the American Ballet Theater that began to change conditions for dancers all round the world. If an art form is to mean anything in the modern world, it must be based on cooperation and respect for the individual, not on authoritarianism and the exercise of personal power.

Main heading

Subheading

First difference stated

Facts on Felicia presented

Short transition

Balancing facts on Jaime

Pointing: what the contrast shows

Subheading

Second difference stated

Facts on Felicia presented

Short transition

Balancing facts on Jaime

Pointing: what the second contrast shows

Subheading

Third difference stated

Facts on Felicia presented

Short transition

Balancing facts on Jaime

Pointing: what the final, key contrast shows

Main heading

Paragraph of overall pointing leading up to . . .

. . . the thesis statement

• Summary: The Flowchart

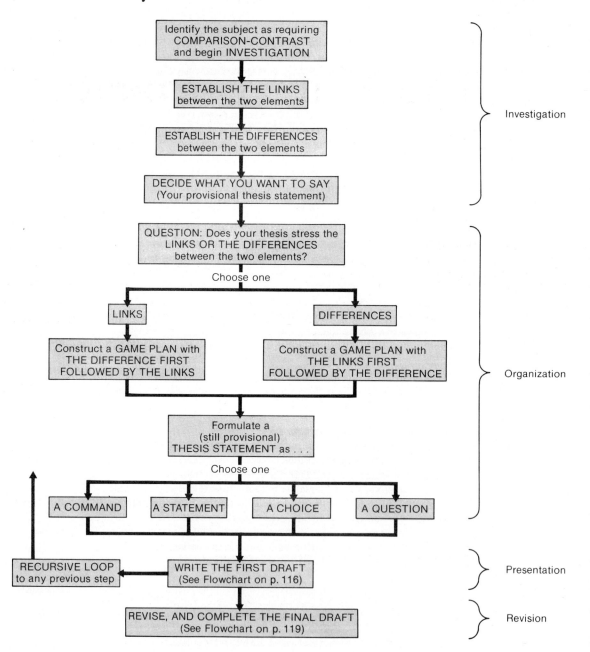

The Multi-Element Paper—Definition

1 •
The Problem:
Pinning Down the Keywords

• Two Kinds of Definition

A scenario: The professor in *Psychology 100* writes on the chalkboard several definitions during each session. Naturally, the students copy them down, certain that these definitions will reappear at examination time. Two students in particular concern us here: Randy and Josephine. This is one definition they both copy with particular care:

> Schizophrenia: Psychosis characterized by the breakdown of integrated personality functioning, withdrawal from reality, emotional blunting and distortion, and disturbed thought processes. (Zimbardo, 1975)

Hearing the word *schizophrenia* rather often during the next few weeks, Randy is smart enough to learn the definition by heart. In the midterm, Question 1 is an essay question. Time allotted: 1 hour. Topic: "Define schizophrenia." Elated, Randy writes:

Schizophrenia is a psychosis characterized by the breakdown of integrated personality functioning, withdrawal from reality, emotional blunting, and disturbed thought processes

When Randy scores only one point of the twenty available for the question, he's annoyed: he was asked for a definition and he's given one, word for word, from the horse's mouth. Where has he gone wrong? To answer that question, we must look at two common uses of the word *definition*.

A dictionary offers explanations of words. Some explanations clarify the function of *function words* such as: *the, to, he, once, which, there, not,* and so on, words that obviously have no definition as such. Other explanations offer the definitions of *reference words*. The most obvious reference words are nouns, the names of things, actions or concepts. (To review *how* dictionaries define nouns, see the *Close-Up* below.) The goal of such a definition is to distinguish the target word from every other word in the language: put another way, the *meaning* of a word is its unique place in the vocabulary of a language. This short, familiar kind of definition, we can label *spot definition*.

In academic writing, a definition is often rather different. Randy's teacher, for example, expected a definition of *schizophrenia* that not only specified the exact place of the word in the vocabulary of psychology but that also explored the concept in depth and in detail. This kind of definition we can label *expository definition*.

Let's see how these two kinds of definition may be useful to you.

A. USING THE SPOT DEFINITION

Almost every academic essay includes technical terms. If, for example, you're taking a sociology course, you cannot escape using the sociologist's jargon. Luckily these terms are clear to the professor; you need not define them unless you're asked to do so. Very often, though, you'll use a word that has *no* agreed-upon meaning; then you must clarify exactly what the word will mean in your essay. For example, you may be discussing the *unemployed*. Who are the unemployed as far as your essay is concerned? Those without work at the time of writing? Without work for more than one month? More than one year? More than five years? Those registered as looking for work? Without a definition, your essay becomes "meaningless" whenever you use the word *unemployed*.

There's another possibility, too: outside the academic context, most technical terms need defining. If, for example, you're explaining to beginners how a camera works, you'll have to define *depth of field, shutter speed, diaphragm* and so on, although such definitions tend to be rough and ready rather than scientifically precise.

Review Assignment

In Need of Definition

In these sentences from student essays, identify the words that require a spot definition. In each case, provide one of the possible definitions.

a. This essay will discuss the way in which product advertising is aimed at the housewife.

b. International protest seems to have shamed the South African government into releasing children held in state prisons.

c. Since 1954, the United States has not been involved in a war anywhere in the world.

d. Has the situation of minorities improved since the heady days of the Great Society programs?

e. Americans take far more vacations than they used to.

B. USING EXPOSITORY DEFINITION

Sometimes it is clear that expository definition is required: a one-hour exam essay with the subject "Define schizophrenia" must obviously go beyond a spot definition. The same subject might be assigned in various ways:

> What is schizophrenia?
>
> Discuss the characteristics of schizophrenia.
>
> What characterizes the schizophrenic?
>
> Outline the components of the schizophrenic condition.
>
> And so on.

In each case, you are asked to discuss a single concept; the context makes it clear that the discussion should be detailed, if not exhaustive, and that it should result in a clear understanding of the term in question. How do you proceed when expository definition is called for?

Close-Up

How Dictionaries Define Words

First, let's be clear what a dictionary definition is *not*—it is not a description. A dictionary seldom brings an object vividly before your eyes (unless there's a picture in the margin). This is because a dictionary defines a *word*, not an *object*. A dictionary has a clear goal: to explain how the target word differs in meaning from every other word in the language and in particular from closely related words. You don't test a definition by asking: "Is the picture clear?" but by asking: "Are there any other words that also fit this definition?" Defining a word involves a familiar process: comparing and contrasting. As an example, this conversation took place between the author and his two-year-old daughter.

ME: What's that, Eleanor?
HER: Issa doggie.
ME: And what's a doggie?
HER: It's a ammamal.
ME: And how do you know it's a doggie?
HER: 'Cos it goes *woof*.

(It's an open question whether the children of psychologists or of linguists have the more dreadful childhood.) Eleanor was led here to *define* the word *dog*. She began with the target word, *doggie*. She then related this term to its class: *animals*. This is a miraculous skill: she has grouped the myriad things she knows into classes, and she can instantly assign a new item (a stray dog she'd never seen before) to its correct class. Within the class of *animals*, Eleanor differentiated dogs by naming one characteristic that dogs alone possess: they bark. (Of course jackals, foxes and pheasants also bark, but Eleanor didn't know that yet.) Dictionary definitions follow this pattern exactly:

$$\text{TERM} \rightarrow \text{CLASS} \rightarrow \text{DIFFERENTIA}$$

Term—the target word is given

Class—the target word is categorized (classified) into a group of comparable items

Differentia—the target word is differentiated from every other word within the class

This is simply comparing (or categorizing) and then contrasting (or differentiating). One further observation: to avoid circularity, most definitions avoid repeating the *term* later in the definition. It doesn't help much to define a *swimming pool* as *a pool suitable for swimming*. Let's see how *Webster's Ninth New Collegiate Dictionary* defines some nouns:

swimming pool—a pool suitable for swimming (Ouch!)

dental floss—a thread used to clean between the teeth

dogcatcher—a community official assigned to catch and dispose of stray dogs

troglodyte—a member of a primitive people dwelling in caves

wittol—a man who knows of his wife's infidelity and puts up with it

Concept Review

Divide the above definitions into their *term*, *class*, and *differentia* segments. Find some further definitions of nouns in your own dictionary and make the same division.

• Expository Definition:
Two Approaches—Top-Down and Bottom-Up

In our imaginary *Psychology 100* class, Josephine also spots *schizophrenia* as a likely subject. She observes that the professor has chosen a definition that lists four distinct components of schizophrenia. During the subsequent lectures, Josephine listens for cases and examples. In preparing for the midterm, she sketches a game plan for a possible essay based on these four components and on her class notes:

Schizophrenia:

Ready-made definition — Psychosis characterized by the breakdown of integrated personality functioning, withdrawal from reality, emotional blunting and distortion, and disturbed thought processes. (Zimbardo, 1975)

First component of Zimbardo's definition — 1. Breakdown of integrated personality functioning
    a. The Dr. Jekyll-and-Mr.-Hyde multiple personality is not schizophrenia. — Negative example
    b. Schizophrenics fail to check that their behavior suits the situation; for example, they don't check that other people believe what they say: delusions and hallucinations result. — Detail

Second component — 2. Withdrawal from reality
    a. Childhood autism is a form of schizophrenia. — Example
    b. The schizophrenic has excessive sensitivity to every incoming stimulus; this bombardment of sensations makes the world utterly confusing—withdrawal from the world is the only way out. — Detail

Third component — 3. Emotional blunting and distortion
    Both prisoners and prison guards must suppress all emotion—the result can be schizophrenia. — Case

Fourth component — 4. Disturbed thought processes
    a. A schizophrenic's language does not follow normal structure because incorrect or "irrelevant" words (which are normally suppressed) bubble to the surface.
    b. Thinking becomes illogical.
    c. The sense of time is distorted. — Various examples

The approach Josephine uses here is called working top-down or working deductively—she starts at the *top* with a ready-made definition and works *down* to the cases. Whenever you are simply substantiating a ready-made definition, you can work in exactly the same way.

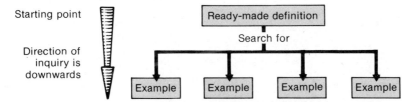

What, then, is working bottom-up or working inductively? Working bottom-up means collecting all the cases, all the information available on a subject, and then working "upwards" toward a definition that embraces everything you've learned.

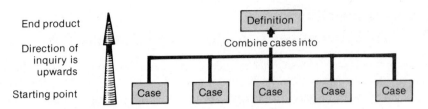

End product

Direction of
inquiry is
upwards

Starting point

Definition

Combine cases into

Case Case Case Case Case

Working bottom-up would be an impossible task for Josephine. She cannot master all the available material on schizophrenia in one semester. On the other hand, a candidate for a master's degree might well adopt this approach: "In the light of everything we know about schizophrenia, what does it appear to be?" To work on a bottom-up example of expository definition, let's pick a simpler case: What is courage?

What is courage? It makes sense to start thinking about a subject like this in terms of *cases*—actions that someone at some time might label *courage*. What do people think of as *courage*? You begin with an obvious case:

a. A woman sees a child in a burning building. She realizes that she has only a few minutes to reach the child. She decides to take the chance and enters the building to save the child. She succeeds and is given an award for courage.

Courage? | Yes | No |

Then you remember a similar case in a recent newspaper:

b. A man standing on a bridge sees a child fall into the river. Instinctively he dives into the water to save the child, remembering only half way down that he himself cannot swim. He is given an award for his courage.

Courage? | Yes | No |

Then there's military courage:

c. In battle an experienced noncommissioned officer is ordered, with his platoon, to take a hilltop position that is heavily defended. For him, it is no big deal. He leads his men and takes the objective. He is decorated for courage.

Courage? | Yes | No |

For you, maybe, the rookie that tries and fails is more courageous:

d. A rookie, new to combat, is so terrified that he crouches down in a foxhole trying to hide. After a moment or two struggling with himself, he forces himself further forward, but again his nerve gives out. This happens several times. By the time he reaches the enemy position, it has already been captured by his fellow soldiers. He is courtmartialed for cowardice.

Courage? | Yes | No |

But you don't have to be in battle to show courage:

e. Two parents have a handicapped child; they decide that they will keep the child at home and give it the best life it can have with its handicap.

Courage? | Yes | No |

What if they make the opposite decision?

f. Two parents have a child in a coma and on a life-support system. The doctors say the child has no chance of recovery. The parents decide to shut off the system.

Courage? | Yes | No |

The TV is on while you are working and you hear the word *courage*:

g. A racing car driver, trying to win the Indy 500 for the fourth consecutive time, has gone out of control on a bend and been killed. The TV commentator speaks of his guts and then of his courage.

Courage? | Yes | No |

A similar case—or is it?

h. A track athlete is brutally spiked on the first lap of a mile race. Despite great pain, she goes on to win the race. A TV commentator speaks of her courage.

Courage? | Yes | No |

Eight cases with eight decisions to make. The pattern of your decisions creates your personal definition of courage. Let's see how. Let's say you answered *yes* to the burning building example but *no* to the bridge. This decision implies a key component in your definition: Courage means being aware of a risk and still taking it. In other words, there are no courageous *instincts*, only courageous *decisions*.

If you said *no* to the noncommissioned officer but *yes* to the rookie, the implication is again clear: Courage means overcoming some inner reluctance. Doing what comes easily is not courageous. Or put another way, there are no courageous *acts*, but only courageous *motives*. If you said *yes* to the parents who kept the child, but *no* to the parents who pulled the plug, the implication is that . . . Well, you decide what that implies. *No* to the driver, and *no* to the track star? This implies . . . Again, you decide.

Of course, you may have answered *yes* in every case, *no* in every case, or any possible combination. Whatever your pattern of *yes* and *no* votes, you must agonize over the material until all the elements of a definition are clear in your mind. Here is one possible interpretation:

i. Courage is not an instinct; it requires conscious awareness of risk. (yes to *a*; no to *b*)

ii. Courage does not lie in the external *act* but in the inner *motive*. (no to *c*; yes to *d*)

iii. Courage is directed to fulfilling duties, not to evading them. (yes to *e*; no to *f*)

iv. Courage must be directed to helping someone else, not just yourself. (no to *g*; no to *h*)

And the definition itself? Based on the answers above, perhaps: "Courage is the mental state in which an individual carries out a moral duty or an action in favor of somebody else, despite a conscious awareness of danger or pain." If you actually wrote this essay, you'd probably develop it as an *inquiry* into the problem, "What is courage?" You'd review the various cases, identifying one by one the elements of your definition. The thesis statement—in this instance clearly belonging at the end of the paper—might simply be the definition as we just formulated it.

Concept Review

Happiness

You are using a bottom-up approach to answer the question: "What do *you* need to be happy?" First, you've sketched out a list—all the things you've ever heard people say make them happy. Now you're ready to put a checkmark against all the things that are essential to *your* happiness—the word *essential* must be strongly stressed:

☐ A lot of money in the bank   ☐ A happy family life
☐ A luxurious home   ☐ Someone to love
☐ An expensive car   ☐ Someone to love you
☐ Holidays in faraway places   ☐ An exotic sex life
☐ Satisfying work   ☐ Excitement
☐ Friends   ☐ Relaxation
☐ Health   ☐ Awareness of God's love
☐ Peace and quiet   ☐ Closeness to nature

Probably you can see how this bottom-up approach would give you the basis for an essay. Now formulate a thesis statement for such an essay based on all your yes answers.

• Negative and Positive Definition

In developing a bottom-up (or *inductive*) definition of courage, we *rejected* several concepts of courage—wrong-headed opinions that did not correspond with our view of the subject. Similarly, in answering the question "What do I need to be happy?" you probably rejected many of the things that other people see as desirable. (If you checked as essential *all* the items on the list, then you have a sure-fire recipe for misery.) These mistaken, rejected ideas are by no means useless material; a strong definition often begins by rejecting a whole string of common misconceptions. (For one example, see the *Close-Up* below.) Let's label the rejection of "mistaken" ideas *negative definition*, and the presentation of "true" ideas *positive definition*. To get a clearer sense of the difference, study the following dialogue; a group of students is brainstorming on the subject "What makes an effective leader?" The students begin by working *negatively*, looking for mistaken ideas about leadership. Since they are also working bottom-up, they try to think of cases, of actual people who believe themselves to be leaders although they obviously are not:

BILL: There's a guy in my office got promoted ahead of me. He thinks just because he's got rank, it makes him a leader. Boy! Is he mistaken.

DONNA: There's someone like that in our office too—she's been there about a hundred years, so she thinks she can tell everyone else what to do.

CHERYL: That's better than some men I know. They seem to think men have some kind of divine right to tell women what to do.

ANN: That's not just men. Most people in my workshop think if they make enough noise it makes them a natural born leader.

ERIC: That's not as bad as some nerd who reads it up in books but doesn't know his elbow from a hole in the ground when he gets on the job.

The list is already impressive. Leadership does *not* come from rank, on-the-job experience, gender, an aggressive personality, or book learning. An essay on leadership might well begin by deflating such common misconceptions. If each point were well-documented, the paper would be off to a flying start. Eventually, however, the reader will expect you to turn to the positive side: what qualities *does* a leader possess?

Close-Up

The Use of Negative Definition

The novelist D. H. Lawrence was accused of writing *pornography* in his most famous book, *Lady Chatterley's Lover*; the book was successfully banned in the United States for more than thirty years. Lawrence tried to defend himself by defining pornography in a strongly worded pamphlet, *Pornography and Obscenity*. In this pamphlet, Lawrence first works negatively, attacking mistaken definitions of pornography. In particular he savagely dismisses any definition that includes "the arousal of sexual feelings" as an essential element. Sexual feelings, he argues, are healthy, not evil; their healthy arousal is no bad thing. Having exploded what he considers wrongheaded ideas, Lawrence switches to positive definition, explaining what pornography *is*: "In the first place genuine pornography is almost always underworld, it doesn't come into the open. In the second you can recognize it by the insult it offers, invariably to sex and to the human spirit." Lawrence's definition has a powerful purpose behind it: if you accept it, then there is no case against *Lady Chatterley's Lover*: the book is a serious attempt to bring sexual love into the open, and to beautify the human spirit by doing so. In fact an American jury in 1959 and a British one in 1960 did accept Lawrence's definition and lifted the ban on his work. Unfortunately, Lawrence had been dead by then for nearly thirty years.

Let's return to our brainstorming session. The group is now on the positive track, trying to find the *defining characteristics* of a leader.

CHERYL: Whatever else, I think a leader has to have a *pleasant personality*.

ERIC: What about General Patton?

BILL: How about Hitler?

ANN: I think *communication* is important.

DONNA: And *fairness*. A leader has to be fair—at least to their followers, subordinates or whatever.

BILL: How about *punctuality*? My boss is late half the time.

CHERYL: That's a side issue. You could have a good leader who wasn't that punctual.

FRANK: To be a real leader, you have to have *integrity*; that's the main thing.

ERIC: How about Nixon?

FRANK: As soon as the people saw he didn't have integrity, he was finished. That's always the way.

DONNA: And *delegation*. Nixon knew how to delegate, but Carter . . . gee. No boss can decide every little thing that comes up.

ANN: Talking of Carter reminds me: I had a boss one time who was *totally indecisive*. She simply couldn't make up her mind.

CHERYL: *Decisiveness* you mean. Yes, I could tell you a story or two about that.

The group is examining each suggested characteristic to see whether it is *essential* to effective leadership or merely *desirable*. Only essential qualities belong in a definition. Lawyers have a similar concept in contract law when they speak of a *conditio sine qua non*. By this they mean a condition that *must* be fulfilled—in fact, unless this condition is fulfilled, the contract ceases to exist. In defining a leader we are also looking for the essential conditions, the characteristics without which leadership cannot exist. The group's list of essential characteristics boils down to this:

Having a pleasant personality	Rejected (non-essential characteristic)
Communication	Accepted (essential characteristic)
Fairness	Accepted (essential characteristic)
Punctuality	Rejected (non-essential characteristic)
Integrity	Accepted (essential characteristic)
Ability to delegate	Accepted (essential characteristic)
Indecisiveness in a bad leader	Rejected (redundant duplicate)
Decisiveness makes a good leader	Accepted (essential characteristic)

Look again at the last two points. They are obviously a single idea expressed twice. Where there are duplicates like this, one of them must clearly be dropped. In all, five separate characteristics emerge. Check the list again. Are all five absolutely essential?

These two brainstorming sessions have produced enough ideas for a full essay on leadership. The first part of the essay would define negatively, attacking common misconceptions; the second part would define positively, presenting the essential characteristics of the effective leader.

Concept Review

The Ideal Husband

In the following group discussion of the ideal husband, decide what the group concludes about each suggestion. Is it a *mistaken idea* that needs correcting? Is it an *essential characteristic*? Is it a *non-essential characteristic* that should be eliminated from the definition altogether? Or is it a *redundant duplicate* of an idea that is better expressed elsewhere?

BILL: So how about the old recipe: high, wide and handsome?
ERIC: You won't find too many men going along with that.
ANN: And not too many women, either.

Mistaken idea	Essential char	Non-essential char	Redundant duplicate

ANN: I think most of us look for commitment in a husband—you know, being committed to make the marriage work.
CHERYL: You're right.

Mistaken idea	Essential char	Non-essential char	Redundant duplicate

CHERYL: And he has to be understanding, too.
ANN: For sure.

Mistaken idea	Essential char	Non-essential char	Redundant duplicate

DONNA: And a good cook.
ANN: That'd be nice—but let's be serious.

Mistaken idea	Essential char	Non-essential char	Redundant duplicate

ANN: One important thing to me: I think a man who cheats on his wife isn't too good of a husband.

Mistaken idea	Essential char	Non-essential char	Redundant duplicate

FRANK: Or you could call it fidelity. I guess most women have that as an ideal.

Mistaken idea	Essential char	Non-essential char	Redundant duplicate

DONNA: What's the word for always bringing you flowers and remembering your anniversary? Attentive? That's part of it.

Mistaken idea	Essential char	Non-essential char	Redundant duplicate

ANN: I knew a couple once—She got interested in jogging and things like that, but he degenerated into a slob. They grew apart, I guess. He mustn't lose interest in his wife; that's important to me.

Mistaken idea	Essential char	Non-essential char	Redundant duplicate

BILL: Turn it around—say a husband has to share his wife's interests.
ANN: It's true.

Mistaken idea	Essential char	Non-essential char	Redundant duplicate

ANN: And you know something else? When I was a kid I used to dream I'd marry the world's greatest lover.
DONNA: Sexual-athlete-wise? Forget it.
ANN: I already did.

Mistaken idea	Essential char	Non-essential char	Redundant duplicate

CHERYL: And a big one we forgot—he has to love you.

Mistaken idea	Essential char	Non-essential char	Redundant duplicate

Altogether there are six essential characteristics. Does that tally with your count?

• Concreteness: The Informal Case Study and the Contrast Module

An essay on leadership or on the ideal husband easily drifts into hot air. The power of the paper to *convince* the reader depends on the concreteness with which each idea is presented. Research will certainly produce relevant studies or statistics, but your own experience should not be overlooked. This is where the *informal case study* comes in. As an example, let's take one component of the leadership essay: fairness. Think for a second: can you recall an occasion when a leader was unfair and thus lost your confidence? Or when a leader gave a tough but fair decision and thus built morale? Using such informal case studies makes the reader feel: "Yes, if I'd been there, I'd have felt exactly the same"—that's good communication. Let's look at two examples, both of them in-class improvisations on the theme of *fairness*. The first writer is Charlene Jackson.

> A leader's fairness can make or break morale. At one time I worked as a switchboard operator, a round-the-clock job where we had to be punctual relieving the previous shift. On our shift of five women, two were persistently late, and they'd both been given a "final warning" by our supervisor. One woman was a single parent with two young children, so the rest of us were ready to cover for her. The other was fresh out of high school; she came late for no reason at all and let us pick up the extra workload. The one thing she could really do was to make eyes at the shift chief. One evening both women were late again. The mother was fired on the spot. She left the building in tears, but we all respected the supervisor's decision. When the girl showed up half an hour later, she was given a "last chance." We couldn't believe it. Most of that night was spent arguing with the supervisor. In fact, the shift didn't settle down again until the branch manager listened to our complaints and agreed to move the supervisor to another job. Leadership, even in a low-level office situation, is impossible without absolute fairness.

Did you feel it too—the effect of this gross favoritism on the morale of the three women? Would you have reacted as the women did, pressing for the removal of the unfair leader? The reader's reaction is the test of a case study. Let's see how an example of a *fair* leader might make the same point. Again, ask if you'd have felt the same way if you'd been in the writer's shoes. If you would, then the writing works. The writer of this piece is Charlene's husband, Tony, who was taking the same class.

> Have you ever felt you had to respect a leader even when he put you down? Some years back I was a draftsman in an all-male, all-white drafting office. There were eighteen of us under Daren James, a boss of the Old School. Then came "equal opportunity," and Personnel sent us a black woman, Wanda. We all saw Wanda as a "token" and thought we'd be carrying her for some time. Whenever she left the room, we gathered round her drawing board, me included, to pick holes in her work and make all the usual remarks. Daren James had never wanted Wanda, but he didn't like all the backbiting. One afternoon he told us to stop signing the work we turned in—we had no idea why. A while later he picked three drawings: one by me, one by Wanda, and one by another draftsman who'd been less than pleasant. Daren had asked the Chief Engineer to stop by and critique our drawings, which he did. Wanda's, he said, was fine. The second drawing was acceptable though not quite centered. But mine had a mistake in it—a right-handed thread drawn left-handed. It hurt, and I was a long time living it

down. Nevertheless, I saw that Daren had been fair, and the backbiting stopped on the spot. Wanda stayed with us for a while: then she finished an engineering degree and moved on. Daren is my idea of a good leader: tough but fair. You can learn something from a man like that.

Two contrasted approaches then—an unfair leader is worthless, while a fair leader is someone you can "learn something from." Either approach works well on its own. Taken together, they can be extremely convincing. In fact, as you probably realized, the two examples together make up a contrast module, a very powerful tool in the process of defining. Charlene, as it happens, did use the two incidents in an essay entitled "What Makes an Effective Leader?" To create a paragraph on fairness, Charlene began by polishing her improvised case study a little. She followed this with a transition: "An incident that happened to my husband some years ago shows the positive effect of fair leadership." She then retold Tony's story in her own words. To end the paragraph, Charlene added some pointing:

Taken together, these two incidents illustrate more than a minor point of office diplomacy. The unfairness of my supervisor left a taint of anger and frustration long after he had gone. It reinforced the feeling that nothing was ever going to change—after all, the mother who was fired went on welfare, while the eighteen-year-old kept her job. On the other hand, Daren James's decision made eighteen men (nineteen if you include Daren himself) rethink their attitudes and scrap some of their prejudices. That is the kind of leadership our society needs at every level.

In this way, Charlene constructed from simple materials a contrast module with some "pulling power."

Review Assignment

Choose one of the characteristics of an effective leader and "free write" a contrast module about it. Then review your piece, paying special attention to the *transition* and to the *pointing*.

2 •

The Personal Voice

In the first thoroughgoing dictionary of English, Samuel Johnson defined a lexicographer as "A writer of dictionaries; a harmless drudge, that busies himself in tracing the origin and detailing the significance of words." Definition encourages compression, polish, and—for some reason—the use of irony. The greatest American practitioner of ironic polish was Ambrose Bierce in his *Devil's Dictionary* (1881–1906). Some samples:

ABASEMENT, *n*. A decent and customary mental attitude in the presence of wealth and power. Peculiarly appropriate in an employee when addressing an employer.

ACQUAINTANCE, *n*. A person whom we know well enough to borrow from, but not well enough to lend to. A degree of friendship called slight when its object is poor or obscure, and intimate when he is rich or famous.

ADMIRATION, *n*. Our polite recognition of another's resemblance to ourselves.

AFFIANCED, *pp*. Fitted with an ankle-ring for the ball-and-chain.

AMNESTY, *n*. The state's magnanimity to those offenders whom it would be too expensive to punish.

BORE, *n*. A person who talks when you want him to listen.

BRIDE, *n*. A woman with a fine prospect of happiness behind her.

CHRISTIAN, *n*. One who follows the teachings of Christ in so far as they are not inconsistent with a life of sin.

CONSERVATIVE, *n*. A statesman who is enamoured of existing evils, as distinguished from a Liberal who wishes to replace them with others.

COWARD, *n*. One who in a perilous emergency thinks with his legs.

DEBAUCHEE, *n*. One who has so earnestly pursued pleasure that he has had the misfortune to overtake it.

DISTANCE, *n*. The only thing the rich are willing for the poor to call theirs and keep.

EDUCATION, *n*. That which discloses to the wise and disguises from the foolish their lack of understanding.

FORK, *n*. An instrument used chiefly for putting dead animals into the mouth.

INVENTOR, *n*. A person who makes an ingenious arrangement of wheels, levers and springs, and believes it civilization.

IRRELIGION, *n*. The principal one of the great faiths of the world.

KLEPTOMANIAC, *n*. A rich thief.

LECTURER, *n*. One with his hand in your pocket, his tongue in your ear and his faith in your patience.

LOVE, *n*. A temporary insanity curable by marriage. . . .

MERCY, *n*. An attribute beloved of detected offenders.

POLITICS, *n*. A strife of interests masquerading as a contest of principles.

SAINT, *n*. A dead sinner, revised and edited.

Review Assignment

The *Devil's Dictionary* Updated

Here are a few suggestions for additions to the *Devil's Dictionary*. Your own wit will probably suggest many other, better ideas.

the news	a terrorist	a spy	the ghetto
a campus radical	a rock star	a scam	social security
equal opportunity	modern Christmas	psychology	an English course

3 •
Writing Workshop—
The Process of Defining

• Choosing a Subject

The questions on this list all begin with the word *What*. This does not automatically make them definition questions. A "what" question could call for analysis of cause and effect ("What causes alcoholism?"), for classification ("What attitudes to drug addiction do you find in your community?"), or for you to make a case ("What is your attitude to the commercialization of Christmas?") Don't judge a question by its external form: instead, find out what exactly you are being asked to do.

First some personal subjects:

1. What do you (personally) need to be happy?
2. What do you (personally) look for in a friend?
3. What do you (personally) have to offer a prospective employer?
4. What do you like about your present job, your present location, or your present school?
5. What would be, for you, the perfect lifestyle?

Now some definitions of roles:

6. What is the proper role of the police force in modern society?
7. What role should a father play in bringing up children?
8. What is the role of the infantry (navy, and so on) in modern warfare?
9. What part does a coach play in a team's success? (Stick to one sport.)
10. What role should a teacher play in educating children? (You may want to limit yourself to one age group or one subject, or both.)

Some definition subjects include such words as *good* or *effective*. This limits the scope, and simplifies the task, of definition:

11. What qualities make a good driver?
12. What qualities characterize an effective leader?
13. What is a true sportsman? (hunter or athlete—not both)
14. What qualities would make an ideal husband (or wife)?
15. What makes a supervisor pleasant to work for?
16. What characterizes a river with good fishing?
17. What makes a store into a pleasant place to go shopping?
18. What makes a holiday resort successful?

19. What qualities are needed to run a profitable small farm?

20. What makes a city pleasant to live in?

Presenting a way of life can be approached as a kind of definition:

21. What are the main characteristics of the Hispanic lifestyle?

22. What characterized the "old South" and its way of life?

23. What are the special qualities of life in the ghetto (or the barrio)?

24. Any place you know well has special qualities. Try to define the special qualities, bringing out what is unique to this place.

And now some *terms* that call for expository definition:

25. What characterizes the "gifted child"?

26. What characterizes love within marriage?

27. What gives a man or a woman upward mobility?

28. What is "natural childbirth"?

29. What is terrorism?

30. What qualities characterize a feminist?

Some subjects are really *re*definitions. Everyone knows, for example, what makes a *singer*, but what makes a *star*?

31. What qualities make a singer (or other musician) into a star?

32. What makes a house into a home?

33. What special qualities does a driver need to become a racing driver?

34. What makes certain athletes "crowd-pullers"?

35. What makes an old car into a *collectible* car?

Finally, if you have taken courses in other subjects, you may have written essays in which you tried to define an important concept in the field. This might be a good time to rework such an essay in the light of what you now know about writing. Of the thousands of subjects possible:

36. What is a sociopath?

37. What is Management by Objectives?

38. What is Cubism?

39. What is irony?

40. What is hysteria?

• Developing a Game Plan

One approach to defining, as we've seen, starts at the "top" with a ready-made definition and documents each component of the definition. This is how Josephine handled her definition of *schizophrenia*. You may encounter two problems if you try this method yourself. The first is finding a usable, ready-made definition; the second is developing a thesis statement that goes beyond the bare definition you decide to use. Phil Alire met both problems in developing a down-to-earth subject: "What makes a successful fisherman?"

Reaching for *Webster's*, Phil found: *fisherman—one who engages in fishing as an occupation or for pleasure.* A few lines below, Phil found: *fishing—the sport or business of catching fish.* Phil was getting no place fast. He then tried to compose a top-down definition of his own. He boldly wrote: "A successful fisherman is someone . . ." A while later he wrote in small print: "who successfully catches fish.

Phil now realized he'd have to use the "bottom-up" method. This meant thinking over his own successes and failures as a fisherman. He came to me with five anecdotes and the inevitable question, "What now?"

Carson River. The time I went camping with Jim and Bob. Bob and I spent the whole day skipping from one spot to the next looking for a "good" place. Jim stayed behind and patiently fished near the campsite. He caught some nice fish; we caught next to nothing.

Beale Air Force Base. I tried for three years to catch a huge large-mouth bass. Then one evening after work I went to try again only to see a kid catch it! He wasn't even watching his line but climbing a tree with his brother. His father had to land it.

My dad's trick. Fish often eat other fish that are injured. Dad used to make a minnow lure look "injured" by jerking it through the water. Once I'd tried *everything* else, and then caught my limit with an "injured" lure.

The summer I bought new tackle. I pumped gas for the whole summer vacation and bought everything brand new from the store. I caught one or two nice fish with that tackle.

Gordon's special spot. One summer we went to a place Gordon knew. It took five hours backpacking in the heat to get there. But it was great. We stayed up half the night fishing with a lantern.

I suggested to Phil that we reduce his experiences to five labels:

Patience

Luck

Readiness to experiment

Good equipment

Determination

Was each point an essential characteristic of the successful fisherman? Phil noticed one problem on his list: the boy who'd hooked Phil's large-mouth bass had used cheap equipment; the same was true of Phil's trip with Gordon—they had caught plenty of fish without the latest in poles and reels. Good equipment was nice, but it wasn't essential, so the point was rejected. Phil's list was down to four.

Patience

Luck

Readiness to experiment

Determination

I asked Phil about negative definition—other people's ideas of success that he could demolish. "I can catch all the fish in a hole with just one stick of dynamite," Phil remembered someone saying. Should he demolish that crazy idea? Phil decided against it: nobody would call the dynamite thrower "a successful fisherman," so he was irrelevant to the subject. Phil stayed with his list of four essential characteristics.

A game plan won't take shape without a thesis. I suggested that Phil turn the four characteristics into a definition and use that as the thesis statement: "A successful fisherman must have patience, luck, and determination and be ready to experiment." Phil thought that was too bland. Then he noticed that three of his qualities (patience, readiness to experiment, and determination) fell together under the umbrella of *persistence*. He could start with *luck*, and then work through the other points to show that "persistence produces results."

Luck → Patience → Determination → Experimentation

And as a thesis: "You can't control your luck, but with persistence you can control almost everything else." Phil's game plan then:

> 1. <u>Luck</u>: The kid who caught "my" bass
>
> 2. <u>Patience</u>: Carson River: how Bob and I wasted a whole day through impatience while Jim caught his limit
>
> 3. <u>Determination</u>: Backpacking in the heat to Gordon's special place
>
> 4. <u>Experimentation</u>: Catching my limit with an "injured" lure
>
> <u>Thesis statement</u>:
>
> You can't control your luck, but with persistence you can control almost everything else.

In developing this game plan, Phil stumbled over most of the obstacles to effective definition. (1) The top-down approach stalled for lack of a workable definition: (2) The bottom-up approach meant a great deal of thinking to produce a list of five words, only four of which were usable. (3) It was difficult to formulate a thesis statement beyond a colorless definition. Don't be surprised if the same problems trouble you.

• Writing the First Draft

A. THE OPENING

As we saw in the Introduction to Part 2, you can present your material in two ways: as a proof or as an inquiry. This choice is especially pertinent in a definition essay: Will you open with the definition and then document each element of the definition in the paper? Or will you open with a question and then piece the definition together bit-by-bit during the essay?

CHAPTER FIVE
The Multi-Element Paper—Definition

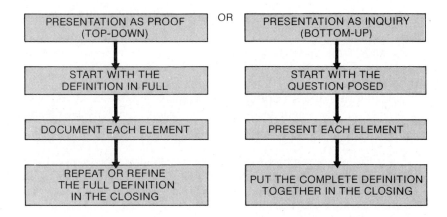

You faced exactly the same choice, top-down or bottom-up, that you faced when you were *investigating* the subject. Should you now *present* your material in the same way that you *investigated* it? Not necessarily. Let's explain this with an analogy. Detective Bottom investigates a series of clues and finally uncovers the killer (that is, he works bottom-up). Detective Top has his killer already behind bars; now he must find the evidence to convict him (that is, he works top-down). When it comes to presenting the case in court, neither detective is obliged to repeat the investigation. Bottom could say: "This is the killer, and this is how I know" (top-down presentation as a proof), while Top could say: "This is my evidence, and it all points to Joseph K. as the murderer" (bottom-up presentation as an inquiry). You, too, have this flexibility.

As a rule of thumb, presentation as an inquiry keeps the reader guessing and interested; it's a good choice where the *whole essay* is a single definition. Presentation as a proof is tighter; it works best when a *definition section* forms part of a longer paper.

B. WRITING

The great temptation in writing a definition is to degenerate into hot air. Be particularly careful about *concreteness*; specific cases, facts, figures, quotations, the results of interviews, the findings of research projects—your essay should be packed with high-quality information.

C. THE CLOSING

If your thesis is the definition itself, it won't need much explanation or other packaging. Let's take an example: you have written an essay on "The role of the modern police force." The essay identifies three essential aspects of this role—the police must:

| Catch criminals | Prevent crime | Work as facilitators |

The essay might well end:

> Accordingly the role of the modern police force is (1) to detect criminals, (2) to prevent crime, and (3) to work with the public as trained facilitators.

In certain kinds of writing, a closing like that is unobjectionable. If you wish to soften things up, you might try *ranking* the various components. Often the reasoning behind this ranking makes a more mellow closing:

> If, as we have seen, a modern police force has three essential tasks, does any one task have priority? Traditionally, the police have enjoyed the support of the public in tracking down criminals and in crime prevention. That support has eroded dangerously during recent years. The police must, as a matter of urgency, develop their role as trained facilitators, working <u>with</u> the public in every way possible. If this does not happen, crime detection and prevention will become virtually impossible.

• Revising

The flowchart on page 119 offers a general scheme for revising your first draft. Re-read this material carefully. The following notes cover the special concerns to bear in mind while revising a definition essay.

A. A SPECIAL CHECK FOR CONTINUITY

a. Headings.   If you are using *headings* in your papers, formulating them for a definition paper is rather easy: each component of the definition generates a new heading. Negative definition may give you pause, however. In an essay on "The Role of the Police" you might well decide to demolish a number of mistaken ideas. Let's take an example:

> Some people mistakenly believe that the role of the police is to enforce the moral values of extremely conservative pressure groups.

Would the normal kind of heading be suitable for this paragraph? This, for example:

> A. The Enforcement of Conservative Moral Values

The danger is obvious: the reader may suspect that *you* hold this view. Some negative wording is important here:

> A. Enforcing Moral Values—No Job for the Police

b. Pointing.   It is particularly tempting in a definition essay to leave each section "hanging." This is the effect that pointing is designed to prevent. What sort of pointing is appropriate in a definition paper? The answer depends, like most other things, on the thesis statement. Let's stay with "The Role of the Police" for an example.

If the thesis is the bald definition, then pointing too can be minimal. At the end of the first section, for example:

The first role of the police is, therefore, to catch criminals.

With a more elaborate thesis, however, you should point each paragraph with special care. Let's say the thesis statement is:

The police must, as a matter of urgency, develop their role as trained facilitators, working with the public in every way possible. If this does not happen, crime detection and prevention will become virtually impossible.

In this case, Section 1 might end with a pointing statement like this:

The first role of the police is to catch criminals—but crime statistics show that the police are less successful at this with each passing year. Why? What stops the police from fulfilling their most obvious duty?

Pointing like this angles the material towards the thesis and gives the essay coherence. *Now reread the tail-end of each section in your own first draft. Does the pointing show how that section fits into the overall line of argument? Does it lead the reader towards the thesis?*

B. A SPECIAL CHECK FOR CORRECTNESS

Your language should always aim at precision, but in a definition essay, you should become fanatical about it. At all costs avoid *ambiguity*—unintended double meanings. There are three main causes of ambiguity: (1) erratic vocabulary, (2) a failure to connect like with like, and (3) poorly placed modifiers.

a. **Erratic Vocabulary.** Watch out for boners like these:

He was caught selling drugs to miners.

The Air Force helps people relive (relieve?) their problems.

Her knees looked as if she had scrapped them.

In the city at night there are very little (few?) people.

b. **Failure to Connect Like with Like.** Can you see, and correct, the problems in these sentences?

The system is just as confusing to the patients as the staff.

We put the sandwiches in the refrigerator as well as the lunch boxes.

To catch slips like these, ask a friend to read your essay and comment on anything that was "hard to follow."

c. **Poorly Placed Modifiers.** Poorly placed modifiers provide most of the humorous errors in English:

He found his slippers *crawling under the bed*.

Having been well spanked, my teachers had no more trouble with me.

After hearing the explosion, my feet carried me quickly away.

The preacher soundly denounced adultery *on Wednesday evening*.

If your baby does not like cold milk, it should be boiled.

Or more seriously:

Having been washed in gasoline, the filter guide is ready to receive the filter.

Taking a warm bath *often* reduces blood pressure.

Do not put the fish into the skillet *until it has been rubbed with butter*.

For a full survey of the possibilities, check *Ambiguity*, *Squinting Modifiers* and *Dangling Modifiers* in your Handbook.

• The Final Draft

Chester Mowery's paper on basketball coaches is brimful of information, yet the organization allows the reader to see instantly how each new fact fits into the overall scheme. Chester has developed each section as a contrast—or rather as a comparison-contrast. The ongoing structure is: "Although on the surface these two coaches used different approaches, in the end they reached the same goal."

What Role does a Coach Play in the Success of a Basketball Team?

1. For a college basketball team, the most basic step towards success is knowing the fundamentals of the game.
   a. Former UCLA coach John Wooden always stressed hard-nosed, man-to-man defense and a fast-break, running offense.
   b. Louisville's Denny Crum believes in full-court, zone-press defense as part of his overall offensive strategy.
2. A basketball coach must be decisive in make-or-break situations.
   a. Gale Cattett, head coach at West Virginia, utilizes experienced players in critical situations.
   b. An "element of surprise" is used by North Carolina's Dean Smith.
3. The key role of a basketball coach is that of motivator.
   a. Jim Valvano of North Carolina has a low-key, relaxed approach.
   b. Bobby Knight of Indiana projects a strong image of authority.

Thesis statement:

There is no magic formula for success in basketball. One thing is clear though: a coach who cannot motivate his team will not have a winning season.

CHAPTER FIVE
The Multi-Element Paper—Definition

Anecdote to catch attention	Is it true, the story of the basketball coach who said to the teacher of freshman English: "You give my guys a B or I'll have you thrown off the faculty"—and they all made B's? If it is true, it shouldn't be: it's not a part of a coach's role to encourage freeloading. But what exactly is the coach's role in leading a team to success?	Inductive method: definition set up as a question

1. Knowledge of Fundamentals

First component introduced	For a college basketball team, the most basic step towards success is knowing the fundamentals of the game. This is where the coach makes his first contribution. For example, former UCLA coach John Wooden, always stressed hard-nosed, man-to-man defense and a fast-break, running offense. Over the years, Wooden led his team to nine national championships. His extraordinary success was based on the premise that if a team can play perfect defensive basketball, the offense will take care of itself.	Example
	There are, naturally, other approaches to strategy. Louisville's Denny Crum, for example, believes in full-court, zone-press defense as the key to a strong offensive strategy. He teaches his players the kind of pressure defense that constantly forces turnovers; once the ball is turned over, a fast-break offense will often follow. Crum is also a successful coach, having led Louisville to one national	Transition to counter-example
		Counter-example
Pointing: first component restated	championship and one runner-up placing. Different as their winning strategies may be, both these coaches show strongly as teachers. An effective coach must understand the basics of the game and be able to instill this understanding into his players.	*Link* between examples stressed

2. Decisiveness

Second component introduced	Then a basketball coach must be decisive in make-or-break situations. Gale Cattett, head coach at West Virginia, uses experienced players when things get tough. He values their extra poise. I rarely saw him play a sophomore or freshman when West Virginia was in a close game. His approach pushed his team to two successive NCAA bids in recent seasons.	Example
	Once again, however, there are alternative approaches. Dean Smith of North Carolina has one national championship and three runner-up placings to his credit. His tactic is to use the "element of surprise." In a game I saw against the University of Arkansas, for example, Coach Smith brought on a relatively unknown player, Jim Braddock, for a last-second shot at winning—even though he had two all-Americans he could have used. In fact, Smith failed to pull it off that time, but the "element of surprise" has saved his team	Transition to counter-example
		Counter-example (as with previous section, a superficial difference leads to a link)
Pointing: second component restated	many games over the last fifteen years. The point is this: in tough situations a coach must make snap decisions. Some coaches are predictable, some are not—it makes no difference. If a coach is decisive, the team is on its way to success.	

3. Skill as a Motivator

Key component as summary of the first three	The key role of a basketball coach is that of motivator. In a sense, this role includes both the others: whether working as a teacher or decision-maker, the coach never stops providing motivation. Here, too, there are many paths to success. A low-key, relaxed approach is taken by North Carolina's Jim Valvano. To him, a single game does not make or break a team or a player. He believes players should enjoy the game and not worry about the inevitable defeats. His philosophy guided his team to the national championship.	Example
	Bobby Knight of Indiana, by way of contrast, projects strong authority. In his games, it is not uncommon to hear his voice rising above the yell of 16,000 fans in the stands. He	Transition to counter-example
		Counter-example
Pointing: key component restated	leaves no doubt in his players' minds about who is boss. Certainly, they play for him: his authoritative style has given him two national championships. There is no single magic way of motivating players; even so, motivating the team is the key role of the coach.	Link stressed

Conclusion

Thesis: Overview and reemphasis of the final key point	A coach has many responsibilities to his team. Although no two successful coaches tackle these responsibilities in the same way, that fact is a lesson in itself—there is no magic formula for success in basketball. One thing is clear though: a coach who cannot motivate his team will not have a winning season.

PART TWO
The Essay

• Summary: The Flowchart

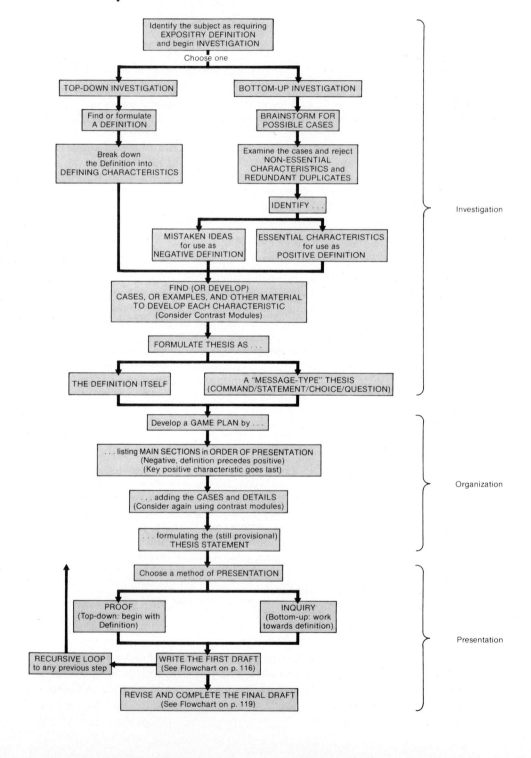

The Multi-Element Paper—Investigating Causes

1 •
The Problem: Discovering *Why*

• The Tangled Chain

Children begin to ask *Why?* from the moment they have a clear grasp of facts. "Why are my eyes blue, Mommy, and yours are brown?" Or "Why are we bigger than mice?" Satisfying childish curiosity is not easy. In fact it was "childish" questions like these that led Gregor Mendel to unravel genetic patterns and Charles Darwin to postulate the theory of evolution. *Why?* (in the sense of *How come?*) is often the question that leads to progress. If the economist can discover *why* American industry is becoming less competitive; if the biologist can discover *why* breast cancer is becoming more common; if the literary scholar can discover *why* poetry is a dying art—then, maybe, such problems can be solved.

As Darwin and Mendel would bear witness, investigating causes is bedeviled by problems. As a writer, you must be aware of these problems before you approach a cause-and-effect investigation. As an illustration, let's look at a "simple" case: Carlotta, a compulsive house cleaner. The situation was this: after a daily routine of fourteen hours of cleaning, Carlotta was exhausted but still unsatisfied—she said that her house was not *clean*. *How come?* What *caused* this frustration? A psychiatrist would be the right person to find out. Her psychiatrist quickly learned that Carlotta was glowingly praised as a child for playing the "little housewife": every time she put on her mother's apron and "cleaned house," her father lavished affection on her. Is this praise the *cause* of her later behavior? Do we have cause and effect?

The professional psychiatrist would have at least three reservations about returning such a simplistic verdict.

First, could it be proved that this childhood praise *caused* Carlotta's present behavior? In the mathematical sense of proof, obviously not; we can discuss human behavior only in terms of probability, not in terms of logical absolutes. How about *legal* proof—proof beyond all reasonable doubt? Here again things are loose: the connection between Carlotta's childhood experience and adult behavior might be merely a coincidence. A lawyer would call the evidence "circumstantial." In fact, proving that linked events fall into a pattern of cause and effect is a perennial headache for all investigators. Does smoking *cause* cancer? Does sex education *cause* sexual experimentation? The arguments still rage because proof is hard to come by. **Rule 1:** *Don't accept one thing as the cause of another until you can demonstrate a cause-and-effect relationship.*

Problem two, to return to Carlotta: if the psychiatrist accepts her father's excessive praise as *one* cause, are there additional causes of her odd behavior? Why, for example, does she *need* praise today? Is she trying to earn praise from an authoritarian husband? Or does she feel she has "lost her looks" and has to compensate? Another line of thought: Carlotta has no children. Is this *because* she likes a clean house? Or does she see her childlessness as a punishment that she can ward off by keeping her house absolutely "pure"? In real life, very few situations result from a single cause. In Carlotta's case, the tidy linkup of one cause and one effect would soon degenerate into a tangled knot of causes and unanswerable questions. Let's say the psychiatrist pins down these main causes of Carlotta's condition. Three causes—is that *all* of them? This is something the psychiatrist will never know: in searching for causes, there is no way to guarantee that *everything* has been taken into account. **Rule 2:** *Search carefully for all the causes, even though you can never be certain that you have them all.*

Thirdly, our investigating psychiatrist would ask a number of questions about the "praise" Carlotta was given as a child. Number one: Was Carlotta really praised so profusely, or is she distorting her memories? If there is distortion, *why*? Or, if Carlotta's memory is correct, *why* is the memory so important to her? And why were her parents like that? Who was trying to prove what to whom? If we surmise that it was Carlotta's father who warped her, why was he that way? Perhaps because his mother warped him—and so on back to "Adam and Eve." (See the *Close-Up.*) Untangling knots like these years after the event is close to impossible. **Rule 3:** *Try to trace the chain of cause and effect back beyond the immediate causes to the root causes.*

These three rules, as we shall see in the next section, form the basis of any serious cause-and-effect investigation.

Close-Up

The Great First Cause

How far back does the chain of cause and effect extend? In ancient times Aristotle, seeing endless motion in the world, reasoned that this motion must have had a *cause*. This cause must be something that does not move itself, but which causes movement in other things: the "unmoved mover" in other words. To Aristotle, this was God—the First Cause of everything. The argument is attractive. Throughout the Middle Ages, the First Cause argument was used to "prove" the existence of God. Alexander Pope, writing *The Universal Prayer* in 1738, addressed God directly as "Thou Great First Cause." The argument is not, however, particularly sound, as the great mathematician, Bertrand Russell, has pointed out. First, it assumes that every series must have a starting point—which is not the case (the series of proper fractions, for example, has no "first term"). More important, although this is a tough logical knot to crack, Russell argues: "To infer a creator is to infer a cause, and causal inferences are only admissable in science when they proceed from observed causal laws. Creation out of nothing is an occurrence which has not been observed. There is, therefore, no better reason to suppose that the world was caused by a Creator than to suppose that it was uncaused; either equally contradicts the causal laws that we can observe."

Concept Review

Rats and Asbestos

In an experiment conducted at the "University of Wiesbaden," a rat was placed in an environment rich in asbestos dust. The air contained about 500 parts per million of asbestos rather than the normal 5 to 10 parts per million. The experiment was repeated 20 times. In each case, the rat contracted asbestosis, a lung disease, within three months.

Questions:

1. Does the experiment establish a chain of cause and effect leading from the dust to the disease, or does it merely indicate the probability of such a chain?
2. Does the experiment imply anything about humans and asbestosis?
3. Which of the following facts might have influenced (and thereby compromised) the result of the experiment?

    a. All the rats were directly descended from the same pair of laboratory rats twelve generations back.

    b. The rats were all fed the same food and water before and during the experiment.

> c. All the experiments were carried out in the same laboratory.
>
> d. All the experiments were carried out by the same scientist.
>
> e. The asbestos dust used in all the experiments was taken from the same consignment.
>
> 4. Given your answers to (3), how much reliance would you place in the results? How close is the experiment to showing cause and effect?

• Cause and Effect: Three Investigations

Whenever an aircraft crashes, whenever a building burns down, whenever plutonium is missing, there is an investigation. *How come?* ask the investigators. The analysis of the causes leads to changes: a better doorlock for the aircraft, improved wiring for buildings, tighter security at atomic plants. During 1986 three dramatic events led to classic investigations of cause and effect: the explosion of the shuttle *Challenger*, the nuclear disaster at Chernobyl, and the eruption of the "Lake of Death" in Cameroon. Each investigation can teach us a great deal about how cause-and-effect analysis works.

INVESTIGATION 1: *CHALLENGER*

On the 28th of January, 1986, nine miles high and moving at nearly 2,000 miles per hour, *Challenger* exploded, killing all seven people on board. What went wrong? Step 1 in an investigation is to decide what exactly is being investigated: in this case, the explosion. Step 2 is to brainstorm for possible causes. Early guesswork about *Challenger* produced many theories: perhaps the ice on the launch pad during the night damaged the shuttle; perhaps a minor accident on the previous Saturday damaged the external fuel tank; perhaps a part in one of the rocket boosters failed under the stress of liftoff; perhaps a fuel line ruptured. (In these diagrams, an ellipse represents a cause and a rectangle an effect. Items in a chain naturally require both notations.)

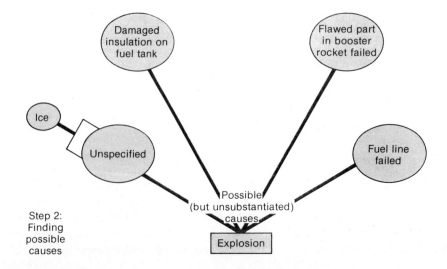

Step 2:
Finding
possible
causes

This "tree" presents the hunches. Step 3 is (a) to establish what actually happened and (b) to prove cause and effect. During February 1986, the presidential commission under William Rogers homed in on the immediate cause of the disaster: cold temperatures on the pad had hardened the "rubber" O-rings that prevent leaks from the booster rockets; the O-rings had failed, allowing hot gasses to escape and ignite; within one minute the whole system was torn to pieces in the air. *Question:* Given the O-ring failure, do we have a provable chain of cause-and-effect? Did this failure cause the crash? After a cautious, four-month analysis of the evidence, the Rogers Commission gave the answer: "Yes, the O-ring failure was to blame." The picture now:

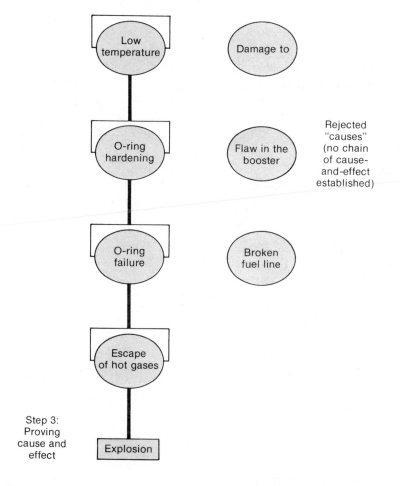

Step 3:
Proving
cause and
effect

The Rogers Commission had established a simple chain of cause-and-effect, but it did not stop there. Rule 2, as we saw earlier, says: look for other causes. Was it *only* the cool morning (38 °F) that caused the crash? It quickly emerged that the O-ring design was faulty, that the engineers knew it was faulty, and that the rings had almost failed before. Richard Cook, a budget analyst with NASA, reported that NASA engineers "held their breaths" during every shuttle launch because of the danger of O-ring failure (*Time*, February 24, 1986, p. 38). A further cause: on the morning of the fatal launch, Allan McDonald, an engineer with Morton Thiokol, who built the rings, argued furiously for the mission to be cancelled on account of the cold, but his warning never reached NASA.

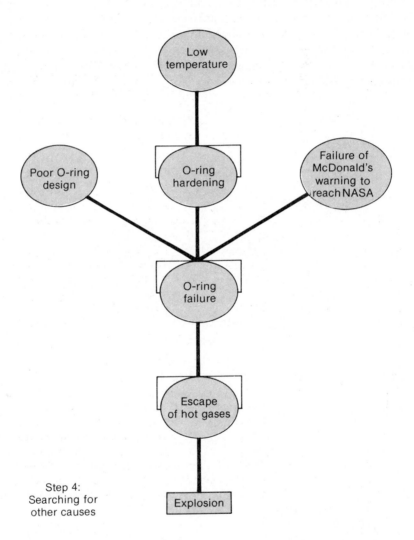

Step 4:
Searching for
other causes

Rule 3 says: pursue the chain of cause-and-effect beyond immediate causes. In fact no investigator could fail to press the question: *how come* the flights went ahead when the bad design of the O-rings was known and when the engineers knew it was too cold for the rings to function? The Commission found two underlying causes at the root of the problem: (1) time pressure—a tough schedule for launches that meant cutting corners, and (2) poor management that blocked lines of communication.

CHAPTER SIX
The Multi-Element Paper—Investigating Causes

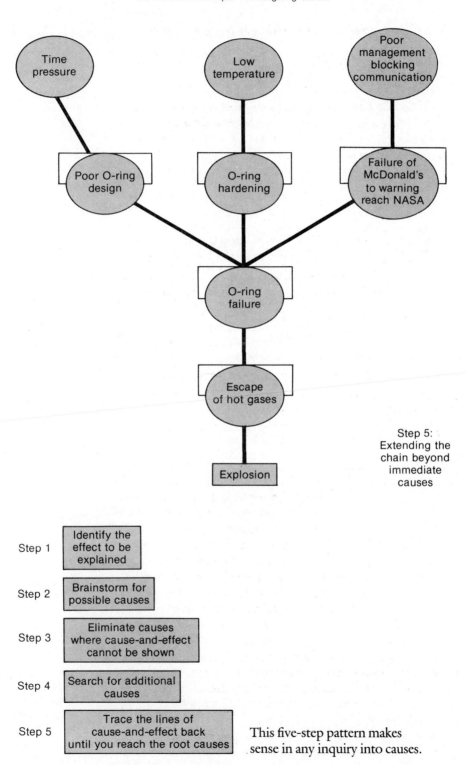

Step 5:
Extending the
chain beyond
immediate
causes

Step 1 — Identify the effect to be explained

Step 2 — Brainstorm for possible causes

Step 3 — Eliminate causes where cause-and-effect cannot be shown

Step 4 — Search for additional causes

Step 5 — Trace the lines of cause-and-effect back until you reach the root causes

This five-step pattern makes sense in any inquiry into causes.

INVESTIGATION 2: NUCLEAR CATASTROPHE IN CHERNOBYL

A second dramatic investigation in 1986 examined the nuclear catastrophe at Chernobyl in the Ukraine. By studying this investigation, we can learn how an academic procedure, the analysis of cause-and-effect, can serve a political aim —the defense of the Soviet nuclear program, the vilification of the Soviet Union, or whatever.

First, a super-brief explanation of nuclear power plants. In essence, fuel rods of radioactive material produce heat. Exactly as in a normal power station, this heat is used to make steam, and this steam is used to power turbines. The turbines in turn drive electricity generators.

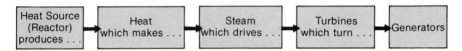

Now the facts. On April 26, 1986, a nuclear reactor at Chernobyl in the Ukraine exploded, showering the Soviet Union, Europe and other parts of the world with radioactive debris. Theories as to the cause of the explosion proliferated until, in August, Soviet investigators presented their findings to the International Atomic Energy Agency in Vienna. They reported a chain of events that ran as follows:

1.	On April 25, 1986, the engineers at the Chernobyl plant began an experiment. They wanted to know how long their turbines would freewheel without steam if a reactor were shut down by an unforeseen emergency. The reactor served eight turbines in all; they would need to test only one. In fact, since the reactor was being shut down for routine maintenance anyway, the time looked right to run the experiment.	1: Turbine experiment conceived
2.	At shutdown time, the experimenters wanted a quick fall in power, so they switched off the automatic control system (which worked very slowly) and used instead the manual control system. This procedure was forbidden. Violation 1.	2: Manual shutdown enabled
3.	Under manual control, the reactor began to shut down too quickly and to overheat. To cool things down, the fuel rods were withdrawn from their housings. Extra cooling pumps were also switched on. These pumps were Violation 2: too much cooling water can weaken or damage the system. The experiment continued.	3: Reactor overheats
4.	The reactor now became too cool, the amount of steam dropped off, setting off an alarm. However, since there was still enough steam to drive the one turbine needed for the experiment, the experimenters switched the alarm off. Violation 3.	4: Reactor is overcooled
5.	The reactor was now working at such a low level that it was dangerous to operate it at all: it should have been totally shut down. Another alarm warned the experimenters of this. They ignored it. Violation 4.	5: Reactor output too low

6. At last, the experiment was ready: a single turbine was being driven by steam, and this steam could be cut off with the turn of a valve. One final safety system was then disconnected to allow a repeat of the experiment if necessary. Violation 5. In a few seconds the experimenters would know how long a turbine freewheels without steam.	6: Final safety system disconnected
7. The valve was closed, cutting off the steam to the turbine. Suddenly pressure began to build behind the valve, and the reactor started up again. The whole system, with all its safety mechanisms disconnected, overheated, went out of control and exploded, showering the Soviet Union and Europe with dangerous levels of radioactivity while the Soviet nuclear bureaucracy looked on in silence.	

A disquieting story. Let's see now how the Soviet investigators angled their material and how Western commentators responded. As a study in the analysis of cause-and-effect, nothing could be more instructive.

Step 1: Deciding What is Being Investigated and
Step 2: Brainstorming for Causes

Step 1 is always the same—deciding exactly what "effect" is under investigation? Is it simply the accident itself? Or is it the disastrous spread of radioactivity, along with the Soviet failure to give due warning? The Soviet investigators in Vienna doggedly restricted themselves to establishing the causes of the accident. With honesty and candor, they presented a simple chain of events leading from the decision to make a technical experiment to the explosion. Most Westerners, on the other hand, wanted the bigger questions addressed: why did the explosion scatter radioactivity far and wide? And why was the world not warned? The Vienna meeting asked these questions, but the Soviet side gave no answers. In fact, the two sides were conducting different investigations:

The accident happened—why?

Radioactive contamination was widespread and hushed up—why?

Deciding exactly what "effect" is under investigation, as you can see, is a very loaded first step.

Step 3: Deciding if There is Proof of Cause and Effect.

The chain of events outlined clearly did cause the accident.

Step 4: Searching for the Whole Range of Causes

To keep things simple, let's accept the Soviet view that only the accident itself should be investigated. How many causes were there? Again Soviet and Western viewpoints differed sharply. Petrosyants, one of the investigators, made the Soviet position clear: "The accident took place as a result of a whole series of gross violations of operating procedures by the workers." (*Time*, September 1, 1986, p. 6) In other words, human error, and human error alone, was to blame. Western commentators disagreed. They spoke of bad design, of incompetent engineers and of ludicrous decision-making procedures. The Western press found other explanations, too. *Time* spoke of a careless attitude to safety: "Soviet engineers and scientists have tended to show much less concern for safety than their Western counterparts." (*Time*, May 12, 1986, p. 14) Economic problems and a shortage of energy were another: ". . . existing nuclear power plants have been forced to pump out more energy than expected, possibly at the expense of routine maintenance." (*Economist*, May 3, 1986, p. 63) If we diagram the Soviet and Western views, the pictures are remarkably different:

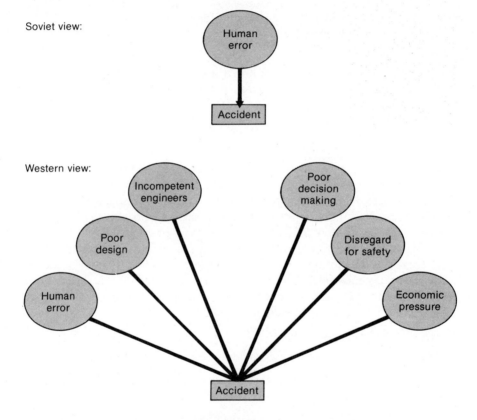

Why the difference? It's a question of goals. The Soviet Union was planning to double nuclear capacity during the next few years; their investigators were saying, in effect: "We have an excellent program, but we also have one or two stupid engineers. If we fire them, the program can go ahead." The goal of the Western press was different: "Let's make the 'other side' look as bad as possible."

Step 5: Extending the Chain Beyond Immediate Causes

The goal of the Soviet investigators was to whitewash their nuclear program by blaming "human error," so they naturally resisted any attempt to extend the chain of causes. The Western press, on the other hand, had a field day extending chains of cause-and-effect in every direction. *Why* are engineers in the Soviet Union incompetent, "the Marx Brothers" according to one *Time* expert? The Soviet educational system, strangulation of technology by the Party bureaucracy, the laxness of the Brezhnev years, the failure of the Soviet system to keep up to date—everything including the imminent collapse of Communism from its own internal contradictions appears in the columns of one newspaper or another. When each contributory cause is traced back in this way, no aspect of Soviet society can escape condemnation as a "cause" of Chernobyl:

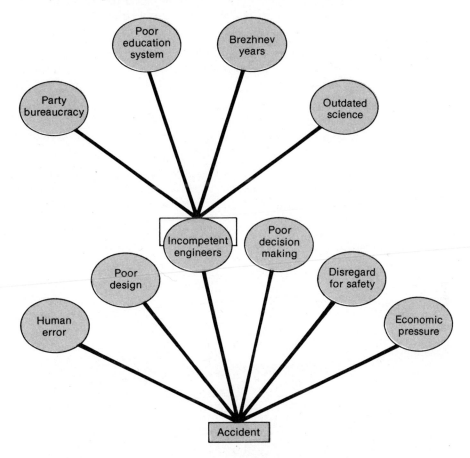

Conclusion. And who is *right*? The Soviet investigators or the Western press? Or maybe the anti-nuclear lobby with its claim that Chernobyl could happen anywhere in the world? The answer depends on how you see the politics of the situation. Nevertheless, an important nonpartisan lesson is clear: the way in which an analysis is conducted depends on the goals of the investigator. Decisions about where to begin an analysis, how many steps to include in it, and so on, may seem to be academic niceties, but they are not. In the real political world, such decisions are the heart of the matter.

Review Assignment

Investigation 3: The Lake of Death

The situation is sudden death in a remote African village. Your task is to sift the evidence and draw a "tree" (like the one in Step 4 of the *Challenger* discussion) showing the pattern of cause-and-effect. (Note that many of the facts given below *cannot* be incorporated into the tree.)

Situation   On the evening of August 21, 1986, in the village of Nios, Cameroon, a smell of burnt gunpowder began to permeate the straw huts of the villagers. It was poison gas. Of the 1,200 villagers, only four survived. All the animals, even the insects, within an area of ten square miles were exterminated as if by a neutron bomb.

The Gas   Investigators established that the gas was a mixture of carbon monoxide, carbon dioxide, and hydrogen sulphide. Carbon monoxide (as in car exhaust fumes) poisons the blood; carbon dioxide suffocates by cutting off oxygen; and hydrogen sulphide (bad-egg gas) affects the central nervous system.

The Source   Where did the gas come from? The village of Nios was built on the slopes of an extinct volcano, the ancient crater forming a blue lake. After the disaster, the lake was a filthy yellow-brown. Somehow, the lake had produced the gas. The gas then spilled out of the crater and, being heavier than air, it rolled downhill, engulfing the village. But how did the lake produce the gas? Two explanations were advanced.

Explanation 1—The Volcano Theory   Perhaps a volcanic eruption at the bottom of the lake shot a huge quantity of gas through the water and out into the crater. Against this theory, one must consider the fact that recording equipment had registered absolutely no seismic disturbances.

Explanation 2—The "Soda can" Theory   In a soda can, carbon dioxide is absorbed and trapped in a liquid; it is trapped by the pressure inside the can. When the can is opened, the pressure is released, and bubbles of gas rise to the surface. The same thing could have happened in the lake. Deep down, gases could have been absorbed by the water and been held in place by the pressure of the lake above. If something disturbed the waters of the lake, the gas would have rushed to the surface. But why was the gas at the bottom of the lake in the first place? Two ideas here: either (1) it had seeped up through the rocks from the core of the volcano deep below, or (2) it was the result of the decay of plant material that had sunk to the bottom of the lake. Probably both explanations are in part correct. But what set the water of the lake in motion, causing the gas to come to the surface? Here investigators found three possible causes: (1) a mini-earthquake, (2) a landslide below the surface of the lake, or (3) the "turnover effect." The turnover effect works like this: gas builds up in the lowest level of water; this process of absorption slowly makes the water "lighter." At a certain critical point, the "light" water starts to rise. This rise could accelerate into an explosion of escaping gas. The turnover effect is generally accepted as the correct explanation.

• Organizing Causes

Having completed your investigation, the next task is organization. Let's take a down-to-earth case: Mitzi Horner is working on a case study for *Sociology 100*: she has been asked to explain why one farm family gave up farming and went to live in the city. The family she chooses is her own. She feels that the fate of her family is typical, and she begins her investigation with a thesis statement clearly in mind: "The small farmer is a dying breed." Her investigation produces this list of causes:

Situation:

In November 1987 the Horners, who had lived in Break's Piece, Indiana, for seventy years, sold out and moved into Bloomington.

1. Abe Horner, the only son, was studying to become a lawyer. The daughter, Mitzi, was training as a journalist. Both lived on the farm during vacations, but neither wanted to take it over when Dan Horner (now aged 60) retired.

2. The barn needed a new roof. In August the bank had refused to lend Dan Horner the money.

3. The selling price for crops was close to production costs in some years.

4. Fuel costs, equipment costs and maintenance costs had all risen to critical levels.

5. Big farming corporations had taken over many farms in the area, and the original farmers had moved away.

6. In October, the Horners were offered an above-market price for their land by John Barleycorn Incorporated.

Mitzi has a list of six causes that must somehow be organized. Order of significance would put the key point last, but with a list of causes, it is often difficult to spot the most "important." Look back for a moment, and try to rank Mitzi's list from least important to most important.

You probably encountered two problems: (1) some causes are very important in the *short term*, while others are equally important in the *long term*, and (2) some causes that hurt badly at the moment might disappear in the future, while others are here to stay. How do you rank the importance of such variables against each other? As so often in writing, analysis of the problem suggests the answer: clustering. In fact, two techniques of clustering emerge from the difficulties just encountered:

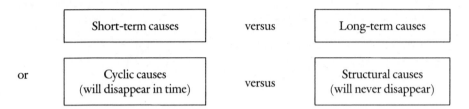

SHORT-TERM AND LONG-TERM CAUSES

First, then, *short-term* versus *long-term* causes. Often a problem grows over the years until something precipitates a crisis. A simple example: Why did John and Mary get a divorce? Because he complained one night about his supper. Obviously, although John's complaint triggered the divorce, it was not the real cause; it was just the last straw that broke the camel's back. With Mitzi's family, there were two "last straws": (1) the refusal of the rebuilding loan for the barn roof, and (2) the sudden offer of a good price for the land. The other four causes are middle- or long-term considerations. This division gives Mitzi two sub-lists:

Short-Term
The refusal of the rebuilding loan
The offer to purchase

Long-Term
Falling prices for farm produce
Rising costs
Increase in big-business farming
The children's refusal to stay on the farm

If she discusses the short-term (or immediate) causes first, Mitzi shouldn't have much problem deciding an appropriate order for the long-term causes; her thesis statement, you remember, is: "The small farmer is a dying breed."

CYCLIC AND STRUCTURAL CAUSES

The second way of organizing causes divides them into cyclic causes (which are virtually programmed to go away) and structural causes (which are here to stay). Farming is in a perpetual boom-and-bust cycle. During the period Mitzi is writing about, farming is "going bust," so the boom is presumably somewhere round the corner: at some stage, crop prices will rise, costs will stabilize, and the banks will be ready to lend money.

Cyclic Causes (Causes that will disappear as the cycle moves on)
The fall in crop prices
The rise in production costs
The difficulties in borrowing money from the bank

Many *structural* changes are taking place in farming, however. Big business is taking over—a change that will not be reversed. Once Dan has sold his land, the children will never get it back. These permanent changes cluster together, probably in the second half of the essay.

Structural Causes (Causes that are permanent)
The takeover by big business
The offer that Dan cannot refuse
The children's unwillingness (and lack of opportunity) to return

Mitzi could use either of these organizing strategies: her choice will depend on the strategy that best supports her thesis statement. Because the cyclic versus structural strategy highlights the offer Dan can't refuse, which is itself part of the takeover by big business, that might be the better choice.

Concept Review

Clustering Causes

Imagine that you are writing about Supersafe Tools, Incorporated. In 1988 the company has a record-breaking year. There are six causes of this success:

a. In 1983 the company decided to spend 25 percent of its profits on training; this policy has produced excellent new people and products.

b. The city where Supersafe has its factory has been a boom town through the mid-eighties, although expansion has now peaked.

c. Last year the old, conservative owner died; the company is now run by his aggressive, talented daughter—a real "whiz kid."

d. Six months ago the company successfully computerized its warehouse, thus making huge cost savings.

e. Demand for the main product lines of Supersafe Tools has been boosted during the last six years by increased military spending.

f. Supersafe had only one serious competitor, Worktools, Incorporated. This company went bankrupt a year ago, an event that helped sales at Supersafe. Unfortunately, other companies are already taking up the slack.

Split up this list into long-term versus short-term causes.
Then split it up into cyclic versus structural causes.

• Case Study or Global Analysis?

Mitzi's sociology professor asked for a *case study* based on the experience of a single family, but he could just as well have asked for a *global analysis* of rural depopulation or "The Current Crisis of the Small Farmer." Let's look at these two terms more closely. A *case study* investigates a single occurrence or situation; usually this special case is typical of the "big picture." The *global analysis* investigates the "big picture" in general terms, drawing on a range of cases and sources. The *Challenger* investigation was a case study, but it could easily be re-run in a general form: "NASA is more accident-prone than it should be; why?" Even Carlotta's excessive housework could become a general question: "Many middle-aged women become excessively anxious about domestic hygiene; why?"

The *organization* of a case study and a global analysis are much the same; even the wording of the thesis statement might be identical, whether you come to it from a single case or from a wide-ranging study. (Mitzi's thesis statement, "The small farmer is a dying breed," is typical in this respect.) On the other hand, the process of *investigation* changes radically if you opt for the case study against the global analysis, or vice versa. For this reason, it helps to decide from the outset whether you are working specifically or generally. Let's say the essay requirement for a class is this:

> **Course Requirements**
>
> An 800-word term paper is required: the subject should be agreed upon with the instructor before mid-term. The paper should address some important social problem in contemporary life.

How should you proceed? Probably you should try formulating a subject in different ways: global analysis formulations follow this pattern:

a. Homosexuals have not achieved full social acceptance; why not?

b. Account for the continuing illegal immigration into the United States.

c. Why do women's earnings still lag behind those of men?

Case-oriented formulations of the same subjects look rather different:

a. Axel Drobbning could not achieve social acceptance in Smallville, Idaho, because of his sexual preference; why was this?

b. Ramon T. is now living and working illegally in southern California. Why has he taken up this dangerous and unrewarding lifestyle?

c. In Petermax Workshops, Incorporated, (where I work) women earn about half of what men earn, just as they did in 1954. What accounts for this failure to change?

Naturally, if you get stuck, you can change horses in midstream. The most common change is that an ambitious global analysis finally settles down as a straightforward case study.

You may have noticed that investigative journalists, looking for human interest, often present a single, highly dramatic case; the reader is expected to accept the case as typical of a trend. This technique becomes questionable if the case is presented as a real one but has actually been "adjusted" to make it more shocking or more representative. (See the *Close-Up* below.) How much should you "adjust" your material? Ethical judgments as well as technical decisions are involved in writing essays.

Review Assignment

Case Study or Global Analysis?

As practice at formulating, reword each of the following subjects into a general, global analysis question.

a. Robert Hutchings tried to escape the ghetto but failed; why?

b. Although she was a promising athlete and in excellent health, Minna Fairfax died of an overdose of drugs. What led to this tragedy?

c. Patrick Ryan, at the age of 22, gave his fortune to charity and went to live in a community of Buddhist monks. What accounts for his behavior?

Conversely, try for a specific, case study formulation of these subjects:

a. Why are increasing numbers of adults returning to schools and universities?

b. Foreign cars are taking an ever-growing share of the U.S. market. Why is this?

c. Normal children are often misdiagnosed as having some kind of learning disability. How do you account for this problem?

Close-Up

Investigating the Investigator

A Pulitzer Prize is the highest recognition a journalist can receive. The competition is fierce. On April 15, 1981, a journalist with the *Washington Post*, Janet Cooke, was given a Pulitzer Prize for an article called "Jimmy's World." This report movingly describes the fate of an eight-year-old boy who is injected with heroin by his mother's boyfriend, a dope pusher, and who becomes addicted. Days later, the *Washington Post* revealed that there was no Jimmy. Janet Cooke resigned, admitting that she had invented Jimmy, and the prize was returned. A number of attitudes to what Cooke had done surfaced during late April and early May. Which attitudes do you find most reasonable?

1. "I am worried about this debacle because it has befouled institutions that are important to me." James Michener.

2. "Other fabrications, on a less spectacular scale, go by every day in news stories. Every day reporters 'embellish' quotes from an individual to make them 'sound better' or to fit the point of the story." Jane Perlez, media critic of the New York *Daily News*. Did Cooke merely "embellish"?

3. "I hope they do better in the future." Richard Nixon, denouncing the *Washington Post* for being "irresponsible."

4. "This newspaper . . . was itself the victim of a hoax." *Washington Post*. Is "hoax" an appropriate word?

5. "I was very firm in my convinction that Miss Cooke's article was part myth, part reality." Mayor Barry of Washington (after the failure of his police department to locate "Jimmy" and give him medical help). Myth?

6. "Miss Cooke . . . would make a fine novelist." James Michener. (Was her work fiction, as such?)

7. ". . . the kid *did* exist—maybe not the specific kid but, somewhere in the city, a kid just like that." Art Spikol (expressing Cooke's basic argument).

8. "I deserved it." Janet Cooke (speaking of her rough treatment when the *Post* found out the truth).

2 •

The Personal Voice

Before their first publication, most magazines develop a preview issue; this issue shows "the stuff we're made of." In the Spring of 1972, *Ms* magazine included in its preview this stunning polemic by Judy Syfers. Although Syfers answers the cause-and-effect question "I want a wife—why?" her unrelenting sarcasm serves other ends.

I WANT A WIFE

I belong to that classification of people known as wives. I am A Wife. And, not altogether incidentally, I am a mother.

Not too long ago a male friend of mine appeared on the scene fresh from a recent divorce. He had one child, who is, of course, with his ex-wife. He is obviously looking for another wife. As I thought about him while I was ironing one evening, it suddenly occurred to me that I, too, would like to have a wife. Why do I want a wife?

I would like to go back to school so that I can become economically independent, support myself, and, if need be, support those dependent upon me. I want a wife who will work and send me to school. And while I am going to school I want a wife to take care of the children. I want a wife to keep track of the children's doctor and dentist appointments. And to keep track of mine too. I want a wife to make sure my children eat properly and are kept clean. I want a wife who will wash the children's clothes and keep them mended. I want a wife who is a good nurturant attendant to my children, who arranges for their schooling, makes sure that they have an adequate social life with their peers, takes them to the park, the zoo, et cetera. I want a wife who takes care of the children when they are sick, a wife who arranges to be around when the children need special care, because, of course, I cannot miss classes at school. My wife must arrange to lose time at work and not lose the job. It may mean a small cut in my wife's income from time to time, but I guess I can tolerate that. Needless to say, my wife will arrange and pay for the care of the children while my wife is working.

I want a wife who will take care of my physical needs. I want a wife who will keep my house clean. A wife who will pick up after me. I want a wife who will keep my clothes clean, ironed, mended, replaced when need be, and who will see to it that my personal things are kept in their proper place so that I can find what I need the minute I need it. I want a wife who cooks the meals, a wife who is a *good* cook. I want a wife who will plan the menus, do the necessary grocery shopping, prepare the meals, serve them pleasantly, and then do the cleaning up while I do my studying. I want a wife who will care for me when I am sick and sympathize with my pain and loss of time from school. I want a wife to go along when our family takes a vacation so that someone can continue to care for me and my children when I need a rest and change of scene.

I want a wife who will not bother me with rambling complaints about a wife's duties. But I want a wife who will listen to me when I feel the need to explain a rather difficult point I have come across in my course of studies. And I want a wife who will type my papers for me when I have written them.

I want a wife who will take care of the details of my social life. When my wife and I are invited out by my friends, I want a wife who will take care of the baby-sitting arrangements. When I meet people at school whom I like and want to entertain, I want a wife who will have the house clean, will prepare a special meal, serve it to me and my friends, and not interrupt when I talk about the things that interest me and my friends. I want a wife who will have arranged that the children are fed and ready for bed before my guests arrive so that the children do not bother us.

And I want a wife who knows that sometimes I need a night out by myself.

I want a wife who is sensitive to my sexual needs, a wife who makes love passionately and eagerly when I feel like it, a wife who makes sure that I am satisfied. And, of course, I want a wife who will not demand sexual attention when I am not in the mood for it. I want a wife who assumes the complete responsibility for birth control, because I do not want more children. I want a wife who will remain sexually faithful to me so that I do not have to clutter up my intellectual life with jealousies. And I want a wife who understands that *my* sexual needs may entail more than strict adherence to monogamy. I must, after all, be able to relate to people as fully as possible.

If, by chance, I find another person more suitable as a wife than the wife I already have, I want the liberty to replace my present wife with another one. Naturally, I will expect a fresh, new life; my wife will take the children and be solely responsible for them so that I am left free.

When I am through with school and have a job, I want my wife to quit working and remain at home so that my wife can more fully and completely take care of a wife's duties.

My God, who *wouldn't* want a wife?

Review Assignment

The Limits of Editorial English

Syfers has not written her piece in "standard, academic, written English," or *editorial English* as it is sometimes called. Some examples: her insistent use of *I* goes against the "rules"; she uses sentence fragments; many sentences begin with *And* or *But*; there are "slangy" forms such as *I guess* or *My God* all through the piece. What justifies Syfers in taking these liberties?

Syfers's personal voice is probably beyond successful imitation (although husbands might try a piece entitled I want a Husband, or mothers might enjoy writing I want a Mother). To get a real sense of how the *voice* of this piece contributes to its effect, try rewriting a part of it in "editorial English" without *I* and without the racy speech forms. You'll probably find that your new version is far poorer.

3 •
Writing Workshop—
Investigating Cause and Effect

• Choosing a Subject

Many of the subjects below could be formulated either in a *specific* form (which calls for a single case study) or in a *general* form (which calls for a global analysis). Be ready to make the necessary change if the formulation does not suit your purposes.

First, investigations based on firsthand observation of a bad situation:

1. A hospital patient known to you died unnecessarily—why?
2. Someone you knew at school or in your workplace was treated as an outcast—why?
3. A marriage you observed closely collapsed—why?
4. A colleague was unjustly passed over for promotion (or unjustly promoted) —why?
5. A promising high school student failed to "make good"—why?
6. Someone known to you became a juvenile delinquent—why?
7. A business you worked for went bankrupt (or was very successful)—why?
8. Morale in an organization known to you was very low (or very high)—why?
9. Someone you know left your church (or joined it)—why?

10. A holiday you once took turned into a disaster—why?

Decisions, especially hard ones, can be analyzed in terms of causes:

11. You may recently have decided to begin a course of study—why?

12. You may have made a career decision: to change to another field, to change employers, to seek promotion—why?

13. Perhaps a "life decision" was involved: engagement, marriage, divorce, starting a family, buying a house—again why?

14. A management decision could also suggest a subject: a decision to go ahead with a project, or to cancel one, to purchase new machinery, to rethink a procedure. Why did you make this decision?

15. As a parent, you may have made an important decision for one of your children: to change schools, to restrict access to television, to seek professional counseling—why?

Questions about our society usually call for a global analysis. Be especially ready here to switch to a specific case study:

16. The small farmer is vanishing from the American countryside—why?

17. City dwellers are moving into the suburbs—why?

18. Homosexuals have not achieved full social acceptance—why not?

19. Church membership has been increasing in recent years—why?

20. The use of (hard) drugs by high school students is declining—why?

21. Society no longer thinks so highly of the soldier as it once did—why?

22. Many people find it hard to discover meaningful sexual relationships—why?

23. Violent crime is on the increase—why?

24. Society is swinging back to "traditional" moral value—why?

25. The women's movement has not achieved a strong working-class following—why not?

26. Unemployment is particularly high in the ghettos—why?

27. Educational standards in the United States have been slipping—why?

28. Enlistment in the armed services has been very strong in recent years—why?

29. Campus radicals are a dying breed; the yuppies are taking over—why?

30. Women are having their first babies much later in life than they once did—why?

Writing on political, economic, or industrial developments usually requires prior knowledge or library reading. Be prepared for research here:

31. The Volkswagen Beetle outsold any other car ever made—why?

32. President Reagan lost a great deal of popularity over the sale of arms to Iran and related issues—why?

33. The Equal Rights Amendment was not ratified—why?

34. Soviet-American relations are less cordial than they once were—why?

35. The boom in the sale of personal computers has slowed down—why?

36. The movement against the use of nuclear power has been gaining strength —why?

37. Society is more aware of ecological issues than it used to be—why?

38. Europeans (especially Czechs) seem to have taken over international tennis —why?

39. The Strategic Defense Initiative (SDI) has failed to gain widespread support, especially among scientists—why?

40. A group (or an individual musician) suddenly faded after an initial success —why?

• Developing a Game Plan

An analysis of cause-and-effect is an investigation. Brainstorming for causes, as we saw earlier, is a systematic process, tracing back lines of causation, working sometimes with a tree diagram to keep a clear overview. To turn a tree diagram into a game plan, you must formulate a thesis statement and decide upon an appropriate structure. First, the thesis statement.

Let's say you're investigating a down-to-earth subject: "Our softball team has lost six consecutive games—why?" Your investigation has three purposes: (1) to discover the causes of the situation, (2) to say how the situation could have been prevented and perhaps to apportion blame, and (3) to suggest action that will end the losing streak. A *positive thesis statement* for a cause-and-effect investigation can derive from any one of these purposes (or from a combination). This gives us three "formulas":

1. These are the causes of the situation.

2. This is how the situation could have been prevented.

3. This is what must be done to prevent a recurrence.

The report on the *Challenger* disaster combined all three: it explained the causes, apportioned blame, and suggested better procedures for the future. Your softball essay could do the same.

If you're examining not a disaster but a success story, then formula number (2) is unlikely to apply, and formula number (3) becomes: What lessons can be learned from this success that can be applied in the future?

A *negative thesis statement* is also possible:

1. We do not know what caused the problem.

2. We do not see how the problem could have been prevented.

3. It is impossible to prevent a recurrence of such problems.

Your softball report might also have come to one (or more) of these conclusions.

Concept Review

Investigation and the Thesis Statement

a. Look back at the poison gas investigation earlier in the chapter. What kind of thesis statement would be appropriate in an essay on that subject? Positive or negative? Type 1, 2 or 3?

b. Look at the Chernobyl investigation once more. How would you word the Soviet explanation as a thesis statement? How would you word the viewpoint of the most pessimistic Western commentators?

c. Mitzi Horner's thesis statement was, "The small farmer is a dying breed." What kind of thesis statement is this?

Let's now follow Chuck Taylor, a beginning student, as he puts together his game plan. Chuck's subject is "The Black Ghetto is Violent, Bitter and Angry —why?" Chuck's firsthand observation suggests three causes which he works into a "tree":

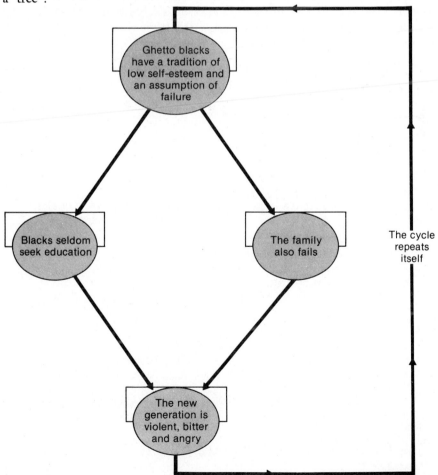

This "tree" is a little odd-looking because Chuck's chain of cause-and-effect is, in fact, a cyclic process. (See Chapter 2 on *dynamic description* to review this kind of process.) This will create a small (but familiar) problem: keeping the reader aware at all times that the cycle is unbroken and unending. The fork may also throw the reader off track unless Chuck handles it carefully: the assumption of failure leads to the lack of education *and* to the collapse of the family; these two things then combine to create the bitterness Chuck is writing about.

What, then, is Chuck's thesis? For years he had watched money being thrown at the problem, but nothing had changed. In Chuck's words: "No welfare, Medicaid, or government housing project has had any impact on the lives of the people I grew up with. When people truly believe in themselves, then, and only then, will their quality of life change, because they will change it themselves."

Developing a structure is easy enough since the flow diagram already contains the pattern. The obvious starting point is an evil tradition—centuries of low self-esteem and a self-defeating assumption of failure. This has two terrible consequences: (1) people ignore their one real chance to escape the ghetto, education, and (2) families fail and fall apart. Deprived of education and family support, the young grow up like their parents, violent, bitter, and angry. The cycle is thus renewed with each generation. Chuck's game plan, then (rewritten in sentence form for greater transparency), is as follows:

Situation:

The violence, bitterness and anger in the black ghetto

Causes:

1. A tradition of low self-esteem has devastated black identity.
    a. During the slavery years, blacks were told that they were less than human, and they were traded like cattle.
    b. The Jim Crow laws operated until recently—blacks were not even allowed to use the same toilets as whites.
    c. The media. Tarzan shows Africans as more stupid than monkeys.

2. An assumption of failure makes blacks give up on education.
    a. There is no pressure in the home to get an education.
    b. Many drop out (me included).
    c. Without education, most fall back on "easy" ways of making money: drug-pushing and prostitution.

3. Broken homes have crippled the black ghetto.
    a. Fathers who were there were often drunk or abusive.
    b. My own home—six children, no father, and an angry, overworked mother.
    c. We felt it was our fault Dad left. He'd tried his best, and failed, and we couldn't help him. We took out our frustration by smashing things.
    d. We had no positive role models. The only "successful" people we saw were criminals.

Thesis:

A handful are lucky and escape, as I did. For the majority, only a new self-respect can break this destructive cycle.

• Writing the First Draft

Writing the first draft of an investigation into cause-and-effect follows the guidelines established in the Introduction to Part 2. All that needs to be added are some thoughts on the opening.

THE OPENING

An investigation starts with a situation. Your essay should do the same. This situation is a *given*; it cannot be in any way debated. Let's say, for example, you're writing on "The Causes of the Increase in Violent Crime." Some criminologists say that there has been no increase in crime—just an increase in reporting. If you agree, then you cannot analyze cause-and-effect. Why not? Because you have no increase in crime to account for.

What makes a sound opening then? Compare for a moment these two openings:

When Alan at the age of fifteen was sent to a New York detention center for juvenile delinquents, it was no surprise to me. I'd watched him grow up through a childhood of abuse and neglect, and I understood his antisocial behavior only too well.

Garbage lines the streets of the neighborhood I grew up in. Walls, signs, even the sidewalks are spray-painted with filthy language. The building next to ours is now an empty shell with a mound of debris where people once lived. Someone is lying face down in the alley where we used to play. A dope addict maybe, or a prostitute—it could even be a friend. Nobody bothers to find out. Why are people like this? Why is the black ghetto so filled with violence, bitterness and anger?

Both of these openings try to "hook" the reader. Each presents a situation that is the result of a chain of cause-and-effect. There are some differences, however. The first opening is from a student essay by Eunice Valentine. It is the classic *Who* (Alan), *What* (sent to a detention center), *Where* (New York), and *When* (at age fifteen) opening. Eunice gets straight into the problem with her second sentence. The second opening is much more descriptive. For a moment the reader half anticipates a work of fiction: this is how a story might begin. But then Chuck (you recognized his subject) picked up his theme with the question *Why?* This is also an effective opening. Either way, in skeleton or in detail, the opening of a cause-and-effect essay presents the reader with the situation under investigation.

• Revising

The Flowchart on page 119 offers a general scheme for revising your first draft. Re-read this material carefully. Revising an investigation of cause-and-effect presents no unique problems. It is worth remembering, however, that a chain of cause-and-effect is very like a dynamic description. If your chain is cyclic (if, like Chuck in the previous section, you want the reader to start and finish in the same place), or if the chain contains branchings, then you might like to review these writing problems and their solutions in Chapter 2, pages 43–51.

• The Final Draft

Our example of an end product is not a high-level investigation into an international disaster but a strictly personal essay. Dawn worked as a therapist in the psychiatric ward of a hospital. The subject she is addressing here is the *frustration, depression and anger* she feels at work. Dawn found it difficult to explain how she'd created her piece—she wrote fiercely and impulsively, often with little evident planning. The structure of her piece is simple: one paragraph on each of her coworkers. The three main paragraphs are, in fact, classic static descriptions: the writing is highly concrete and ruthlessly filtered. Dawn did not use section headings; her paper is very personal, and she wanted to avoid the stiff, formal framework that section headings usually create. (As always, each writing decision is a matter of judgment based on your current purposes.) The strength of Dawn's writing is the way it forces the reader to take her side. After reading it, you'll probably feel: "Yes, if I were in her situation, I'd feel frustrated too." How is the effect achieved? Probably through the concreteness and the lively sarcasm of the description: Sheila, Janey, and Mack come horribly alive.

Psychiatry Blues

Who, What, Where and When opening

Two years ago I started work as a therapist in the psychiatric ward of a large general hospital. I enjoy working with the patients but, even so, my days on the ward are filled with frustration, depression, and anger. — **Lead-in sentence**

First cause introduced (Sheila causes frustration)

The frustration is supplied by Sheila. According to the organization chart on her office wall, Sheila is in charge of the ward. Sheila is a lumpy woman of no particular size or shape, with mousy hair and eyes that never make contact with mine. She pads about the ward, closing the doors silently behind her. Her impact as a supervisor is as indefinite as her footsteps. Sheila has a hard time deciding where to have lunch, which typewriter to use, which speed the fan should be on, and where to post a note so that everyone will see it. Her inability to make simple decisions usually disrupts her life more than it disrupts mine, but when her indecisiveness interferes with patient care, then frustration strikes the whole ward, nurses and patients alike. One example: traditionally Friday afternoons are not devoted to arts and crafts but to a fun activity of some sort. Most Friday afternoons I spend watching Sheila trying to decide on the activity. The patients sit at the tables, listening apathetically while Sheila lists endless activities that <u>might</u> be possible; she expects these mental health patients to assume her burden of decision-making. I have tried to be assertive and make suggestions. I think I become most frustrated when Sheila can't decide (as a preliminary to evaluating my idea) whether a mere therapist has the necessary training to suggest ideas at all. — **Descriptive detail using the controlling filter** *indecisive* — **Anecdote begins** — **Pointing: extreme level of frustration**

Second cause introduced (Janey causes depression)

The second factor that interferes with my work is depression. The depression would probably interfere less if it were my own; as it is, Janey has enough for the entire hospital. Janey is Sheila's "right-hand man." Janey is tough-looking and sturdy, with cropped hair and hard-tanned skin. Appearances can be deceptive. Underneath, Janey is as soggy as a rectal suppository. About once a week Janey's husband is unpleasant to her: he will have forgotten a lunch date or ignored her in the hallways of the hospital. First she becomes angry. Pacing back and forward across the carpet, she showily snaps No. 2 pencils. Her cheeks turn bright red before she begins to cry. I try to comfort her, agree that men are scoundrels, and move the patients' progress notes before they become a blotchy, inky mess. After Janey has calmed down, we spend a great deal of time discussing her feelings. By the time she is secure again and ready to face the day, I am depressed and longing for the day to end. — **Descriptive detail using the controlling filter** *depressive* — **Pointing: the end product of Janey's depressive-ness**

Mack just makes me angry. Like me, he is employed as a therapist, but he seems to despise the

CHAPTER SIX
The Multi-Element Paper—Investigating Causes

Third cause introduced (Mack causes anger)

job. Instead he attends to the mundane needs of the clinic, and especially to Sheila's needs, since his only chance of promotion depends on her. Mack has the beer paunch typical of the unpromotable failure; he wears inch-and-a-half-thick eyeglasses on his nose and taps on his heels. Things can become hectic on a psychiatric ward, and then I need a backup. Often I have sighed with relief hearing those taps hit the stairs, only to become angry as Mack walks by. If I ask for help, Mack is busy "checking something in the records." Sometimes when I am helping a patient, Mack shouts out for me to fetch him an extension cord, a Phillips screwdriver, or more document protectors. At this point my anger boils over. I exhaust my locker room vocabulary on Mack and then try to calm down for another day of basketweaving with my patients. It isn't always easy.

Descriptive detail using the controlling filter *unsupportive*

Pointing: the anger overflows

Wrap-up: there is no escape

Personnel problems are Janey's responsibility; however, when I complain to her about Mack, she reminds me that husbands are just as unsupportive towards their wives, and that the lack of support from a mere colleague should not surprise me. When I go to the top, Sheila can never decide if her pencil is sharp enough to take notes or if she is undermining Janey's "authority" by listening to me at all.

General discussion leading to the thesis statement. (In this case the thesis does *not* relate the case study to some general principle)

The result of this frustration, depression and anger is that I dread going to work and often have a headache soon after I arrive. The problem is not equipment, organization, time, or money: it is people. My job is interesting and worthwhile, but the attitudes of my coworkers limit my productivity, disturb my mood, and hamper my ability to deal with my patients.

PART TWO
The Essay

• Summary: The Flowchart

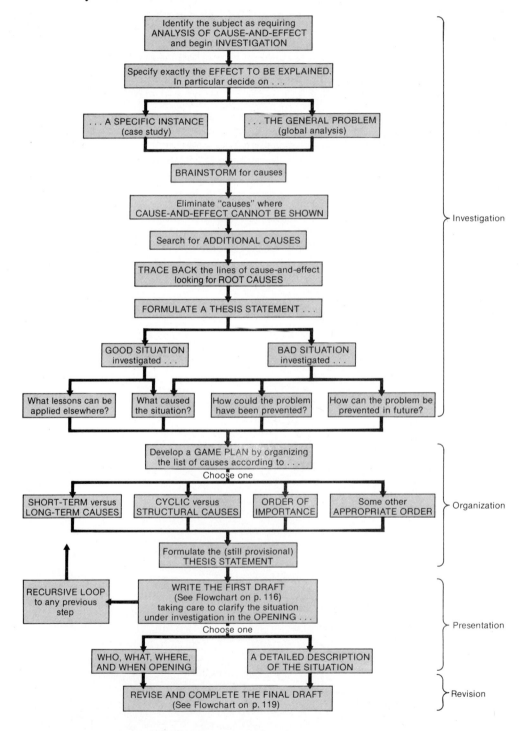

SEVEN

Getting Them All—Classification

1 •
The Problem:
The Riddle of the Unknown Number

- **Sorting and Filing: The All-Inclusive System**

SCENE: An Office during the summer vacation period
CAST: The Boss
       The Secretary
       The Temporary standing in while the Secretary is on vacation

ACT 1: LOVE, ANGIE

TEMPORARY: What do I do about this letter?
BOSS: File it.
TEMPORARY: Where though?
BOSS: I thought Marie went over filing with you before she left.
TEMPORARY: She did, but I don't think this letter has a file.
BOSS: Impossible. I designed the filing system myself.
TEMPORARY: Okay, but I still don't know where to file it.

BOSS: (Angrily) What's it about then?
TEMPORARY: It just says "You were great—Love, Angie."
BOSS: Give that to me!!

ACT 2: HOLIDAY CLEANUP

BOSS: You've been standing in front of that filing cabinet for the last hour. What's the trouble now?
TEMPORARY: Another letter I don't know where to put.
BOSS: Who's it from this time?
TEMPORARY: The window cleaner. It's his vacation schedule.
BOSS: Then put it under Vacation Schedules.
TEMPORARY: There's no such file. How about Building Maintenance?
BOSS: Vacation Schedules, I said.
TEMPORARY: Or Hired-In Services?
BOSS: You heard me.
TEMPORARY: Or Cleaning? Or Auxiliary Personnel? Or Office Hygiene? Or Local Contractors? Or . . .
BOSS: Put it in my Pending tray—okay?

ACT 3: PARTY LINE

SECRETARY: Anything you couldn't find while I was gone?
TEMPORARY: He wanted to know what the Christmas Party cost last year.
SECRETARY: Oh, the party. That goes in a kind of a joke file. He broke his leg on the same day as the party one year, so we always file party stuff under Broken Legs.
TEMPORARY: Broken Legs!
SECRETARY: I thought everybody knew about it.
TEMPORARY: Everybody except me and the boss.

Anyone who has worked in an office knows problems like these. A filing system must foresee every eventuality and allow for it. With Angie's little note, the system collapsed. This gives us *Rule 1* for filing systems: *Everything must have a slot somewhere within the system.*

Letters are sometimes lost, even in the best operated filing systems. Why? The problem is "multiple entry." The window cleaner's vacation schedule can enter the filing system in too many places. And so: *Rule 2: Nothing must fit into two slots equally well.*

The final problem is that systems become too "personalized"—the file names should be clear even to outsiders. *Rule 3: The names used for the slots must be readily understandable.*

It's clear that these three rules apply to filing systems; but how do they apply to academic essays? Many essay subjects are so general that neither you nor your instructor can know how many elements are actually involved. An example: "Discuss the tactics that have been used against terrorists." How many tactics are involved here? An indefinitely large number. How can you cope? Choosing a few of the more interesting is a fatal mistake since the question asks you to discuss them *all*. In fact, in analyzing terrorist tactics, the three rules that govern an office filing system also apply: You must (1) cover *all the tactics*, (2) allow *no overlap*, and (3) use *understandable labels* for the categories. How would you set up such an analysis?

The pie graph, now a familiar feature of computer graphics, provides the answer. A pie graph is simply a circle representing 100 percent of whatever is being analyzed. Like a pie, a pie graph is cut into slices, with each slice representing a distinct part of the whole. One possible idea among many:

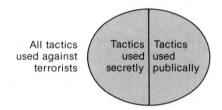

All tactics used against terrorists | Tactics used secretly | Tactics used publically

All tactics used against terrorists

Ignoring the *exact* percentages, we can show that this division follows the three rules closely:

> **Rule 1:** *Everything must have a slot somewhere within the system.*
> Is every conceivable tactic that could be used against terrorists either *public* or *secret*? It seems so.
>
> **Rule 2:** *Nothing must fit into two slots equally well.*
> Could any tactic be both public and private at the same time? It seems unlikely.
>
> **Rule 3:** *The names used for the slots must be readily understandable (or easily definable).*
> The labels *public* and *secret* are easy to grasp; any problems could be resolved with a few words of definition.

The process of "slicing the pie," or *classification*, to use its formal title, is a powerful tool once you know how to use it. Let's explore a little further by looking at some pie graphs and asking if they follow the rules or not. *Movies* make a convenient subject. Below are five pie graphs that classify movies from five different perspectives: the first looks at *cost*, the second at *use of color*, and so on. This perspective is called the *rationale* of the classification. Each graph is critiqued using the three rules. Study each graph and try to understand *why* it is critiqued as it is.

Five Ways of Looking at Movies

Rule 1: Everything must have a slot somewhere within the system.

Rule 2: Nothing must fit into two slots equally well.

Rule 3: The names used for the slots should be readily understandable (or easily definable).

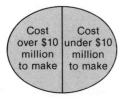

Rationale: Cost
Breaks Rule 1 (A movie that cost exactly $10 million would have no place in the circle.)

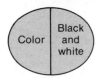

Rationale: Use of Color
Breaks Rule 2 (Some movies, for example, *The Wizard of Oz*, fit both slots.)

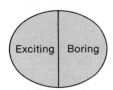

Rationale: Entertainment value
Breaks Rule 3 (What is exciting to one person may bore someone else; closer definition of the terms would be difficult.)

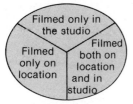

Rationale: Place of filming
Must be okay (There are only two places a film can be made: in the studio or outside the studio, that is, on location. With studio plus location allowed, there can be no other possibilities.)

Rationale: Subject Matter of the Movie
Offends all the rules
Rule 1: What about documentaries? War films? Children's movies? Home movies?

Rule 2: Combinations exist: a comedy-western, a sci-fi drama, a musical comedy.

Rule 3: A spy movie versus a thriller? The difference is not immediately clear and could not easily be defined.

Concept Review

Classifying

This time the subject is cars. In each case, give the *rationale* behind the classification, and then critique it according to the three rules, just as movies were critiqued on the previous page. Further, if you find errors, then improve the classification.

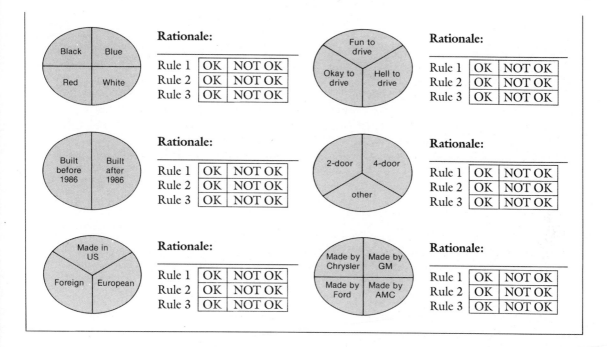

Top-Down and Bottom-Up Classification: A Problem of Verification

Using pie graph classification, nothing is simpler than to take a subject, slice up the circle, and get writing. Two student improvisations show the idea:

Men Who Drink Beer

There are three types of male beer drinkers: slow, normal and fast. The slow type is the sipper. The sipper is either a truly delicate person or someone who hates beer. The sipper never finishes his beer. His routine is to lift the can cautiously to his mouth and allow the beer to moisten his lips. He may tilt the can back to impress you, but his mouth is closed and nothing enters. He then sets the can down with a thoughtful expression on his face. Next, the sipper engages in a long conversation or leaves the drinking area on some pretext. When he returns, or when he has nothing more to say, he repeats his non-drinking routine once more. The second type of beer drinker is the normal person. The normal person spends ten to twenty minutes drinking his beer. He picks up the can and raises it to his lips in a normal manner, taking a normal swallow. After each swallow, he sets his beer can down in a normal way, says a few normal words to the people around him, and then repeats the swallowing process. The fast type is the guzzler. The guzzler is a person from whom it would be possible to make a living simply by selling him beer. The guzzler attacks his beer. He empties the can so fast it collapses because of the unequal pressure. Although the guzzler saves time on drinking, he must waste several seconds wiping foam from his nose and chin. After the wiping process, he belches and is ready for his next beer.

Guy Mitchell

Dancers

At a dance the other night, I spotted three types of dancers. The first was the studio dancer. These people whirled about the floor, the epitome of grace, never missing a step. They probably learned to dance this way in studios run by washed-out ballet dancers. Their eyes swept snobbishly round the room, pausing only when they caught their own reflections in a mirror. Those little pauses were the only spontaneous movements they made during the whole evening. Then there were the careful dancers. These people kept their eyes fixed on other dancers, comparing their own movements, and revising their performance accordingly. Their jerky, second-hand steps became ever more grotesque as the evening wore on. Finally, the windmills. The windmills were wholeheartedly in the "let-it-be" movement. They flailed their way across the floor, with arms and legs flying in improbable directions. Their eyes were closed: they had escaped all constraints of space—and of common courtesy. They danced with the pillars, the floor, the PA system, with virtually anything except a fellow human being. Normal dancers? I didn't see one.

John Williams

Do these two classifications follow the rules? In the case of Guy's paragraph on beer drinkers, the answer is "Yes" without any reservations. The classification is logically perfect: fast, normal, slow. It is logically impossible for any beer drinker to remain outside these categories, and a clear line can be drawn between the categories to prevent overlap. Guy's approach to classification is (to use a now familiar term) *top-down*. He begins with a perfect system and then sketches in appropriate detail about each category.

John Williams' paragraph on dancers is more difficult to evaluate. He is working *bottom-up*, trying to remember an actual dance and the types that he actually saw there. Did he get them *all*? Obviously neither he nor the reader can be sure. At best John can say: "As far as I can recall, there were no other types."

For you as a writer, the significance is this: working top-down you can verify your classification *logically*; you can be sure you're on absolutely safe ground. Working bottom-up (which in practice most writers do) makes verification tough: you can verify your classification only *empirically*, and you run the risk that a better informed reader (your instructor!) may find it defective. The two terms then: *logical verification* allows you to prove logically and beyond all argument that your classification (normally top-down) is correct; *empirical verification* forces you to work harder, trying to find categories missing from your (normally bottom-up) classification.

Another point that applies to both paragraphs: they have a problem with the thesis statement. What are these two writers *saying*? Nothing. They are simply classifying. This problem besets many classification essays: they are "perfect," but they are meaningless. More on this later in the chapter.

Concept Review

Students

For each of the following classifications, say whether it is logically verifiable or empirically verifiable. The subject is "Students."

Review Assignment

Writing a "Meaningless Paragraph"

Take some humdrum, million-times-repeated activity, and classify the ways of doing it on a pie graph. Then free-write a paragraph based on the pie graph. When you've finished the paragraph, decide whether or not it is "meaningless." Subjects might include the ways of:

Eating spaghetti	Changing a baby	Avoiding saying hello
Making a bed	Parking a car	Smiling
Cleaning shoes	Blowing one's nose	Avoiding wrinkles
Getting a pay raise	Cleaning one's teeth	Drinking soup
Excusing late papers	Reading a newspaper	Complaining about grades

• How Many Slices? A Problem of Hierarchy

Imagine that you're taking *Psychology 310: Perception* and that the professor sends the class to the zoo. The purpose of the trip is to study the ways in which the visitors look at (or perceive) the animals. Let's say you go to the zoo with no preconceptions, ready to work bottom-up. After an hour or two of studying the visitors, you have a list of ten different observation styles. Your rationale is *the kind of animal each visitor showed most interest in*. The list:

1. Watched *nothing*—walked straight ahead without turning the head
2. Watched only *teenage specimens* (human)
3. Exclusively a *bird* watcher
4. Exclusively a *mammal* watcher
5. Exclusively a *fish* watcher
6. Watched only animals that were actively *playing*
7. Watched only animals that were *eating*
8. Watched only *grotesque* or sinister animals
9. Watched only *cuddly*, storybook animals

10. Watched *everything*, even the sparrows feeding in the trash bin
(Note: These were the pure types. Many visitors fell into no clear single category; these visitors have been categorized according to their most common pattern of observation.)

Turning these ten observation styles into a worthwhile essay will be difficult: a "laundry list" of ten items makes a dull reading. Unfortunately selection is impossible, since a classification means getting them all. To progress any further, you must understand the idea of hierarchy:

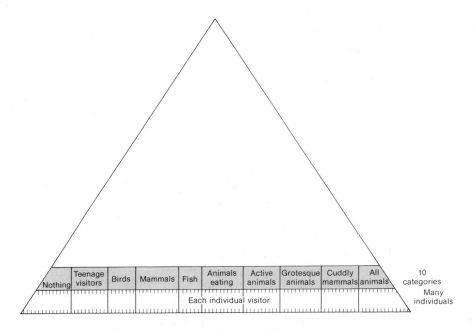

The *hierarchy* here starts with an unknown but large number of individual visitors at the bottom of the pyramid. Each category in your ten-part classification includes some of these visitors. But, as we said, ten categories are too many to make an effective essay; in other words, this classification is *too low down in the hierarchy*. The solution is to *reclassify*—to take the ten-category division and rework it higher up the pyramid. For example, a three-category reclassification is possible: *Interested in No Animals, Interested in Special Animals, Interested in All Animals*. (See opposite page.)

Unfortunately, this three-part classification has gone to the other extreme and is now too *high* in the hierarchy: obviously, *Interested in Special Animals* clusters too many types together. Let's try again, this time allowing more categories in the *Special Interest* sector. For example we could say: (1) Some observers showed interest in a particular genus (birds, mammals, fish); (2) some observed primarily actions (moving and eating); (3) others watched animals that gave them an emotional reaction (cuddly mammals and grotesques). Including the Watched-Everything and the Watched-Nothing groups, this plan yields five categories.

CHAPTER SEVEN
Getting Them All—Classification

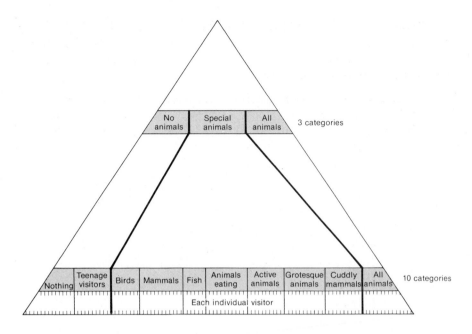

Five categories are a manageable number, and they should prove interesting to discuss. The classification is now *at the right level in the hierarchy.*

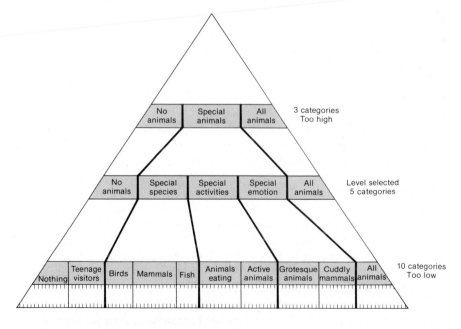

The same problem, too many categories, may well arise in your own essay. If it does, then reclassify your material higher up the pyramid. Above all remember; don't delete anything from your list. A classification must "get them all."

Concept Review

Reasons for Getting Married

This list contains eleven reasons for getting married. First, empirically verify that it is complete (that's a fancy way of saying: "See if any reasons have been left out"). Then, because a list of eleven or more reasons would make a tediously long essay, reclassify the reasons "higher up the pyramid." And so, people marry:

1. Because their parents arranged the marriage
2. Because of peer pressure (the rest of the gang was married already)
3. Because of loneliness
4. Because of a wish to start a family
5. Because a family is already on the way
6. Because of a desire for "unlimited sexual access" to a special partner
7. Because of love
8. Because the desired partner was rich (or better off)
9. Because of a bad family life with mom and dad
10. Because two together can live more cheaply than two separately
11. Because some jobs require a spouse when "entertaining" company guests

• Using Classification to Say Something

We've already seen that classification can produce "meaningless" essays. Unless you're sure that a particular classification will produce a worthwhile thesis statement, don't pursue it beyond the pie graph stage.

Each problem form tends to produce certain kinds of thesis statement; classification is no exception. If, for example, you're writing on "The Reasons for Getting Married," you might well suggest that one reason is better than all the others—let's say *love*. Accordingly you put *love* as your last category leading into the thesis statement: "Of all the reasons for getting married, love is the only one that really matters." Or as a command: "Marry for love, or you'll be sorry." Such a thesis statement depends on *ranking* the categories in order of importance.

On the other hand, you may study the list of reasons for marrying and find no single super-reason; you may, for example, have seen marriages for the "wrong" reasons turn out very well, and marriages for the "right" reasons go sour. In this case, your thesis statement might be: "There is no way to predict the outcome of a marriage from the motives of the couple contracting it." A thesis like that derives from the *impossibility of ranking* the different categories in your classification. If ranking is impossible, you might also consider an *open thesis*, which, like an open verdict, reaches no conclusion at all. (See the *Close-Up* below.)

A thesis statement formulated as a choice is common in classification essays, especially in technical disciplines. Again it's a question of ranking, but this time with a split decision. As an example, let's say that you're studying aeronautics and that you're faced with the subject: "Discuss the types of propellors available for small aircraft." A suitable rationale for the classification would be *adjustability*. (A brief technical explanation: the blades of a propellor can be set to a harsh angle so that they really bite the air, which is good for climbing, or to a flatter angle, which is good for economical cruising. To achieve *both* ideals, a propellor must be adjustable.) Looked at from the perspective of adjustability, there are three types of propellors: (1) preset in the factory and not adjustable; (2) adjustable on the ground by means of special tools; and (3) adjustable during flight by means of a lever in the cockpit. Type (3) is the most efficient but by far the most expensive. The thesis statement might, therefore, take the form: "Full in-flight adjustability is extremely expensive: on-the-ground adjustability is cheaper, but far less advantageous. In each case, the costs must be weighed against the benefits."

Concept Review

Classification and the Thesis Statement

Let's return to Guy Mitchell's subject, "Men Who Drink Beer." This is a standard classification subject: an unknowable number that must be divided into categories before discussion can begin. Study these five possible classifications. Which rationale do you see as the most likely to produce a worthwhile thesis statement? How exactly would you formulate this Thesis Statement?

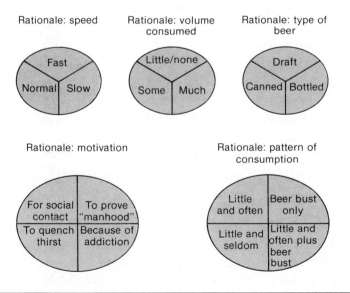

Close-Up

The Case for the Open Thesis

Good tactics (and an instinct for survival) sometimes rule out a strong thesis statement. An article in *Time* magazine, July 21, 1986, illustrates such a case. In the summer of 1986, the Meese Commission made its report on pornography, recommending curbs on several kinds of sexual material. Part of responsible news reporting is explaining how significant segments of the public react to an event. In this case, *Time* presented feminist reaction under the headline: *Pornography: The Feminist Dilemma*. The article begins:

> According to various feminists, the Meese commission report was good for the women's movement (Law Professor Catherine MacKinnon), bad for the movement (A.C.L.U. Attorney Nan Hunter) or basically irrelevant to feminist interests (Movement Pioneer Betty Friedan).

This is standard classification. How does the journalist, John Leo, proceed? He gives each viewpoint roughly equal time, presenting the arguments of the three camps. And his thesis? It's a classic *open thesis*, the I-have-no-idea conclusion:

> Says Deborah Chalfie, a Washington attorney active in Feminists Against Pornography: "I still have problems with defining what we are trying to get at."

Question:

Does John Leo's technique here reflect fairness and open-handedness? Or is he sitting on the fence? In general, when do you think an open thesis is justified?

• Keeping Things Parallel: The Extended Balance Sheet as Game Plan

A contrast, as you remember, "scores points" only if each idea about *A* is *balanced* by the contrasting idea about *B*. (Telling the reader that Fido is a poodle means nothing unless Bill's breed is also given.) A classification should also be kept parallel. John Leo, for example, in classifying feminist attitudes to the Meese Commission report, (see *Close-Up*) found equally prestigious speakers for each viewpoint and allowed them the same exposure; anything else would have looked like prejudice. How can you, in an essay, set up the parallels and keep them going? Let's look at a case, using it first to review the ideas we've discussed so far.

Pat Cunliffe was a medical secretary. During her working life, she'd met hundreds of general practitioners, some admirable and some not. The idea of categorizing these doctors in order to say something about them appealed to Pat. Her subject is, therefore, *general practitioners*; her rationale for classifiying them: *The attitudes of doctors towards their patients*. Working bottom-up, she found four attitudes in all:

1. A doctor might be burned out and indifferent towards patients.
2. A doctor might see patients simply as a way of making money.
3. A doctor might enjoy playing "god in a white coat."
4. A doctor might have a genuine concern for the health and welfare of each patient.

This classification cannot be logically verified, but empirically it makes sense: probably there are no other types, and no doctor is likely to play two roles at the same time with the same patient. Four categories are a manageable number, so the concept of hierarchy need not be brought into play. The next step is to make sure that this classification leads to a (at this stage provisional) thesis statement. It does:

Any licensed doctor is allowed to practice medicine; the best doctors are not those who make the most money from the profession but those who care about their patients on the human level.

This thesis is based on *ranking* the four types in order of effectiveness:

1. Burned out (absolutely ineffective)
2. God in a white coat egomaniacs (sometimes dangerous)
3. Moneygrubbers (safe but uncaring)
4. Doctors with a genuine interest in patients (most effective)

All Pat's decisions so far depend on concepts discussed earlier in the chapter. The next step is to decide how each type will be presented and how the four presentations can be kept parallel. Pat decided to use a specific doctor to represent each type—an informal case study. Owen, Beck, Stewart, Ramirez: there was no shortage of examples. To keep things parallel, Pat hit on the idea of using dynamic description: a step-by-step account of a patient's visit to a general practitioner. Five steps covered the territory:

Pat now had a strong game plan to work from. As an "extended Balance Sheet":

1. BURNED OUT (Dr. Owen)	2. GOD IN A WHITE COAT (Dr. Beck)	3. MONEY-GRUBBERS (Dr. Stewart)	4. GENUINELY CONCERNED (Dr. Ramirez)
Arrival and reception	Arrival and reception	Arrival and reception	Arrival and reception
Waiting room	Waiting room	Waiting room	Waiting room
Explaining symptoms	Explaining symptoms	Explaining symptoms	Explaining symptoms
Diagnosis and treatment	Diagnosis and treatment	Diagnosis and treatment	Diagnosis and treatment
Departure	Departure	Departure	Departure

The final decision now: should Pat use block presentation (one doctor at a time) or switch presentation (one topic at a time)—*Arrival* for example. (To review block and switch presentation, see Chapter 3.) In Pat's case, introducing the doctors one by one seemed more natural. If you want to read Pat's essay, you'll find it at the end of this chapter.

Review Assignment

The "Extended Balance Sheet"

Draw up a pie graph classification for one of the following subjects. Then set up an appropriate game plan as an "extended balance sheet." To develop each "slice of the pie" you'll probably want to use either the pattern of static description or of dynamic description.

a. The ways of traveling from New York to New Orleans

b. The ways of robbing a bank

c. The ways of keeping a garden free of weeds

d. The ways of losing weight

• Balance Sheet into Evaluative Grid: An Advanced Technique

A game plan set up as an "extended balance sheet" is enough to get you writing. Let's go a step further and see how the "balance sheet" can assume an even stronger shape. Ron Tolley sold stereo equipment. Many customers asked him about the new compact disc system and about how it compared with traditional records and tapes. Ron decided to write for his customers a handout entitled "Sound Systems Today." Ron's customers had four systems to choose from:

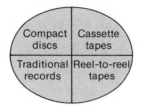

Ron had identified five criteria that customers use (informally) to evaluate sound systems against each other:

a. Wide frequency response (*Frequency response* = the highest and lowest notes the system can adequately reproduce)

b. Freedom from distortion (*Distortion* = factors that change the music, including wow, flutter, crosstalk, and similar technicalities)

c. Cleanness of the sound (The music must be free of clicks, plops, hisses and rumbles.)

d. Low wear and tear (The system should have a lifetime of many years *at its maximum potential.*)

e. Value for money (The system should give the "biggest bang for the buck.")

Ron first set up a "balance sheet," much like Pat's in the previous example; he put his four types down the righthand side and his five criteria along the top. Instead of filling in with parallel facts, Ron now penciled in simple, evaluative comments using the scale A through F:

	Frequency Response	Distortion	Cleanness of Sound	Wear and Tear	Price
Cassette tapes	C	B	C	C	B
Traditional records	B	B	C	D	B
Reel-to-reel tapes	A	A	B	B	C
Compact discs	A	A	A	A	A

An evaluative grid like this makes an excellent game plan. It is also interesting to note that the vertical list is a *classification*, while the horizontal list of criteria offers a *definition*: "What qualities make for a good sound system?"

Should Ron use block presentation (covering each piece of equipment in turn) or switch presentation (covering each criterion in turn) to write up this game plan? (To review block and switch presentation, see Chapter 3.) In this kind of essay, block presentation is definitely *out*. It scatters statistics on price, frequency response and so on, far and wide throughout the piece. The reader would be forced to scan up and down the article, searching for the relevant comparisons. Readers don't do that—they give up. In technical reporting, switch presentation usually produces a clearer picture.

Ron's article suggests how you might refine your subject, particularly if it concerns machinery or some goal-oriented task. The formula question becomes: "What is the best . . . ?" Some examples:

1. What is the best camera for a beginner/for a hunting trip/for underwater photography?
2. What is the best handgun for a police officer on patrol duty?
3. What is the best printer for a particular kind of computer?
4. What is the best way for a working mother of three to stay in shape?
5. What is the best way of learning to drive?

The procedure again:

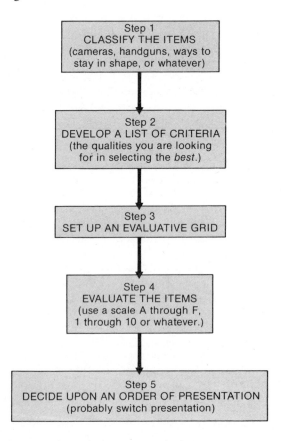

2 •
The Personal Voice

Classification is an academic technique derived from formal logic. This almost scientific rigor can lend authority to ideas that might seem, at first glance, subjective or even opinionated. Most writers, on occasion, need to become "judgmental"—to take a strong line on a subject. The danger is that the reader may simply say: "Well, that's your opinion. I think otherwise." In the passage below, Margaret Fuller, one of the great nineteenth-century essayists and a pioneer of the women's movement, tells the American reader in no uncertain fashion what is the "correct" attitude to travel in Europe. Her finger-wagging lecture might easily seem opinionated, but she neatly ducks the problem by *classifying* attitudes to European travel. The reader can find no logical escape from her three-part classification; given her three types, the reader has even less chance of escaping her conclusion. Fuller's combination of a strong personal voice and a strong objective structure is overwhelming.

AMERICANS IN EUROPE

There are three species. First, the servile American—a being utterly shallow, thoughtless, worthless. He comes abroad to spend his money and indulge his tastes. His object in Europe is to have fashionable clothes, good foreign cookery, to know some titled persons, and furnish himself with coffee-house gossip, by retailing which among those less travelled and as uninformed as himself he can win importance at home. I look with unspeakable contempt on this class—a class which has all the thoughtlessness and partiality of the exclusive classes in Europe, without any of their refinement, or the chivalric feeling which still sparkles among them here and there. However, though these willing serfs in a free age do some little hurt, and cause some annoyance at present, they cannot continue long; our country is fated to a grand, independent existence, and, as its laws develop, these parasites of a bygone period must wither and drop away.

Then there is the conceited American, instinctively bristling and proud of—he knows not what. He does not see, not he, that the history of Humanity for many centuries is likely to have produced results it requires some training, some devotion, to appreciate and profit by. With his great clumsy hands, only fitted to work on a steam-engine, he seizes the old Cremona violin, makes it shriek with anguish in his grasp, and then declares he thought it was all humbug before he came, and now he knows it; that there is not really any music in these old things; that the frogs in one of our swamps make much finer, for they are young and alive. To him the etiquettes of courts and camps, the ritual of the Church, seem simply silly—and no wonder, profoundly ignorant as he is of their origin and meaning. Just so the legends which are the subjects of pictures, the profound myths which are represented in the antique marbles, amaze and revolt him; as, indeed, such things need to be judged of by another standard than that of the Connecticut Blue-Laws. He criticises severely pictures, feeling quite sure that his natural senses are better means of judgment than the rules of connoisseurs. . . .

[The third class] is that of the thinking American—a man who, recognizing the immense advantage of being born to a new world and on a virgin soil, yet does not wish one seed from the past to be lost. He is anxious to gather and carry back with him every plant that will bear a new climate and new culture. Some will dwindle; others will attain a bloom and stature unknown before. He wishes to gather them clean, free from noxious insects, and to give them a fair trial in his new world. And that he may know the conditions under which he may best place them in that new world, he does not neglect to study their history in this.

Margaret Fuller
From *At Home and Abroad*

Review Assignment

Language and Value Judgments

a. Construct the pie graph that underlies Fuller's analysis.

b. Fuller does not formulate her "thesis statement" in so many words. Try formulating a thesis for her as a command, a statement, a choice, and a question.

c. Try rewriting one of Fuller's three paragraphs in *non-judgmental* language. When you've finished, compare the effect of the two styles. What place do you think Fuller's style of judgmental writing might have in academic essays?

3 •
Writing Workshop:
The Process of Classification

• Choosing a Subject

Often choosing a rationale for a classification is more difficult than choosing a subject. To help solve this problem, many of these suggestions below contain a built-in rationale: *Reasons for* . . . , *Ways of* . . . , or *Attitudes of* . . . .

First, *reasons for* or motivations:

1. Reasons for using a personal computer in the home
2. Reasons for smoking marijuana
3. Reasons for taking up addictive drugs
4. Reasons for selling a house
5. Reasons for getting married
6. Reasons for getting divorced

7. Reasons that men (or women) enlist (or reenlist) in the military

8. Reasons for buying a dog

Important Note. Be careful to distinguish classification subjects like these from similar-looking subjects that call for a cause-and-effect analysis. For example, Subject 8 might take the form: "I bought a dog—why?" If it did, it would no longer call for classification. The cause-and-effect analysis says: "I did this because . . . *and* because . . . *and* because . . . ." Classification says: "People do this because . . . *or* because . . . *or* because . . . ." Cause-and effect analysis creates a list every item of which applies; it is an *and structure*. Classification separates items so that they cannot overlap; it is an *or structure*. One consequence is that a cause-and-effect analysis has both a general form ("People buy dogs . . .) and a specific form ("I bought a dog . . ."), while a *classification has no specific form*; it is impossible to classify "My reasons for buying a dog," or any comparable subject.

Next, the *ways of*:

9. Ways of spending Christmas (or some other festival)

10. Ways of investing savings

11. Ways of laying out (or keeping up) a garden

12. Ways of keeping a car in running order

13. Ways of refusing a date

14. Ways of breaking off a love affair

15. Ways of earning a little extra money

16. Ways of writing (that is, actually composing) computer programs

A final group of subjects with a built-in rationale, *attitudes of*:

17. Attitudes of teenagers (or some other group) toward authority

18. Attitudes of men toward a woman boss

19. Attitudes in society toward "househusbands" (that is, men who keep house while their wives earn the family income)

20. Attitudes of parents toward drug-taking by their children

21. Attitudes of students toward a particular subject (for example, English, math)

22. Attitudes of husbands toward working wives

23. Attitudes of society toward unwed mothers

24. Attitudes of society toward accepting welfare payments

Subjects without a built-in rationale are here divided into two groups: people-oriented and issue-oriented. If you choose one of these subjects, you might want to try reformulating the subject using *reasons for*, *ways of*, or *attitudes of*.

25. Local priests or ministers or rabbis or other religious leaders

26. School teachers (or university lecturers)

27. Child abusers

28. Hospital nurses (or doctors)

29. Liars

30 Crusaders for a good cause (Be specific about the cause.)

31. Store clerks

32. Photographers' models

33. Driving styles

34. Styles of popular music (or of rock music, or of country and western, and so on)

35. Personal computers

36. A sporting item (for example, skis, surfboards, dirtbikes)

37. Cameras

38. Styles of furnishing

39. Cities

40. Novels

• Developing a Game Plan

A. THE CLASSIFICATION ITSELF

In the first stages of classifying, there are red lights for *no-go* and amber lights for *proceed with caution*, but no green lights.

After you have chosen a subject and a rationale, you'll set up the pie graph. Test the classification carefully: if it is defective, *now* is the time to correct it. Every minute spent developing a faulty classification is a minute wasted. If the classification is good, amber light.

The next question is: do you have too many categories for a manageable essay? If so, then you must think of a way to reclassify your material "higher up the pyramid." If you're still in good shape, amber light.

Another question: does the classification mean anything? Does it lead to a worthwhile thesis statement, or is it merely a sterile exercise? If you have a shrewd idea what you want to say, amber light. It's amber because you may still have a *research gap*.

B. THE RESEARCH GAP

In a classification essay, each category requires equal and parallel development, but—do you *know* enough to develop the categories equally? If not, you have a *research gap*. To see what this means, let's follow Chris Leech investigating the subject "Reasons for using a personal computer in the home." Working bottom-up, Chris thought of the people he knew who had a PC and then tried to figure out their principal reason for using it.

THOUGHT	TYPE
Chris had a son, Danilo, who had a reading disability. Chris bought a PC and the software recommended by Danilo's teacher to help the boy overcome his problem. Chris's wife, Marcia, then discovered a typing program and learned to type.	For: Education Examples: Danilo and Marcia
Shortly after Chris bought his PC, a neighbor, Derek, stopped by to look at it. A week later Derek also had a PC, larger and more impressive than Chris's. Sadly, Derek never got beyond the super demonstration program that came with the PC.	For: Prestige Example: Derek
Across the street from Chris lived a young girl known as The Hacker. Chris seldom saw her because she spent all her free time with her PC. Unfortunately, Chris had no idea what she actually *did* during all that time.	For: Hacking Example: "The Hacker" across the street
Chris knew that many PC addicts devoted hours to playing arcade games and other computer "sports." Chris did not know why anyone would do this, or what games a computer could play.	For: Game playing Example: ?
Another type was Chris's cousin, George. George kept his household accounts, wrote letters, bought and sold shares, and kept track of his tape collection with his PC. George's wife even used the PC to store recipes.	For: Running useful programs Example: George

These five types produce a five-part classification circle:

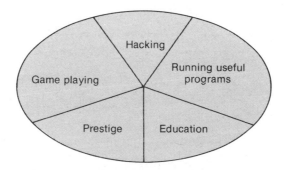

The classification looks fine, the number of categories is manageable, and Chris knows what he wants to say. His problem is ignorance. He knows that people play games on computers, but not *what* games they play (or what kind of pleasure they get from doing so). Similarly with the hacker: Chris knows that hackers exist, but not what they do. There is only one way to fill the research gap: research. In this case Chris interviewed a hacker and a games player and got his answers.

In general terms, try to spot a potential research gap as early as possible. If filling the *research gap* will take more time than you have at your disposal, then abandon the subject. If your subject is still "up and running," you'll have:

> A formally correct
> classification

> A thesis

> All the information you need
> (or the time to research it)

The green light at last.

C. THE "EXTENDED BALANCE SHEET"

Chris can easily set up an "extended balance sheet" (like the one Pat used for her essays on doctors earlier in the chapter). A static description of each type fills the bill. These might be the headings:

a. The *type of computer* used

b. The *time spent mastering* the computer

c. The *time spent using* the computer

d. The *ultimate value of* the computer to the user

e. The *effect on the user*

A full game plan is now only moments away.

Two common categories can sometimes stop you in your tracks, so we should look at them: the negative category and the combination category.

The Negative Category.   A classification often contains a negative category. A classification, for example, of "The ways of spending Christmas" might include not only positive categories such as:

> Celebrating with the close family
> Celebrating with the extended family
> Celebrating with friends
> Celebrating with acquaintances
> Celebrating alone

but also the negative category:

> Not celebrating at all

This group, the non-celebrators, carry on as normal, making no change in their routine. Obviously a non-celebration cannot be discussed under the same headings as a celebration. A different kind of comment, possibly much shorter, would be appropriate for this group.

The Combination Category.   A related problem occurs with categories that merely combine others. The report based on the trip to the zoo (discussed earlier in this chapter) would encounter this problem. Many of the visitors fall into a clear category: they watched only cuddly animals, or they watched only teenage humans. Other visitors seem to belong to one category at one moment and to another category the next. These "mixed types" cannot be totally ignored; they must be explained away:

> Many visitors were inconsistent in their behavior. This essay, however, will discuss only the "pure," consistent types. The inconsistent should be considered a separate category combining any two or more of the other types.

Having said that, probably in the opening, the matter is closed.

• Writing the First Draft

Writing the first draft of a classification essay follows the guidelines established in the Introduction to Part 2. (See flowchart on p. 116.) Only the opening and the closing need further comment.

A. THE OPENING

In its most skeletal form, the opening simply announces the subject and the number of categories to be presented. Often, however, a classification essay requires a little more "up front." Let's return to Ron Tolley's discussion of sound systems for an example. Ron's customers have a major problem: they do not understand how the new compact disc differs from earlier systems. To help them out, Ron must describe the new system—but where should be put this explanatory material? There are two options: up front, or somewhere in the body of the paper. Ron, in fact, described the compact disc system in the opening—that way, all four sound systems "started level" when he began his analysis. The general principle is this: Be ready to handle in the opening anything the reader must know to make sense of the essay.

B. THE CLOSING

One student writing on "Reasons for getting married" concluded with a seven-word paragraph:

In marriage, love is all that matters.

What more need be said? On the other hand, a classification often needs detailed and careful discussion before it yields its inner meaning. A preacher, for example, might classify his congregation into *sheep* and *goats* and make it clear who belonged in each category. It is unlikely, however, that the preachment would end there. Having established the classification, most preachers would find a great deal more to say by way of comment and analysis. If the closing of your classification essay turns out longer than earlier closings, this is no cause for alarm.

• Revising

The Flowchart on page 119 offers a general scheme for revising your first draft. Re-read this material carefully. In revising a classification essay, you'll need to watch two extra points.

A. A TIP ON CONTINUITY: SECTION HEADINGS

The use of section headings is particularly appropriate in a classification essay. Unless there are strong reasons not to, simply headline each category with its name. Classification is a formal structure, and the labels stress the logical rigor of this approach.

B. A SPECIAL CHECK FOR CORRECTNESS: THE AGREEMENT OF COLLECTIVE NOUNS

Collective nouns are group words: *herd, committee, labor union, Congress*, and so on. The collective nouns that occur most frequently in classification essays are: *type, group, category*, and so on. Are these words singular or plural? Look at these two sentences:

a. This category of people do their best to achieve results.

b. This category of people does its best to achieve results.

Both sentences are correct. If you don't know why, review your Handbook under *Agreement of Collective Nouns* or *Collective Nouns*.

• The Final Draft

Our example of an "end product" is Pat Cunliffe's essay on doctors. We met this essay earlier when it was just a game plan.

1. The Burnout (Informal Case Study: Dr. Owen)
    a. My reception was chilly.
    b. The waiting room was uncomfortable and hideous.
    c. I never fully explained my symptoms.

    d. The diagnosis was cursory.

    e. My departure was also chilly.

2. God in a White Coat (Informal Case Study: Dr. Beck)

    a. The setting was impressive.

    b. My reception was less impressive than it was meant to be.

    c. I explained far more symptoms than I really had.

    d. Diagnosis and prescription were an anticlimax.

    e. I felt I'd been used.

3. The Moneygrubber (Informal Case Study: Dr. Stewart)

    a. The "Treatment Center" was a science fiction nightmare.

    b. I foresee that reception will one day be fully computerized.

    c. Symptoms will be described to, and analyzed by, a machine.

    d. The doctor will preside over a computer diagnosis.

    e. The patients will be overwhelmed, confused, and humiliated.

4. The Real Doctor (Informal Case Study: Dr. Ramirez)

    a. His practice was low-key and easily accessible.

    b. His receptionist had the right human touch.

    c. Patients told him their worries as well as their symptoms.

    d. His warmth as a human being was as much a cure as his prescriptions.

    e. He courteously saw everyone to the door.

Thesis statement:

Medicine must reassert the value of concerned care and the value of treating the whole human being.

Quotation as opening

"The art of medicine," Voltaire once said, "consists of amusing the patient while nature cures the disease." Voltaire sounds equally cynical about all doctors. In my own experience, doctors fall into four categories, three of which are not particularly admirable.

Four-part breakdown indicated

The Burnout

Arrival shows that Owen is not *admirable, although the exact "label" for this type comes later*

I once visited a certain Doctor Owen one February morning in Chicago. There were only three parking spots outside his office, and he had parked his car so that it occupied all three. Shivering on the doorstep, I rang his bell and waited while his secretary unchained it. I was a new patient, and his secretary noted down what I told her on a yellow scratch pad. Although I was his first appointment, Doctor Owen kept me waiting for twenty minutes. There were no magazines in his unheated waiting room and nothing on the walls but faded diplomas and two hideous charts showing the blood circulation in cattle and horses. When at last a buzzer rasped and a red light blinked, I pushed my way into the doctor's office. There was a tray on the desk and a cup of coffee that had a smell of hot cognac to it. Doctor Owen looked at me with a hostile stare. I began to explain my rather vague symptoms: a mole on my cheek had begun to itch and change color, perhaps from overexposure to a sun lamp . . . . I could not voice my secret fears to Doctor Owen. He glanced at the mole, sighed, and reached for his prescription pad. "Three times a day," he said. I went out through the still empty waiting room into the icy street. The prescription remained in my pocket, unused; typically of the man, he never sent me a bill, and I would not have paid it if he had. Doctor Owen represents a tragic pattern: burnout. When burnout strikes, doctors should give up medical practice. They do more harm than good.

Pointing: General comment on this type of doctor

Who-What-Where-When

Arrival

Waiting room

Explaining symptoms

Diagnosis and treatment

Departure

PART TWO
The Essay

God in a White Coat

A second group of doctors love the feeling of power they get from dealing with life and death. Doctor Beck was like this. I visited him once when my own doctor was on vacation. Doctor Beck's office was in a highrise in the best part of town. The lobby of the building was palatial; it had a waterfall and a jungle of exotic plants. Doctor Beck's office was just as impressive, with oriental rugs and oil paintings. His secretary was glamorous but no friend of her computer to judge by the way it buzzed when she tried to use it. Doctor Beck himself wore a crisp white coat; he had a stethoscope round his neck and a worried expression on his face. He listened to my symptoms (lower back pain) stroking his face thoughtfully. He asked searching questions about my drinking habits; he asked how many people in my family had died of cancer; he asked about my diet, especially about eggs. After each answer, he gave a sad little nod of understanding. After ten minutes, all I could see ahead was decline and early death. Finally he prescribed some salve: "I don't <u>think</u> it's serious," he said. "Just be very, very careful, that's all." I could hardly believe my luck. "Thank you, doctor," I said. "Thank you so much." When I collected my prescription, I found it was for a deep-heat salve I could have bought over the counter. My moments of agony in Doctor Beck's office had simply boosted the doctor's ego at my expense. Doctors of this type, the gods in white coats, do little physical damage to their patients, but the emotional damage can be considerable. They are not a credit to their profession.

The Moneygrubber

Moneymaking doctors, the third group, seldom hunt alone; they work in packs. Doctor Stewart was a member of a rich group practice—it called itself a "treatment center"—in Florida. When I visited her some years ago, the Center was already a science fiction fantasy. I can imagine it in twenty years time. Every corridor will pulsate with energy like a large hospital during a nuclear catastrophe. Nurses, assistants and doctors will stride in all directions, telephones will beep, and computer readouts will be flushed from printers. Patients will sit in front of computers, answering the machine's remorseless questions. Then the moment of truth: fifty seconds with Doctor Stewart, now an elderly woman seated on a platinum throne. She will glance at the computer diagnosis, tap a few numbers on her desktop terminal, and wait in silence while a laser printer spews out a ten-page explanation of the disease exactly adapted to the patient's IQ and reading level. The patient will retreat, overwhelmed, confused, and humiliated. My visit in 1985 was bad enough; what the future holds is unthinkable. What satisfaction, I wonder, do moneymakers like Doctor Stewart get from their work—apart from the money, that is? Surely this super-efficiency forgets the most ancient principle of medicine: that the doctor should treat the whole patient, not just the disease.

The Real Doctor

Before he retired, my family doctor was someone who, in my view, got things right. He lived and practiced in an old, comfortable house in the middle of our community. His waiting room was large, well-lit and cheerful, and there were magazines for all tastes as well as toys for children. His assistant was a middle-aged, motherly woman, who knew how to calm other mothers with small, sick children, or to create the right atmosphere for shy teenage girls to tell their "unique" troubles to the doctor. Doctor Ramirez was a busy man, but he made time to listen not only to his patients' symptoms, but to their worries as well. He knew how often a physical ailment has an emotional cause, and his sympathetic ear probably cured as many people as his prescriptions. Unlike the other doctors, he took time to explain to each patient what was wrong and how he planned to put it right. He saw each patient courteously to the door of his office, rich and poor, young and old alike. Doctor Ramirez, and doctors like him, represent the medical profession at its best—humane, caring, and concerned with the whole person.

CHAPTER SEVEN
Getting Them All—Classification

Conclusion: Comment on the three less admirable types

Conclusion

Modern medicine has developed powerful drugs, all-seeing diagnostic machines, and superb techniques of management; however, this has led to a depersonalization of medical treatment that might, in the end, lead to worse results rather than to better. The apathetic doctor and the egomaniac will not be able to halt this trend. Medicine must reassert the value of concerned care and the value of treating the whole human being if advances are to be made in the future.

Thesis statement

• Summary: The Flowchart

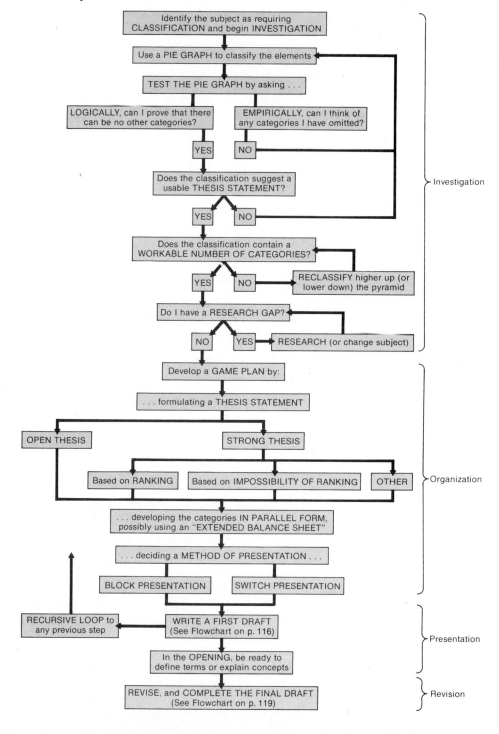

EIGHT

Making a Case

1 •
The Problem:
Getting the Reader on Your Side

• The Blind Negotiation

Many goals are unreachable. However brilliantly you write, you will not convince the Pope to marry, you will not convince the Soviet leaders to allow multi-party elections, and you will not persuade the Toyota Corporation voluntarily to stop exports to the United States. Two factors weigh against such fruitless attempts: (1) you are addressing an immovable reader, and (2) you are asking too much. Somehow you must improve your chances in both these areas. But how?

Let's begin by analyzing the problem. Two situations require you to make a case: a *debate* and a *negotiation*. In a debate, you win by convincing 51 percent of the audience that your point of view makes more sense than that of your opponent; you must convince half the audience, not the speaker for the other side. In a negotiation, on the other hand, your goal is to reach agreement with the other side—a much tougher assignment. A successful negotiation has no winner and no loser, just two winners. Making a case in writing is a kind of negotiation: you must convince a doubtful reader. But it is more: it is a *blind negotiation*. To succeed, you must reach agreement with a reader whom you cannot see, cannot hear and from whom you receive no feedback. Further, the reader can win the argument outright by one simple action: ceasing to read. (In the academic context, of course, the professor is obliged to read to the bitter end—but that won't help a badly made case.) The challenge, then, is to conduct a successful blind negotiation.

CHOOSING THE RIGHT "NEGOTIATING PARTNER"

The immovable reader is beyond your powers of persuasion, so you must pick a more promising "neogtiating partner." The first step is to study the complete range of attitudes to your question. An immediate stop to the import of Japanese automobiles, for example, has powerful proponents and powerful opponents. Convenient labels would be: Owen Bieber, President of the United Automobile Workers (in favor of the stop) and Eiji Toyoda, the Chairman of the Toyota Corporation (against). Let's put them at the ends of a vector:

President of the UAW		Chairman of Toyota

Which side are *you* on? Let's say you favor a drastic curb on the import of Japanese cars. Who, then, is your ideal "negotiating partner"? The Chairman of Toyota is immovable. The boss of the UAW is also out of range though for a different reason: writing for him is simply "preaching to the converted." You cannot convince him because he is convinced already. Halfway along the vector is a point of balance: the genuinely undecided. That group and the next, that is, *those who are against you but who will listen to your arguments*, represent your best chance. To simplify things further, anything you write for the slightly hostile group also covers the undecided, so the "Hostile But Will Listen" are your ideal target.

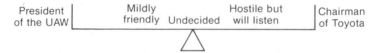

Who falls into this off-center group? Probably Americans who like the option of buying a Japanese car, but who normally buy American. A reader who intended to buy a Japanese car for economic reasons would be more hostile and much harder to convince. We shall study readership analysis in detail in Part 3 of this book. For now, it's enough to say that you should have a clear picture of your target reader in mind, and that you should shape your arguments to influence just such a person.

Our present concern is academic writing; in fact, a formal essay follows much the same lines. The reader, your professor, will listen to your arguments, but will listen with a "red pencil" in hand, trying to spot the weaknesses in your case. Whether the professor happens to agree or disagree with you makes no difference: the academic reader is *always* on the other side.

In a "blind negotiation," then, academic or otherwise, *the target reader is someone who inclines to the other side, but who is ready to listen to your arguments*.

SETTING A REALISTIC GOAL

Targeting the right reader improves your chances. Setting a realistic goal improves them still further. What is your goal? The minimum goal is what diplomats call "frank and wide-ranging talks." This is code: it means that each side now understands exactly where the other is coming from. If you achieve this, your piece is already quite successful. The next level up the diplomatic code is "constructive and useful talks." This means that the positions of the two sides have moved somewhat closer. The blind negotiator is unwise to aim higher. You won't change your reader's mind completely; the reader won't finish your piece thinking exactly as you do. Be more humble: *if the reader moves perceptibly in your direction, then you have "made your case."*

Concept Review

The Target Reader

This piece by George Bernard Shaw is part of the preface to his play, *Androcles and the Lion*. This famous preface begins with a question: Why not give Christianity a chance? Shaw then argues that "nobody has ever been sane enough to try his (Jesus's) way" because Jesus's way would undermine every kind of worldly power. It is a controversial idea. In this extract, Shaw argues that even the apostles did not "try his way."

> Take, for example, the miracles. Of Jesus alone of all the Christian miracle workers there is no record, except in certain gospels that all men reject, of a malicious or destructive miracle. A barren fig-tree was the only victim of his anger. Every one of his miracles on sentient subjects was an act of kindness. John declares that he healed the wound of the man whose ear was cut off (by Peter, John says) at the arrest in the garden. One of the first things the apostles did with their miraculous power was to strike dead a wretched man and his wife who had defrauded them by holding back some money from the common stock. [Ananias and Sapphira; Shaw names them at the end of the extract. Ed.] They struck people blind or dead without remorse, judging because they had been judged. They healed the sick and raised the dead apparently in a spirit of pure display and advertisement. Their doctrine did not contain a ray of that light which reveals Jesus as one of the redeemers of men from folly and error. They cancelled him, and went back straight to John the Baptist and his formula of securing remission of sins by repentance and the rite of baptism (being born again of water and the spirit). Peter's first harangue softens us by the human touch of its exordium, which was a quaint assurance to his hearers that they must believe him to be sober because it was too early in the day to get drunk; but of Jesus he had nothing to say except that he was the Christ foretold by the prophets as coming from the seed of David, and that they must believe this and be baptized. To this the other apostles added incessant denunciations of the Jews for having crucified him, and threats of the destruction that would overtake them if they did not repent: that is, if they did not join the sect which the apostles were now forming. A quite intolerable young speaker named Stephen delivered an oration to the council, in which he first inflicted on them a tedious sketch of the history of Israel, with which they were presumably as well acquainted as he, and then reviled them in the most insulting terms as "stiffnecked and uncircumcized." Finally, after boring and annoying them to the utmost bearable extremity, he looked up and declared that he saw the heavens open, and Christ standing on the right hand of God. This was too much: they threw him out of the city and stoned him to death. It was a severe way of suppressing a tactless and conceited bore; but it was pardonable and human in comparison to the slaughter of poor Ananias and Sapphira.

Questions

1. Working backwards from the text, do you think any kind of reader would be *offended* by Shaw's remarks?
2. Do you think any kind of reader would be *shocked but still interested*?
3. Do you think any kind of reader would simply *agree* with Shaw?
4. Which group do you think contains Shaw's *intended reader*?
5. Do you think Shaw has angled his material well for his intended reader?

• Tactics

In the medieval schools of rhetoric, students were trained in debate. A subject was announced, usually something unprovable either way, such as "Did Adam have a navel?" Speakers were picked—but the speakers were not told which *side* they were on until seconds before the debate began. Students trained in this way had a keen sense of the arguments for the other side. A writer conducting a blind negotiation must be just as sensitive.

The arguments for your side—the arguments for the other side: no other material is available to you. How should you handle the material? What approach is a reader likely to find convincing? First, six tactical schools that are best avoided:

1. The Forthright School: "I think this way, and anyone who thinks differently must be a confounded fool."
2. The Totalitarian School: "There is only one correct opinion—mine; anyone who disagrees will be liquidated." (Smith and Wesson beats four aces.)
3. The Traditional School: "My opinion must be right because this is the way people have always thought."
4. The School of Authority: "I know I'm right because 1,236 sources, all by Ph.D.s, say the same thing."
5. The Charm School: "How could someone as sweet and lovely as me possibly be wrong?"
6. The Boat Stabilizing School: "Anyone who disagrees with me is going to rock the boat—and we're all team players, aren't we?"

Although these tactics often work in face-to-face argument, none of them is likely to work in writing: a blind negotiation gives the reader too much power. Adherents of these schools make two mistakes: (1) they never admit that the other side has worthwhile arguments, and (2) they never admit that their own case is anything but perfect. Let's look closer.

HANDLING THE CASE OF THE OTHER SIDE

By scorning the reader's viewpoint, a writer implies that the reader is at best misguided, at worst stupid or perhaps deliberately devious. Probably the argument is already lost. The reader can win the argument by ceasing to read—and nobody enjoys being called misguided, stupid or devious.

Effective tactics are altogether more civilized and reasonable. Normally, it's fair to assume that the reader's beliefs, although different from yours, are held for sane and valid reasons. You must work hard to understand these reasons; unless two negotiators understand each other, they will not reach a satisfactory agreement. Let's take a simple case.

John and Amy win $5,000 in a lottery. John wants to spend the money on a holiday in Thailand; Amy wants to send the money to her elderly, disabled mother. If Amy accuses John of being nothing but a selfcentered, materialistic pig, she is likely to hear that she is nothing but an impractical, cranky halfwit. As long as neither tries to see the other's point of view, they are unlikely to reach agreement. If, on the other hand, Amy says: "You're right, we need a holiday, but . . . ," and if John says: "You're right, we should do something for your mother, but . . . ," then there is a chance of compromise. John will suggest that Amy's generosity, though admirable, goes too far, and Amy will suggest that John's idea of taking a vacation, though justified, is extravagant. Now the two sides are not just bickering; they are negotiating. "You're right, but . . ." This formula is the clue to a respectful handling of your opponent's point of view.

As a practical procedure, try to think through the case for the other side under three headings: What are the arguments for the other side? How far are they true? How far can they be demolished? A game plan based on those questions will avoid the arrogance and brutality (conscious or unconscious) of the "six schools."

WHAT ARE THE ARGUMENTS FOR THE OTHER SIDE?	HOW FAR ARE THEY TRUE?	HOW FAR CAN THEY BE DEMOLISHED?

THE CASE FOR YOUR OWN SIDE

Now the case for your own side. The danger here is perhaps a hangover from high school. At high school, you were probably asked to give your opinion on a subject and then to "back up your opinion with facts." The posture here is essentially: "This is why I hold this opinion, take it or leave it." This exercise may be an aid to intellectual growth, but it is not the same thing as making a case. When you're making a case, the goal is to *convince* the reader. To achieve this, you must present your case in a way that invites the reader to understand it and perhaps to agree with it. This means looking at your own case critically, through the eyes of your opponent.

In every case that can be argued two ways, there are weaknesses; otherwise everyone would have the same opinion. There will always be weaknesses in your own case, some obvious and some that you must work hard to discover. Once you know your weak spots, what then? Do you conceal them, or do you admit them? In a debate, you would conceal them, although you'd be ready with counterarguments in case of awkward questions. In a blind negotiation, the reader will certainly raise objections, although the writer, unfortunately, does not know what they will be. For this reason, it is wise to address honestly and fairly all the problems you know about. No reader will be convinced by an argument full of loopholes that you've left undefended. Having admitted your weaknesses, of course, you'll play them down, showing that they do not destroy the main thrust of your argument. To show this in action, let's take an example in some detail, two versions of an office memo about a new policy.

```
                              Memo


From: Bert Faddler, Office Supervisor
To: Kate Corn, Personnel Manager


Problem:    The new management policy on clocking in late has
created considerable confusion among the staff.  Many claim
that they cannot understand the policy, and a great deal of
time has been wasted explaining it to individuals.

Solution:  A half-hour meeting of staff and management on
Friday afternoon would allow the management to present the
policy and to answer questions.  After this meeting, we could
assume that staff knew the policy, and we could take appropriate
action against those violating it.
```

There are several objections to this plan. They surface when Kate Corn asks Bert Faddler to stop by her office to talk over his idea:

CORN: I sent out a written notice on this. Did everyone get it?
FADDLER: Sure they got it.
CORN: Did they read it?
FADDLER: I guess they did, but they didn't seem to get the point. It was a bit long and complicated for some of them.
CORN: And you want a half-hour meeting for the *whole* staff? That's 86 work hours, you know.
FADDLER: We've already lost more than that, and there's still a lot of bad feeling around. Some people I counseled called in sick two days running.
CORN: Well, I still don't like the idea of a meeting. Maybe I should send out another letter.
FADDLER: I think that'd make things worse.
CORN: You don't have much faith in my writing, do you? But I think we'll try it my way even so.

CHAPTER EIGHT
Making a Case

You can see what's happening here. Corn raises a basic objection to Faddler's suggestion: time. This means she is taking a stand *against* him, and this puts her prestige "on the line." Faddler offers counterarguments, but if Corn accepts them, then he has "won," and she has "lost." Even if she knows she is wrong, she may still want her own way simply to defend her prestige. Faddler would be better off if he'd anticipated her objections in his memo. This is how the memo might then have looked:

```
                              Memo

    From: Bert Faddler, Office Supervisor
    To: Kate Corn, Personnel Manager


    Problem: The New management policy on clocking in late has
    created considerable confusion among the staff.  Many claim
    that they cannot understand the policy, and a great deal of
    time has been wasted in explaining it to individuals.

    Solution: A half-hour meeting of staff and management on
    Friday afternoon would allow the management to present the
    policy and to answer questions.  After this meeting, it would
    be assumed that staff knew the policy, and appropriate action
    could be taken against those violating it.

    Possible Objections:

    1. A written explanation of the policy from the Personnel
    Manager has been distributed to the staff.  The length
    (four pages) may have discouraged reading; further, the large
    number of exceptions and special situations listed may have
    obscured the general line of policy.  Additional written
    clarification would probably add to the confusion.  For this
    reason, a short oral presentation of the policy followed by
    questions seems the best way to clear things up.  Several
    staff have already requested this.

    2. The number of work hours consumed by a half-hour meeting
    is 86.  Last week discussions of the policy with individuals
    and with groups took approximately 60 work hours.  Two
    individuals counseled called in sick two days running--a loss
    of 28 hours.  The situation is not improving.  A staff meeting
    to clear the air will ultimately save a great deal of time.
```

The new memo is longer, but it avoids putting Corn on the defensive. The principle is a general one: if you point out and then minimize the objections to your idea, your reader will have less trouble accepting it. In a blind negotiation, where you have no chance to answer your reader's objections, this technique is essential.

The grid below will help you in making a case: it ensures that you think your case through from the reader's point of view.

WHAT POINTS DO I WANT TO MAKE?	HOW CAN I ENSURE THAT THE READER UNDERSTANDS THE POINT?	WHAT OBJECTIONS ARE THERE TO THIS POINT?	HOW CAN I ANSWER THESE OBJECTIONS?

Concept Review

Love and the Progress of Science

Below are two passages that make a case. To help you assess them more open-mindedly, no author or source is given. Critique each passage by asking:

1. Exactly what case is the writer making?

2. In handling the other side's ideas:

   a. Does the writer in fact present the case for the other side?

   b. If so, is the other side's case fairly presented? Or is it simply ridiculed?

   c. Do you think that readers who disagree with the writer will feel that their side of things has been understood and fairly handled?

3. In handling the case for the writer's own viewpoint:

   a. Has the writer made any special effort to ensure that his or her case is accessible to the target reader?

   b. Has the writer admitted any weaknesses in his or her case?

   c. If so, how has the writer tried to lessen the effect of these weaknesses?

4. Overall, do you find the piece convincing?

A. **Falling in Love**

In our society, young men and young women are taught that "falling in love" (which is simply a fancy name for lusting after a sexual partner) is the noblest and most worthwhile of all human activities. If you don't believe me, then look at our art and literature. Young people devote the best part of their waking hours to "love," the men spotting, pursuing and finally possessing (in marriage or outside it) the women they find most attractive, and the women luring and entrapping men into marriage or into bed.

In this way, the creative energy of youth runs to waste in an activity that is not merely unproductive but positively harmful. Most of the waste and senseless luxury in our world spring from this pursuit. Men squander their time in idleness, and women behave like common whores, decorating and exposing their bodies simply to arouse male sensuality.

And I think this is wrong.

It is wrong because climbing into bed with a sexual partner, idealize it as we may, is no more a noble human aspiration than gorging oneself on delicious food, which some people also make their life's chief concern.

The conclusion I draw from this is that we must stop glorifying sexual love; we must understand that sexual intercourse, whether inside or outside marriage, helps no one achieve any worthwhile goal, be it the service of humanity, of our country, of science or of art—not to mention the service of God. Exactly the opposite: falling in love and then neglecting everything but the pursuit of the beloved, whatever poets and novelists say to the contrary, prevents us from achieving any goal worthy of a human being.

B. Does Science have a Future?

Nobody denies that we are passing through a crisis during these last weary and angry years of our century. It has been a century of frenzied activity aimed at knowing and recording everything. Science, we thought, would free mankind of its ancient evils and build a new world of justice and happiness. Now, after a century of progress, it is clear that we are no nearer justice and happiness than before. So, in despair, people are abandoning the old idea that knowledge leads to happiness. Perhaps it is not surprising: every action has an equal and opposite reaction; this is the exhaustion that accompanies every long journey. People sit at the roadside, gazing at the endless plain of another century ahead of them, and despair of ever reaching their destination. They doubt that they are on the right road, and they grieve that they didn't stop along the way to sleep forever in a hayfield under the stars. Why go forward when the goal never gets any nearer? Why know anything when so much remains hidden? It is better to stay free and innocent, happy like an ignorant child. And so science, because it failed to bring happiness, has been declared bankrupt.

But *did* science promise happiness? I doubt it. Science promises truth—but can you reach happiness by way of truth? A few philosophers can, perhaps. Meanwhile, the rest of humanity howls in despair. The truth has cheated us, so give us lies and illusions. We hate this abominable life on earth, so give us another world where the wicked are punished and the good rewarded! Nature is unjust and cruel, science creates appalling weapons, every social structure is a form of dictatorship, technology is a perversion—it brings nothing but ugliness and crime! Hounded by thoughts like these, many people plunge into dreamland as the only hope . . . .

This despairing cry for happiness touches me closely, but for all this lamentation, science has not stopped in its tracks. What reassures me is that the social soil of our country is still the same as it always was—the democratic soil in which our century was born . . . . And so I believe that the next century will continue the work of our own time, the rapid advance of democracy and science.

• Fair and Unfair, Logical and Illogical Argument

It is not easy to argue fairly; it is even more difficult to argue logically. Many students lack even a rudimentary training in the principles of reasoning, but they are still expected to be logical in their thinking and writing. The purpose of this section is to warn you about some of the logical pitfalls that occur in day-to-day academic writing. In Part 3, this theme will be explored again from the perspective of the researcher.

In making a case, the fundamental question is this: Do I want to win the argument, or do I want to establish the truth? If you merely want to win the argument, then you can use any material, however fallacious, stupid or despicable, as long as it convinces the reader. Ouch! If you draw the line at deliberately using what is fallacious, stupid or despicable, then you are trying to establish the truth—a much tougher assignment. The Romans and the medieval scholars who pioneered the study of logic gave these two techniques Latin names: *solutio ad hominem* or *making a case that satisfies the audience* and *solutio recta* or *making a case that establishes the truth*. (Many of the old Latin terms are still in common use—*non sequitur*, for example. Where the Latin name for a trap in logic still has some currency, it is given in parentheses.) Let's play devil's advocate, then, and set some traps for the unwary.

A. MAKING A CASE THAT SATISFIES THE AUDIENCE AND IGNORES THE TRUTH

First, let's look at a group of seven arguments that fail to convince *you* but that may be clinchers for the *reader*.

Argument Using an Accepted Authority *(Argumentum ad Verecundiam)*. Let's say the reader is a devout Roman Catholic and you are an atheist (if the devil's advocate can be an atheist); in this case, you might use an edict of the Pope (on contraception or abortion, perhaps) knowing that your reader *must* accept it. In the extract below, this technique is used by a journalist to give credence to the idea of reincarnation.

> Even such practical Western thinkers as Benjamin Franklin and Henry Ford shared a belief in reincarnation. And J. Paul Getty, the late oil billionaire and art collector, was rumored to have fancied himself a reincarnation of the culture-loving Roman emperor Hadrian. General George Patton was also a vociferous believer.

Franklin, Ford, Getty (a rumor only), and Patton are all great authorities. But on what *subjects* are they authorities? Eighteenth-century science, cars, oil, and tank battles. Their personal opinions on a subject where they claim no expertise have no possible bearing on the truth or falsehood of reincarnation. Even so, the superficial reader will probably fail to notice the trick.

Argument Based on Prejudice *(Argumentum ad Invidiam)*. The comp-lementary tactic is to mobilize the reader's negative prejudices—for example, "He's a communist! How can you believe anything he says?" *Communist, fascist, women's libber, male chauvinist*—any smear that makes the reader see red can be used to bait a trap. Obviously an argument should be judged on its validity, not on the "acceptability" of the person advancing it. Prejudices numb the power of reason. A case in point: under the headline *Polling the Unhappy Poles, Time* magazine, November 24, 1980, ran an article that reported a public opinion poll taken by a French reporter in Poland. Some of the results of the poll:

> Only 3% said they would vote for the Communist Party in free elections, compared with 34% for the Christian Democrats, 27% for Socialists, and 19% for Liberals . . . .

Apparently, two-thirds said they would "actively resist" a Russian invasion. Many questions could be asked about such a poll: Who was polled? *Time* says the group was a "representative sample of 500 Poles." But how did a French reporter obtain a "representative sample"? How, in fact, does a foreigner administer a public opinion poll in a communist country? Since Poland has no "Christian Democrats" (or a Western party system), what do the votes mean? And so on. For many *Time* readers, their prejudices and the figures line up so nicely that no questions are asked. Prejudice is a powerful weapon in numbing the voice of reason.

Argument Based on a Concession *(Argumentum ex Concesso).* A related method is to wring a concession from your unwary reader, and then to build a case on it. In discussion, the technique is familiar:

DEVIL: So you believe in freedom?
VICTIM: Sure.
DEVIL: And democracy?
VICTIM: Everyone does.
DEVIL: And the right of free speech? And the right to free assembly?
VICTIM: That's part of it.
DEVIL: Then the Nazi Party of America has the right to march through Jewish areas shouting anti-Semitic slogans.
VICTIM: Now hang on . . . .
DEVIL: You just admitted it!
VICTIM: I guess so.

In writing, this maneuver works in much the same way.

Argument Based on Fear, on Pity, or on Greed *(Argumentum Baculinum, ad Misericordiam, ad Crumenam).* Fear, pity and greed are powerful emotions; they can easily confuse the truth. The argument based on fear is essentially the schoolyard threat: "You shut up. My dad can lick your dad any day." The Holy Inquisition (and its later imitators) used this very persuasive argument in its torture chambers. The same argument occurs in political debates. One example: speaking in Cheyenne, Wyoming, President Reagan defended an increase of 18 percent in military spending, claiming that this increase will "buy peace for the rest of the century and beyond." This argument successfully mobilizes fear. A few sentences later, Reagan uses another emotion, pity: the 18 percent increase will insure that "no young Americans will have to bleed their lives into some battlefield." This is a classic use of an *argument based on pity*. These two emotions cloud the listeners' sense of reason. To say: "Well maybe a 17 percent increase would work just as well" sounds ghoulish and disloyal, unconcerned about the young Americans threatened with death in battle. The facts and figures are not discussed; they are overpowered by emotions. (But when you think about it, the difference between a 17 percent and an 18 percent increase is almost $3 billion.)

Greed can also swamp facts. The money argument is used to switch a discussion about rights and wrongs to a discussion about ways and means. In a debate, for example, on the *rights* and *wrongs* of capital punishment, someone inevitably says, "Well it's a heck of a lot cheaper than keeping them in jail all their lives." This argument will sway many people: they can be tricked into deciding an issue of *right and wrong* simply on the grounds of *cost*. It's illogical, but it works well enough.

Argument Based on Unverifiable Information *(Argumentum ad Ignorantiam).* When the reader cannot verify the facts, the writer may be tempted to twist them. The most blatant cases involve faking the results of scientific experiments. A more subtle approach is revealed in an interview Donald Regan, President Reagan's former chief of staff, gave to the New York *Times*:

> Some of us are like a shovel brigade that follows a parade down Main Street cleaning up. We took Reykjavik and turned what was really a sour situation into something that turned out pretty well. Who was it that took this disinformation thing [American plans to attack Libya] and managed to turn it? Who was it took on this loss in the Senate and pointed out a few facts and managed to pull that? I don't say we'll be able to do it four times in a row. But here we go again, and we're trying.

Regan's "here we go again" refers, of course, to the sale of arms to Iran and the diversion of payments to the Contras. Regan is assuming that the public has no way of knowing what *really* happened, so the "shovel brigade" can twist or suppress information as it sees fit. The gravity of Regan's misjudgment is now history.

These seven logical traps are deliberately set by the propagandist; as a student writer, you'll use such traps only by accident. It's important to check your work thoroughly for such "accidents": the reader does not know your intentions—and a dirty trick is a dirty trick, whether you intended it or not.

B. THE NON SEQUITUR: CONCLUSIONS THAT DO NOT ARISE FROM THE EVIDENCE

A second group of traps comes under the umbrella of the *non sequitur*, a Latin phrase meaning "It does not follow." They occur when facts are given and a conclusion is drawn—but the conclusion simply does not follow.

Confusion of Chronology with Causality *(Post hoc ergo propter hoc).* When one thing follows another in time, it is easy to imagine that the first event caused the second. For example, a student says: "Last week I had a run-in with my history teacher, and the next week I made a D on my essay test. That guy is really out to get me." A quarrel *followed by* a bad grade is not necessarily the same thing as a bad grade *caused by* a quarrel. "Ever since you went to college you've treated your home like a hotel!" says the angry mother. She implies that going to college has *caused* the change of attitude, ignoring the fact that her offspring is growing up anyway. You can see the problem: if one thing follows another, there *may* be a cause-and-effect relationship—or there may not. If you are arguing honestly, you have to prove the pattern of cause-and-effect, not just gloss over it.

The Broken Chain of Cause and Effect (The pure *non sequitur*).   Product advertising often ruptures the chain of cause-and-effect. For example, Romany Bride, the latest pop idol, uses a certain brand of soap; an advertisement implies that by using this soap the reader will . . . . Who knows what unrealizable dreams the advertisers mobilize in us? In fact, the soap will clean your body, but that's all it will do. Let's look at a more subtle example. An advertisement for typewriters once offered this argument:

> In an independent survey of high school and college instructors, fifty per cent agreed: Students who type usually receive better grades . . . . Though a student's ability and the subject being taught are factors, fifty per cent of the instructors agreed . . . . students who type usually receive better grades. If there is a student in your family, wouldn't this back to school time be the perfect time for you to purchase a typewriter?

This argument is worth looking at closely. First the statistics. Half the instructors agreed—half disagreed. Students, it is said, *usually* received better grades. Without a definition of *usually*, we can take it to mean 51 percent of the time (or possibly more). So, in about 25 percent of cases, students receive better grades. Better than what? The implication is that the grades are better than those of other students, but this is not put into words: "better" could simply mean that a typed essay receives a better grade than the same essay untyped. Since many classes *require* typed papers, that should come as no surprise. Now for the cause-and-effect argument: buying a typewriter will *cause* the student in your family to receive better grades. The case is full of holes. First, it is not buying a typewriter that improves grades, but using it. Next, there is no evidence that it is the *typing* that improves the grades. It could be that the kinds of students who type their papers are inherently better students: they have a better attitude to academic work; they are more concerned with presentation; they come from wealthier typewriter-owning backgrounds where academic performance is valued and where there are fewer financial worries. Ultimately, we must say *non sequitur*—it does not follow. Where, in fact, is the burden of proof? Very much with the writer. The reader can reject the whole idea simply by saying: I see no conclusive evidence that buying a typewriter improves grades.

The False Analogy.   Another kind of false conclusion arises from *argument by analogy*. An analogy is a comparison used as a clarification. In itself it proves nothing. A simple example is the fable of the tortoise and the hare; this story shows that slow and determined can beat quick and cocky. Can we go further? Does the story show, for example, that a thick shell guarantees determination or that long ears are a sign of cockiness? Certainly not. No case can be built on an analogy; an analogy is simply an example. Often, however, a writer uses an analogy as though it does make a case. An example occurs in an article on art forgeries by Thomas Hoving. He poses an interesting question: "*If* a forgery can fool everyone, even the experts, why isn't it as valid as the work it pretends to be?" Hoving deftly answers in this way: "As for fakes being the real thing, I can only say that art collecting is a love affair, and when you find out that your lover has been deliberately lying to you for years, it's all over." (*Connoisseur*, November 1986, p. 41) That's a neat analogy, but it's not a sound argument. The fake picture is compared to a cheating lover, but in fact the picture has not been "deliberately lying," nor has it been fornicating with another collector. The *faithfulness* of the picture is not the issue, but its *beauty*. "Why is a discovered forgery no longer a beautiful picture?" That's the question. A lover who has been lying for years is no less beautiful because this behavior is exposed. Hoving's argument by analogy fails to tackle the question. For you as writer, the message is plain: check carefully whenever you use a comparison (an analogy) to make a point clear. The analogy proves nothing and you can go nowhere with it; it is simply an illustration.

C. THE USE OF MISLEADING OPTIONS

A common and effective maneuver is to limit the options available to the reader and to make one option totally unattractive. In this way, the reader can be stampeded into your camp.

The All-or-Nothing Choice. An *all-or-nothing choice* is like a zero-sum game, the final of the World Soccer Cup, for example—either you win or you lose. All or nothing. Life is seldom like a World Cup Final: usually there are options other than winning or losing. One common political all-or-nothing maneuver occurred in an earlier example:

> President Reagan said that the nation will risk war if his request for an 18 percent increase in military spending is reduced by Congress as a way to cut the deficit.

Eighteen percent, all of it, or risk war! A car salesman might use the same technique: "We never haggle about prices. You pay the sticker price, or no sale." Both the salesman and President Reagan are conducting their business legitimately, but not with scrupulous honesty. A small reduction in the defense budget will not drastically increase the risk of war; an offer to buy ten cars will lead to a quick reconsideration of the sticker price. We are seldom in an all-or-nothing situation, whatever claims are made to the contrary.

The False Dilemma. A similar trap lurks in most dilemmas. Occasionally, there are genuinely two choices: for example, you can go swimming either naked or clothed. Usually, however, there are many options. Artificially narrowing the choice creates a *false dilemma*. An example: an encyclopedia salesman will offer you a choice—*950 Great Books of the World* for $1,750 or the *Encyclopedia Universa* for only $1,600. You have other choices, of course, principally to buy nothing at all, but these options are seldom mentioned by the salesman. The old bumper sticker similarly poses a *false dilemma*: "America—love it or leave it." As a writer, ensure that you don't railroad the reader by excluding available, but inconvenient, options.

CONCLUSION

Your goal when making a case is to move the reader in your direction. Most readers are highly "sales resistant" when it comes to ideas with which they disagree. You will certainly lose your "customer" at the first sign of deliberate trickery on your part. In the same way, weak or illogical arguments will destroy your case. Students seldom deliberately set the traps we have just discussed for their instructors; usually the trap is set by accident, and it is not the instructor but the student who blunders into it. Work hard to spot such basic errors in your arguments, and then eliminate them.

SUMMARY

The logical traps we have discussed are:

A. Making a case that satisfies the audience (but ignores the truth).

a. Argument Using an Accepted Authority
   Example: "You are a Lutheran. Luther says do this. You have to do it."

b. Argument Based on Prejudice
   Example: "You hate communists. He is a communist. You can't believe what he says."

c. Argument Based on a Concession
   Example: "Do you believe in absolute free speech? You do! Okay, then you have to allow me the right to shout 'Fire' in a crowded theater."

d. Argument Based on Fear
   Example: "Only Hitler can prevent the Reds from murdering you in your bed. Vote for him."

e. Argument Based on Pity
   Example: "You can't put him in jail for five years. He has a wife and twelve children who will starve."

f. Argument Based on Greed
   Example: "It is *right* to execute criminals because it *costs* too much to keep them alive."

g. Argument Based on Unverifiable Information
   Example: "I have seen a secret CIA plan for the assassination of Margaret Thatcher."

B. Using a non sequitur: a conclusion not based on the evidence.

a. Confusion of Chronology with Causality (*post hoc ergo propter hoc*)
   Example: "After the war the bikini came into fashion, so war obviously has a liberating effect on beachwear."

b. The Broken Chain of Cause and Effect (the pure *non sequitur*)
   Example: "Movie stars divorce and remarry often. If I go through a couple of divorces, it will help me become a movie star."

c. False Analogy (using a comparison as more than an illustration)
Example: "The crow who wanted to be a swan could not become one; so white birds are better than black birds."

C. **The use of Misleading Options.**
a. All or Nothing
Example: "The sticker price or nothing—we never haggle."

b. False Dilemma
Example: "America—love it or leave it."

Concept Review

Traps in Logic

The following extracts, mostly adapted from student essays, demonstrate each of the errors in the list above. One perfectly logical sentence has also been included. Attach the appropriate error label (or labels) to each sentence.

1. If you admit that America is a Christian country, then you have to agree that our society should shape itself in accordance with the rules laid down in the New Testament. [Let's assume the reader agrees to this. Ed.] St Paul clearly states that women are inferior to men. "The head of the woman is the man . . .; neither was the man created for the woman, but the woman for the man." (I Corinthians 11) Our society has a duty to follow Christian teaching in this respect as much as in any other.

2. There are no prizes for coming second in the business world; only coming out on top really counts.

3. The use of drugs by singers has had a devastating effect on record sales. Jimi Hendrix died in 1970. Since then sales of phonograph records have gone steadily downhill.

4. For reasons of security I cannot give the source of my information, but a report exists showing that over three-quarters of American servicemen are threatened by alcoholism.

5. Our society is wrong to ban the use of "controlled substances." There is nothing inherently wrong in their use. After all, Washington, Jefferson and Franklin all used opium. [As a painkiller. Ed.]

6. The Strategic Defense Initiative is our only hope. Unless we have an effective nuclear shield before the end of the century, we will inevitably fall victim of a Soviet first strike. [*Two* strikes against this one. Ed.]

7. The South African system of apartheid is disgusting; no sane person doubts that. So when the South African government talks about black terrorists infiltrating their country from Mozambique, they are obviously lying.

8. Two choices confront us: either we can continue with (or even expand) our use of nuclear energy, or we can begin to phase it out.

9. The United States was right to pull out of South Vietnam—democracy has to be defended, but not when it means increasing income tax in America.

10. A human brain is exactly like an enormously powerful computer. With a computer, the programing is what counts. We should educate children with the same care that we write computer programs—in that way we could prevent crime and produce happy, perfectly functioning citizens.

11. There is no way of predicting who is liable to turn into a rapist: I would advise a woman never to get into a car with a man unless she has a knockout spray or something similar in her purse.

12. Unmarried mothers have an extremely harsh and difficult life; the government should guarantee them at least the same standard of living as that of the average middle-class family.

13. It is an established fact that smokers have lower college grades than nonsmokers. [This *is* a fact. Ed.] It follows, therefore, that by giving up smoking, you will improve your grades.

2 •
The Personal Voice

Joseph Heller's *Catch-22* is set in Italy toward the end of World War II. In this extract, an army flyer, Yossarian, is making a case. He is trying to prove, to Major Sanderson, the unit psychiatrist, that he is insane. Sanderson is the first speaker.

"This fish you dream about. Let's talk about that. It's always the same fish, isn't it?"

"I don't know," Yossarian replied. "I have trouble recognizing fish."

"What does the fish remind you of?"

"Other fish."

"And what do other fish remind you of?"

"Other fish."

Major Sanderson sat back disappointedly. "Do you like fish?"

"Not especially."

"Just why do you think you have such a morbid aversion to fish?" asked Major Sanderson triumphantly.

"They're too bland," Yossarian answered. "And too bony."

Major Sanderson nodded understandingly, with a smile that was agreeable and insincere. "That's a very interesting explanation. But we'll soon discover the true reason, I suppose. Do you like this particular fish? The one you're holding in your hand?"

"I have no feelings about it either way."

"Do you dislike the fish? Do you have any hostile or aggressive emotions toward it?"

"No, not at all. In fact, I rather like the fish."

"Then you do like the fish."

"Oh, no. I have no feelings toward it either way."

"But you just said you liked it. And now you say you have no feelings toward it either way. I've just caught you in a contradiction. Don't you see?"

"Yes, sir. I suppose you have caught me in a contradiction."

Major Sanderson proudly lettered "Contradiction" on his pad with his thick black pencil. "Just why do you think," he resumed when he had finished, looking up, "that you made those two statements expressing contradictory emotional responses to the fish?"

"I suppose I have an ambivalent attitude toward it."

Major Sanderson sprang up with joy when he heard the words "ambivalent attitude." "You do understand!" he exclaimed, wringing his hands together ecstatically. "Oh, you can't imagine how lonely it's been for me, talking day after day to patients who haven't the slightest knowledge of psychiatry, trying to cure people who have no real interest in me or my work! It's given me such a terrible feeling of inadequacy." A shadow of anxiety crossed his face. "I can't seem to shake it. . . .

"I'd like to show you some ink blots now to find out what certain shapes and colors remind you of."

"You can save yourself the trouble, Doctor. Everything reminds me of sex."

"Does it?" cried Major Sanderson with delight, as though unable to believe his ears. "Now we're *really* getting somewhere! Do you ever have any good sex dreams?"

"My fish dream is a sex dream."

"No, I mean real sex dreams—the kind where you grab some naked bitch by the neck and pinch her and punch her in the face until she's all bloody and then throw yourself down to ravish her and burst into tears because you love her and hate her so much you don't know what else to do. *That's* the kind of sex dreams I like to talk about. Don't you ever have sex dreams like that?"

Yossarian reflected a moment with a wise look. "That's a fish dream," he decided.

Major Sanderson recoiled as though he had been slapped.

"Hasn't it ever occurred to you that in your promiscuous pursuit of women you are merely trying to assuage your subconscious fears of sexual impotence?"

"Yes, sir, it has."

"Then why do you do it?"

"To assuage my fears of sexual impotence."

"Why don't you get yourself a good hobby instead?" Major Sanderson inquired with friendly interest. "Like fishing. Do you really find Nurse Duckett so attractive? I should think she was rather bony. Rather bland and bony, you know. Like a fish."

"I hardly know Nurse Duckett."

"Then why did you grab her by the bosom? Merely because she has one?"

"Dunbar did that."

"Oh, don't start that again," Major Sanderson exclaimed with vitriolic scorn, and hurled down his pencil disgustedly. "Do you really think that you can absolve yourself of guilt by pretending to be someone else? I don't like you, Fortiori. Do you know that? I don't like you at all."

Yossarian felt a cold, damp wind of apprehension blow over him. "I'm not Fortiori, sir," he said timidly. "I'm Yossarian."

"You're who?"

"My name is Yossarian, sir. And I'm in the hospital with a wounded leg."

"Your name is Fortiori," Major Sanderson contradicted him belligerently. "And you're in the hospital for a stone in your salivary gland."

"Oh, come on, Major!" Yossarian exploded. "I ought to know who I am."

"And I've got an official Army record here to prove it," Major Sanderson retorted. "You'd better get a grip on yourself before it's too late. First you're Dunbar. Now you're Yossarian. The next thing you know you'll be claiming you're Washington Irving. Do you know what's wrong with you? You've got a split personality, that's what's wrong with you."

"Perhaps you're right, sir," Yossarian agreed diplomatically.

Joseph Heller
From *Catch-22*

Review Assignment

Dialogue

This dialogue bears the true stamp of Joseph Heller—the kind of demented logic that has passed into the language as catch-22. (*Webster's Ninth New Collegiate Dictionary* spends eleven lines defining *catch-22*.) In this extract, Yossarian finally agrees that he is Fortiori—Fortiori living under the delusion that he is Yossarian. This admission of insanity may achieve the desired discharge from the military, but for Fortiori, not for Yossarian himself.

The use of dialogue takes our experiments with voice to their logical conclusion. Think of a situation in which one character has to make a case, and then try to develop the argument as a *dialogue* between two contrasted characters. (The first twenty suggested assignments in the next section offer some possible situations.) Try to stay away from narrative, and try also to keep the speech turns short. Heller is a model in these respects.

3 •
Writing Workshop: Making a Case

• Choosing a Subject

Research. Making a case can entail extensive research. Until research techniques have been presented in Part 3, you should probably limit yourself to subjects on which you already have plenty of information.

Readership Analysis. A writer never makes a case in a vacuum; there is always a target reader. In an academic paper, the target reader is a known person with known expectations. In other contexts, the reader may be someone altogether different. We'll explore the problem in depth in Part 3. In the meantime, some of the subjects below have been coupled with a target reader. If you write on one of those subjects, angle your arguments for the target reader, not for your instructor. As to style, formal, academic, written English is appropriate in all cases.

Making a Personal Case.   In day-to-day life, we often make a case for something that affects us personally:

1. *Reader:* your "boss." *Goal:* to be awarded a pay raise or a promotion.
2. *Reader:* a neighbor. *Goal:* to achieve cessation of some objectionable behavior.
3. *Reader:* a university (or college). *Goal:* to be given academic credit for some noncredit training or activity.
4. *Reader:* a tax authority. *Goal:* to be released from some kind of tax assessed against you.
5. *Reader:* an insurance company. *Goal:* to be reimbursed for some kind of loss arguably covered by your policy.
6. *Reader:* a firm that has sold goods to you. *Goal:* to achieve repair or replacement of the goods, although the warranty situation is unclear.

In your personal correspondence file, you may find a case that you lost. Perhaps you could now try to present your case more effectively.

Making a Social Case.   Citizens have the right to lobby for their interests. How would you argue one of these cases, or a similar case known to you?

7. *Reader:* the nuclear energy committee of a state legislature. *Goal:* to prevent the building of an atomic waste disposal facility in your state.
8. *Reader:* the top management in your company. *Goal:* to have a workplace free of tobacco smoke.
9. *Reader:* a bus company. *Goal:* to prevent the closure of a rural bus route.
10. *Reader:* a water company. *Goal:* to provide customers with a monthly chemical analysis of their drinking water.
11. *Reader:* the commander of a military base. *Goal:* to cease overflights by helicopters after 5:00 p.m. and on weekends.
12. *Reader:* the publisher of a magazine. *Goal:* to cease accepting some kind of advertising that you think objectionable: for alcohol, tobacco products, and so on.
13. *Reader:* a bookstore. *Goal:* to cease the sale of material that is pornographic or demeaning to women.
14. *Reader:* a school principal. *Goal:* to restore to the library important works of literature removed on the grounds of "indecency."
15. The President of the United States and your representatives in Congress are keen to hear the views of ordinary citizens. Draft a letter that makes a case on a subject of concern to you.

Making a Suggestion. Nothing is perfect. The subjects below offer suggestions for improving things at your place of work. A suggestion usually begins with a clear statement of the problem; this is followed by a concise statement of your suggestion. Then you must make a case for your idea.

16. Suggest a way of improving morale in your office or workplace.

17. Suggest a way of using less raw material or fewer supplies.

18. Suggest a way of saving work hours.

19. Suggest a way of making a machine more productive.

20. Suggest a way of solving an administrative or technical problem that has arisen.

Making an Academic Case. The subjects below are simply controversial statements. Followed by the word *Discuss*, each could appear as an essay subject in an academic course of some kind.

21. The use of a quota system to achieve racial or sexual equality does not work.

22. The space program is an expensive luxury that should be discontinued.

23. America will never have a woman president.

24. The United States should leave Nicaragua to its fate.

25. Inferior people are happier as slaves than they are as free people.

26. The defense of Israel plays too big a role in American foreign policy.

27. *All* murderers should be executed.

28. The United States should get out of nuclear power generation immediately.

29. Television is destroying what is left of family life.

30. War toys should be banned.

31. The sale of pornography to men threatens the safety of women.

32. Computers are not labor-saving devices; they force users to work harder.

33. There is no point in making treaties with the Soviet Union since the Soviets cannot be trusted to abide by their commitments.

34. The United Nations should be scrapped.

35. The video tape recorder will kill normal television broadcasting.

36. The U.S. Army and Air Force have no reason to be in Europe.

37. Alcoholism is not a disease; it is a sign of a weak character.

38. Nobody has the right to tell me what I can read/to tell me what I can do in the privacy of my own bedroom/to tell me what I can put into my own bloodstream.

39. AIDS is a punishment sent by God.

40. A married couple should never stay together "for the sake of the children."

• Thinking Things Through—The Game Plan

No two cases are ever made in quite the same way; everything depends on the subject and on the target reader. Nevertheless, following one student through the process of making a case will give you an idea how to proceed.

Background.   Abel Townshend worked in a library. He had two children in high school when he began his bachelor's degree. During his English 101 class, his children told him that a number of classic books had been silently withdrawn from their high-school library. Included were works of fiction, such as *Lady Chatterley's Lover* and *The Catcher in the Rye*, as well as scientific works by Freud and Havelock Ellis. Abel telephoned the school and confirmed that this was so; some parents, he was told, found sexually explicit material unacceptable in a school library. Abel was indignant and asked me what I thought. I told him to write a letter to the school principal making a case and to solicit signatures from other parents.

Readership Analysis.   The high school principal had already made a decision under pressure from a group of parents. Abel saw that an about-face restoring the books to the library would be difficult for the principal. Abel would have to make his case respectfully and without showing the anger he felt. His real weapons would be a strong list of signatures and the veiled threat of a stormy session at the next Parent-Teacher Association meeting.

The Case for the Other Side.   Abel used the brainstorming sheet suggested earlier in the chapter to think through the case for the other side:

Subject: The removal of library books
My Point of View: Against

What are the arguments for the other side?	How far are they true?	How far can they be demolished?
They believe that sexually explicit material may "put ideas into children's heads."	Some extreme books (de Sade) should be kept away from immature teenagers.	Most children already have the ideas. Sensible adult books will give these ideas a mature framework.
There is enough sexually explicit material in "the environment" without adding to it in the school library.	This is true — there is an excess of cheap, degrading material around.	The books in question are not cheap, but major works that put the physical side of sex in perspective.

Abel's Own Case.   Similarly Abel developed his own ideas. Taken together, the two brainstorming sheets made an effective game plan.

What points do I want to make?	How can I insure that the reader understands the point?	What objections are there to this point?	How can I answer these objections?
Education should lead to tolerance.	Students already see the removal of the books as intolerant and repressive.	Toleration can go *too* far.	These book are not extreme, but mainstream. Students should evaluate such things themselves.
Sex without a moral background can be very destructive.	Children mostly encounter sex <u>divorced</u> from morality.	Deciding *which* morality is a problem.	Let the students have access to, and evaluate, *all* reasonable standards.

• Writing the First Draft

Before writing his first draft, Abel did not conduct formal, library research, but he talked things over with his wife and with other, like-minded parents; they gave him a number of ideas. His first draft was simply each segment of the game plan written up as a paragraph. The opening, the transition and the short closing (see the final draft at the end of the chapter) were all added later.

• Revising

The Flowchart on page 119 offers a general scheme for revising a first draft. Revising a case means paying particular attention to the logic of argument. Abel was especially anxious about this problem because he was writing to the high school principal, a trained academic. Let's look at some of the changes Abel made.

A. In his first draft, Abel spotted a classic logical error:

These fifty books have been paid for out of the library fund to which many parents contribute. These contributions were made so that books should be available to students, not so that books should be withdrawn and locked up.

A financial argument has been brought in here to settle a question of right and wrong. This is the argument based on greed. Obviously Abel could not use this argument because that would commit him to the view that *any* book that had been paid for, however vile, must stay on the shelves. That was *not* his position. He dropped this idea altogether.

B. Another formulation that Abel rejected was this:

> Unless these fifty books are restored to the shelves, the students will lose all faith in the authority of the school.

This is the all-or-nothing fallacy twice over. There are other choices than restoring all fifty books (restoring forty-nine of them, for example), and there are other possibilities than that all the students will lose all their faith in the authority of the school (some of them might lose some faith, perhaps). This idea finally appeared as:

> Books have been withdrawn, and many students see this action as intolerant and repressive. Whenever authority is seen as repressive, young people (and older ones too) tend to rebel against it. Prohibition simply doesn't work.

C. Abel spotted a *non sequitur* in this sentence:

> School spirit has already suffered, as can be seen by the poor attendance at the wrestling match last Saturday.

Abel suspected that the poor attendance was caused by the trouble over the books, but he had no way of proving it. The idea was better left out.

Conclusion. Making a case depends heavily on the quality of your argument. Work hard to pick holes in your own work. If you don't do it, you can be sure the reader will do it for you.

• The Final Draft

Abel's case was finally made in the following letter. (The principal, by the way, brought up the matter at the next Parent-Teacher Association meeting. Abel's group was well represented, and the books were restored to the library.) Your own final draft may not be in the form of a letter, but it might easily follow the same structure as Abel's piece. If your essay is based on library research, then your sources may require annotating; consult your instructor on this problem.

	Dear Principal:	Full letterhead is not given here
Who-What-Where-When	Recently about fifty books were removed from the shelves of the library of Deighton High School. Your administrative assistant told me on the telephone that a number of parents found the sexual	
Lead-in to the problem	explicitness of these books "unacceptable" in a school library. I, and the other undersigned, are not happy about this decision.	
Point 1 for the other side mentioned	I understand the concern of the parents who want the books removed, and in a large measure I share it. These parents feel that reading sexually explicit material might put wrong or even perverted ideas into the heads of their children. That is indeed a danger. There are books, those of the Marquis	Admission that the point is partly true
Counter-argument offered	de Sade for example, that might distress or harm immature teenagers. But the fifty books in question are simply not in this category. I know of nothing in any of the withdrawn books that is not already "in the minds" of my two children and their classmates. What teenagers need is a mature framework	

for the ideas that they already have. A book such as <u>Lady Chatterley's Lover</u> puts physical sex into the framework of a committed, adult relationship. Surely, there is nothing wrong in exposing our children to an idea such as that.

Pointing: Wrapup sentence

Point 2 for the other side

Some parents are unhappy about the way their children are endlessly bombarded with sexual material in advertising, in the media, in movies and so on. They feel that a school has no business increasing this pressure, and I agree with them. But these books were not in the library to increase this pressure: they were there to make sense of it, to give the students some way of putting it all in perspective. One of the missing books, <u>Jokes and their Relation to the Unconscious</u>, by Sigmund Freud, was brought home by my son, aged 17. After he'd read it, he passed it on to me. It was an unusual book. Freud repeats some very vulgar stories in that book, but he then tries to explain why people need to tell such jokes. Surely that's what a school is for—to help students understand the world they already know. They hear dirty stories all day every day, but now a book that helps them understand <u>why</u> has been removed from the library as "unacceptable." That can't be right.

Counter-argument offered

Admission that the point is partly true

Pointing: Wrap-up

Transition: Switch to Abel's viewpoint

I know the parents who have asked for the removal of the books, and I understand their point of view, but I think the action they have asked for is wrong. I want to suggest why the books should be put back on the shelves.

Abel's first point

Argumentation

Loophole closed

For me, education means learning to tolerate other people's ideas. Books have been withdrawn, and many students see this action as intolerant and repressive. Whenever authority is seen as repressive, young people (and older ones too) tend to rebel against it. Prohibition simply doesn't work. I'm not arguing for the removal of all control: toleration can obviously go too far. But when titles such as <u>To Have and Have Not</u> by Ernest Hemingway and <u>The Naked and the Dead</u> by Norman Mailer are silently removed from library shelves, I start to panic. This is <u>1984</u> all over again.

Admission of weakness

Pointing: Wrap-up

Abel's key point

Argumentation

Loophole closed

My final point is the most important. Outlawing explicit sexual discussion from the school means that dirty jokes, "adult" magazines, biology classes and Hollywood movies will be allowed to form an even greater part of our children's attitudes to sex. This is a disaster. If sex is to enrich life, then it must be understood against a moral background of some sort. Without moral control, sex easily becomes dangerous and destructive. I agree that there is a problem—whose morality? In answer to that, I would say that high school students are old enough to understand and evaluate various moral viewpoints for themselves. Removing sane, adult books from the library is not a step towards moral understanding; it is a big step away from it.

Admission of weakness

Pointing: Wrap-up

I understand that it may be difficult for you to reverse your decision to remove the books. Accordingly, I and the other undersigned, would like the subject raised at the next PTA meeting.

Closing: Simple request for action

Sincerely,

Abel Townshend

The list of many signatures is not given here

• Summary: The Flowchart

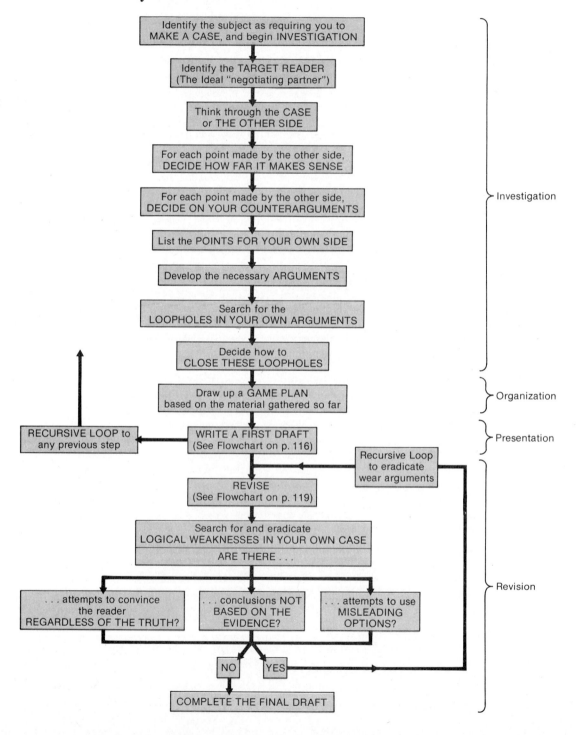

Conclusion: A Survival Kit

1 ·

The Problem: Survival

A survival kit will get you out of the desert alive—although the going can still be rough. The first two parts of this book have been intended as a "survival kit" for the academic desert (or jungle) ahead. Let's look at this kit one last time and see what went into it.

• Survival Kit Item 1: Invisible Language

Good academic writing does not draw attention to itself; it is "invisible" in the sense that the *ideas* and not the *words* come across to the reader. *Ideas* not *words*. Anything that diverts the reader's attention away from your argument and toward your language is a distraction and carries an automatic penalty. If you've completed most of the assignments so far, then you've probably mastered "Editorial English"—the invisible language of the academic essay. If you've attempted the exercises on personal voice, you'll know that different situations demand different styles, and you'll be on your way to achieving the necessary range.

• Survival Kit Item 2: Structures that Mean Something

An instructor assigns an essay question to test your understanding of the way the facts fit together. Because most academic essays serve this rather limited purpose, they are more highly structured than most other kinds of writing. You've studied the basic structures in their stripped-down, skeletal form, and you've solved the problem of fleshing out the skeleton with "relevant" and "appropriate" information—information that is relevant and appropriate to a thesis statement. The essays that you write in your future classes should make a strong point and make it well. That is what instructors are looking for.

• Survival Kit Item 3: The Right Tool for the Job

You've studied how to describe. You have studied how to use descriptions to build essays. You have studied the five most common problem forms and the corresponding answer structures. You should now be able to look through any list of essay questions and decide for each question how the answer should be (or might be) organized. Knowing the right tool for the job gives you a head start in tackling any writing assignment. To check that the trick really can be worked, let's look at a short examination containing ten typical essay questions. Your assignment is to decide for each topic which of our five structures might form the backbone of an answer. The first five shots are easy to call; thereafter it's more difficult. (Don't be discouraged if you know nothing about the subject; you should still be able to spot the appropriate structure.)

CONCLUSION: A SURVIVAL KIT

English 241: Introduction to the Novel Final Examination Answer three questions. Time allowed: two hours.	ESSAY TYPE				
	Comparison and Constrast	Definition	Cause and Effect	Classification	Case
1. Define "naturalism" in fiction.					
2. Hemingway leaves out of his novels everything that is not *essential* to understanding them; Trollope includes everything he can think of, much of it *inessential*. Compare and contrast any two novels by these writers in the light of this different of technique.					
3. Try to classify novels according to the public for whom they were written.					
4. After the First World War, a new kind of fiction emerged. What caused this change of technique?					
5. "Nobody takes literature seriously any more." Discuss.					
6. Novel writing can be broken down into three main periods. Discuss each of these periods and the kinds of novels that it produced.					
7. What is "defamiliarization" in the novel?					
8. Discuss Jean-Paul Sartre and Albert Camus as "existentialist" writers.					
9. Hemingway has been adulated as the patron saint of modern literature and denigrated as a macho sham. What is your opinion?					
10. Victorian novels are often extremely long and episodic in structure. Why?					
11. What distinguishes "Socialist Realism" from "Realism" as it is understood in non-communist countries?					
12. How do you account for the large number of successful women novelists in the nineteenth century?					

• Survival Kit Item 4: A Systematic Approach to Writing

Perhaps you'll forget every scrap of specific advice in this book, every technical term, and the name and shape of every structure. If, nevertheless, you've learned how to think through a writing assignment, then you've absorbed the most important lesson of all: *good academic writing is nothing more than systematic thinking recorded on paper.*

· PART THREE ·

The Research Paper

Introduction

What is Research?

Research is a glamor word. A plain biologist sounds like a dull sort of person, but upgrade the label to research biologist and the horizons immediately widen: romantic images arise of Watson and Crick cracking the genetic code, or maybe even of Frankenstein in his laboratory in Ingolstadt.

What is research? "Going to the library and reading up on things," a student once told me without enthusiasm. That may be *part* of a research project, although it does not have to be. But it is not the same thing as research. *Research is simply the start-to-finish process of handling information, however it is acquired and however it is used.*

Efficient research depends on asking the right questions at the right time. Two questions, in fact, arise before you can begin research at all:

1. Who is my reader?
2. What is my subject?

Who is my reader? The instructor, surely. The instructor is obviously the target reader for a standard student research project, but there are other, richer possibilities, too. It's a mistake to see research as a narrow, classroom activity that has no real-world applications. To broaden your perspective on target readers, Chapter 9 will show you how to take a profile of the reader and how to angle your material to this profile.

Researching a subject that interests you is in itself rewarding and enjoyable. Developing your work as a research project can be just as worthwhile—but there are dangers. A research project is shamelessly heavy on your time, and it can quickly erode your motivation. Careful planning is essential to ensure that you have a manageable subject that realistically fits your time schedule. Chapter 10 will help you with the crucial first decisions.

Once you are under way, research falls into four steps, each of which requires a special skill. None of these steps comes naturally, so Chapters 11–16 take you systematically through the skills a researcher needs. First, a familiar word of caution: a research project seldom proceeds step by step. There is inevitably, and desirably, overlap among the steps, and frequent recursion. Although we shall study it as a simple process, research is highly complex. The four steps then:

• Step 1: Finding Information

Unsurprisingly, research begins with finding information. Tracking down information takes two forms: (a) *field research*, which means conducting interviews and experiments in search of *new* information, and (b) *library research*, which taps a reservoir of information in a *prepackaged* form. Chapters 11 and 12 present the special skills you'll need in these two situations.

• Step 2: Storing Information

As you discover the material you need, you'll invoke Step 2, storing information. How can you store information so that it is immediately retrievable no matter how many times you rethink your project? That is the problem tackled in Chapter 13.

• Step 3: Evaluating Information

Once you begin reading, you'll be making notes on a deluge of facts, figures, and arguments. Some of this material will make perfect sense and some will be blatantly ridiculous; in many cases, however, you'll be hard pressed to decide *what* to believe. Chapters 14 and 15 will help you here.

• Step 4: Using Information

When all the facts are in and evaluated, then Step 4, Using Information, comes into play. This part of the process takes two tracks: (a) documenting your sources to help later researchers verify your work, and (b) putting your own ideas across with the aid of your source material. Sometimes you can simply follow your source; sometimes you must subject your source to destructive criticism. You'll learn how to do this in Chapter 16.

• Summary: The Flowchart

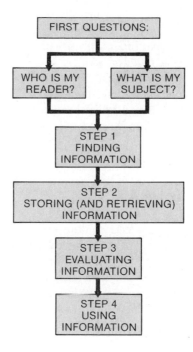

NINE

Researching the Reader

1 •

The Problem:
Reaching the Target Reader

• Editorial English: One Dialect Among Many

How to Speak Southern is the title of a book by Steve Mitchell. Is "Southern" a language? The book is in the form of a dictionary and includes such entries as:

HOW TO SPEAK SOUTHERN

Airs: Mistakes. "That shortstop's made two airs, and the game's not half over yet."

Bawl: What water does at 212 degrees Fahrenheit. "That gal can't even bawl water without burnin' it."

Cyst: To render aid. "Can Ah cyst you with those packages, ma'am?"

Earl: A metal device used to improve radio and television reception. "You could pick up a lot more stations if you had a higher TV earl."

Hard: To secure employment. "Ah didn't get that job. They hard somebody else."

Idinit: Term employed by genteel Southerners who wish to avoid saying "Ain't." "Mighty hot today, idinit?"

Madge: A state of wedlock that any preacher can put you into, but only a lawyer can get you out of. "Seems like a lot of madges end in divorce these days."

Orta: Should. "You orta see her in that bikini."

Spear: The opposite of inferior. "Ah couldn't get no satisfaction from that clerk, so Ah asked to see her immediate spear."

Zackly: Precisely. "Ah don't zackly know where he is."

So that's "Southern." The next question is addressed to all fair-minded north-erners: Is there anything *wrong* in speaking this way? Instinctively most people answer: "No, you can speak as you like." Then, on second thought: "Unless people can't understand you." This reservation implies a major principle: *language is acceptable if it achieves communication, but it is unacceptable if it does not.*

This principle, if true, is of great importance to you as a writer: it means that mutual understanding between writer and reader is all-important; this in turn implies that the "rules" of language depend not on the grammar book but on achieving mutual understanding. But where does that leave "Editorial English," the English we aimed at in Parts 1 and 2 of this book? Are English grammar and usage fixed, or is a writer allowed discretion and latitude? A specific case will help answer that question.

James Baldwin's *Go Tell it on the Mountain* is a novel. Many of the characters are Southern blacks displaced to the North early in this century. Baldwin carefully recalls their speech in many patches of dialogue. The dialogue below has been rewritten in play form to produce the undiluted flavor of this now-dead dialect:

SISTER PRICE: Is we first?

ELISHA: No, Sister Price; Brother Johnny here was the first. Him and me cleaned up this evening.

SISTER McCANDLESS: Ain't but you two who cleaned the church?

ELISHA: Lord, Sister McCandless, look like it ain't never but us two. I don't know what the other young folks does on Saturday nights, but they don't come nowhere near here.

SISTER McCANDLESS: It sure is time we had a revival among our young folks. They cooling off something terrible. The Lord ain't going to bless no church what lets its young people get so lax, no sir.

It's obvious that these three characters are in full and perfect communication. To achieve perfect communication, the speakers must be using a consistent set of rules for "encoding" and "decoding" their ideas. These rules may not be consistent with the rules of "Editorial English," but they must be self-consistent; otherwise there would be no communication. So—is there anything *wrong* with their grammar? Most linguists would say, "As long as these people are having no problems, the question of right and wrong does not arise." In other words, the rules of communication that a particular speech community adopts are valid rules within that community. (See the *Close-Up* below.)

That's not the end of the argument, however. Let's imagine that Elisha (or Sister Price) uses this dead dialect to write a letter applying for an office job. (With apologies to Baldwin) it looks like this:

```
Lord, Brother Rockerfellow:

Is you still holding that job open what I see in the newspaper?
It sure look good to me.  Ain't no way I going to pass up a job
like that if I can help it, no sir.  If you folks wants to see
me, I ain't hard to find--me and my old lady is generally home,
so you don't have to do nothing but call.

sincerely,
```

The grammar used in the letter above is much the same as Elisha used in the church, but now it is definitely wrong. Why? Because it is disastrously *inappropriate* to the situation. A job application requires standard written English. Elisha's letter will not achieve 100 percent communication with Mr. Rockerfellow. Why not? Will Mr. Rockerfellow have difficulty understanding it? A little, perhaps, but nothing serious. The real problem is that Elisha is communicating far *more* than he intends. His language projects the message: "I am not a suitable person to work in the business community."

Generalizing, we can say that language is "wrong"—that is, it is unacceptable, when it is inappropriate to the communication situation. Conversely, language is "right" when it fits the situation. One last glance at Elisha in the church will establish the point. Imagine the reaction of the two sisters if Elisha had said: "Good gracious, Sister McCandless, who do you imagine has been performing these lustrations if not Johnny and I. It's a perfect mystery to me how the juvenile portion of our congregation spends its Saturday evenings, but they seem to me particularly conspicuous by their absence." No "errors of grammar" now, but probably not much communication either. For you as a writer the principle is clear: *Language is a means to an end; to be effective, it must be adapted to the overall communication situation.*

Close-Up

Grammars and Grammarians

In 1693 the great poet John Dryden wrote that English lacked "a tolerable dictionary or a grammar, so that our language is in a manner barbarous." The next hundred years produced innumerable *grammars* aimed at fixing the English language once for all. In 1729, for example, Thomas Cooke's *Proposals for Perfecting the English Language* demanded abolition of all irregular verbs. Rules were laid down, many of them in defiance of normal speaking and writing practice. Alternative forms were abolished, the "correct" form being chosen either logically (as with the abolition of the double negative) or by appeal to the rules of Latin (as with the attempt to abolish "It's me" in favor of "It is I.") A grammar that ignores what native speakers do and tells them what they *should* do is called a *prescriptive grammar*.

In the nineteenth century, it was realized that all the Indo-European languages, starting with Sanskrit, are interrelated. To work out these interrelations, a new concept developed: *descriptive grammar*. A comparison of languages must ignore questions of "right" and "wrong" and simply say: this is what this group does (or did); this is their grammar. Descriptive grammar went a stage further in the early years of this century when Franz Boas and Edward Sapir began to collect American Indian languages before they died out. In this situation, the linguist lived with the tribe, describing each language from scratch.

The writer should keep *both* concepts of grammar in view: prescriptive grammar keeps you within the conventions of written English; descriptive grammar alerts you to many stylistic options.

Concept Review

Alternative Grammars

Many speakers ignore the rules of Editorial English in favor of familiar alternative rules. Look, for example, at this sentence: "I ain't ready yet, and Joe ain't ready either; we ain't going to make it on time." The alternative rule used here is apparently: "The present tense of the verb *to be* becomes *ain't* in its negative forms." Look now at these clusters of sentences. Each cluster illustrates a common "alternative rule." Basing yourself on these sentences, try to put this "alternative rule" into words.

a. She didn't have no money, I didn't have no time, so we didn't do nothing—I can't take no more weekends like that one.

b. I like donuts, and he likes donuts—him and me like donuts.
Mary, she likes jogging, and I like it too—me and her go jogging together most days.

c. Is we meeting Tuesday? We sure *are*—we're going to the movie.
Is you ready? You're late, you know—you're always late.

• Style and the Communication Situation

So far in this book the communication situation has been tightly controlled: academic essays written in Editorial English for a single reader, the professor who grades them. Writing effective term papers is essential to your success as a student, but your potential as a writer is far richer. Let's look at one student who had to master several "Englishes" to do an effective job. None of these Englishes was as extreme as that used by Baldwin's characters, but the range was still considerable.

Tracy was studying Computer Science. She was good enough to be asked to write a program to handle the departmental library. She wrote the program in Pascal, but as soon as the bells and whistles all functioned correctly, Tracy needed English—not one English, but three. First she had to write a training manual for the student librarians using the program. That was English 1: easy-to-read, layman's language, very personal and supportive, but at the same time logical and systematic—definitely not the language of the term paper. Then, since Tracy was at the end of her senior year, she had to leave a description of the program so that a later programmer could repair or alter it. That was English 2: the super-precise, technical prose of the professional programmer—again, not the style of a term paper. Finally she had to prepare a reference manual for experienced users, describing each procedure, the error messages and so on. That was English 3: a discontinuous style, allowing the reader to start reading *anywhere* and avoiding "flow" at all costs; snappy imperatives and fragmentary sentences pumped out the information fast. Not one of these Englishes was the Editorial English of the term paper; in fact term-paper English would have been *wrong* every time.

Developing the right English for any given communication situation depends in part on understanding what exactly comprises a "communication situation." The famous linguist, Roman Jakobson, identified six elements that are present whenever communication takes place. Jakobson's six communication elements are:

A. *Sender* In every communication situation there is a *sender*.

B. *Message* The sender must send something: the *message*.

C. *Receiver* Until the message is received there has been no communication. Obviously, we need a *receiver*.

D. *Contact* The message must be physically transmitted from the sender to the receiver, so there must be a means of *contact*.

E. *Context* No message is complete in itself. For example, a telegram that says SEND THE GOODS is meaningless unless both parties know the nature of the goods and their destination. These unexpressed "mutual understandings" are the *context*.

F. *Code* The sender and receiver must use a mutually understood *code* (or language), or there can be no communication.

Adapting Jakobson's ideas to our present purpose, we can say that the first five items on his list make up the "communication situation" for which the writer is "encoding." The choice of the "code" or language, item *F* on the list, depends on how the writer assesses the first five items. Let's look at each element in the communication situation and see how it might influence the writer's choice of language.

A. ASSESSING THE SENDER: WHO ARE YOU?

You, as writer, are not a fixed entity. In every piece you write, you're role-playing to some extent: a letter to your parents is not written in the same language as a letter to a lover; a complaint to a noisy neighbor is not written in the same style as a prayer. How do you want to come across to your reader? Or, a more sophisticated question: given your reader and your message, what would be an appropriate *persona* (assumed identity) for you as writer? A reader always reaches for the *persona* behind the words. Your choice of *persona* strongly influences your style.

B. ASSESSING THE MESSAGE: WHAT EXACTLY IS YOUR MESSAGE?

Like your choice of *persona*, your choice of message also depends on the target reader. Given this reader, is your message essentially a lecture, an argument, a story, a joke, a tearful plea, a set of instructions, a friendly chat, or what? Obviously the answer to these questions strongly influences the style of English you choose.

C. ASSESSING THE RECEIVER: WHO IS THE READER?

This question warrants a section of its own—everything depends on the target reader. See Profiling the Target Reader below for details.

D. ASSESSING THE CONTACT: HOW WILL THE READER HAVE ACCESS TO THE MESSAGE?

Some examples of the way contact influences style: a servicing manual for a car need not be as attractive as a sales flyer delivered with the junk mail; a textbook must reach a greater range of readers than a letter home; the instructions for a computer program are designed so that the reader can start anywhere, while a novel begins at the beginning. The way in which the piece will be *used* strongly influences the style in which you write it.

E. ASSESSING THE CONTEXT: HOW MUCH DOES THE READER ALREADY KNOW ABOUT THIS SUBJECT? WHAT ATTITUDE DOES THE READER HAVE TOWARD IT?

A piece for a novice uses different language from a piece for an expert; a piece defending motherhood is not as argumentative as a piece defending pedophilia. Building in the appropriate amount of information, reassurance, persuasion, or arm-twisting requires you to adapt your language carefully.

Concept Review

An Investigation of Style

These three passages are in radically different styles. After each passage are questions on the sender, the receiver, and so on.

A. Rabbits

This is a fierce bad Rabbit; look at his savage whiskers, and his claws and his turned-up tail. This is a nice gentle Rabbit. His mother has given him a carrot.

The bad Rabbit would like some carrot. He doesn't say "Please." He takes it! And he scratches the good Rabbit very badly. The good Rabbit creeps away, and hides in a hole. It feels sad.

This is a man with a gun. He sees something sitting on a bench. He thinks it is a very funny bird! He comes creeping up behind the trees. And then he shoots—BANG! This is what happens—But this is all he finds on the bench, when he rushes up with his gun.

The good Rabbit peeps out of its hole, and it sees the bad Rabbit tearing past—without any tail or whiskers!

Beatrix Potter
From *The Story of a Fierce Bad Rabbit*

a. *Sender* Potter is role-playing in this piece. *What* role?

b. *Message* The language of this story is strongly influenced by its message. What is the message? And how has it influenced the language?

c. *Receiver* What are the probable age, sex, socio-economic level, and general background of Potter's target reader?

d. *Contact* How do you imagine Potter's reader(s) would actually *use* this story? Do you see any traces of its original form as an illustrated book.

B. The Perfect Office

Desk. Keep the desk clean. It is a workbench, not a catchall. Never allow a lot of old-fashioned relics to accumulate on a desk. File everything away in its natural place, and dispose of all obsolete things. Keep current papers in a pending folder or basket with explanatory notes clipped to them. Beware of piling papers in file boxes and forgetting them. The more papers on a desk, the more to remember. Cover all papers or letters of a confidential nature when leaving the desk. Leave the desk clean at night. See that the typewriter is covered or closed in a desk.

Chair. An armchair is not a convenient chair for typing. A swivel chair with a good *back rest* is the most practical and restful. Chairs are often too high or too low for ease in typing. Adjust the height until the chair seems comfortable.

Lois Hutchinson
From *Standard Handbook for Secretaries*

a. *Sender* What picture do you form of Hutchinson from the tone of her piece?

b. *Message* The language of these instructions creates a "super-message" for Hutchinson's readers. It is not about desks or chairs but about their personal behavior. What is this "super-message"?

c. *Receiver* Profile Hutchinson's target reader: age, sex, socio-economic level, educational level, period in history.

d. *Context* How much shared knowledge is Hutchinson assuming in her reader? What kind of motivation would a reader need to stand up to this barrage of orders and snappy remarks?

C. Home

Home, home, home, it was home I was wanting, and it was HOME I came to, brothers. I walked through the dark and followed not the town way but the way where the shoom of a like farm machine had been coming from. This brought me to a sort of village I felt I had viddied before, but was perhaps because all villages look the same, in the dark especially. Here were houses and there was a like drinking mesto, and right at the end of the village there was a malenky cottage on its oddy knocky, and I could viddy its name shining on the gate. HOME, it said. I was all dripping wet with this icy rain, so that my platties were no longer in the heighth of fashion but real miserable and like pathetic, and my luscious glory was a wet tangle cally mess all spread over my gulliver, and I was sure there were cuts and bruises all over my litso, and a couple of my zoobies sort of joggled loose when I touched them with my tongue or yahzick. And I was sore all over my plott and very thirsty, so that I kept opening my rot to the cold rain, and my stomach growled grrrr all the time with not having had any pishcha since morning and then not very much, O my brothers.

Anthony Burgess
From *A Clockwork Orange*

a. *Sender* Burgess wrote this piece, but he is obviously role-playing an I-character whose name, in fact, is Alex. What picture do you form of Alex?

b. *Message* Alex uses many words of Russian origin; in most cases the meaning is clear from the context. Does this use of Russian words convey any special message to the reader?

c. *Contact* Judging by these few lines, what kind of book do you think *A Clockwork Orange* must be?

d. *Context* I once asked Burgess *why* he'd used Russian words when very few of his readers would know any Russian at all. He admitted he was unhappy about "losing" his readers, but he happened to know Russian, and it somehow fitted well with the character. Do you see this lack of "mutual understanding" between reader and writer as a serious problem?

• How Styles Vary

We've seen that language should be adapted to the communication situation, and we've looked at the factors in the communication situation that influence the choice of language. Turning now more closely to language: what are the variables? How exactly does one kind of English differ from another? The variables of style can be divided into two groups: (**A**) words themselves and (**B**) ways of phrasing things.

A. STYLE AND WORDS

To avoid drowning you in options, let's look only at the two key choices involved in picking words: plain versus fancy words, and non-specialist words versus specialist.

Some words are definitely fancier than others: *residence* or *domicile* as opposed to *house* or *home*; *companion* as opposed to *friend*; *prefabricated* as opposed to *ready-made*. Most of our day-to-day words come from Anglo-Saxon, the dialect of the Germanic tribes who conquered England after the Romans went back to Italy around 400 A.D. In 1066 A.D., England was once again conquered, this time by a group of French-speaking Vikings known as the Normans. For several centuries after the Norman Conquest, Anglo-Saxon was the language of the depressed peasantry while French was the language of the court, the legal system, and the administration. Ultimately, of course, the two languages merged into a creole known as "English." Modern American English preserves this ancient class distinction: peasant Anglo-Saxon words are still our "ordinary" words, while aristocratic French words, even today, have a more official or a more "impressive" sound to them.

Should you as writer systematically prefer one kind of word to another? Some writers on style advise using "Anglo-Saxon" words in preference to "French" ones, arguing that what is simple is always better than what is complex. But that misses the real point: a writer's choice of words should be subject to the total communication situation. Rather than using a rule of thumb, you should try to monitor your language word by word; the essential question should be: "Is this the right word to get this message across to this reader?" Usually the mix of words comes out differently for each piece you write.

Concept Review

Anglo-Saxon or Norman-French?

The paragraph you just read contains a fair mixture of "plain" words of Anglo-Saxon origin and "fancy" words that come from French. In many cases, it would be possible to find a synonym from the "other language." For example, what French-derived words, could you substitute for:

most (of), word, (this) time, after, today?

And what words of Anglo-Saxon derivation could you substitute for:

opposed (to), language, centuries, ultimately, illustrate?

Note: Check your substitute words in a dictionary to confirm their origin.

Jargon can be irritating, especially the jargon of a group from which one feels excluded. You may cringe, for example, when you hear a crowd of computer fanatics discussing a new 32-bit-addressable machine with a built-in modem and ten expansion slots. In fact, such jargon is unobjectionable: it is a series of precise terms for specific objects. Most new technologies find it more effective to create a new jargon than to force old words into unfamiliar, specialized meanings. When writing for your fellow experts, jargon is not a problem. For any other readership, however, these specialized words create a stiff and unapproachable style. "Keep out—specialists only," they seem to say. In general, keep specialized words for specialists.

Concept Review

Specialist Language

The expressions below are sometimes used by experts in addressing non-specialists. What "normal" word might be preferable in such a context?

A heavy meal can lead to a *cardiac arrest*.

The computer displays information on the *CRT*.

Mountaineers often communicate by means of a *transceiver*.

You can use a *potentiometer* to brown out a light bulb.

Phlebotomy usually reduces fever.

The summer months see little *precipitation activity*.

B. STYLE AND PHRASING

Words cluster into phrases, and style is often a matter of phrasing rather than of word choice. Again, let's simplify the question of phrasing to two vectors:

| Abstract | | | | | | | | | | | | | Concrete |

| Formal | | | | | | | | | | | | | Informal |

Abstract and *concrete* stand at the two ends of a continuum; every intermediate stage is also a possible choice. The differences between a concrete style and an abstract one have already been exhaustively discussed in the first two parts of this book; it's probably enough to repeat that for many purposes your style will gravitate toward the concrete end of the vector. Again, this is not a rule of thumb; your choice of style should be based on achieving your goals in the light of the overall situation.

Formal and *informal* writing are distinguished by their relative closeness to *spoken* English. The essays you have written so far have probably pulled away from spoken English and toward the formal end of the vector—but not to the furthest extreme. Absolutely formal language, the language of a legal contract, a diplomatic note or a scientific experiment, would be inappropriate for the subjects you've been tackling.

Concept Review

The Appropriate Style

What would be the appropriate degree of concreteness/abstraction for the following?

a. A recipe for Spaghetti Bolognese

b. A review of a book entitled *Making Money in Difficult Times* for publication in *The Wall Street Journal*

c. Instructions for changing the film in a camera

d. A two-page summary of the current state of the fight against AIDS

e. A twenty-word definition of irony

What would be the appropriate degree of informality/formality for the following?

a. The advice given in an Ann Landers type of column

b. A letter accepting an invitation to a movie premiere

c. A recipe for Spaghetti Bolognese

d. An application for a job interview as personal secretary to the head of a small company

e. A contract for the sale of a house

C. STYLE AND THE ACADEMIC RESEARCH PAPER

The three passages we studied earlier in the chapter were not offered as style models for writing academic research papers; in each case their language would be grossly inappropriate. But why? The reasons for excluding them offer some interesting clues about stylistic choices.

a. Exclusion of "Rabbits". As a style for research papers, Beatrix Potter's story is clearly out of court. Not only would its baby sentences sound odd in a research paper, but, far worse, they would make subordination (in the grammatical sense) impossible. Many ideas are almost impossible to express in very short sentences. For example, try reducing the following sentence to a string of super-short sentences:

> Once we ask ourselves what is involved in choosing a man or a woman *for the rest of one's life*, we see that to choose is to wager.
>
> Denis de Rougemont

b. Exclusion of "The Perfect Office". Hutchinson's style mixes short, sharp declarative sentences (such as "It is a workbench, not a catch-all") with a tidal wave of commands. She is depending on an authority structure that hardly exists in the modern western world. (She was writing in the 1930's when jobs were *really* scarce). No professor would tolerate this kind of thing from a student—and few students would tolerate it from a professor. She makes no attempt to *persuade* the reader. She is concerned simply with hammering out *information*.

c. Exclusion of "Home". Anthony Burgess/Alex not only uses a private vocabulary, he phrases his ideas in a wild and poetic way "Home, home, home, it was home I was wanting, and it was HOME I came to, brothers." Creative, poetic, impulsive language, language not bound by forms but rebelling against them, is not the language of academic research. The grammar of this piece is deviant, words are omitted that a complete sentence would normally include (this is called *ellipsis*), and speech rhythms are strongly marked, as you will see if you read the text aloud. The third strike against Burgess's language is its emotional charge. Emotion seldom has a place in academic writing, although it can be vital elsewhere—the last sections of the *Delcaration of Independence* for example.

D. SUMMARY

Let's summarize all these ideas about style and language in the form of a style analysis sheet. This sheet can be used either to evaluate an existing piece of writing or to map out the stylistic choices for an upcoming assignment.

STYLE ANALYSIS

Word choice

1. The words are predominantly

"Anglo-Saxon"				"French"

2. Specialist words are

Included			Excluded

Phrasing

1. The language is predominantly

Concrete			Abstract
Standard			Deviant
Excluded			Included

2. The grammar is
3. Ellipsis is

4. Patterns of *spoken* English are

Excluded			Included
Standard			Poetic/inventive
Scientific			Emotional
Allowed to flow			Kept short
Included			Excluded
Non-authoritarian			Authoritarian
Informative			Persuasive

5. The language is
6. The language is
7. Sentences are
8. Subordination is
9. The style is
10. The style is

Concept Review

Analyzing Style

Study the following passage. Then analyze its style using the style analysis sheet above.

The Legend of Junior Johnson

It was Junior Johnson, specifically, however, who was famous for the "bootleg turn" or "about-face," in which, if the Alcohol Tax agents had a roadblock up for you or were too close behind, you threw the car up into second gear, cocked the wheel, stepped on the accelerator and made the car's rear end skid around in a complete 180-degree arc, a complete about-face, and tore on back up the road exactly the way you came from. God! The Alcohol Tax agents used to burn over Junior Johnson. Practically every good old boy in town in Wilkesboro, the county seat, got to know the agents by sight in a very short time. They would rag them practically to their faces on the subject of Junior Johnson, so that it got to be an obsession. Finally, one night they had Junior trapped on the road up toward the bridge around Millersville, there's no way out of there, they had the barricades up and they could hear this souped-up car roaring around the bend, and here it comes—but suddenly they can hear a siren and see a red light flashing in the grille, so they think it's another agent, and boy, they run out like ants and pull those barrels and boards and sawhorses out of the way, and then—Ggghhzzzzzzzzhhhhhhgggggggzzzzzzzeeeeeong!—gawdam! there he goes again, it was him, Junior Johnson! with a gawdam agent's sireen and a red light in his grille!

Tom Wolfe
From *The Kandy-Kolored Tangerine-Flake Streamline Baby*

• Profiling the Target Reader

A reader is, in one sense, a customer. The task of the seller (the writer) is to present a "product" that the customer wants at a price (an investment of time) that the customer can afford. So far we have suggested that language must be adapted to the reader—but there is more. The ideas must be made *accessible* to the reader with suitable cases and examples; the means of presentation must be suitably *attractive*; and the reader must find the arguments *motivating*.

As yet we have a faceless, featureless readership. To advance, we need a technique for accurately profiling the readership. Many professional writers use a checklist or "inventory" of some sort—that way nothing important is forgotten.

READERSHIP PROFILE

How many readers? One ☐ 2–50 ☐ Many ☐

Sex — All male ☐ Most male ☐ Equal mix ☐ Most female ☐ All female ☐

Age — Young ☐ Middle ☐ Old ☐ Mix of _____

Family — Married ☐ Single ☐ Mix of married and single ☐

Ethnicity — Predominantly _____ Mix of _____

Nationality — Predominantly _____ Mix of _____

Income — Well off ☐ Middle-income ☐ Poor ☐ Mix of _____

Education — Bachelor's or higher ☐ High School ☐ Dropout ☐ Mix of _____

Occupation — All the readers are _____

The readers are a mix of _____

The readers have no common occupation ☐

Interests — All the readers share an interest in _____

The readers have no common interests ☐

Politics — Conservative ☐ Liberal ☐ Radical ☐ Mix of _____

Who am I in relation to my reader? _____

How much do my readers already know?

Little ☐ Some ☐ Much ☐ Mix of _____

What is their attitude to my message?

For ☐ Against ☐ Neutral ☐ Mix _____

In what form will my reader have access to my work? _____

Special features of this readership are _____

_____

A. ADAPTING YOUR LANGUAGE TO THE PROFILE

Getting your language right means adapting to your reader's (a) *capabilities* and (b) *expectations*.

a. Capabilities.   Two questions are important in evaluating the capabilities of the readership: What is its level of education? And how much does it already know about the subject?

If you are dealing with a single level of education (if, for example, all members of the readership are high-school dropouts, if they are first-year students, or if there is only one reader), then adjusting the level of language is really no problem. Difficulties begin when the readership has mixed abilities: a computer manual, for example, might be used by ninth graders or by university professors. When working with a *range*, you have two choices: you can pick a single level and stick to it, or you can vary the level to provide "something for everybody." Probably, it is best to stay at a single level—somewhere in the middle—not impossibly hard for the weakest and not offensive to the strongest. Once you've decided on a level, you'll have to experiment with your language, fine-tuning to get it right. If necessary, for example if you're writing instructions, field-test the work to ensure that it's comprehensible *to the reader.*

Your answer to the question "How much do my readers already know?" affects your style in a way that we have already discussed: the novice will be scared away by heavy, specialized terminology, while the old hand will resent the substitution of loose, inaccurate words for familiar, accepted terminology.

b. Expectations.   The expectations of the "audience" also affect your style. Let's take a blatant case. Before class, a group of twenty students are gossiping, using fairly earthy language. Would it, then, be appropriate for the lecturer to begin class with a string of cuss words? No. Students do not *expect* to be spoken to in this way; most of them would find the lecturer's style insulting. Similarly a letter from a company to a customer normally uses Editorial English, even if the customer is known to use a strong dialect; for the company to write a dialect letter might offend the reader's expectations. The question that provides the clue is: "Who am I in relation to my reader?"

The reader also has expectations that you can approach through another of the checklist questions: "In what form will my reader have access to my work?" Between the covers of a textbook, a reader expects (or will put up with) one kind of language; in a novel with a lurid cover and a title such as *Hitman for the Crazy Garter*, a different style altogether is expected. The physical form that your work takes often implies an appropriate style.

B. ADAPTING THE MATERIAL AND THE MESSAGE TO THE PROFILE

A writer, as we said earlier, is "selling" an idea to a reader. To be marketable, your material must: (a) be accessible to the reader, (b) be attractively "packaged," and (c) fulfill some need that the reader has.

a. Accessibility.   Often a reader understands all the words but misses the concept. This is usually a problem of examples, cases, and details. Either there are not enough examples and details to make the point clear, or the explanatory material passes the reader by. The key question in this case is: "How much do my readers already know?" The less they know, the more material you must include.

The next problem is this: what *kind* of material will work best? This is mostly a matter of common sense. Study the readership profile and see what suggests itself as useful or dangerous. If, for example, your subject is professional sport and your readers are all female, it is senseless to harass them with endless macho boxing stories; without stereotyping, you should pick examples that reflect "women's concerns." If your subject is cash flow and your readers are top managers, they will readily grasp an example taken from the federal budget, while the budget problems of welfare newlyweds would be foreign to them. Conversely, the problems of a pensioner deciding how to finance a second swimming pool will not grab the interest of evening students struggling to make ends meet. The checklist tells you what to go for and what to avoid. In discussing language, we said that if you have a *range* of readers, it is best to stick to a single language level; with explanatory material, the opposite is true: faced with a range of readers, try to provide something for everyone.

b. Packaging. Illustrations, graphs, tables, flowcharts, headings, the amount of text on each page, the appearance of the cover page, the binding—all these considerations are part of *presentation*. With an academic essay, you have little flexibility. In most other assignments, you're on your own. The general rule is to approach your reader from as many angles as possible: a picture, a chart, a passage of argument, a quotation, a dialogue—variety sustains interest. Headings break the text up into manageable chunks so that it seems less "threatening." In a word, does your work look *inviting*? Would it encourage "dipping" by a casual reader? Normally, it should.

c. Motivation. "Why should the reader agree with, or be interested in, what I'm saying?" Students writing academic papers rarely ask themselves this question (unfortunately). A writer outside the academic world who fails to ask the question—and to follow up by finding a convincing answer—will not reach the reader. Once again, a close study of the readership profile may clarify dangers and opportunities. If, for example, your subject is "Punk Rock" and the readership is well off and elderly, you can see at once the danger: you have a "hard sell" on your hands. Conversely, if your subject is "Loopholes in the Tax System" and your readership is middle-income, middle-aged parents, you can assume a high level of interest, and you can target your material very close to home. Once again, common sense and sensitivity towards people are the guidelines. Let's take an analogy from fishing. An argument is a baited hook; you are the angler, the reader is the fish. What bait are the fish taking today?—that's the crucial question. I personally like avocado, but there's not a fish in the world will touch it. The rule is: *the bait must taste good to the fish, not to the angler*. If I put forward arguments *I* find convincing, details that *I* find interesting, but that ignore the interests, the preconceptions, or even the prejudices of my reader, then I'm baiting my hook with avocado. The simple advice is—don't.

Concept Review

Constructing a Readership Profile

Read the following passages. Working backwards, try to reconstruct from one of them a readership profile.

1. The Pregnant Father

Unless you're reading this book under false pretences, you have just become a pregnant father. Traditionally, this is a time in a man's life when he becomes a rather uneasy background figure, hovering on the fringes of the great event. From time to time, catalogues of baby's clothing and equipment may be thrust under his nose; or his opinion may occasionally be sought on the size and design of the crib or the baby carriage.

But in between helping to conceive the child and giving out cigars at the other end of the process, very little attention has been paid to the man's side of pregnancy.

And, most definitely, there *is* a man's side.

For the first-time father, pregnancy can be puzzling, tiring and sometimes hurtful, and a frequent strain on the patience and the digestion.

The most unsettling fact to face is that your dear, familiar wife will change. She will change not only in shape, but also in disposition. She will be subject to uncharacteristic moods and fancies, often following one another with confusing speed.

She smiles, she weeps, she feels ravenous or bilious, she wants company, she wants solitude—all in the course of the same day and quite possibly even before lunchtime.

You, sir, have months of this to cope with.

Peter Mayle
From How to be a Pregnant Father

2. Leeches in Modern Medicine

When the leech attaches itself to a host, it pierces the skin with three teeth—one on each corner of a triangle—leaving a mark like the Mercedes-Benz logo. Because skin is elastic, it peels back, forcing wide the hole through which the leech reaches the blood supply. An enzyme in the creature's saliva slackens the blood vessels. The sensible leech keeps a low profile. Its saliva contains an anesthetic which numbs the wound, keeping feeding time quiet.

There are more than 600 species of leech. All are fairly long, thin, worm-like and drink blood—but some are more useful than others. To man, *Hirudo medicinalis* is the most useful. In its saliva are two compounds which make dinner-time less hard work for leeches—and microsurgery more like feeding time at the zoo. The first is an enzyme called orgelase, which dissolves the tissue-cement that binds cells together. As the cells separate, the saliva, containing the anesthetic and an anti-coagulant, can move more freely through the host's blood stream. The second is the anti-coagulant itself. For blood to clot, fibrinogen, a protein dissolved in the blood, is precipitated at the site of the wound as fibrin when acted on by an enzyme called thrombin. Hirudin, a non-enzyme produced in the leech's gut and secreted in saliva, inactivates the thrombin. This breaks the link in the blood-clotting chain and keeps blood fluid for up to 24 hours.

That property is making leeches useful in operating rooms.

From "Leeches find their niches"

3. Slavery

The devil white man cut these black people off from all knowledge of their own kind, and cut them off from any knowledge of their own language, religion, and past culture, until the black man in America was the earth's only race of people who had absolutely no knowledge of his true identity.

In one generation, the black slave women in America had been raped by the slavemaster white man until there had begun to emerge a homemade, handmade, brainwashed race that was no longer even of its true color, that no longer even knew its true family names. The slavemaster forced his family name upon this rape-mixed race, which the slavemaster began to call "the Negro."

Human history's greatest crime was the traffic in black flesh when the devil white man went into Africa and murdered and kidnapped to bring to the West in chains, in slave ships, millions of black men, women, and children, who were worked and beaten and tortured as slaves.

Malcolm X
From *The Autobiography of Malcolm X*

2 •
Writing Workshop:
The Double Readership

Nothing is more vital to a writer than a clear sense of the reader. Researching the reader is Step 1; adapting your work to the reader is Step 2. This workshop challenges you to present one message to two radically different readerships. This will mean first analyzing the two readerships; then you'll have to adapt your language, the specific information you use, the way you present the material, and your "selling psychology" to two readerships.

• Two Readers: Two Pieces—Choosing a Subject

Group 1. With the first group of subjects described below, there is a clear split between a sympathetic readership (an easy sell) in the lefthand column and a hostile readership (a hard sell) on the right. (Questions 3 and 5 are reversed, of course.) The problem here is to discover and build on the right *motivation*.

1. A manufacturing company with 900 employees (97 percent white in an 80 percent white community) is suspected of practicing racial discrimination in hiring. You write a handbill to be passed out at the factory gate calling on *all* employees to take one-day strike action against discrimination.	You explain the necessity of the strike, but this time in the form of a short article for a hometown newspaper read mostly by minorities.
2. The PTA at your local high school is trying to fire a teacher because he (or she) has openly admitted to being a homosexual. You write an open letter to all PTA members defending the teacher.	You write a Letter to the editor of *Gay News* denouncing the attitude of the PTA and defending the teacher.

3. The same as 2, except that you *support* the PTA and attack the teacher for both readerships.	
4. *Young Feminist*, a national magazine, has called for a public forum about abortion on demand. You decide to write to the forum attacking such abortions (though not abortion under *all* circumstances).	*Catholics Awake*, again a magazine with national distribution, has also called for a forum on the same topic. Again you decide to write attacking abortion on demand.
5. The same as 4, except that your message is pro-abortion for both readerships.	

Group 2. These subjects create a different problem of motivation: *interest*. Here, the readership on the left has no real interest in the subject, while the readership on the right will be spontaneously interested in your piece.

6. You come from a small rural town, and you are at present working (or studying) abroad. Your hometown newspaper asks you for a short article on what things are like out there.	You are still working (or studying) abroad, but this time your firm (or your stateside university) asks you to write a short article for employees (students) about to be assigned to your part of the world.
7. Your company newspaper has a column entitled "Family Vacation Ideas." After a two-week vacation trout fishing in Canada, you decide to write an article for this column.	You are a subscriber to *Fly Fishing* magazine. After your two-week vacation in Canada you write an article on "Trout Fishing in Manitoba."

Group 3. The next two subjects show the difference between a *negotiation* and a *debate*. In a negotiation you must convince your negotiating partner, *the person on the other side*; in a debate you must convince *third parties* that you are right and that the other side is wrong. (The negotiations are on the left; the debates are on the right.)

8. The *Fascist Monthly* has published an article denying that large numbers of Jews were killed in Nazi concentration camps. You write a letter of protest to the editor.	Your local radio station has a 10:00 p.m. program called "What's Bugging You?" Listeners call in with three-minute complaints. How exactly would you word your protest under these circumstances?

9. You are taking HISTORY 492: *The Contemporary Middle East*. The professor is a male Arab and a devout Moslem. As a "short answer" in the final exam, he includes the topic: "Should women go veiled in public?" Your answer is *No*.	The same course, same subject, same message—but this time you have to make a three-minute oral presentation to the class.

Group 4. The next two subjects highlight problems of accessibility. The readership on the left will have no problem understanding the material; the readership on the right will need much more help.

10. You work in a dental clinic. You are asked to write a short piece reminding parents of the benefits of good oral hygiene for their children.	You are also asked to write a piece on the same subject for the children themselves.
11. Write a set of operating instructions for booting a specific program on a specific personal computer.	Describe for the novice who has never used a personal computer how programs are booted. (Stick to one model of computer.)

Group 5. In the final group of subjects, style becomes crucial. Your language will be markedly different for the two readerships. The information you use, the physical appearance of the two pieces, and your "motivational strategy" will also contrast strongly.

12. Recently, there have been disturbances on campus involving students and police. You write an article for the campus student newspaper calling for a more helpful attitude toward law enforcement officers.	The same message, but this time as a 200-word essay answer during the Final Examination for LENF 230: *Criminal Law in Action*.
13. The same as 12, except your message is that police have no place on a campus.	
14. You must give a five-minute oral presentation to your English class on the topic: "Problems I am having with my research paper." Draft the text of your speech.	Present the same problems, only this time as a letter of complaint to the head of the English department at your school.
15. Write a short description of an automobile you know well for *Motoring Enthusiast* magazine.	Write a short review of the same car for *Nursery Day*, a magazine aimed at young mothers.

If one of the suggestions in the previous section appeals to you, then you are ready to go. If not, set up your own subject using one kind of problem as your starting point:

a. Put a message across to a readership that is strongly hostile, and then to a readership that is on your side.

b. Put a message across to a readership that is interested in what you have to say, and then to a readership that really couldn't care less.

c. Put a message across in a negotiating situation, in which you must convince the other side, and then in a debate, in which you must convince third parties.

d. Put across a message to a readership that already knows what you are talking about, and then to a readership that is ignorant of the material.

e. Put across a message to two readerships with widely different interests in the material (technical versus non-specialist, for example).

f. Put across a message in an academic and in a non-academic context.

g. Put across a message in oral as opposed to written form.

• Thinking the Assignment Through

Once you have a satisfactory subject, you may know how to proceed "instinctively." On the other hand, it may help you to work systematically. In this case, the first step is readership analysis. The checklist below poses the questions raised earlier in the chapter. Go through the checklist twice, once for each readership.

READERSHIP CHECKLIST

1. What exactly is my message?

(Remember, the message stays the same for the two readerships.)

2. Who is my reader?

How many readers? One ☐ 2–50 ☐ Many ☐

Sex	All male ☐ Most male ☐ Equal mix ☐ Most female ☐ All female ☐
Age	Young ☐ Middle ☐ Old ☐ Mix of _____
Family	Married ☐ Single ☐ Mix of married and single ☐
Ethnicity	Predominantly _____ Mix of _____
Nationality	Predominantly _____ Mix of _____
Income	Well off ☐ Middle-income ☐ Poor ☐ Mix of _____
Education	Bachelor's or higher ☐ High School ☐ Dropout ☐ Mix of _____
Occupation	All of the readers are _____
	The readers are a mix of _____
	The readers have no common occupation ☐

CHAPTER NINE
Researching the Reader

Interests   All the readers share an interest in _____

The readers have no common interests ☐

Politics   Conservative ☐ Liberal ☐ Radical ☐ Mix of _____

Special features _____

Review your answers and then ask:

a. Do I have any mixes that will create problems of *range*? If so:

What level of language should I stick to?

Should I try to motivate *all* my readers (something for everybody), or should I limit myself to a target group?

b. How much do my readers already know?

Little ☐ Some ☐ Much ☐ Mix of _____

How technical should my language be?

Do I have problems of accessibility?

What clues in the checklist help me to choose examples?

What clues in the checklist warn me what to avoid when I choose examples?

c. What is the attitude of my reader to my message?

Positive ☐ Neutral ☐ Hostile ☐ Mix of _____

What motivational strategy is appropriate?

What kind of language will help?

3. **Who am I?**

a. Does my reader have any negative preconceptions about me?

b. What kind of language style might confirm these negative prejudices?

c. Will these prejudices make it hard for me to put my idea across?

d. How can I overcome this barrier?

e. How do I *want* my reader to perceive me?

f. What language style would be right for the *persona* I want to assume?

4. **How will the reader have physical access to my message?**

a. Does this kind of contact impose any constraints on length?

b. What are the reader's preconceptions about this means of contact?

c. How can I work with (or work around) these preconceptions?

d. What kind of language is appropriate to this means of contact?

When you've answered all these questions, you'll be overloaded with considerations, and there may be inconsistencies among your answers that you can't resolve until you have a first draft in front of you. What now?

The game plan for most of the subjects suggested would be little more than a list of key words. Prepare whatever seems convenient for the subject in hand; then write.

• Writing a First Draft

This assignment is rather different from earlier assignments. In a strictly academic context, the language is fixed, the appearance of the work is fixed, and the need for a well developed motivational strategy is slight. With so few variables, turning a good game plan into a good essay quickly becomes second nature. In the present assignment, everything has become a variable. With so many variables and some subtle psychological problems to solve, you'll find that presentation and revision require concentrated thought. This is true no matter how skillful or experienced a writer you are.

From your readership analysis, you know roughly what style you are shooting for, what points you should make, and what motivational strategy will best "sell" your ideas. The best tactic now is to "get something down in writing," in the assurance that this first draft will need several major rewrites. Try to form a picture of your reader in your mind's eye, and project your message to that reader fluently and confidently.

• Revising, and Writing the Final Draft

After the usual cooling-off period, review your first draft in the light of your goals. Study your answers to the checklist questions, and review your first draft to see where you have succeeded and where you still have work to do. In a piece that involves complex motivational problems, even a professional writer needs plenty of time for revisions and afterthoughts. As a final check, the detailed questions can be simplified to four "meta-questions":

1. Is the language right for the readership?   Yes☐ No☐
2. Are the ideas accessible to the intended reader?   Yes☐ No☐
3. Is the material suitably "packaged" in the physical sense?   Yes☐ No☐
4. Overall, will the reader be motivated to accept the message? Yes☐ No☐

If the answers are yes, then the assignment is nearly complete. If the answers are no, there is more work to do.

Naturally you must also revise for "correctness." Earlier in the chapter, we stressed that language is correct only for a given communication situation; even "English grammar" is not a monolithic set of inflexible rules. Check your language for its appropriateness to the *situation*, not for its appropriateness in a term paper.

• A Case Study

Judd Springfield was in charge of a workshop that serviced heavy farm equipment. Judd was told by his management to find ways of cutting costs. He had observed that the cotton waste used as cleaning rags was generally thrown away after a single use, long before it was really dirty. Since cotton waste cost the workshop $200 a month, Judd figured that using each rag two or three times could save the workshop at least $100 a month.

The idea left Judd's office in two written forms: a *memo* to the management and an *instruction* for the mechanics. How did the two pieces differ?

Most obviously, the *packaging* differed. In Judd's company, office memos simply followed a set form. In "packaging" the instruction, Judd had more options. He could pin up a notice on the board—but not everyone reads notice boards. He could circulate a single copy of the instruction and have each mechanic sign it; this struck Judd as too formal—he needed good-natured cooperation. A third possibility was a low-key personal note to each mechanic; that was the approach Judd chose.

As to *style*: the memo used tough, easy-to-read sentences, drained of emotional overtones. The personal note needed a warmer tone, friendly, persuasive and colloquial.

Motivation was Judd's major problem. The management would see little point in his suggestion, since it saved only $100 a month, while the workforce would see no point in it at all: the mechanics stood to gain nothing whatever by economizing. Judd realized that an *order* to use each rag until it was dirty would be ludicrous and unenforceable: he couldn't see himself picking over the trash cans for half-used rags. Judd needed a positive motivator. He decided that for every $100 saved, $30 should be allocated to the Sports Fund. That way the mechanics would benefit from economizing. That left Judd with a final battle: persuading the management to surrender the $30.

This is how the two pieces turned out:

```
                        MEMORANDUM

     From:      Judd Springfield, Workshop Manager
     To:        Amy Drew, Assistant to the General Manager
     Date:      February 15 1988, 4:00p.m.
     Subject:   Cost Savings
     Reply:     Required


     Suggestion

     In addition to the suggestions for cost saving submitted last
     week, a further idea: The workshop at present spends $200 per
     month on cotton waste as cleaning material.  If mechanics
     used this cotton more economically, savings of up to 50 percent
     of this cost could result.

     Action Required

     Since the mechanics will not effect this economy without some
     incentive, I suggest that $30 in every $100 saved be transferred
     to the Sports Fund.  Please confirm in writing that this can
     be done.

     Justification

     The sum saved will not exceed $70 per month, but the measure
     will directly affect the working procedures of the staff.
     Along with the other measures to be taken, it will make them
     more economy-minded, and that, according your January Management
     Directive, is our main goal.
```

Workshop Manager's Office

23 February 1988

If you've heard about the financial trouble the company's in, you probably think: Okay, so what can I do about it? Not a lot. Still, there are ways we can all do something to help.

What I'm going to suggest to you is one small idea, but it can't hurt. Last year our workshop spent $2,400 on cotton-waste. $2,400! We could easily save half of that--if we stop throwing away a handful of perfectly good rags every time we wipe a speck of oil off something. Just keep the rag by you a couple of times instead of throwing it out--and we could save upwards of $1,200 a year.

I've suggested to the management that they support us on this. If we make a saving, they've agreed to put some of it into the Sports Fund for new equipment. So we'll be getting back 25 cents out of every dollar we save. That could be $300 or $400 a year coming right back to us.

Think about it. Hang onto your rag a few minutes longer--and we'll all be better off. It sounds like a joke, but it's true.

Sincerely,

Judd Springfield

CHAPTER NINE
Researching the Reader

• Summary: The Flowchart

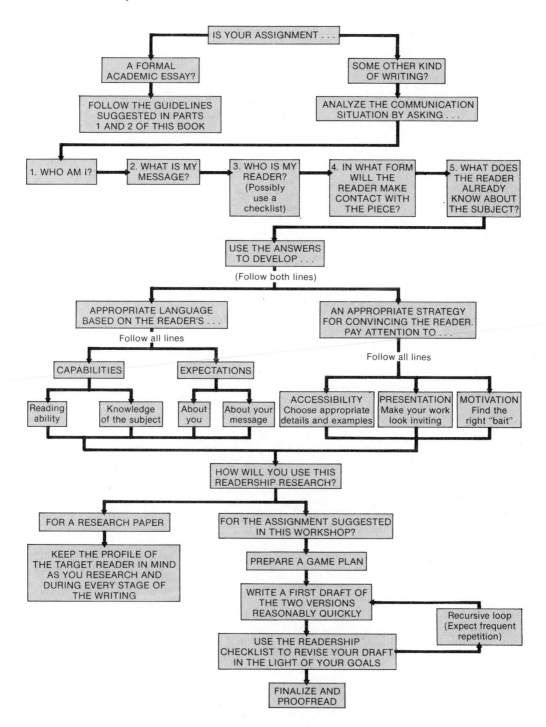

IS YOUR ASSIGNMENT . . .

A FORMAL ACADEMIC ESSAY?

SOME OTHER KIND OF WRITING?

FOLLOW THE GUIDELINES SUGGESTED IN PARTS 1 AND 2 OF THIS BOOK

ANALYZE THE COMMUNICATION SITUATION BY ASKING . . .

1. WHO AM I?

2. WHAT IS MY MESSAGE?

3. WHO IS MY READER? (Possibly use a checklist)

4. IN WHAT FORM WILL THE READER MAKE CONTACT WITH THE PIECE?

5. WHAT DOES THE READER ALREADY KNOW ABOUT THE SUBJECT?

USE THE ANSWERS TO DEVELOP . . .

(Follow both lines)

APPROPRIATE LANGUAGE BASED ON THE READER'S . . .

Follow all lines

AN APPROPRIATE STRATEGY FOR CONVINCING THE READER. PAY ATTENTION TO . . .

Follow all lines

CAPABILITIES

EXPECTATIONS

Reading ability

Knowledge of the subject

About you

About your message

ACCESSIBILITY Choose appropriate details and examples

PRESENTATION Make your work look inviting

MOTIVATION Find the right "bait"

HOW WILL YOU USE THIS READERSHIP RESEARCH?

FOR A RESEARCH PAPER

FOR THE ASSIGNMENT SUGGESTED IN THIS WORKSHOP?

KEEP THE PROFILE OF THE TARGET READER IN MIND AS YOU RESEARCH AND DURING EVERY STAGE OF THE WRITING

PREPARE A GAME PLAN

WRITE A FIRST DRAFT OF THE TWO VERSIONS REASONABLY QUICKLY

Recursive loop (Expect frequent repetition)

USE THE READERSHIP CHECKLIST TO REVISE YOUR DRAFT IN THE LIGHT OF YOUR GOALS

FINALIZE AND PROOFREAD

Your Research Project: First Decisions

This chapter is about choosing a subject for a research project. It is based on the assumption that you will, indeed, be writing a paper. After you have studied the chapter, your research should be off to a flying start.

1 •
The Problem:
Starting Off on the Right Foot

Senator Proxmire's famous Golden Fleece award singled out federally funded projects where the cost involved did not seem to justify the result. His most celebrated Golden Fleece was a study which, in part, explored class relationships in a brothel in the Peruvian Andes. Perhaps the project had scientific merit, perhaps not. Whatever the truth of the matter, there are good reasons, purely selfish ones, to avoid becoming a candidate for a Golden Fleece of your own. A research paper, even a short one, represents a large investment of time. Your motivation will flag on occasions; most subjects lose their glamor before you have licked them into shape. Prepare for the honeymoon to end by choosing a subject that is important to you. Talk over the subject with your instructor. A badly chosen subject will create the sensation that you're wasting time, and the project, if you ever finish it, will give you no feeling of satisfaction.

• Subjects and Approaches

The two questions "What *kind* of research?" and "Research on what *subject*?" are inseparable; for example: "I'm going to Egypt in the autumn, and I'd like to do something before I go on how they built the pyramids." Such a subject comes with library research, formal academic presentation, and dynamic description as part of the package. Or: "I've been asked at work to find out why people use drugs on the job and to recommend what we can do about it." This subject will be researched primarily outside the library and will take the form of a non-academic recommendation report. For the sake of convenience, the research suggestions below use a "method priority" approach.

A. AN INVESTIGATION

Investigation is one of the classic forms of research. Three types of ideas follow.

a. Some puzzling aspect of recent history might persuade you to begin an investigation:

The cult of Elvis, or the cult of the Beatles

The entanglement and fall of President Nixon

The failure of the Equal Rights Amendment to achieve ratification

The disappearance of the hippies and flower power

The failure of the American Indians to preserve much of their culture

The apparent lack of resistance to Hitler among so many European Jews

b. More speculatively, you might try to explain some puzzling phenomenon of our own time:

The increase in cults of unreason

The successes of the "moral majority"

The swing away from college education

The paralysis of the United Nations

The cult of physical fitness

The continuance of the ghettos

c. A real-life investigation could arise from any number of situations in your personal or working life. For example you might investigate:

Why a product marketed by your company no longer sells well

Why a particular company has not achieved racial or sexual balance in hiring

Why some necessary action on the part of your local town hall has not been taken

Why patterns of enrollment have recently changed at your college or university

Why your church has gained (or lost) members recently

Why the industries of a particular area are dying (or booming)

The most common structure for an investigation is the analysis of cause-and-effect, a process that we discussed in Chapter 6. How does a "research paper" differ from the essay suggested there? In several ways, none of them major. First, an academic research paper is unlikely to concentrate on a single case; normally research leads to a broad treatment of the subject.

The second difference is in the opening section. A short essay normally begins with a statement of the *situation* to be explained. In a research paper, this opening section tends to be longer and more detailed. You must establish the facts beyond dispute before trying to explain them. Imagine, for example, you are writing a research paper on the increase in child abuse in recent years. Your paper will be meaningless unless you can show that child abuse has actually increased; your opening must address such questions as: what has really increased, child abuse or the *reporting* of child abuse? And: has the commonly accepted *definition* of child abuse changed in recent years?

Finally, a research paper tends to produce "findings"—that is, it generates a significant conclusion or recommendation. This often means that the thesis statement, as well as the reasoning that builds up to it, expand dramatically.

B. A SURVEY OF INFORMED OPINION OR A COMPARATIVE SURVEY

A viewpoint is not worth much unless it is grounded on an understanding of the way experts in the field see the problem. This is where a *survey of informed opinion* comes in. Some suggestions:

a. Take some aspect of knowledge where there are conflicting theories; define the terms of the problem and fill in the background (if necessary); classify and present the various theories; draw some conclusion.

Who was "Jack the Ripper"?

Who assassinated John F. Kennedy, and why?

Is there life on other planets?

Could NATO hold out against an attack by conventional Soviet forces?

What effect does television violence have on children?

What were the circumstances surrounding the death of Marilyn Monroe?

b. Think of a topic where facts are not in dispute but where moral values differ widely. A classification of viewpoints often contains two groups with violently antagonistic views, as well as a don't-care group and a confused group. Remember, this is a survey; you are not *primarily* making a case.

Should abortion on demand be against the law?

Do industries have the right (or duty) to seek a profit at all costs?

Should the possession and use of marijuana be legalized?

Is professional sport destroying itself?

Should American schools offer basic courses (such as math) in the mother language of the students, or teach all courses exclusively in English?

Should the United States support anticommunist guerilla groups?

c. Chapter 7 presented a technique for conducting a comparative survey under the title, *Balance Sheet into Evaluative Grid*. Use this technique to decide:

Which organization has achieved most for a particular minority in recent years.

What piece of equipment (car, camera, weapon, motorcycle, sewing machine, and so on) is best suited for a particular task.

What computer language is best suited for some particular application.

What is the best way of treating some disease or mental condition.

What is the best way for a particular purchaser to finance a particular purchase.

Like the investigation, the survey also has a classic structure: classification. A full research paper differs from the classification paper explained in Chapter 7 in that it requires a more elaborate opening and closing. In the opening, you may find it necessary to define your key terms or to provide extensive background information, or both. After this opening, the paper moves to a classification of the various viewpoints. In reaching a conclusion, you may want to make a case for one particular viewpoint, or you may conclude that the case is *moot*—that is "undecidable." This, therefore, is the normal structure for a survey:

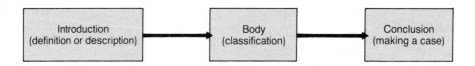

C. AN ATTACK OR A DEFENSE—MAKING A CASE

In Chapter 8 many arguable cases were suggested, most of which had a strong research component. Review the list.

D. EXPLODING A MYTH

Who is not occasionally outraged by the unthinking repetition of some myth that is dead but won't lie down? Some examples (hold on to your hackles) are:

That men are better drivers than women

That government officials are above the law

That Americans have no culture (this is a European myth)

That America is the policeman of the world

That snakes are vermin

That the space program pays for itself in spinoffs

Exploding a myth is a special form of making a case. Obviously it concentrates most fully on dismantling the viewpoint of the other side. It may help you to read Chapter 16 on writing the reasoned reply before embarking on a topic of this type.

E. AN EXPERIMENT

Ruling out experiments in the natural sciences, experiment papers fall into two groups: those based on observation and those based on some kind of opinion poll. Both techniques need a firm grasp of statistical inference, so don't try anything complicated unless you know what you're doing. In any case, *discuss the structure of your experiment with an expert before you spend time collecting data or soliciting answers*. You'll find a discussion of the special techniques involved in Chapter 11, Field Research. Following are some suggestions for experiments.

> If your place of work is considering some change of operating procedure (for example, different opening hours, a different system of payment, a change in the goods stocked or services offered), set up an opinion poll to verify that the change is worth making.

> If you live or work in an area where there are many buildings and a network of paths, observe the pattern of pedestrian movement and the "beaten tracks" with a view to relocating the paths where people want them.

> Smoking-allowed sections in cafeterias and workplaces are often controversial. Try to establish by observation and by means of an opinion poll if the current smoking/nonsmoking setup meets the needs of the people concerned.

> Many buildings have an entry with multiple doors. Observe the way in which these doors function during high-traffic and low-traffic periods. Do the doors help or impede the flow of people?

> Find a children's playground. By observing the behavior of the children, and by means of an opinion poll aimed at both children and parents, critique the design and equipment of the playground.

Most experiments are set against a background of existing research; the experiment paper tends to begin with an explanation of the latest thinking on a subject; it then explains why and how the current experiment was set up; next comes a description of the experiment itself and its results; finally, some conclusions are drawn, often in the light of the research described in the opening section.

Review Assignment

Formulating a Subject

Think of a general subject that it might interest you to research. Formulate a specific subject in various ways: as an investigation, as a survey of informed opinion or a comparative survey, as an attack or a defense, as the explosion of a myth, and as an experiment.

• The Research Project: First Decisions

As soon as you have a subject in mind, you can give direction to the project by looking at your research options. Three main choices confront you. The first concerns your sources of information, the second your message, and the third your readership.

CHOICE 1: LIBRARY RESEARCH, FIELD RESEARCH, OR A MIX

For many students in the humanities, *research* is synonymous with *library research*. Some projects are, indeed, tied to the library: a paper on medieval Latin love lyrics will not take you out of doors very often. Many subjects, however, allow some degree of field research, especially in the verification of theories found in books. The research paper printed at the end of this book, for example, contains some useful field work. For an idea of the possibilities, you might like to glance ahead at Chapter 11, Field Research.

Often your options are limited by purely physical considerations: you cannot survey the attitudes of Eskimos unless you are in the Far North; you cannot analyze Mussolini's brilliance as a speaker unless you understand the finer points of the Italian language. In practical terms, don't go ahead with a project until you're sure you'll access to what you need.

If your project depends on the library, read Chapter 12 on Library Research, and then visit your local libraries. Do they have the bulk of what you need? Ask if the gaps can be filled *within your time frame* by material ordered from other libraries. If you are working in a campus library, you may find that the local city library is better suited to your needs, and vice versa. If you are studying outside the United States, you should check into the libraries of local universities and into libraries set up by the United States Information Services (USIS) and the British Council. If the material you need for an in-depth study of your subject is not available, change your subject.

If you want to conduct original research, clarify very early that you'll be *allowed* to carry out your plans. A door-to-door survey may be out of the question in an expensive condominium; a street survey may be forbidden by the police in a busy thoroughfare; hanging around a children's playground may invite suspicion unless you first clear it with the police department.

Library research? Original research? Or a mix? Decide where your project is going and quickly check the terrain. Many promising ideas founder because "you can't get there from here."

CHOICE 2: STRONG THESIS VERSUS OPEN QUESTION

Should the project depend upon a strong thesis, or will it survey informed opinion and finally leave the question open?

Strong Thesis: UFOs have landed
Open Question: What opinions are there on whether UFOs have landed?

CHAPTER TEN
Your Research Project: First Decisions

You may know from the outset which option to choose, or you may be unsure. Since successful reading and note taking depend on knowing what you are looking for, think carefully about this option.

If you can't decide, or if you know very little about the subject, then work provisionally on the assumption that you are posing an open question. Your reading will then remain broad and balanced. If you later decide to switch to a strong thesis, you'll have all the material you need. On the other hand, if you've worked on a strong thesis, your reading and note taking may have been too narrow to allow you to change your mind.

CHOICE 3: ACADEMIC RESEARCH OR A REAL-WORLD PROJECT

Who is the end user of your project? As we saw in the last chapter, the reader is the most important variable when it comes to presenting your material. If the project is purely academic, then you'll have little discretion over language or presentation; the form is set. If, on the other hand, you decide to venture outside the classroom and to write for a different readership, you'll have to make many decisions about presentation. The technique of readership research outlined in Chapter 9 will be important in developing a real-world project.

Concept Review

A Sense of Direction

Formulate a specific subject on which you might write a research paper. Make three choices for this subject:

a. Library research ☐   Field research ☐   Mix ☐

b. Strong thesis ☐   Open question ☐

c. Academic research ☐   Real-world project ☐

Do you see any problems that could arise from your choices?

2 •

Writing Workshop: A Project Proposal

Let's make a favorable assumption: that your instructor has set aside time to talk over your project with you personally. To ensure that this discussion is worthwhile, some instructors suggest that you bring along a formal *project proposal*. The project proposal is an excellent way of thinking through the first stages of a research project. What goes into a project proposal?

A. THE TITLE PAGE

A title page should be attractively laid out. It is the smile that you exchange with the reader on first meeting. The title itself is (roughly):

Proposal to Write a Report on:

This is followed by your title, your name and whatever other information is appropriate.

B. AN OVERVIEW

In a paragraph or two (ten to fifteen lines?), you should explain the general direction of your project, why you want to write it, who it is for, and so on. In his project proposal, John Wilson, a student working on his first research project, included the following overview:

OVERVIEW

I would like to write a research project on the rights of homosexuals within American society. The paper would be academic and written within the framework of a course such as SOCIOLOGY 105: Introduction to Contemporary Social Issues. I would like to examine the subject purely from the legal point of view, presenting the subject objectively and scientifically.

I find this particular topic interesting because of the conflict of moral values involved; I have heard many quite violent arguments about homosexuality. After studying all aspects of the problem, I would like to reach a decision as to whether our society puts homosexuals at a legal disadvantage, and, if so, how serious the disadvantage actually is. I will try to base this decision on the strength of the arguments, not on my personal inclinations.

C. THE PROFILE OF THE TARGET READER

With an academic paper, a readership analysis is unnecessary. With any other kind of project, it is essential. Your instructor can give you no guidance until you have pinned down your readership. The readership checklist in Chapter 9 offers a framework for your analysis.

D. STATEMENT OF RESOURCES

Are the resources you need available? A reconnaissance trip to a library (or to several) is necessary to find out. Possible interview sources should be noted, as well as experiments that you hope to conduct. John Wilson again:

STATEMENT OF RESOURCES

Books and Articles already found

Akers, Ronald L. Deviant Behavior: A Social Learning Approach. Belmont: Wadsworth, 1973.
Egerton, Brooks. "Gay Politics: A Time to Take Stock." The Progressive May 1985: 25+.

Hettlinger, Richard F. "Sex, Religion and Censorship." Censorship and Freedom of Expression. Ed. Harry M. Clor. Chicago: Rand, 1971.

Pious, Richard, ed. Civil Rights and Liberties in the 1970s. New York: Random, 1973.

Interview

Since the military has a policy of discharging known homosexuals, I have requested an interview with Captain Bohuslav Sinkiewicz of the Judge Advocate General's office at our local Air Force base.

Survey

I want to ask (by mail) the personnel officers of all the companies in this country employing more than 400 people if they follow any guidelines on the employment of homosexuals.

The instructor will study these items with the eye of experience. Some problems, in fact, "stand out a mile," as you'll see if you think through the following questions.

Study Questions

a. Look at the *dates* of John's sources. Do the dates suggest a problem?

b. Can you foresee any obstacles to John's getting the interview he wants?

c. John's survey looks like a good idea. Do you think he will have any problems conducting it? Do you think he will receive enough replies to form any worthwhile conclusions?

d. If you foresee problems, suggest some alternative tactics.

E. A TIMETABLE

The most common problem in writing research papers is running out of time. This has two causes: (a) a faulty estimate of the time required, and (b) laziness, the tendency to postpone work with a feeble rationalization such as "I work best under pressure." Try to include in any timetable a generous (50 percent?) allowance for "slippage." John's timetable correctly lists the main stages in an academic project, although his timings reflect some inexperience. Scan the dates critically. Do you see any problems?

a. Discussion of project proposal	April 10
b. Completion of basic reading, note taking, and interviews	April 29
c. Firm working outline	April 30
d. First draft of text	May 5
e. Supplementary reading completed and deadline for survey results	May 19
f. Completion of final draft and final deadline	May 21

F. THE GAME PLAN

John's first game plan was interesting in that it contained almost all the characteristic mistakes of first-time researchers. The game plan is given here in its first form, and then in the form it assumed a few days later.

SUBJECT: HOMOSEXUALITY

1. The history of homosexuality

    A. Homosexuality in the ancient world

    B. Homosexuality in the Bible

    C. Homosexuality in Europe until 1800

    D. Homosexuality in modern America

2. The Churches and homosexuality

    A. The doctrine of the Roman Catholic church

    B. The doctrines of Protestant churches

    C. Other religious attitudes

3. Common social attitudes to homosexuality

    A. Fear

    B. Lack of understanding

    C. The AIDS crisis

4. Limitations imposed by society on homosexuals

    A. Social sanctions

    B. Economic sanctions

    C. Legal sanctions

5. Gays fight back

    A. Organizations

    B. The Bill of Rights

6. The Origin of Current Laws

    A. Federal

    B. State

7. Conclusion: Sexual preference should be irrelevant when it comes to the rights, privileges and freedoms of Americans. At the present time, homosexuals do/do not enjoy the same rights as other citizens.

Study Questions

a. The game plan lacks "transparency"—that is, the instructor will not be able to guess what each section will contain. Where in particular do you see this lack of transparency?

b. In his overview John said that he wanted to look at the subject "purely from the legal point of view" with the goal of deciding "whether our society puts homosexuals at a legal disadvantage." Go through the game plan section by section. How much of John's material deals *strictly* with his declared goal?

c. John does not define *homosexual* in his outline. Why is a definition essential? And where should it be situated?

SUBJECT: DISCRIMINATION AGAINST HOMOSEXUALS IN AMERICAN SOCIETY

1. Definition: What is a homosexual?

    A. Some psychologists see a homosexual potential in everyone.

    B. Many "straights" have had some homosexual contacts.

    C. Many homosexuals have not come out of the closet.

    D. Discrimination can take place only against known and identifiable homosexuals. In this paper, homosexuals are defined as those publicly practicing a homosexual lifestyle.

2. Introduction: Gays claim that three kinds of discrimination are practiced against them: social, economic, and legal.

3. Social discrimination

    A. What gays complain about.

    B. Are the gays' complaints justified? Arguments.

    C. Do the churches discriminate against gays? Arguments.

    D. The situation has worsened dramatically since the AIDS epidemic.

4. Economic discrimination

    A. Are gays discriminated against in hiring? Arguments. Survey results.

    B. Does the tax system discriminate against gay "marriages"? Arguments.

5. Legal discrimination

    A. State laws rather than federal laws are aimed specifically against homosexuality. Some examples.

    B. Are these laws enforced? Should they be repealed? Arguments.

    C. There is no constitutional guarantee of one's right to a sexual preference. Should there be? Arguments.

6. Conclusion: Sexual preference should be irrelevant when it comes to the rights, privileges and freedoms of Americans. At the present time, homosexuals do/do not enjoy the same rights as other citizens.

The game plan is now transparent; the material is limited to John's immediate concerns, and the main theme is adequately developed—at least, it is adequate for this preliminary stage. The purpose of the game plan is to direct reading and note taking. Now that he knows roughly what he is looking for, John can work confidently at finding it.

PART THREE
The Research Paper

Review Assignment

As soon as you have firmed up your plans for a research project, draft a project proposal and submit it to your instructor.

• Summary: The Flowchart

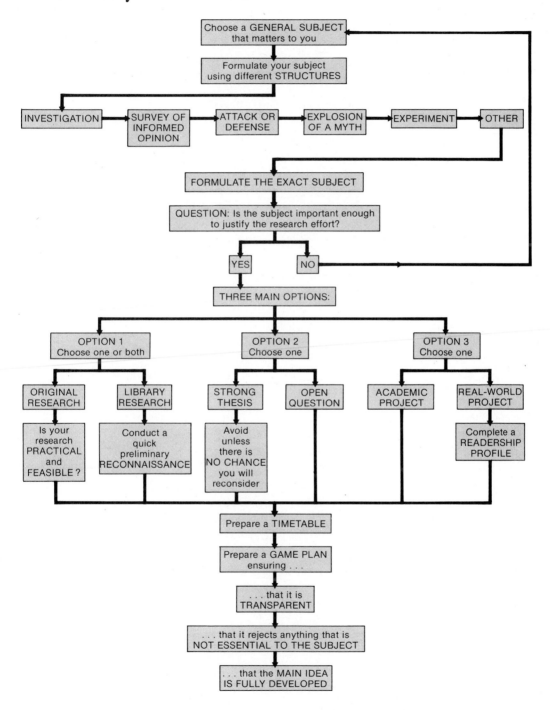

Finding Information 1: Field Research

The Problem: Exploring Unknown Paths

Most people have a healthy suspicion of "book learning": luckily there is no law that says research must be "bookish." This chapter covers the kind of research that takes place *outside* the library; in the next chapter we shall deal with the challenge of library research itself. Original research (if we exclude experiments in the natural sciences) offers three avenues of exploration: (1) tapping the knowledge of experts by means of interviews, (2) making experimental observations, and (3) conducting an opinion poll. Although few research papers are based *exclusively* on these techniques, any one of them can add zest and legitimacy to your researches.

1 •
Interviewing

Two kinds of people get interviewed: celebrities and authorites. Unless the interviewee is a celebrated authority, the two types should not be confused.

• The Celebrity and the Authority: Two Kinds of Interview

The *celebrity interview* is the province of the journalist. Normally the interviewer asks general, easy-to-answer questions aimed at making the celebrity appear witty (or at least intelligent) and personal questions aimed at giving the public something to gossip about. The reader is assumed to be interested in the interviewee's opinions on fashion, famine in Africa, divorce, breakfast cereals—anything. The text of celebrity interviews is notoriously creative.

Actual Interview

INTERVIEWER: Terrible weather we're having, aren't we?
CELEBRITY: I guess so.
INTERVIEWER: Like the old joke—everyone talks about the weather but nobody does anything about it.
CELEBRITY: Yes, it is.
INTERVIEWER: Do you have a favorite kind of weather?
CELEBRITY: Not really.

Published Text

> Even the thunderstorm outside didn't dampen the spirits of Diggory Venn. "Everyone talks about the weather, but nobody seems to do anything about it," he quipped. Diggory can be happy in just about any kind of weather, he told me, smoothing down those mutton-chop whiskers that have spun the world into a whole new fashion spiral.

Leave this kind of interviewing to the professional journalist. An *authority interview*, on the other hand, is not creative gossip with the rich and famous: it is a basic tool of the journalist reporting the news and of the researcher hunting for information. The journalist is constantly pressing for *anything newsworthy*. The research interview is a little different. It is a series of structured questions aimed at gathering *information or ideas* known exclusively to the interviewee. The tone of the interview is undramatic and businesslike. The authority is not asked for facts that the researcher could find in any almanac or encyclopedia, or for opinions outside his or her area of competence. *The end product of the research interview is information that is unavailable in quite the same form from any other source.*

• When to Use an Interview in Your Research

Interviews cost a great deal of time. It would be wrong to ask a professor, a professional worker, or a business executive to set aside time for an interview without good reason. An interview can do two things for you:

a. Provide information not otherwise available
b. Confirm information that is otherwise in doubt

If the information you need has never been made public, then it's fair to question someone who knows the facts. Similarly, if you have reason to doubt published information, it's fair to question an authority on the subject. Let's look at an example. (In this example, the names have been changed for obvious reasons.)

COUNSELING FOR RAPE VICTIMS

Rose Lanark became involved in her research subject through a friend, her roommate Melanie. After a party, Melanie was the victim of an attempted rape. Rose went with Melanie to the Crisis Center on campus and later accompanied her to the police department to report the attack. Rose was shocked at the seeming heartlessness of the whole procedure: she'd thought things were "better these days." She decided to find out how the professionals saw their role in helping the victims of rape and to report her findings in a research paper. To prepare for the interviews, she read some of the extensive literature on rape counseling and found many discrepancies between the sensitive and sound advice she found in books and what she had seen in practice. Finally Rose sent a copy of her completed research paper to the Crisis Center and the police, with positive and valuable results.

The research pattern that Rose followed suggests some guidelines. First she was confronted by a problem that earnestly bothered her; writing on it kept her motivation high. Then she established a clear research subject: how professionals see their role in helping rape victims. Next came library research into the *theory* of the subject. Rose's field research concerned itself with the *practice*. The thesis of Rose's essay was, obviously, the ugly discrepancy between theory and practice. This pattern, particularly the relationship it suggests between theoretical research in the library and practical research in the field, might well give shape to your own work.

• Securing an Interview

"What's in it for me?" That's the question every potential interviewee is bound to ask. The normal answer is: "Not much." Remember this when you call or write a letter to ask for an interview. As would-be interviewer, you have two problems: (a) to minimize obstacles in the way of the interview, and (b) to provide some kind of motivation for the interviewee to help you out.

A. MINIMIZING OBSTACLES

The main obstacle between you and your interview is *time*. How much time can you fairly ask a busy person to surrender to you? Probably not more than about fifteen minutes—or, at the very most, half an hour. Think of it from the other person's point of view: most working people simply don't have a spare half hour in their day for fringe activities. You should also be flexible about the time and place of the interview: the convenience of the interviewee is the only important factor.

B. PROVIDING MOTIVATION

If you can touch any responsive chord in the interviewee, this may get you the interview. Did the interviewee attend your university, for example, or study the same subject as you, or make a successful public appearance that you attended? Anything that links you with the interviewee may break the ice. If your research might benefit the interviewee, that is a point worth stressing. Sometimes you can use a negative motivation, suggesting that the interviewee has "a case to answer."

Concept Review

Gaining Access

Rose Lanark wrote this letter to the director of the Crisis Center where Melanie was "processed." Read it, and then answer the questions.

> Dear Ms. Creecher:
>   The successful operation of your Crisis Center is a major concern of all the women on our campus. I brought a friend of mine, Melanie Dorner, to the Center on the night of February 19th after she had been attacked. To be honest, neither Melanie nor I felt that she gained much help or support by talking to your counselor. I am sure that you will be very concerned to hear this.
>   I feel, as do quite a number of my fellow students, that we should know more about what happens to rape victims here, and why. This is the reason for my making this request to you. I am at present writing a report on rape victims on our campus. Naturally, there are a number of questions I cannot answer myself. I would be very grateful if you could find time to talk to me about some of these problems. In fifteen minutes, you can probably put me right on most of the things that puzzle me. Naturally, I'll send you a copy of the completed report; it may contain feedback that will be of value to you.
>   I can be free at any time that suits you, and I can promise not to take more than fifteen minutes of your time.
>
> Sincerely,

a. Where can you see Rose trying to remove the obstacles that might prevent her from getting the interview?

b. What positive motivation is she offering Ms. Creecher?

c. Is she suggesting that Ms. Creecher has "a case to answer"? If so, do you think this makes the tone of the letter too negative?

• Preparing for an Interview

During the election campaign of 1976, Jimmy Carter was interviewed by *Playboy*. The last interview session was apparently over; the last question had been about Carter's puritanical image. Then Carter put the cat in the henroost with his now famous afterthought: "I've looked on a lot of women with lust. I've committed adultery in my heart many times." For the interviewer, Robert Scheer, this was an extraordinary stroke of luck. No interviewer could plan or prepare for such a confession. What can an interviewer legitimately expect? How should you plan an interview?

PLANNING FACTOR 1: DOING YOUR HOMEWORK

An interview is set up when there is no other way to plug the gaps in your knowledge. It follows that reading comes *first*. In his book *Keys to Successful Interviewing*, Stewart Harral says: ". . . the success of your efforts is likely to be in direct proportion to your knowledge of the subject. If you don't know the subject well enough, the interviewee may fear that he will be misquoted. Or worse, he may feel that he is wasting his time." That is sound advice.

PLANNING FACTOR 2: TIME—PREPARING YOUR QUESTIONS

To secure her interview with Ms. Creecher, Rose Lanark stressed that she would need only fifteen minutes. In practice, you may get more time than you requested, but you should be prepared to stick to your bargain. That means preparing questions very carefully. The general rule: You seldom get the time you'd like, so really use the time you get. Because she had done her homework, Rose could plan her questions rather precisely. They included:

1. What strategies do counselors at the Center routinely use to combat the effects of shock in rape victims?

2. Is it Center policy that the counselor sits formally behind a desk when talking to victims?

3. What proportion of your counselors are male? Followup question: Shouldn't all the counselors be female?

4. Melanie was talked through a checklist of questions. What is the purpose of this checklist? Followup question: Are statistics compiled from the answers?

5. What was the source of the pamphlets given to victims? Followup question: Is the clinical, take-it-or-leave-it style in these pamphlets used for any *reason*?

6. Are rape victims counseled about what to expect at the police department and how to cope with it? Followup questions: If so, why was Melanie not counseled? If not, why not?

Several of these questions are, of course, veiled criticisms. This arises from the nature of the problem. Note, however, that Rose's questions, although critical, are still fair questions—they are not statements masquerading as questions. She does not ask, for example:

Wouldn't it have been better if the counselor had talked to Melanie in an informal, relaxed setting rather than from behind a desk?

> Experts agree that a counselor's job is to find out what concerns the
> victim, not what interests the counselor—so why did the counselor use
> a checklist of questions?

Those are not questions, and Ms. Creecher will not respond to them in a way that helps Rose write her paper. For a fifteen-minute interview, you should prepare between ten and fifteen questions. If that seems a lot, remember that some answers may be short and others may be simple "no-comments." The technique for posing questions face to face is our next concern.

• Conducting an Interview

A. ARRIVAL

The most basic rule—always arrive a little early.

B. EQUIPMENT

Unlike professional reporters, most research interviewers use a portable tape recorder. Unless you are a stenographer, you should use one too. It should be small and unobtrusive, battery operated (to avoid hassles with power cables), and ready to go. Always mention the tape recorder to the interviewee, and confirm that you may use it. "That way I won't misquote you," is a graceful arm twist.

C. GETTING GOING

Some friendly words to get things going on the human level are important, but don't overdo it. Every minute counts.

D. INTERVIEW VERSUS CONVERSATION

The ideal outcome of a fifteen-minute interview is fourteen minutes of answers to one minute of questions. You are not conducting an argument, a debate, or a conversation; you are collecting data.

E. QUESTION-AND-ANSWER TECHNIQUE

Question-and-answer technique is a gift that develops with practice. There are no rules, but there are guidelines.

a. **Open versus Closed Questions** A "closed" question is one that can be answered in one word, often *Yes* or *No*. If you want your interviewee to talk, then ask "open" questions—that is, questions that call for an *explanation*. A typical open question is Rose's:

> What strategies do counselors at the Center routinely use to combat the
> effects of shock in rape victims?

b. **One Question at a Time** Don't cluster questions; separate them. It is unproductive to ask: "Can you tell me how many people work here, how you choose them, what their qualifications are, and how you monitor their work?"

c. **The Two-Shot Question** Often a closed (yes/no) question draws an "admission" from the interviewee. Rose achieves this when she asks:

> Are rape victims routinely counseled about what to expect at the police department and how to cope with it?

The answer *Yes* or *No* allows Rose to ask the appropriate follow-up question.

d. **Generalizing** If the interviewee gets into too much detail, then the interviewer asks:

> Could you sum up the general idea in just a sentence or two? Something I could quote you on, maybe.

e. **Particularizing** If the interviewee offers only woolly abstractions, the interviewer asks:

> Could you give me a specific example?

f. **Repeating** Whether by accident or design, the interviewee may sidetrack a question. The interviewer can then say in all fairness:

> We seem to have lost track of my question. Let me repeat it for you.

g. **A Fight to the Death** If the interviewee is reluctant to answer a question, don't try to exert pressure. Simply pass to your next question. If you're over-persistent, you'll quickly poison the atmosphere.

h. **Courtesy** The great rule is to be polite, easy and natural. After the interview, a short letter of thanks may be appropriate. If you send the interviewee a copy of your paper, a covering thank you letter is always in order.

Concept Review

Question-and-Answer Technique

The following interview is a disaster. Critique the questions asked by the interviewer to find out what went wrong. The subject of the interview is a new day-care center for the children of employees at a large chemical factory. The interviewee is John Marx, the personnel officer of the company. When we join the interview, little more than "Good mornings" have been exchanged.

INTERVIEWER: First, how do you think a day-care center should be financed?
MARX: Shouldn't we first talk about whether we want a center or not?
INTERVIEWER: Okay. Do we want a center?
MARX: That depends who you mean by "we."

INTERVIEWER: You used the word, not me!

MARX: Let me ask *you* a question: Who do you think wants the center?

INTERVIEWER: Mothers with small children.

MARX: Right.

INTERVIEWER: How many such people are there?

MARX: I don't know exactly.

INTERVIEWER: Roughly?

MARX: I really don't know. We haven't collected any figures.

INTERVIEWER: But you must have a rough idea.

MARX: Seriously, no.

INTERVIEWER: If you don't know how many women are involved, how do you know if there's a demand for the center?

MARX: The company doesn't believe there is a serious demand.

INTERVIEWER: Can I quote you on that?

MARX: No.

INTERVIEWER: Listen, I've talked to at least five women with little kids, and they all jumped at the idea. How do you respond to that?

MARX: I don't have to. Look, do you know how many kindergartens and nursery schools there are in this town?

INTERVIEWER: No. How many?

MARX: I rather think you should have checked up on a thing like that. There are enough, and they all have vacancies!

INTERVIEWER: Oh . . . . Let me ask you another question, then: Would you agree that your company has a bad image with regard to employing mothers? What exactly are your policies about maternity leave, for instance? And why do you have so few women in management positions? Are you refusing to build this day-care center because the company is doing badly at the moment, or is there another reason?

MARX: We don't need a reason for *not* doing something that we don't have to do. Is that all?

INTERVIEWER: I guess. Thanks for your help.

Review Assignment

The Research Interview

Choose one of the five research projects given below. List the specific people—the real people in your world—that you'd interview. Then list the questions you'd ask each of your "victims." You can carry the assignment a stage further by role-playing interviewer and interviewee.

a. Choose one of your classes in which there is a certain amount of dissatisfaction among the students. You want to find out (a) what is causing this dissatisfaction, (b) how widespread it is, and (c) what can be done about it.

b. Students normally have little influence in deciding what courses will be scheduled for a particular semester. You believe that students would appreciate a greater say. (a) Establish that this is so, (b) find out what problems this might create, and then (c) collect ideas on how student input might best be channeled.

c. You wish to set up (or expand) a day-care center at your place of work, on campus, or in your community. You must establish (a) that the demand for the center exists and (b) exactly how the center could be set up.

d. An attempt to organize a "rock fest" on campus or in your community has been turned down by the authorities. You want to establish (a) whether there is any real demand for a "rock fest," and (b) under exactly what circumstances the authorities would allow a future "rock fest."

e. A dispute has arisen about the parking of cars on campus or within your community. You want to establish (a) whether parking is generally seen as a problem; then you want (b) to know the exact nature of the dispute and (c) to collect suggestions for resolving it.

2 •
Experimental Observation

Many problems have no book answer. This is particularly true of small-scale, local problems. Improving the layout of a warehouse, making the food in a cafeteria more acceptable to customers, optimizing the opening hours of a library, organizing the flow of work through a repair shop—the general theory for solving such problems has been studied by experts, but *applying* the general theory calls for detailed, experimental observation. As an example, let's take a case that does not, in fact, involve library research; the problem must be solved by first-hand field research. The three steps involved here follow a standard, problem-solving pattern.

• Case Study: Going Up

Jeff Ogilvy works in a twenty-story building. His company has its offices on the eighth floor. The building has two elevators, and Jeff realizes that during the morning and evening crush these elevators are not shifting people as efficiently as they should. At present, during heavy traffic periods, Elevator A serves floors 1 through 10 exclusively, and Elevator B serves floors 11 through 20 exclusively. Jeff decides to watch the elevators to see what is happening.

STEP 1: RECONNAISSANCE

Jeff sits in the entrance lobby at 7:30 A.M., watching. He first observes that the crush outside Elevator A ("his" elevator) is about half that outside Elevator B. By 8:10, however, Elevator A has a huge crowd waiting beside it, while the crowd outside Elevator B is about the same size as before. This situation peaks at about 8:20. Thereafter, the Elevator A crowd shrinks rapidly, while the Elevator B crowd does not tail off until about 9:30.

Jeff is now sure that there really is a problem. How should he develop his initial observations? In two ways: quantify them and then try to interpret them. After that, a recommendation may be possible.

STEP 2: QUANTIFICATION AND VERIFICATION

Luckily, the elevator problem can be quantified without a sophisticated knowledge of statistics. Jeff's obvious task is to *count* the two groups. If he counts them every five minutes and keeps a careful log of the numbers, he'll know if his subjective impression is supported by the figures.

One set of observations can seldom be trusted: too many coincidental factors can arise. In verifying his elevator observations, Jeff would obviously check the evening pattern. It should be a mirror image of the morning one. He should also check that the pattern repeats itself every day—let's say for a week. The general rule: whenever you make observations, repeat them several times to verify them.

Let's assume that Jeff collects figures over five workdays and then takes their mean average:

	MEAN AVERAGE NUMBER OF PERSONS WAITING	
	Elevator A	*Elevator B*
7:30	3	12
7:35	6	10
7:40	4	13
7:45	7	14
7:50	7	15
7:55	9	16
8:00	11	15
8:05	14	14
8:10	24	15
8:15	30	14
8:20	45	13
8:25	40	13
8:30	30	14
8:35	10	14
8:40	8	12
.	.	.
.	.	.
.	.	.

The crush at 8:30 a.m. is now a "scientific fact," established beyond dispute. Jeff must now investigate the *cause* of the problem.

STEP 3: INTERPRETATION AND RECOMMENDATION

One possible explanation of the figures is that more people work in the lower half of the building; Jeff asks the building management about this—but in fact the building is evenly occupied. Jeff searches for another interpretation. Obviously employees are arriving in different patterns. Jeff wonders if more of the companies in the top half of the building use flextime (that is, they allow employees to arrive and leave when they like as long as they work a set number of hours). Jeff makes a number of phone calls, and he confirms that this is the case.

What, then, does Jeff recommend to the building management? He discovers that the companies on floors 9 and 10 do not use flextime: so, armed with his figures, he suggests that overcrowding in the lobby will improve if, during rush hours, Elevator A serve floors 1 through 8, and Elevator B serve floors 9 through 20. Since his figures indicate that this would even out the flow, his idea might well be accepted.

• Summary

Situations differ radically, but the technique of experimental observation remains fairly constant:

1. RECONNAISSANCE

Examine the problem. Confirm that the problem really exists, and form a theory (or several theories) about what is happening. Collect some tentative data.

2. QUANTIFICATION AND VERIFICATION

Plan to collect data in the form of easy-to-compare figures. Unless you are at home with statistics, plan to count whole groups and to avoid taking "samples." (This problem is highlighted in the next section.) Then, start counting.

Confirm data, where possible, by carefully repeating the observation procedure. If you obtain several sets of data, it often makes sense to average them.

3. INTERPRETATION AND RECOMMENDATION

Avoid drawing conclusions from data unless the figures support the conclusion beyond all possible doubt. All figures contain a "margin of error." Until you are thoroughly at home with statistics, assume that this margin of error is large.

If you have a theory about your figures, try to verify it from another source (for example, the telephone calls in our elevator study confirmed that flextime was favored in the upper stories). A recommendation backed by good statistical research—the simpler, the better—carries a lot of weight.

Review Assignment

An Experiment

Is there anything that irritates you? Maybe there are not enough parking spots in the car park. Maybe a bus schedule causes unnecessary waiting. Maybe your bank does not provide the information you'd like about your bank account. Maybe there are never enough checkouts open at your grocery store. Or maybe the checkout desk at the library is understaffed at peak times. Whatever the problem, design an experiment that would:

a. Establish that the problem actually exists
b. Put a number value on the size of the problem
c. Produce data on which you could base a recommendation

3 •
Opinion Polls and Questionnaires

An important technique for establishing whether a problem exists is the opinion poll. If, for example, three or four students complain to the librarian that the library closes too early, the librarian might poll users of the library to find out if *most* students think this way. A store might poll customers to find out which departments are perceived as doing a good job and which are below par.

One problem with polls is their "unreliability." For example, just before Ronald Reagan took the presidency from Jimmy Carter by a landslide, the pollsters said the election was "too close to call." And they were *right*: given the blunt weapon of the public opinion poll, the election could have gone either way and stayed within the pollsters' "margin of error." The professionals make no sweeping claims for the accuracy of their methods. A research survey conducted by an "amateur" is even more prone to error. Let us, nevertheless, look at a practical case to see what can be done.

Deidre Morris works in the admissions department of a small hospital. She has to listen to many complaints and gets very little praise from customers when she does her job well. She (and her boss) would like to carry out a poll on the subject of "customer satisfaction." How should they proceed?

• Getting a "Fair Sample"

The goal of an opinion poll is to approach a fair cross section of the public and to find out what this "sample" thinks about a particular subject. This is not easy, for reasons that we'll study more closely in Chapter 15. In Deidre's case, she will have to compose a questionnaire of some sort and then ask a cross section of her customers to complete it. In practical terms, how might she do this?

A common way of soliciting public opinion is to leave a questionnaire lying about where those concerned will find it. If Deidre did this, 10 out of every 100 customers might fill in the questionnaire. Is this a fair cross section? Almost certainly it is not: satisfied customers will tend to ignore the questionnaire while disgruntled customers will seize on it. When the answers are analyzed, the picture will be unduly negative.

Another technique would be for Deidre to pass out a questionnaire to every tenth customer, with a request to fill it in. This would create a better cross section, but, in practice, Deidre is unlikely to pass out a questionnaire to every tenth customer. If the tenth customer is argumentative and crabby, she may instinctively save the questionnaire for the eleventh. If the ninth customer is a sweet little old lady, Deidre may give her a questionnaire out of turn. Anyone who has worked on a public opinion poll knows how easy it is for human feelings to "skew" a sample. In this case, the results would be unduly positive.

The best technique would be to give *everyone* a questionnaire. Not everyone will complete it, but, over a month, the results would be reasonably significant. For amateurs, it is generally better to poll *everybody* (what statisticians call a "population") rather than to select a few in the hope of creating a "representative sample." Total polls avoid many statistical traps.

• Asking the Right Questions

Opinions are recorded by means of a questionnaire. How many questions should a questionnaire contain? Many questionnaires begin by asking the sex, age, nationality, mother language, and "other identifying features" of the respondent. Often, collecting this data is a waste of time. In Deidre's case, for example, does her department need to know if females are happier than males with the way they are treated? Or if young people are happier than old? If she won't use information on age, sex and so on, she should not solicit it. In any case, too many facts makes analyzing the information tedious. Realizing this, Deidre and her boss decide on a simple approach—they want to know if customers are satisfied with the speed, courtesy and efficiency of the admissions department.

The wording of the questions determines the value of the answers: writing good opinionnaire questions is perhaps the toughest of all writing assignments. Let's look at the problems.

A. PREAMBLE

Most questionnaires begin with a few words explaining their purpose. For example:

Version 1:

> The Admissions Department of this hospital is extremely concerned that you have the best possible attention. Your kindness in answering these questions will help us to help you. You may return the completed sheet to the person who just helped you with your admission.

Version 2:

> You are kindly requested to complete the questions below and return the completed sheet to the Central Admissions Desk. Thank you in advance for your cooperation.

Version 3:

> Complete this questionnaire and return it promptly to the main desk.

Study Question: How might each of these wordings influence the answers to the later questions?

B. BLANKET VERSUS SPECIFIC QUESTIONS

Questions are worth asking only if the answers contain usable information. Study these four ways of asking Deidre's key question:

a.
> **1.** Was your admission handled with speed, courtesy and efficiency?
> Yes ☐ No ☐ Don't know ☐

b.
> **1.** Was your admission handled with speed, or were there delays?
> Yes ☐ No ☐ Don't know ☐
>
> **2.** Were personnel courteous to you, or did you experience rudeness?
> Yes ☐ No ☐ Don't know ☐
>
> **3.** Was your admission efficiently handled, or were mistakes made?
> Yes ☐ No ☐ Don't know ☐

c.
> **1.** Was your admission handled sufficiently quickly?
> Yes ☐ No ☐ Don't know ☐
>
> **2.** Were personnel courteous to you at all times?
> Yes ☐ No ☐ Don't know ☐
>
> **3.** Was your admission handled efficiently?
> Yes ☐ No ☐ Don't know ☐

d.
> **1.** Were there any unnecessary delays during your admission?
> Yes ☐ No ☐ Don't know ☐
>
> **2.** Was anyone discourteous to you at any stage during your admission?
> Yes ☐ No ☐ Don't know ☐
>
> **3.** Were any mistakes made during your admission?
> Yes ☐ No ☐ Don't know ☐

Study Questions

i.   One of these formats provides no usable information at all. Which one?

ii.   Another format provides a meager amount of information. Which one?

iii. The third and the fourth format contrast positive wording and negative wording. Will this influence the answers? Will it influence the amount of information generated?

C. THE FORM OF THE QUESTION

The same question can be posed in several ways. The direct question, *a* below, is the most obvious. A statement set up for agreement or disagreement, as in *b*, or a range of statements, as in *c*, sometimes make the question clearer. A rating system, as in *d*, is the most sophisticated approach. The open question, *e*, creates a different kind of information altogether.

a.
> Was your admission handled sufficiently quickly?
> Yes ☐ No ☐ Don't know ☐

b.
> Would you agree with this statement: "My admission was handled with sufficient speed"? Yes ☐ No ☐ Don't know ☐

c.
> Which of the following statements most closely represents your opinion?
>
> **1.** My admission was handled with sufficient speed. ☐
>
> **2.** My admission could have been handled somewhat more speedily. ☐
>
> **3.** My admission was handled too slowly. ☐

d.
> Rate the speed of your admission on the five-point scale below:
>
> Fast   1   2   3   4   5   Slow

e.
> In the space below, please comment on the way your admission was handled.

Study Questions

i.   Which of these techniques would allow an unscrupulous researcher the most leeway for influencing the result?

ii.   Which form is the most difficult to evaluate once the results are in?

iii. Which form would be most suitable for Deidre's purpose?

D. THE LOADING OF THE QUESTION

We have already seen that questions can be "loaded" to generate certain answers. Look at these questions:

a.
> Our staff members are trained to work courteously with you. Do you agree that we are doing a successful job?   Yes ☐ No ☐ Don't know ☐

b.

> Our staff members are trained to work courteously with you. Do you think we are doing a successful job? Yes ☐ No ☐ Don't know ☐

c.

> A successful cure depends in part on good relations between hospital staff and patient. Has the Admissions Department created a good impression on you? Yes ☐ No ☐ Don't know ☐

d.

> Have you been treated courteously by everyone in the Admissions Department? Yes ☐ No ☐ Don't know ☐

e.

> Have you been treated courteously by everyone in the Admissions Department? Yes ☐ No ☐ Don't know ☐
> If No, we would greatly value a comment to tell us where we slipped up. Please—it really would help:

Study question.   Rank these five forms starting with the most manipulative and finishing with the most straightforward.

Review Assignment

The Opinion Poll

Look again at the research subjects listed in the Review Assignment on page 306. In each case, an opinion poll might be the best way to handle part of the research. Choose one of these subjects and set up an appropriate questionnaire. Consider carefully the number of questions to be asked; the kind of information that the questions will generate; the form that the question and the answer should take; and how best to avoid loading the questions.

•   Summary: The Flowchart

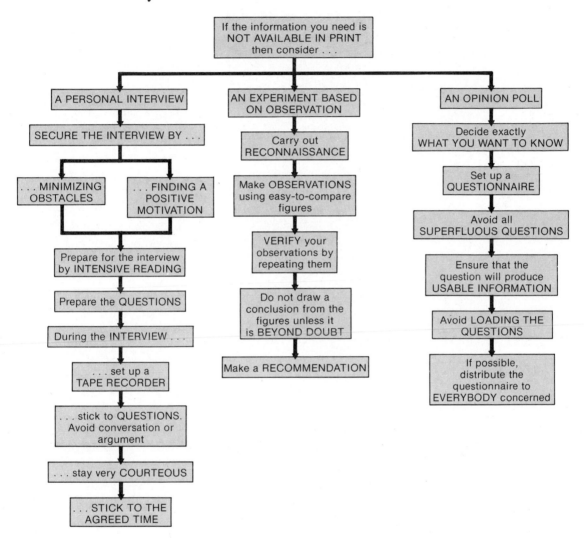

Finding Information II: Library Research

The Problem: Tracking Down Sources

This chapter deals with library research—that is, research from published sources. Your goal as a researcher is to put your hand on exactly the material you need in the minimum amount of time. Research skills take years to develop; this chapter will simply "show you the ropes." As you discover the information you're looking for, you'll want to take notes. For this reason you should glance ahead at Chapter 13, *Storing Information*, before you begin serious library work.

1 •

The Information Avalanche

• The Obstacles between You and Your Sources

The last person who was familiar with *everything* known to his generation was probably Aristotle, and he died in 322 BC. Since then, people have had to look things up. Today the problem of "looking things up" has become nightmarish. The Library of Congress, for example, now contains more than 60 million items, 15 million of them books. The number of serious journals and magazines published throughout the world is at least 68,000. Yet, for many students, the problem is not having too much information, it is having too little. If you understand the obstacles to the flow of information, you can plan your research to avoid them.

Obstacle 1: Secrecy.   Not all information is public. The activities of the government, of companies, or of research workers in universities are largely secret— or inaccessible. Not even the FBI always beats the keeper of the secrets to the shredding machine.

Obstacle 2: Dispersion.   No library in the world contains *everything* that a researcher might need for a project. A request to another library for a photocopy of an obscure article or book can take months to produce results. Even if you know exactly what you want, there may be no quick way of getting it.

Obstacle 3: Concentration.   Most libraries specialize. This is an excellent thing if you hit a library with the same specialization as yours. In other subjects, you may find that quite basic texts are not in the catalog.

Obstacle 4: High Demand.   High demand is the problem on most campus libraries. If thirty students are writing a term paper on Greek Red Figure Vases, they will all be using the same handful of works. First come, first served.

Obstacle 5: Excessive Supply.   The "information avalanche" is the final problem. In a week, one could read everything Hemingway published; to tackle what scholars have written *about* Hemingway might take years. Hemingway's short story, *The Killers*, for example, is ten pages long; Walker's *Twentieth-Century Short Story Explication* (1979) lists no fewer than forty-two scholarly articles— thousands of pages of text—about that one story. And the mountain grows daily.

• Strategies for Coping

You will probably encounter *all* these problems during your first research projects. Three simple tactics help work round them: (a) reconnaissance, (b) a fast start, and (c) expert advice.

COPING STRATEGY 1: RECONNAISSANCE

Reconnaissance means spying out the land. Good reconnaissance avoids researching subjects for which the supply of information is inadequate. Let's say, for example, that you want to write on the damage caused by sulphur emissions from a chemical factory in your city. You can be certain that the necessary data are "a company secret." Without wasting time, reformulate your topic, shifting, perhaps, to a general study of the damaging effects of sulphur. Then check your library to ensure that it has the necessary materials. In general: *Study the strengths and weaknesses of your sources of information and plan your subject accordingly.*

COPING STRATEGY 2: A FAST START

"The early bird catches the worm." If one text is in demand, the first student at the library gets it; the second student is first on the waiting list. Less selfishly, if your library must borrow a book via the interlibrary loan system, then a fast start means you'll have the book in time to use it. The general rule: *Procrastination hurts*.

COPING STRATEGY 3: EXPERT ADVICE

Obtaining expert advice does not mean asking your professor exactly what you should read. A better tactic is to list what is available and ask your professor what items will be most helpful. (You can also ask if you've missed anything important, of course.) More advanced students in your discipline may have some tips, too. Coping with the information avalanche is just as much a problem for the expert as it is for the novice; don't be afraid that asking for help will make you "look bad." Exactly the opposite is the case.

2 •
Getting On Track

Imagine some day in the distant future when all 60 million items in the Library of Congress are one huge computer database. The researcher will touch a few keys to begin a rapid and enormous search: for example, one could ask for a copy of all the letters written between 1924 and 1931 that mention Hemingway's story "Cat in the Rain," or for details of all the lawsuits brought anywhere in the world between 1850 and 1890 that involved the right of a married woman to own property. A dream, or a nightmare?

This glance into the crystal ball shows you the ideal research situation: *a rapid search of all the relevant sources for the information and ideas that you need*. Finding information in the traditional library falls well short of this ideal; yet some researchers can find what they need in a few hours, while others flit from subject to subject complaining: "The library didn't have anything, so I changed my topic." What are the secrets of a good library technique?

Better than generalized advice and "counsels of perfection," let's take a case. The case concerns a beginning student, Jasmine McKenzie, who had no prior knowledge of how a library functions. Her mistakes and successes will suggest a procedure for a fast, efficient library search.

Jasmine McKenzie was taking a course on child psychology. As a subject for a short research paper she chose the psychological effect of war toys.

• Resource Option 1: An Encyclopedia as Overview

At home Jasmine had the *Encyclopaedia Britannica*. A general encyclopedia like this, or a specific one dealing with psychology, agriculture, literature, or whatever, is a reasonable starting place. Especially useful in encyclopedia entries are the *names of authorities* and the *keywords* that are used. Jasmine read the *Britannica* article on toys. Two ideas gave her food for thought: (a) probably the most common use of toys through history has been training in "the use of weapons." Jasmine saw that her problem was not a new one. (b) Each technological development quickly affects toy design: as soon as the Chinese invented gunpowder, they also invented exploding toys. Jasmine began to see her subject in a wider perspective—the typical result of using an encyclopedia.

• Resource Option 2: The Book Collection

At her local (non-computerized) library, Jasmine asked the librarian on duty: "Where can I find something on war toys?" The librarian checked a list: "Toy Making is at 745.592. Or try the catalog." Jasmine now made two common mistakes; reading about them will cost you far less time than making them yourself.

TACTIC 1: BROWSING THE STACKS

Theoretically, books in a library are grouped in the book stacks according to their "subject." Books on the Second World War are stacked together, books on Japan, books on toys, and so on. Each subject has a code number; most libraries use the number system invented by Melvil Dewey in 1876. Some newer libraries have adopted the Library of Congress system, which combines numbers and letters. These code numbers often mislead the beginner: they seem to imply that every book is about just one subject, and that it is physically possible to group together *all* the books on a certain subject. This is patently not the case. Where, for example, would you look for a book on the survivors of Hiroshima?

> Japan—history
>
> Atomic warfare—moral and religious aspects
>
> World War 1939–1945
>
> Or elsewhere altogether?

Categorizing books by subject is a giant-sized classification headache. Benjamin Custer, editor of the *Dewey Decimal Classification and Relative Index*, recognizes that most books are "multi-subject." He advises librarians to classify a multi-subject book according to its "chief emphasis." If it has no "chief emphasis," then the book should be put into a general category that covers all its subjects. If that fails, the various subjects should be listed, and the book should be given the *lowest* of the available numbers. As you can see, all the books stacked under the same number will have something in common, but not all the books with something in common will be stacked under the same number. For this reason browsing the stacks *might* produce useful material, but you are far more likely to miss the titles you need. (In many libraries, the stacks are in fact *closed*, and readers must request books from a central desk.)

Jasmine located the stack numbered 745.592, Toymaking. (Under the Library of Congress numbering it would be TS 2301.T7.)

These numbers are worth analyzing because they show how librarians are trained to think. In the Dewey system, any 700 number is concerned with *The Arts*. The 740's all concern *Drawing and Decorative and Minor Arts*. The number 745 itself indicates *Decorative and Minor Arts*. The numbers after the decimal point target the subject ever more precisely. The number 745.5 deals with *Handicrafts*, while 745.59 refers to *Making Specific Objects*. The final stack number, 745.592, contains books on *Toys, Models, Related Objects*. The Library of Congress system works in much the same way.

Jasmine began to take down the books: *Making Dolls from Waste-Paper*; *Royal Amusements: Copying Queen Victoria's Toys*; *Radio-Control for Model Builders* —Jasmine ran (not quite screaming) to the catalog. She'd learned lesson 1: the stacks are not the place to begin. (On the other hand, once you find a really good book, scan the shelves on either side—you may well find more.)

TACTIC 2: THE BOOK CATALOG

Most people have used the card catalog (or computer catalog) that indexes a collection of library books. Each book in the collection is indexed on at least three cards: a card for the author, a card for the title, and usually several cards for the subject(s).

Have you ever wondered where these cards come from? Many years ago they were typed up in the library itself, but today they are mostly supplied, preprinted, by the Library of Congress or by private firms. This has led to a welcome degree of

NUCLEAR AMERICA. Copyright © 1984 by Gerard Clarfield and William M. Wiecek. All rights reserved. Printed in the United States of America. No part of this book may be used or reproduced in any manner whatsoever without written permission except in the case of brief quotations embodied in critical articles and reviews. For information address Harper & Row, Publishers, Inc., 10 East 53rd Street, New York, N.Y. 10022. Published simultaneously in Canada by Fitzhenry & Whiteside Limited, Toronto.	Title, year of copyright (symbolized by ©), and the names of the authors
FIRST EDITION	Edition number (first edition in this case)
Designed by Ruth Bornschlegel	
Library of Congress Cataloging in Publication Data	
Clarfield, Gerard H.	Name of main author (for card)
Nuclear America.	Name of the work (for card)

Bibliography: p.
  Includes index.
  1. United States—Military policy. 2. Atomic weapons.
3. Atomic energy—United States. I. Wiecek, William M.,
1938- . II. Title.
	Three subjects (for three subject cards)

UA23.C558 1984 355'.0335'73 84-47565	Stack number under Library of Congress and Dewey systems

standardization among libraries. Instead of looking immediately at the cards, let's look at the second title page, the *copyright page* as it is called, of a modern American book.

The first paragraph deals with publication and copyright matters. Then follows the Library of Congress data. Most important are (a) the author, (b) the title, and (c) the subject(s). In this case the items numbered 1, 2, and 3 are the *three* subjects that have been identified in the book, *Nuclear America*, by Gerard Clarfield and William Wiecek. A master card, or author card, is made out on the basis of this information. Four further cards are produced by typing an extra line above the author's name: a title card and three subject cards. These five cards provide the researcher with five access routes to the book. Let's look at the cards themselves:

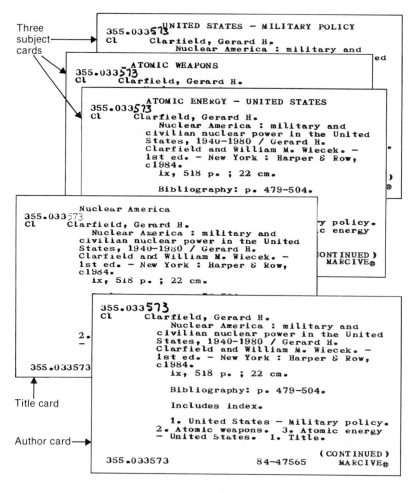

Three subject cards

Title card

Author card

The author card and the title card are useless to a researcher like Jasmine, who knew neither the titles nor the authors of any relevant books. For her, the *subject cards* were the only line of access. She started with the subject *toy manufacture*.

Here she encountered her friends from the stacks once more, plus additional titles with other code numbers. She leafed through the index cards. She was still working randomly, hoping that a title would strike her eye. Nothing did. Discouraged, she returned to the central desk and explained her problem in more detail; this time the librarian gave her a useful lead: "Check the *Library of Congress Subject Headings.*"

Concept Review

Catalog Cards

Imagine that you are a librarian preparing catalog cards for this book—that is, *Writing: Process and Structure*. Where would you find the information you need? How many cards would you prepare, and what would be the main heading on each card?

TACTIC 3: SUBJECT HEADINGS

Researchers approach a card catalog with an astonishing range of keywords in mind. To standardize things, the Library of Congress has listed most of the keywords a researcher might use and suggested the "correct" keyword. This enormous word list is called the *Library of Congress Subject Headings*. (Another similar work is called *Sears List of Subject Headings*.) Below each entry on the list are cross references and the keywords that the Library of Congress itself uses to index the subject. (Many Dewey-based libraries use the Library of Congress headings while keeping the Dewey numbering.)

Jasmine's experience shows how different the idea of a researcher can be from that of a congressional librarian. She first checked *toys* and found a long list of *toy*-related material: only *toy pistols* and *toy soldiers* had any relevance to her topic. *Toy soldiers* was cross-referenced to *military miniatures*, which in turn was cross-referenced to *miniature arms*. If Jasmine had spent all day playing Rumplestiltskin with the card catalog, she might still have missed *miniature arms* as the keyword for *war toys*.

Armed with an authentic keyword, Jasmine returned to the card index. Most of the items indexed under *miniature arms* concerned collecting tin soldiers, but one title arrested her attention: *The Psychology of War Toys*. The *call number* (that is, the exact number allocated to this book) and the map of the library told her where to find the book.

TACTIC 4: BIBLIOGRAPHIES

A bibliography is a list of books and other sources. A prepackaged reading list obviously speeds things up; the problem is to find one. This is where the *Bibliography Index* comes in. This index tells you, for a given subject, where the "reading lists" can be found. Many of these reading lists are at the backs of books, presented under various aliases: *List of Works Cited*, *Suggestions for Further Reading*, and so on.

Her librarian showed Jasmine where the *Bibliography Index* was located. She began with the volume for 1986, searching under *toys* and *military miniatures*. Finding nothing, she worked back through the years. Her first find was in the Index for 1980: the *Encyclopedia of Toys* by Constance King apparently contained a good bibliography. Jasmine found this encyclopedia in the reference room, but the 83 titles in the bibliography simply concerned the history of toys; not a single title looked useful. Returning to the Index, Jasmine worked back year by year. Finally in the 1971 Index she found:

> ogy, and therapeutics for physicians and medical
> students. 4th ed Macmillan '70 incl bibliog.
> TOY soldiers. See Military miniatures
> TOYS, Hazardous
>   Swartz Edward M. Toys that don't care Gambit '71 p371-7
> TRACE elements
>   Pinta, Maurice. Detection and determination of trace
>   elements; absorption spectrophotometry, emission

Luckily Jasmine's library had a copy of *Toys that Don't Care*. The book itself was useful. In its bibliography (*Selected References*), it listed about 110 works with such suggestive titles as:

> *Assault on Childhood*
>
> *Play and Playthings for the Preschool Child*
>
> "What Toys Mean to Your Child"
>
> "Transmission of Aggression through Imitation of Aggressive Models"

The first two titles are books; the two remaining titles bring us to the next resource option: periodicals.

• Resource Option 3: The Periodicals Collection

Periodicals (or *serials* as librarians often call them) appear "periodically"—weekly, monthly, and quarterly are the normal intervals. Let's look at two of Jasmine's titles and see how she tracked them down.

TACTIC 1: FINDING KNOWN TITLES

Periodicals are of two types: *journals*, in which professionals report their latest research for the benefit of other professionals, and *magazines*, which are aimed either at the general reader or at a special interest group. Let's first track down one of Jasmine's magazine items:

> Olds, Sally. "What Toys Mean to Your Child." *Today's Health* Dec. 1969: 22+.

Most modern libraries keep current magazines for a few months and then trash them. Many magazines are printed on biodegradable paper and last only a short time anyway. Magazines are usually stored on *fiche* (pronounced *feesh*). Fiche is familiar to most people from banks and spare-parts stockists. It is like a large photographic slide about four by six inches. On one piece of fiche, up to 98 pages of text are printed. An actual magazine (usually called the *hard copy*) occupies up to 400 times as much space as a copy on fiche. (Microfilm, long rolls of 35 mm film, was also popular for a while, but it is bulkier than fiche and harder to use.) The appropriate fiche is taken from the cabinet. A fiche reader, a machine like a large slide projector, is used to find the correct spot on the fiche and to project the page onto a screen. On many fiche readers, pressing a knob marked PRINT delivers a copy of the page in a few seconds.

Next, an item Jasmine needed from a scholarly journal:

> Bandura, A., Dorothea Ross and Sheila Ross. "Transmission of Aggression through Imitation of Aggressive Models." *Journal of Abnormal Social Psychology* 63 (1961): 575–582.

Journals are stored on fiche, but less often. Many libraries bind the numbers for each year into book form. Journals are generally stored in a periodicals room; a photocopier is used to copy an article.

Jasmine had no trouble locating the 1961 volume of the *Journal of Abnormal Psychology*. She scanned the article quickly to see if it was too technical. Luckily it was not, so she photocopied it.

An Important Tip. Let's look ahead for a moment. One of the last tasks in finalizing your project will be to compile a bibliography listing everything you've quoted in your project. Whenever you make a photocopy or a fiche copy, make sure that your copy contains the name of the magazine it came from, the date, the page number, and, in the case of journals, the volume number. If these data are not printed on the original page, then add them in pen on your copy; this can save you a lot of trouble later on.

TACTIC 2: FINDING NEW MATERIAL: THE PERIODICAL INDEXES

The librarian asked Jasmine if she had enough material. Jasmine was unhappy that her finds were so old—twenty years or more. She needed more recent material. The librarian took Jasmine to the Index desk, one of the more battered and untidy corners of the library.

Ulrich's International Periodicals Directory (1986–87 edition) lists some 68,800 magazines, journals, newsletters and other periodicals that are published worldwide. To access this enormous body of information, the researcher needs some kind of index. In fact there are so many indexes that finding the right one is a challenge in itself. How exactly does an index work? An index picks a selection of periodicals, typically between 100 and 400. The general tendency of its list gives each index a particular bias. (See the *Close-Up* below.) The *Business Periodicals Index*, for example, specializes in business magazines—about 400 of them; five titles from the *A* section give you the flavor:

Advertising World

American Journal of Agricultural Economics

Antitrust Law and Economics Review

Audio-Visual Communications

Aviation Week and Space Technology

Naturally there is overlap; many periodicals are listed in more than one index. Some indexes have been computerized; this speeds up your search, but it can be expensive as most libraries charge for each search you make.

The most general of the indexes is the *Readers' Guide to Periodical Literature*. It is based on a list of some 199 popular news magazines ranging from *Scientific American* to *Harper's Bazaar*. Every two weeks or so, all the articles published in all the selected magazines are listed alphabetically under author and under subject. Every three months, the most recent indexes are consolidated; finally each year a consolidated listing for the whole year appears. The *Reader's Guide* is a common place to begin a search; its great advantage is that most libraries stock most of the magazines it indexes. Let's see what happened when Jasmine tried to find material on war toys.

The *Reader's Guide* for 1985 (March 1985–February 1986, to be precise) is a green book of more than 2,000 pages. Jasmine first checked *War toys* but with no luck; there was no such heading. Recalling the Library of Congress Headings, she tried *Military miniatures* and *Miniature arms*: this produced nothing of interest. Under *Toys* she found this *See also* list:

> **Toys**
> *See also*
> Balloons, Toy
> Beanbags
> Dolls
> Playgrounds, Home—Equipment
> Pogo sticks
> Teddy bears
> Toy and game industry
> Yo-yos

Then came a list of articles, several of which looked interesting:

> The 14th annual guide to the best new toys. E. Sweet. il *Ms* 14:75-6 D '85
> Ambivalence in toyland. B. Sutton-Smith. *Nat Hist* 94:6+ D '85
> The best toys for kids (and the worst). B. Spock, il por *Redbook* 166:16+ N '85
> Black toys: they've come a long way since 1945. il *Ebony* 41:355-6+ N '85
> Build HM's Baby Bugatti. il *Home Mech* 81:14-15 S '85
> Cement truck. G. Hamilton and S. Wolgemuth. il *Fam Handyman* 35:108-10 S :

Item 3 on the list can serve as our example. As a baby of the Spock generation, Jasmine recalled Spock's antiwar sentiments; his article might be useful to her. The entry in the index told her the *title* of the article: "The best toys for kids (and the worst)." It gave the author as B. Spock. The abbreviations *il* and *por* indicated that the article was *illustrated* and contained a *portrait*. (The abbreviation *bibl*, which does not appear here, means *bibliography included*, a specially important clue.) The article appeared in *Redbook*; to be exact in Volume 166 of *Redbook*, on p. 16 and subsequent pages (16+). This issue appeared in *N '85*—obviously November 1985. (Since 1986, the *Reader's Guide* has offered a new service: a short summary or "abstract" of every article indexed is available on microfiche. This enables the researcher to preview the article and decide if it is worth finding.)

Jasmine noted down the relevant facts about several articles from the 1985 index, and then worked backwards through the 1984 and 1983 indexes, collecting more titles. Before physically searching for the articles, she decided to try two more relevant indexes: the *Business Periodicals Index* and the *Education Index*. In presentation, these follow exactly the same pattern as the *Readers' Guide*. In the *Business Periodicals Index* under the heading *Toy and game industry—Marketing*, Jasmine found this entry:

> War toy invasion grows despite boycott. C. Kooi, *Advert*
> *Age* 57:44 Mr 3 '86

The *Education Index* produced an article on selecting toys that looked interesting:

> Choosing good toys for young children. S. Feeney and
> M. Magarick. il *Young Child* 40:21-5 N '84

Armed with her list, Jasmine now tracked down the articles in the fiche collection in her library.

Close-Up

The Indexes

Do you have fun reading lists? Even if you don't, knowing what indexes are available will give you a head start when you need to track down something in *your* special field. Is this list complete? No, it is representative, and, with one exception, lists only indexes that are still alive and well.

Air University Library Index to Military Periodicals 1949 onwards

Applied Science and Technology Index 1958 onwards

The Art Index 1929 onwards

The Bibliographic Index 1938 onwards

Bibliography and Index of Geology 1933 onwards

Biological and Agricultural Index 1964 onwards

Black Studies Index (See *Index to Periodical Articles by and about Negroes*)

Book Review Digest 1905 onwards

Book Review Index 1965 onwards

Business Index 1979 onwards

Business Periodicals Index 1958 onwards

Current Book Review Citations 1976 onwards

Drama Index (See *Play Index*)

The Education Index 1929 onwards

Engineering Index 1881 onwards

Essay and General Literature Index 1934 onwards

General Science Index 1978 onwards

Geology Index (See *Bibliography and Index of Geology*)

Granger's Index to Poetry 1982 (Major poems until that date)

Humanities Index 1974 onwards

Index to Legal Periodicals 1908 onwards

Index to Periodical Articles by and about Negroes 1950 onwards

Law Index (See *Index to Legal Periodicals*)

Medical Index (See *Quarterly Cumulative Index Medicus*)

Military Index (See *Air University*)

Music Index 1949 onwards

New York Times Index 1913 onwards

The Philosopher's Index 1969 onwards

Physical Education Index 1978 onwards

Play Index 1978 (All major plays to that date)

Poetry Index (See *Granger*)

Poole's Index to Periodical Literature 1802–1907 (historians take note)

Popular Periodicals Index 1973 onwards

Public Affairs Information Service 1914 onwards

Quarterly Cumulative Index Medicus 1927 onwards

Short Story Index 1953 onwards

Social Sciences and Humanities Index 1965–73

Social Sciences Index 1974 onwards

Sports Index (See *Physical Education Index*)

Wall Street Journal Index 1957 onwards

Some of these indexes are available as computer databases. A computer search is quicker, but it can be expensive.

TACTIC 3: THE ABSTRACTS

An *abstract* is the essence of a thing. Almost every academic discipline has some organization that publishes regular *abstracts* of important articles. Only the bigger libraries stock all these abstracts, but judicious use of the abstracts can save you a great deal of reading: the abstract tells you if it is worthwhile to locate and read the complete article. The *Psychological Abstracts* are a good example. Each year some 30,000 articles are "abstracted," so browsing is definitely ruled out.

Following the suggestion of the librarian, Jasmine checked up the references under Toys in the *Psychological Abstracts*. She came across an abstract of "Choosing good toys for young children," the article she'd found in the *Education Index*:

> 25189. **Feeney, Stephanie & Magarick, Marion. Choosing good toys for young children**. *Young Children*. 1984(Nov), Vol 40(1), 21-25. —Presents suggestions for parents, grand-parents, teachers, and others who buy toys for 2-6 yr old children. Characteristics of good toys are identified. Typical abilities and interests of children of various ages are described, and how they can be enhanced or developed by toys and play materials is considered. Good toys are attractive and interesting to children; well-constructed, durable, and safe; matched to children's abilities and good for children of various ages; and useful in various ways. Adults affect children's play by their selection of and storage methods for toys. Sensory materials; active play equipment; construction materials; dolls, stuffed animals, and dramatic play; books and recordings; and art materials are discussed in terms of how they contribute to children's development. Examples of appropriate types of toys are presented for each of 3 age groups (2-3, 3-4, and 4-5 yrs) in tabular form. (6 ref) —*H. Hall.*

The abstract alerted Jasmine not to pursue this item—it had nothing to do with war toys. Another item, however, looked more interesting:

> 8894. **Rubin, Kenneth H. & Howe, Nina.** (U Waterloo, Canada) **Toys and play behaviours: An overview.** *Topics in Early Childhood Special Education*. 1985(Fal), Vol 5(3), 1-10. —A literature review on children's toys and the types of play activities associated with them shows that art materials tend to elicit solitary and constructive play forms, whereas dress-up clothes, vehicles and dolls are associated with sociodramatic play. Realistic toys are more conducive to facilitating pretend play in young children than abstract toys; however, with increasing age, less structured, more abstract toys may encourage pretense activities. Other factors that affect children's play include play space, density, the number of toys available, the presence of familiar vs unfamiliar peers, and the sex of the play partner. It is concluded that children's toys do have an impact on play behaviours but that there are still many unanswered questions regarding the relations between the two. (31 ref)—*Journal abstract.*

The question raised at the end of this abstract is one of the things that had been worrying Jasmine: what impact do toys have on the way children behave?

• Resource Option 4: Information Services

Information is a marketable commodity, and many weekly, monthly, and annual publications compete to keep the reader up to date. Most people are familiar with *The World Almanac and Book of Facts* or the *Associated Press Almanac* as sources of statistics and other data. Other publications are more elaborate or more special-ized. *Current Biography*, as its name implies, keeps tabs on people in the news. *Keesing's Contemporary Archives*, *Newsbank*, *Facts on File*, and so on deal with current affairs. Other information companies supply files of magazine articles on particular topics: *SIRS* (Social Issues Resources Series) is typical. These services are expensive, so not all libraries subscribe to all services. If you want a particular kind of information, explain your problem to a librarian who will tell you what is available.

Jasmine tried using the *SIRS* information bank, but with only modest success: it is intended for high school libraries rather than for serious research. The bank itself is a small wall of ring binders with titles such as *ENERGY*, *WOMEN* and *YOUTH*. The only title relevant to Jasmine's research was *YOUTH*. In the index to *YOUTH* she found nothing under *Toys*, but there were two references under *Games*:

G
Gambling, teenage, 7
Games, 9, 49
Gault, Gerald, 1
Gender identity
   See Sex role
Generation gap, 25, 79, 85,
      88, 91
Gifted children, 17
Guidance counseling
   See Counseling programs;
      School, Guidance
      counselors

One of these items turned out to be an article from the *Indianapolis Star*, (June 14, 1981) about a game called Killer. In this game college students use toy guns to "murder" victims. The article was marginally relevant, and Jasmine photocopied it.

• Summary

Like many beginning students, Jasmine had only the haziest idea of how to track down what she needed. Having completed one research project, she understood how a library functions, and she was beginning to find what she needed more easily. That is the goal of any researcher: fast access to necessary information.

Concept Review

Choosing Promising Titles

Using the indexes takes practice. The first box below explains how index entries are read. The other boxes contain entries on the general subject of "computer-phobia." Look at the entries, and then answer the questions.

How to interpret an entry in an index

(All three of these indexes are published by the H. W. Wilson Company. Other indexes are similar.)

Marriage contracts
  Start your next marriage here [prenuptial agreements] L. B. Eichler. il. *50 Plus* 25:47-9+ F '85

An article on the subject **Marriage contracts** entitled "Start your next marriage here," by Lawrence B. Eichler, will be found, with illustrations, in the periodical *50 Plus,* volume 25, pages 47-49 (continued on later pages of the same issue) in the February 1985 issue. A title enhancement. "prenuptial agreements," has been added by the indexer to clarify the meaning of the title. Square brackets are used to indicate these editorial interpolations.

Sample subject entry

Explanation

Psychological aspects

The ambivalent miseries of personal computing. A. Kleiner. *Whole Earth Rev.* no44:6-9 D/Ja '84/'85
Just me and my machine; the new solipsism. L. Winner. *Whole Earth Rev* no44:29 D/Ja '84/'85
The monkey trap or the mystical engine? B. Walsh. *Whole Earth Rev* no44:inside front cover-1 D/Ja '84/'85

Humanities Index, 1985–6

Psychological aspects

Computers, corporate culture and change. J. C. Linder. *Pers J* 64:48-55 S '85
Cosmos vs. chaos: sense and nonsense in electronic contexts. K. E. Weick. *Organ Dyn* 14:50-64 Aut '85
Distress and the other stress [eustress: positive response to problem-solving and challenge] J. E. Beaver. *Comput Decis* 17:56-7 Ag 27 '85
Don't be afraid of computer phobia. E. S. Ely *Comput Decis* 17:98-101 S 10 '85
Getting comfortable with your computer [misconceptions cause managers to shy away from computers] P. Margarita. tab *Manage World* 14:18-19 My '85
Getting started in computing—without fear. D. B. Dibrell. *Natl Underwrit (Prop Casualty Insur Ed)* 90:30-1+ F 21 '86
Human-oriented implementation cures cyberphobia, E. Gardner and others. tabs *Data Manage* 23:29-32+ N '85
Managing computerphobia. T. C. Little, Jr. *Superv Manage* 30:8-12 Je '85
The psychological costs of master computer. W. A. Wagenaar. tab *Datamation* 31:157+ Jl 1 '85

Business Periodicals Index, 1985–6

PART THREE
The Research Paper

<table>
<tr><td colspan="1">Psychological aspects</td></tr>
</table>

> **Psychological aspects**
> Addiction. S. R. Alpert il *Comput Electron* 23:4 Mr '85
> Combating cyberphobia. G. W. Bracey. *Phi Delta Kappan* 66:508 Mr '85
> Computers and the family [mental health] A. Naiman. il *Pers Comput* 9:19 S '85
> Computers on the couch [views of S. Turkle] D. Hellerstein, il por *Esquire* 104:360-3+ D '85
> Getting started. O. Edwards. il *Pers Comput* 8:86-7+ F '84
> The new computer anxiety. A. Naiman, il *Pers Comput* 9:31 Ja '85.
> Sherry Turkle. L. Van Gelder, il por *Ms* 13:48-9+ Ja '85
> Using computers leads us to look at minds as machines. S. Turkle, il por *U S News World Rep* 98:67 Ja 14 '85

Readers' Guide to Periodical Literature, 1985

Magazine Titles in Full

Computer Decisions

Computer Electronics

Data Management

Datamation

Management World

Ms

National Underwriter

Organizational Dynamics

Personal Computing

Personnel Journal

Supervisory Management

U.S. News and World Report

Whole Earth Review

a. Imagine you are writing an essay on why people are afraid of computers. Pick the *four* articles that look the most interesting for your project.

b. Imagine that your articles must be ordered from another library. What information will the librarian need to place the order? List the necessary information for your chosen articles.

CHAPTER TWELVE
Finding Information II: Library Research

• Summary: The Flowchart

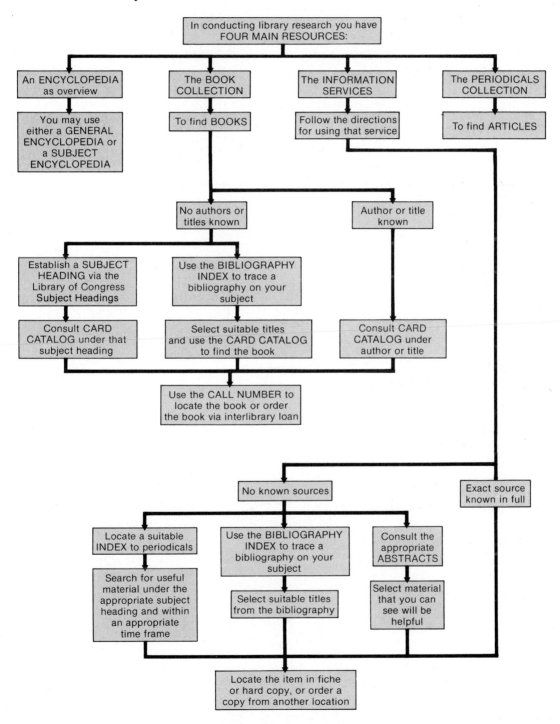

CHAPTER

• THIRTEEN •

Storing Information

The Problem: Keeping Track

When Theseus entered the maze that concealed the flesh-eating Minotaur, he secured one end of a ball of wool at the mouth of the labyrinth and used it to track his way out. You will need something comparable when you begin to lose yourself among the intricacies of your research project. To keep track, you'll need a running bibliography for your sources and an information store for your finds. This chapter shows you how to work with these essential tools.

1 •

The Running Bibliography

• The Running Bibliography: Design and Purpose

A running bibliography is simply a list of every source you have found so far. If the list is to be accessible, it must be in alphabetical order; if it is to be updateable, then it must accept new material at any point. An *alphabetical*, *updateable* list will be a card index or, if you work on a word processor, a computer listing. (See the *Close-Up* below.)

Close-Up

Bibliographies and the Word Processor

Bibliography software is available for most systems. The programs work in an obvious way: for each item you wish to add to the bibliography, the program prompts you to enter all the relevant data. When you want a printout, one keystroke gets a perfect bibliography first time. More commonly, a researcher keeps for each project a separate textfile with a filename such as BIB. Each item (book, article, and so on) is entered alphabetically, using the "correct" bibliographical form. (See the next section for details.) Since this file is identical in structure with a card index, little need be said about it except to record two reservations. Reservation 1: unless you have a lap-top computer, you will not be able to use your word processor in the library. This means you must make detailed bibliographical notes in the library and *without fail* transcribe them at home. Don't forget. Reservation 2: unless your computer allows multi-tasking, you will not be able to access the bibliography file while you are writing on the screen. This can be inconvenient. The problem is solved (at least for a short bibliography) by reprinting the bibliography each time it is updated.

The card index is a familiar device—an alphabetical stack of index cards (3 by 5 inches usually). On each card are the data about one book, article, or whatever. Before we study the data more closely, let's tackle a question that every student asks at some stage: why? Why is so much stress laid on bibliographies in academic research papers?

A student expects to learn not just facts, but the methods—or the *methodology* as it is called—of an academic discipline. Lab work, for example, is highly methodical, not for the sake of method, but because a poorly run lab seldom produces worthwhile results. In each discipline, an important part of the methodology is the way in which knowledge is *accumulated*: researchers suggest ideas, argue about them, test them and finally accept or reject them. Without accumulation of knowledge, each generation would have to reinvent the wheel. One essential technique of accumulation is to ensure that the sources of information used by one researcher are accessible to other researchers for comment, analysis and criticism. This is the role of the bibliography; it is one of the dragons that guards the temple of academic truth.

A bibliography provides the information a later researcher will need to track down your sources and review them. This means that each time you offer a quotation, a statistic, or a research finding, you have a duty to explain exactly where you found this material. Some years ago this was done with footnotes (at the foot of the page) or endnotes (at the end of the essay). This cumbersome apparatus has for the most part been dismantled, as you'll see in Chapter 16, Presenting Information. Today in most disciplines, writers use *sourcenotes*, short insertions in the text that refer the reader to the bibliography. The bibliography is the heart of a streamlined system aimed at making tracking operations speedy and efficient. The next question then: what information does a later researcher need in order to run a trace action?

• Adequate Documentation—Support for a Trace Action

To trace *exactly* the source you used, a later researcher needs (or might need):

1. *The type of source.* Is the source a book, a magazine, a database, an interview, or what? Obviously, the researcher needs this physical information before beginning a trace action.
2. *The name of the source person.* For a book or article, this is the name of the author; for an interview, the name of the interviewee, and so on.
3. *The title of the source.* Published sources always have a title of some sort.
4. *The publication data of the source.* Publication data explain exactly where the source originated. If different forms of the same source exist (reprints and so on), publication data clarifies exactly which version you used.

To give you a closer idea, let's develop the documentation for a book that Jasmine McKenzie used, one by Erich Fromm on destructiveness. The most obvious data on this book are these:

1. Type of source: **book**
2. Author: **Erich Fromm**
3. Title: ***The Anatomy of Human Destructiveness***

No problems here. Next, the publication data. What exactly is needed? First, a glance at what is *not* needed. Many facts about a book—whether it is hardbound or paperback, how many pages it has, and so on—are interesting, but they will not help a trace action. *Publication data offer the minimum necessary to trace the source.* What is this minimum?

4a. The date and/or the edition number: **First edition, 1974.**
As knowledge increases, new books are written or old ones are updated. An update is called a new *edition*. Obviously, a later researcher must know which edition you are using. Not all books carry the edition number, and so it is essential to include the date of publication as well.

4b. The publisher: **Jonathan Cape Ltd.**
The rights to a book are often traded among publishers. A book may appear simultaneously in different countries from different publishers. This is especially true of cheap paperback reprints. The trace action must be able to locate the version *you* used.

4c. The city of publication: **London**
Is this *really* necessary? Yes indeed. Many books are brought out in different versions in different countries. A book published simultaneously in London

• **338** •

PART THREE
The Research Paper

and New York, even by the same publisher, contains not only different spellings but often quite radical revisions.

Different sources require different trace data, but the principle is always the same: the researcher provides the minimum data for a successful trace action.

• Standardized Documentation—Academic Shorthand

If you compare half a dozen books with bibliographies, you'll see that these bibliographies differ in layout, sometimes drastically. A recent book by John Howell, *Style Manuals of the English-Speaking World*, lists some 226 separate manuals issued by commercial publishers, university presses and professional bodies—226 ways of documenting sources. Fortunately, academic researchers are beginning to standardize, although, as with videorecorders, there are rival standards and the standards are incompatible. At present two academic standards have large followings: the so-called *MLA* and *APA* standards. *MLA* is promulgated by the Modern Language Association, *APA* by the American Psychological Association. You should find out what standard documentation *your* discipline uses—your professor, or Howell's book, will help you. At this stage, however, let's stick with the *MLA* standard: it is the norm for the humanities, and especially for English.

The *MLA* documentation for Fromm's book looks like this:

Fromm, Erich. The Anatomy of Human Destructiveness. London: Cape, 1974.

Let's examine this entry carefully. Thereafter, the patterns for other entries should make sense without detailed comment.

1. *The type of source.* Where is it made clear that this item is a *book*? This is not expressly stated because the documentation for a book always looks exactly like this—no more is needed. Only if the source were in some way unusual (a Ph.D. dissertation, for example, or a computer program) would this "oddity" be noted.

2. *The name of the source person.* Because authors' names are used to alphabetize a bibliography, the author's name is given first, and it is reversed so that the family name heads the entry. The punctuation is invariable: family name, comma, given name (and/or initials), period.

3. *The title of the source.* The title of the work is given next. It is underlined (or printed in italics) and followed by a period.

4. *The publication data of the source.* The layout of the publishing data is arbitrary but has a long tradition behind it: City, colon, publisher, comma, year, period. Let's confirm that *MLA* provides adequate documentation:

   a. *The date and/or the edition number.* *MLA* puts the date of publication last. Where is the edition number? To save space, an edition number is given only if a second (or subsequent) edition is used. The absence of specific information means: "First edition."

b. *Publisher.* The name of the publishing house is given in the shortest recognizable form. *Jonathan Cape Ltd* is cut back to *Cape.*

c. *City of Publication.* The book was published in London.

If you followed the way in which one standard entry is put together, other kinds of entries should present no problems.

• Documenting your Sources: The *MLA* Standard

The *MLA* standard is normally used for work within the humanities. If you must use a different standard, see the next section (p. 348) for the names of the principal manuals of style.

You will encounter three puzzles in putting together most entries:

A. What to use as the name of the author?
B. What to use as the title of the source?
C. What to include as publication data?

Name of Author? Title of Work? Publication Data?

Each puzzle must be solved independently. A book with four authors, with a subtitle, and in its third edition creates three independent problems. No list of specimen entries can cope with all the millions of possible combinations. The only solution is to create three lists covering each problem in turn. To these three lists, a fourth list has been added: it deals with less common sources such as recordings, pictures, broadcasts and so on. *You should quickly scan the list below right through: that will give you a sense of the various kinds of entries.*

A. The Name of the Author

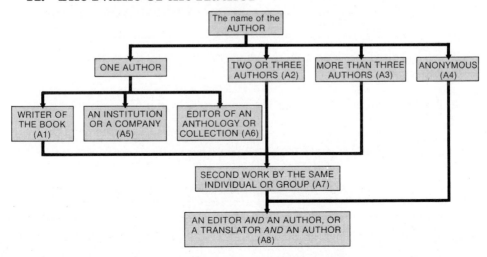

1. A Book, Article or Other Source with One Author

Fromm, Erich. The Anatomy of Human Destructiveness. London: Cape, 1974.

Kooi, Cynthia. "War Toy Invasion Grows Despite Boycott." Advertising Age 3 Mar. 1986: 44.

Hillier, Mary L. "Toy." Encyclopedia Americana. 1985 ed.

The form of the name is normally that given on the title page. You might wish to fill out initials or unmask the user of a pseudonym. If so:

Lawrence, D[avid] H[erbert].
Orwell, George [Eric Blair].

2. A Book or Article with Two or Three Authors

McCord, William, Joan McCord and I. Zola. Origins of Crime. New York: Columbia, 1959.

Feeney, Stephanie, and Marion Magarick. "Choosing Good Toys for Young Children." Young Children Nov. 1984: 21–25.

Two or three authors are all named *in the order given on the title page* or in the byline. Only the first name has the order reversed because only that name is alphabetized. (Here *MLA* differs from *APA*.)

3. A Book or Article with Four or more Authors

Adler, Richard, et al. The Effects of Television Advertising on Children: Review and Recommendations. Lexington: Heath, 1980.

Lansky, L. M., et al. "Sex Differences in Aggression and its Correlates in Middle-class Adolescents." Child Development 32 (1961): 45–58.

If a book or article has four or more authors, the abbreviation *et al.* (and others) is used to save space.

4. An Anonymous Book or an Unsigned Article in a Magazine or Other Source

Sir Gawain and the Green Knight. Ed. J. R. R. Tolkien and E. V. Gordon. London: Oxford UP, 1925.

"Foul Smell in the Cabbage Patch." Economist 20 Dec. 1986: 94.

"Toy." Encyclopaedia Britannica: Macropaedia. 1982 ed.

Anonymous material begins with the title of the work; the item is alphabetized using the first word of the title (ignoring *A* and *The*).

5. A Book or Other Work by a Government Agency or Other Institution

> Department of Defense. Automated Data Systems (ADS) Documentation (DoD-STD-7953). Washington:
>   Dept. of Defense, 1983.

Where a company, a university, a government department, or any other institution issues a work, this institution is given as the "author."

6. A Collection with an Editor

> Bliss, E. L. ed. Roots of Behavior. New York: Hafner, 1968.

Many modern books are really anthologies of articles by specialist contributors. In this case, the editor who chooses the contributions counts as the "author"—the abbreviation *ed.* makes the situation clear. An anthology of poems or stories uses the same form.

7. A Second Book or Article by the Same Author or Authors

> Fromm, Erich. The Anatomy of Human Destructiveness. London: Cape, 1974.
> - - -. The Sane Society. New York: Holt, 1955.

The same name is not repeated; three hyphens are substituted. The three hyphens (no more) are also substituted for a group of collaborating authors. A cluster of several works by one author (or collaboration) is normally alphabetized, although you may use chronological order if you prefer.

8. A Book or Article that has been Edited or Translated

> Virgil. Aeneid. Trans. Rolfe Humphries. New York: Scribner, 1951.

> Shakespeare, William. The Complete Works of William Shakespeare. Ed. W. J. Craig. London: Oxford UP,
>   1905.

Where there is an author *and* an editor, the author normally "outranks" the editor. Nearly all new editions of older works have an editor whose job it is to check the original text and correct errors.

B. The Title of the Work

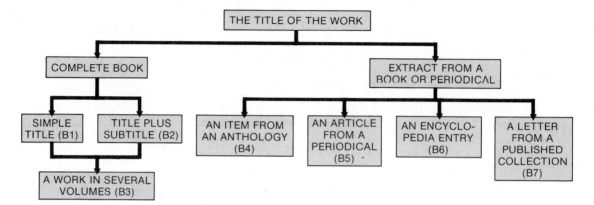

1. A Book with a Simple Title

Fromm, Erich. The Anatomy of Human Destructiveness. London: Cape, 1974.

2. A Book with a Subtitle

Fromm, Erich. The Crisis of Psychoanalysis: Essays on Freud, Marx, and Social Psychology. New York:
　　Holt, 1970.

Many books have subtitles. If, on the title page, the subtitle is separated from the main title by a colon (as in this example), then the subtitle should be included in the bibliography as part of the title.

3. A Book in Several Volumes

Orwell, George. The Collected Essays, Journalism and Letters of George Orwell. 4 vols. Ed. Sonia Orwell
　　and Ian Angus. London: Secker, 1968.

If you made use of only one volume, this is noted at the end of the entry:

Orwell, George. The Collected Essays, Journalism and Letters of George Orwell. 4 vols. Ed. Sonia Orwell
　　and Ian Angus. London: Secker, 1968. Vol. 3.

4. An Article, Story, or Other Piece Anthologized in a Book

Lorenz, Konrad. "Ritualized Aggression." The Natural History of Aggression. Ed. J. D. Carthy and
　　F. J. Ebling. New York: Academic, 1964: 45–58.

The title of the article (or other item) is put in quotation marks; the title of the book is underlined.

5. An Article in a Periodical or Newspaper

> Kooi, Cynthia. "War Toy Invasion Grows Despite Boycott." Advertising Age 3 Mar. 1986: 44.

> Purdum, Todd S. "Coleco Smitten by 'Rambo.'" New York Times 1 Aug. 1985, sec. 4: 1+.

The name of an article is given in quotation marks. The name of the publication is underlined. The title of a news item is often a headline. *MLA* capitalizes all the keywords in the title (whatever form the original article used); *APA* capitalizes only the first word.

6. An Entry in an Encyclopedia

> "Toy." Encyclopaedia Britannica: Macropaedia. 1982 ed.

> Hillier, Mary L. "Toy." Encyclopedia Americana. 1985 ed.

7. A Letter in a Collection of Published Letters

> Baker, Carlos, ed. Ernest Hemingway: Selected Letters, 1917–1961. New York: Scribner, 1981.

C. Publication Data

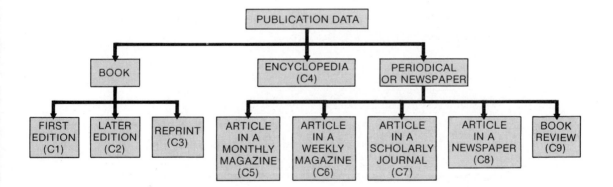

1. The First Edition of a Book

> Fromm, Erich. The Anatomy of Human Destructiveness. London: Cape, 1974.

Publication data begin with the city. If many cities are given on the title page, use the first one. For a book published in a less well known city (for example,

Glenview, Illinois, is the home of the publisher Scott, Foresman) use simply *Glenview* as the city. Do not add *IL*.

The name of the publisher is kept as short as possible. For a university press use, for example:

Oxford UP
U of Chicago P

The date of publication is often given on the title page. If not, use the copyright date. If the second title page (copyright page) lists many *reprints*, or *impressions*, by the same publisher, these dates should be ignored. If the book has no city, no publisher, or no date, then in the appropriate slot use one of the following abbreviations: *N.p.* (no place); *n.p.* (no publisher); *n.d.* (no date). (You may have to use all three!)

2. The Second (or Later) Edition of a Book

Dewey Decimal Classification and Relative Index. 19th ed. Ed. Benjamin A. Custer. Albany: Forest, 1979.

An *edition* of a book is a full reworking. An *impression* or *reprint* is a new printing of exactly the same text. Only *edition* numbers are of any importance.

3. A Reprinted Book

Collins, William Wilkie. Man and Wife. 1870. New York: Dover, 1983.

For all reprints, the original date should be added after the title. A paperback edition of a hardback original uses this form.

4. The Edition of an Encyclopedia

"Toy." Encyclopaedia Britannica: Macropaedia. 1982 ed.

5. An Article in a Monthly (or Bi-Monthly) Magazine

Feeney, Stephanie, and Marion Magarick. "Choosing Good Toys for Young Children." Young Children
Nov. 1984: 21–25.

Spock, Benjamin. "The Best Toys for Kids (and the Worst)." Redbook Nov. 1985: 16+.

The month (abbreviated) is given after the name of the magazine (May, June and July are written in full); a colon follows, and then the page numbers are given. If the article is paged continuously, the numbers of the first and last pages are given. If the article is broken up, then only the first page is given with the symbol +. If the pages aren't numbered, then use the abbreviation *n.pag.* (no pagination).

6. An Article in a Weekly (or Biweekly) Magazine

> Kooi, Cynthia. "War Toy Invasion Grows Despite Boycott." Advertising Age 3 Mar. 1986: 44.

This differs from a monthly publication only in that the exact date of publication (the date on the cover) is added.

7. An Article in a Scholarly Journal

> Bandura, A., Dorothea Ross and Sheila Ross. "Transmission of Aggression through Imitation of Aggressive Models." Journal of Abnormal Social Psychology 63 (1961): 575–582.

Many journals are published monthly, quarterly or erratically. Each year, the issues are collected into a "volume." In this case the volume number is 63, and the year concerned is 1961. It is helpful to give both figures because libraries bind and label journals differently: some use the volume number, some the year, some both. Most journals are paged continuously through a volume; if each issue is separately paged, you should add the issue number to the volume number. In the case below, 5.3. means Volume 5, Number 3.

> Kenneth A. Rubin and Nina Howe. "Toys and Play Behaviors: An Overview." Topics in Early Childhood Special Education 5.3 (1985): 1–9.

8. An Article in a Newspaper

> Purdum, Todd S. "Coleco Smitten by 'Rambo.'" New York Times 1 Aug. 1985, sec. 4: 1+.

Some newspapers are printed in sections with independent page numbering; the *New York Times* article is in Section 4 (the business section) on page 1 and later pages.

9. A Book Review

> Sanborn, Sara. "Driven by a Desire for Sheer Destruction." Rev. of The Anatomy of Human Destructiveness by Erich Fromm. New York Times Book Review 18 Nov. 1973: 3+.

D. Documenting Less Common Types of Sources

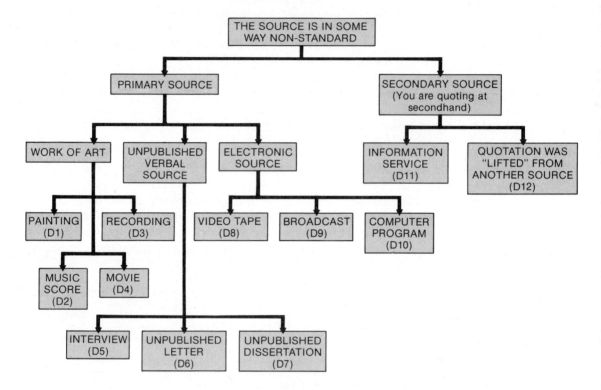

Books, periodicals and newspapers are, for many research papers, the only sources. Odd situations, such as "secondhand quotations," can still arise, however. With other, non-print sources, the goal is to give whatever information will help trace the item. The *MLA Handbook* covers many obscure eventualities. If you need even more detail, a book by Eugene Fleischer, *A Style Manual for Citing Microform and Nonprint Media*, covers the field exhaustively. The list below covers typical items you might need to document.

1. A Painting (or other Art Work)

> Cassatt, Mary. Two Children on the Seashore. National Gallery of Art, Washington, D.C.

If you found the work as a reproduction in a book, then the book must also be documented:

> Vermeer, Johannes. The Lacemaker. Louvre, Paris. Plate 26 in Vermeer of Delft. By Albert Blankert.
> Oxford: Phaidon, 1978.

2. The Score of a Musical Composition

> Bartok, Bela. Concerto for Orchestra. Hawkes Pocket Scores 79. London: Boosey and Hawkes, n.d.

3. A Recording of a Musical Composition

> Bartok, Bela. Concerto for Orchestra. Cond. Georg Solti, London Symphony Orch. London, CS 6784, 1965.

> Cohen, Leonard. "Story of Isaac." Leonard Cohen: Live Songs. CBS, 65224, 1973.

This is the minimum entry. You should add any other information that is relevant to your purposes.

4. A Movie

> Tess. Dir. Roman Polanski. Columbia Pictures, 1979.

This is the minimum entry. You should add any other information (stars, screenwriters, and so on) that is relevant to your purposes.

5. An Interview

> Moordike, Angela. Personal interview. 7 May 1988.

> Dole, Elizabeth. Telephone interview. 12 Aug. 1987.

6. An Unpublished Letter

> Dole, Elizabeth. Letter to the author. 14 Aug. 1987.

The form for *published* letters is given earlier.

7. An Unpublished Dissertation

> Arborough, Leonid. "War Toys and their Effect on the Behavior of Pre-Schoolers." Diss. U of Mainz, 1987.

8. A Videotape

> Jane Fonda's Prime Time Workout. Videocassette. Karl Home Video, 1984.

9. A Television Program

> CBS Evening News. Written and narrated by Dan Rather. 10 May 1987.

10. Computer Software

> "Apple III Pascal." Cupertino: Apple Computer, 1981.

11. Information Service

> Cavinder, Fred D. "Killers on Campus." Indianapolis Star 14 Jun. 1981, mag. sec.: 8+. Rpt in YOUTH 2.
>   Ed. Eleanor C. Goldstein. Boca Raton: Social Issues Resources Series, Inc, 1985.

This item from a newspaper was reprinted by the information service, *SIRS* (Social Issues Resources Series). The first part of the reference follows that for a newspaper; the latter part begins with the abbreviation *Rpt* (Reprinted) and refers to *SIRS* itself. Each information service constructs its data bank differently: some give advice on the way their material should be referenced—*SIRS* does, for example. In other cases you may have to improvise the reference.

12. Material from a Secondary Source

One of your writers will often quote material from sources inaccessible to you. Rubin and Howe, for example, in "Toys and Play Behaviors: An Overview" (1985) quote a 1932 text by the great child psychologist, Jean Piaget. If you want to use this quotation from Piaget, the bibliography simply lists the work where you found the quotation. It makes no mention of Piaget. The reference to Piaget occurs in the essay itself; it looks like this:

Piaget was the first to distinguish between cognitive play and social play (qtd. in Rubin and Howe: 2).

The abbreviation *qtd.* means *quoted*. The bibliography entry is:

> Kenneth A. Rubin and Nina Howe. "Toys and Play Behaviors: An Overview." Topics in Early Childhood
>   Special Education 5.3 (1985): 1–9.

• Documenting your Sources: Other Approaches

At least 25 disciplines require a particular style of documentation, some of them rather idiosyncratic. The most prestigious discussion of the various possibilities occurs in *The Chicago Manual of Style* (13th edition, 1982). If you need to know more, that is the place to start looking. To give you a taste of the *kinds* of differences that arise, let's glance at some of the variations between the *MLA* standard and its chief rival, the *APA* (American Psychological Association) standard.

a. **Names.**   While *MLA* allows an author both a family name *and* a given name, *APA* allows only the use of family name and initials. If several authors are involved, *MLA* inverts only the name of the first (for example, Freud, Sigmund), while *APA* inverts *all* the names.

b. **Quotation Marks.** *MLA* requires the use of quotation marks around the title of an article; *APA* forbids it.

c. **Capitalization.** *MLA* requires all the main words in the title of an article to be capitalized; *APA* capitalizes only the first word.

If you feel like groaning at the triviality of all this, you are not alone. Freelance writers who submit essays to different publications using different standards sometimes curse the "powers that be."

In practical terms, if you cannot use *MLA*, then consult a manual appropriate to your discipline; some disciplines have several manuals. Some of the major manuals are:

Agriculture:	American Society of Agronomy. *Handbook and Style Manual for ASA, CSSA, and SSSA Publications*. 6th ed., 1976.
Biology:	Council of Biology Editors. *Council of Biology Editors Style Manual*. 4th ed., 1978.
Business:	Moyer, Ruth, Eleanour Stevens, and Ralph Switzer. *The Research and Report Handbook for Managers and Executives in Business, Industry and Government*. 1981.
Chemistry:	American Chemical Society. *Handbook for Authors of Papers in American Chemical Society Publications*. 1978.
Mathematics:	American Mathematical Society. *A Manual for Authors of Mathematical Papers*. 7th ed., 1980.
Medicine:	*Information to Authors, 1980–1981: Editorial Guidelines Reproduced from 246 Medical Journals*. Eds. Harriet R. Meiss and Doris A. Jaeger. 1980.
Physics:	American Institute of Physics. *Style Manual for Guidance in the Preparation of Papers for Journals Published by the American Institute of Physics*. 3rd ed., 1978.
Psychology:	American Psychological Association. *Publication Manual*. 3rd ed., 1983.

Review Assignment

Compiling an *MLA* Bibliography

For a short paper on the future of the whaling industry, Lee Chubbin came up with a number of items. They are described in the paragraph below. Your assignment is to prepare an *MLA*-style bibliography for these eight items. Remember two things: (a) not all the information available about a source will be needed to document it, and (b) a bibliography must be in alphabetical order.

The inspiration for Lee's paper was the movie, *Moby Dick*. *Moby Dick* was made in 1956 by the director John Huston for Warner Brothers; it starred Gregory Peck and Richard Basehart. The first written source Lee tried was the article on whaling in the *Encyclopedia Americana*, 1985 edition; this article was by Richard C. Kugler. Having read this piece, Lee realized that he knew nothing about how whales eat, sleep, navigate and reproduce, so his first specialized book was a "heavy." *Whales* by

E. J. Slijper is a classic written originally in Dutch. It was translated into English by A. J. Pomerans and published by Basic Books Publishing Company, Incorporated, of New York in 1962. On the dust jacket of the book, but nowhere else, is a subtitle: *The Biology of the Cetaceans*. Lee felt a growing disgust at the idea of killing whales, so he decided to seek out the arguments for a ban on whaling. Two books helped him. The first was *A Whale for the Killing* by Farley Mowat. This book was published in 1972 in Boston, Massachusetts, by Little, Brown and Company. Lee then used the second edition of a book by Faith McNulty, *The Great Whales*. This edition was published in 1983 by Doubleday and Company, Incorporated, in Garden City, New York. (The original edition had appeared in 1973.) Realizing that much of this book material was rather old, Lee researched the periodicals indexes. He found a *Newsweek* report entitled "Trying to Save the Whale." The article had no byline. It appeared on page 39 of Volume 106, Number 20 of the magazine, dated November 11, 1985. In the bi-monthly periodical *Oceans*, Lee found "Pilot whale killings: tradition versus conservation." The authors were Sean Whyte and Margaret Whyte. This was the January/February 1986 issue, Number 1 of Volume 19 of *Oceans*. Page numbers were 8 and 9. Finally, in the *Ecology Law Quarterly* for 1985 (Volume 12, Number 4), Lee found a long article (pp. 937–975) that helped him greatly. It was by Patricia Birnie and was entitled "The role of developing countries in nudging the International Whaling Commission to encouraging non-consumptive uses of whales."

2 •

Keeping Track of Information

• Strategies that Don't Work

Let's begin by watching three research clowns make their slapstick errors.

JOEY BOOKMARKER

Joey doesn't take notes. As he reads, he simply marks the page where anything catches his attention—even in library books. Joey Bookmarker soon has a stack of (overdue) books and magazines with hundreds of places marked. Three days before his deadline, his mind is a blur of information, none of which he can readily trace back to a source. His research paper will be, at best, a statement of his present opinion on his subject. How he *arrived* at his opinion, and whether his opinion is based on information or on fairy tales, no one can tell.

MARY NOTEPAD

Mary buys six pads of legal-sized notepaper before embarking on any project. As she reads, she uncritically copies every single scrap of information she finds. After a month of back-breaking work and three days before her deadline, she has filled all her notepaper from edge to edge and on both sides of the paper. She is now no better off than Joey Bookmarker. Like him, she has a mass of information, but it is unsorted and probably unsortable in the time remaining. Her research paper will be an incoherent pasteup of painfully researched detail.

BURN FASTTRACK

Burn leaves a cloud of blue smoke as he pulls away from every stop light. He does not take notes; instead, he reads a little and then transforms this material into a "completed" paragraph. He then reads a little more, writes a little more, and so on. Unfortunately, as he uncovers new sources of information, his piece demands extensive *rewriting*. Rewriting bores rubber-burners, and so Burn loses interest in the project. His end product is incoherent, contradictory, and, in a word, worthless.

From these three cautionary tales, we can sketch the four requirements of a workable information storage system:

A. **Expansion.** The system must allow for indefinite expansion; related facts must be easily clustered next to each other. (All three clowns fail here.)

B. **Ease of Organization.** It must be easy to organize or to reorganize facts; it must be easy to restructure the game plan. (All three clowns again fail here.)

C. **Instant Access.** All the facts needed at writing time must be *instantly accessible*. (All three clowns will have problems *finding* material.)

D. **Ease of Transcription.** The facts must be stored so that writing is as simple and straightforward as possible. (All three clowns will find writing a final draft a slow and forbidding task.)

The only system that meets all four requirements is *an indexed file of notecards set up so that each card contains a single item of information*. The system should be backed up by a *copyfile*.

• Keeping a Copyfile

Using a photocopier, a fiche copier and, perhaps, a text scanner (a clever device that reads a page of a book and converts it directly into a word processor file), you can quickly assemble a mini-library on your subject. This collection is called a *copyfile*. A copyfile has several advantages:

A. You can work at home in the evenings and at weekends when the library is closed.

B. Working at home is also a big plus if you use a word processor.

C. In case of doubt while writing, you can put your hand on the original source in seconds.

D. You can avoid a last-minute hunt for lost trivialities, such as a date or page number.

It helps to note on the bibliography card the fact that you made a copy:

> SPOCK, Benjamin
>
> "The Best Toys for Kids (and the Worst)"
> _Redbook_ Nov. 1985: 16+.
>
> COPY IN COPYFILE
> Teacher Training Center Library: Fiche

Copies must be paid for, but a copyfile for a research project costs little more than a trip to the movies—and it's much better for your health.

• Setting Up and Using an Information Store

A card index is an ideal information store: it allows indefinite expansion; it is easy to organize or reorganize; it allows instant access to information; and, at writing time, the information you need for each paragraph is ready to go. (For some thoughts on using a word processor as a store, see the _Close-Up_ below.) If you have never created such an index, a case study will give you the idea.

Close-Up

The Word Processor and the Information Store

Many students experiment with methods of storing research data using a word processor. Typically an outline is entered, and then facts, as they come in, are added at the appropriate place in the outline. When all the facts are in, rewriting and editing slowly develop a readable text; continuity and analysis are provided as necessary. The steps are:

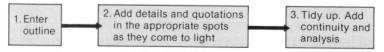

With luck, a good report can be written in this way—but there can be problems. The first is memory. Notes cannot be taken _indefinitely_, since all computer memories are limited. If the project has to be split into two or more segments, then the transfer of material from one section to another becomes difficult and time-consuming, at least with most word processing programs. In general, finding, moving and reorganizing are tricky. A bigger problem is the information you decide _not_ to use; if this is struck from the piece, it is usually beyond recovery; if material is not struck but stored, the store quickly becomes a wilderness of incomprehensible file- and path-names. All these problems can be solved with enough memory and sophisticated software. In general, however, students seem to get the most out of a word processor when they use it *in conjunction with* a traditional card index.

Will Hampshire is studying agriculture with a special emphasis on the problems of the third world. Will believes that many modern techniques are too sophisticated for the third-world farmer; accordingly, he is researching the farming techniques of older civilizations to see what might be worth resurrecting. Will has talked through this problem during a seminar, and so he already has a rough game plan in mind:

1. Agriculture

    1.1. Plowing

    1.2. Sowing and crop rotation

    1.3. Irrigation and fertilization

    1.4. Harvesting

2. Animal Husbandry

    2.1. Type selection

    2.2. Stabling and other housing

    2.3. Breeding programs

    2.4. Disease control

    2.5. Slaughtering

Thesis:
Older methods may be more suited to third world farmers than advanced American technology.

The neatest way of working is for Will to set up a system of *subject dividers* based on his game plan. A normal index card measures 3 by 5 inches (or the larger 5 by 8 inches); the section dividers should be about a third of an inch higher. Accordingly, Will's information store looks like this:

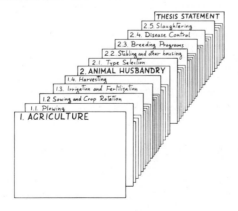

Three kinds of notes then begin to "plump up" each section: (A) notes about useful facts or statistics, (B) direct quotations, and (C) summaries of arguments or descriptions. Let's look at an example of each.

Will is working with a modern translation (1914) of a book by the ancient Roman writer, Vitruvius. Vitruvius' *Ten Books on Architecture* have many tips on finding and transporting water. This "lost technology" is relevant to Section 1.3. of Will's information store, Irrigation and Fertilization.

A. USEFUL FACTS OR STATISTICS

Each individual fact is recorded on a card of its own. Don't be tempted to record two facts on one card: you'll have problems if the facts have to be "split up" later.

> 1.3. Irrigation and fertilization
>
> Signs of places to sink wells:
>
> A fleece placed overnight in a hole will become damp if there is water in the ground.
>
> Vitruvius, p. 228 (Full text in Copyfile)

B. DIRECT QUOTATIONS

Short quotations can be copied by hand. It saves time if longer quotations are photocopied and pasted onto the card.

> 1.3. Irrigation and fertilization
> Signs of places to sink wells:
>
> Dig out a place not less than three feet square and five feet deep, and put into it about sunset a bronze or leaden bowl or basin, whichever is at hand. Smear the inside with oil, lay it upside down, and cover the top of the excavation with reeds or green boughs, throwing earth upon them. Next day uncover it, and if there are drops and drippings in the vessel, the place will contain water.
>
> Vitruvius, p. 228

C. SUMMARIES

Vitruvius often goes into too much detail for Will's needs. When this happens, a summary will be enough to remind Will of the key ideas. He can return to the copyfile for the details if need be.

> 1.3. Irrigation and fertilization
>
> In supplying an ancient city, water was brought long distances. Hills were normally tunneled through, while depressions were crossed either by an arched aqueduct or by a totally closed pipe acting as a siphon. Vitruvius favors the aqueduct because a pipe made of lead might poison the water supply.
>
> Vitruvius pp. 244-246 (full text in Copyfile)

If a section acquires too many cards, it can be split into subsections. If it acquires none at all, it may have to be dropped. If a new idea altogether emerges (for example, Will has nothing on the storage and distribution of crops), a new section can be added. In other words, the game plan develops with the reading.

Beginners are sometimes reluctant to make such detailed notes early in their reading; old hands know how much time it saves later.

Review Assignment

Creating an Information Store

In the fall of 1984, Cullen Murphy, managing editor of *The Atlantic*, visited an experimental farm on Butser Hill in England. On this farm a team of archeologists led by Peter Reynolds is trying to recreate the exact conditions of Iron Age agriculture, 300 years before Christ. This extract is from Murphy's report.

Your assignment is to make four notecards from this extract. Pay special attention to *labeling* the card for easy filing in Will Hampshire's information store on page 353.

An Iron Age Farm

[p. 21:]
To begin with, Reynolds needed a site that was free of contamination by artificial pesticides, herbicides, and fertilizers. One of the spurs radiating from Butser Hill, known as Little Butser, met that criterion, and Reynolds was able to persuade local farmers not to spray their crops when the wind was blowing toward it. Little Butser possessed an additional advantage: it is marginal land, 800 feet above sea level, with a soil cover less than half a foot deep on a base of hard chalk. These adverse conditions guaranteed that the farm's performance would not be enhanced by accidents of environment. . . .

Before planting his fields Reynolds needed livestock, both for traction and for manure. Because many Iron Age species, such as Celtic shorthorn cattle, are extinct, and others, such as Old English goats, are nearly so, Reynolds had to search for close approximations—substituting Exmoor ponies, say, for the horses of Iron Age times, or mating wild boars and Tamworth pigs in an effort to "back-breed" something like the prehistoric porker. He also had to acquire the appropriate technology and to become proficient in its use. Often working from scanty evidence, perhaps a fragment of rock carving, Reynolds fashioned mattock hoes and digging sticks and wooden ards to stir the soil. He crafted neck yokes and horn yokes, and trained cattle to them both.

For sowing Reynolds had to procure not only the right kinds of food crops but also the right kinds of weeds. Paleobotanists working with carbonized seeds or with seed impressions fired into pottery had already identified the major varieties of wheat grown in pre-Roman Britain, notably emmer and spelt, now cultivated only in remote regions of Asia Minor. Reynolds obtained samples of these rare cereals, which are cultivated at Butser under a
[p. 22:]
variety of experimental regimes: manured and unfertilized, sown in spring and in autumn, raised on plots cleared variously by ax and fire. In certain fields weeds are permitted to grow naturally; in others special varieties, long extinct in the British countryside, are deliberately introduced. (One field at the farm is reserved exclusively for the propagation of unusual weeds.) The purpose of this diversity is to evaluate the degree to which the variables tested affect yields. Most of the experiments have been planned to last for at least twenty seasons, to ensure a valid annual average. Some of the trials have by now been under way for eleven or twelve years.

The preliminary results have surprised both archaeologists and historians. Though Butser's crops have been planted on unimproved ground and tended with primitive tools, Reynolds has been getting enormous yields—larger, for example, than any yields indicated by written records from medieval times, and almost as large as those that British farmers were achieving on the eve of the First World War. The Iron Age Briton, it would appear, was no subsistence farmer.

Consider the spelt wheat sown every October in Field No. 2. Reynolds has never added manure to this field and never allowed it to lie fallow. He has not rotated the grain with Celtic beans, which fix nitrogen in the soil. Cultivation to control weeds has deliberately been kept to a minimum. Apart from planting seed in soil that ards have stirred and scored, virtually nothing has been done in Field No. 2 to enhance the viability of its crop. And yet the field has been producing, on average, more than three quarters of a ton of spelt wheat per acre every year. Wheat farmers in the United States last year did not produce much more: a little over a ton per acre.

Parcels of woodland are put to the torch and then observed over time as plant life returns. Trenches are dug and earthworks erected; then they are left alone and allowed to erode. Reynolds is obsessed with what, in his own words, "shows up in the long term." That is one reason why he experiments continually with pits, which are found by the hundreds, in a variety of shapes and sizes, whenever an Iron Age site is excavated.
[p. 23:]
Pits: if not for rubbish, as is often supposed, then what were they for? Reynolds has established, among other things, that a chalk-lined hole five feet deep and four feet wide, when sealed airtight with moist clay and topsoil, can safely preserve a ton of grain for years. Pits may also have been used for tanning leather and storing water, for making silage and salting meat. Perhaps some harbored potter's clay. Others may have served as larders.

Cullen Murphy
From "The Butser Experiment." *Atlantic*, August 1985: 20–23.

• Summary: The Flowchart

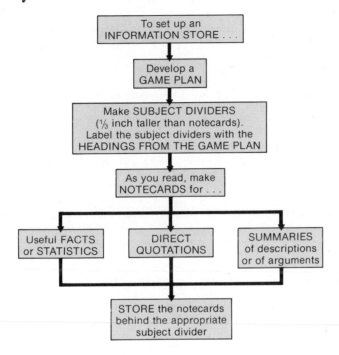

CHAPTER

• FOURTEEN •

Evaluating Information

1 •
The Problem:
Knowing What Makes Sense

There are three kinds of professional writers: the careful, the unconcerned, and the crooks.

The careful try to create a reliable and truthful text: every detail is checked, and any doubts are indicated by such words as *probably* or *there is some evidence that*. Careful writers make mistakes. This extract from *Time* magazine, for example, is absurd:

> At a food processing plant near Prague, a middle-level executive is responsible for overseeing the production of 2 million tons of canned meat a day. But his workers actually produce less than half that amount. So he lies; he marks down 2½ million tons a day. He has no fear of being caught and punished. "That's my boss's problem," he says with a shrug. "He probably fiddles with his figures too."
>
> *Time*, January 10, 1983

Why is it absurd? Because 2 million tons of canned meat a day is about 250 pounds a day for every man, woman and child in Czechoslovakia. (The error was corrected in the next issue of the magazine.) Careful writers make mistakes, but not with malice aforethought.

The unconcerned do not deliberately cheat the reader, but they present convenient half truths without comment, or they uncritically copy ideas from other writers without checking them out. Let's glance, for example, at Robert L. Whiteside's *Face Language*, which appeared in 1974. In this book, facial features (such as large eyes, thin lips, wrinkles, or a hooked nose) are said to predict behavior patterns. How do you personally rate material like this?

A. If your wife is large-eyed and you forget to kiss her goodbye, you have hurt her, because she is a romantic and needs a daily demonstration of how much you care. (p. 14)

B. If your nurse has tight, thin lips, you can expect her to tear off just enough bandaging and just enough tape to cover the wound. She won't waste any material or any time. (pp. 56–57)

C. Commercial-minded people share the Roman or hawk nose. They are naturally more administrative and like to talk business and prices . . . . If your husband has the commercial build, make him glow with happiness by telling him how you have saved some money in the way you have shopped. (p. 110)

What evidence does Whiteside have for these cheap generalizations? In the book, he offers none at all. Unfortunately his vicious perpetuation of negative stereotypes (for example, the hawk-nosed person thinks only about money) takes his book beyond the boundaries of the merely ridiculous.

The crooks have an axe to grind: they will cheat and lie either in the service of some cause or because they are paid to "make a case." Most readers can identify lying propaganda, especially that of the *other* side, but even great international authorities are sometimes shown up as liars. The art historian Bernard Berenson apparently accepted bribes to lie about the authenticity of art works—a story documented in Colin Simpson's book, *Artful Partners*. The educational psychologist, Sir Cyril Burt, faked scientific studies, with devastating results for the education of ethnic minorities. (See the *Close-Up* below.)

Your library contains material by the careful, the unconcerned and the crooks. As a researcher, your problem is to tell them apart.

Close-Up

The Faker Unmasked

The story of Professor Sir Cyril Burt and the identical twins is worth retelling, if only to hone the edge of your suspicious nature.

Between 1955 and 1966, Sir Cyril Burt, an international authority on educational psychology, published three reports on a total of 53 pairs of identical twins separated at birth or shortly afterwards. Intelligence Quotient tests carried out on the twins "proved beyond doubt" that IQ is largely hereditary and influenced only slightly by environmental factors. The social significance of the figures is obvious: in 1969, for example, Arthur Jensen used Burt's figures to argue that, since intelligence is largely inherited, compensatory educational programs aimed at minorities are probably a waste of effort.

In 1972, Leon Kamin, a Princeton psychologist, was urged by a student to read one of Burt's papers. "The immediate conclusion I came to after 10 minutes of reading was that Burt was a fraud," Kamin said. Kamin began a destructive analysis of Burt's "researches." Some of Kamin's observations: although Burt conducted three separate studies, they all produced *exactly* the same figures—a flagrant improbability. Burt had failed to give the age or sex of the twins, the age of testing, and other vital data. In a 1973 lecture, Kamin announced: "The numbers left behind by Professor Burt are simply not worthy of scientific attention."

Then a bombshell. Many of Burt's later works were co-authored by Margaret Howard and Jane Conway; in *The Sunday Times* of London (October 24, 1976), Oliver Gillie reported that neither of these women could be traced. (Howard later surfaced, although not as co-author.) Then a search for Burt's research records came to nothing: they had been trashed by his housekeeper shortly after his death in 1972.

Close analysis of Burt's figures by D. D. Dorfman shows him "beyond reasonable doubt, to have fabricated data on IQ and social class." Burt's reputation as a faker is now educational folklore. His case shows how much power is wielded by an accepted authority. It shows too that a spirit of scepticism—like Kamin's when he read Burt's paper—is your only safeguard against being "taken in."

Sources:

Dorfman, D. D. "The Cyril Burt Question: New Findings." *Science*, September 1978: 1177–1186.
Wade, Nicholas. "IQ and Heredity." *Science*, November 1976: 916–919.

2 •
Two Basic Checks

Before you invest time in a full evaluation of a text, you should ask two questions: (a) is the text up-to-date? and (b) is it a primary source or a secondary source?

• Check 1: Is Your Source Up-to-date?

Today's newspaper is the most up-to-date written source. The speed with which newspapers (and newscasts) rush the facts to the public automatically creates problems of reliability. A typical case was the AP report on November 18, 1986, that the North Korean leader, Kim Il Sung, had been assassinated. AP did all it could to verify the story, which originated from the South Korean Defense Ministry: a welter of denials, affirmations, and "no-comments" filled out the story. Next day (November 19), AP reported that Kim had made a public appearance welcoming the president of Mongolia. The *latest* news is not always news at all.

Less up-to-date, but generally more reliable, are articles by scholars and investigative reporters. They take the time to get the story right and *then* publish it. In general a gap of six months to two years separates the start of an investigation from publication. For you as researcher, such a time lag is usually acceptable; the trade-off, increased reliability, is worth the wait.

Books run in the slow track. The process of book production and distribution works at a snail's pace. From two to three years normally separate the start of investigation from the appearance of the finished product. Nevertheless, a well-written book is an ideal source. Unlike a single article, a book gathers together many strands of research, and it usually represents years of thought, study, and discussion.

As a researcher, how can you test the "up-to-dateness" of your material? The date of publication is a poor test: sometimes a brand new book, especially on a subject such as computers, is outdated even before publication. On the other hand, older works are often far from outdated; sometimes they are essential classics. Try running the following "up-to-dateness check" on any source you're unsure about, especially if it's more than about ten years old.

THE UP-TO-DATENESS CHECK

a. Read reviews by scholars in the field. (You can track down the necessary reviews in the *Book Review Digest* or the *Book Review Index*.)

b. For an older book, check *Books in Print* (your librarian will help you) to see if an updated edition has appeared.

c. Check a recent *critical bibliography* to see what rating the book receives. If such a bibliography exists, you can track it down by using the *Bibliography Index*. (See Chapter 12 for details.)

d. Compare what the author says with what you are finding in the most recent scholarly journals on the subject.

e. Ask your professor for guidance.

• Check 2: Is your Source Primary or Secondary?

A *primary source* is a work containing original thinking or experimentation carried out by the author in person. A *secondary source* is a work reporting on or analyzing a primary source. (Tertiary sources, reports on reports on reports, are also common.) Wherever possible, you should try to use the primary source. An example shows why. In the previous chapter, Will Hampshire used an ancient Roman writer, Vitruvius. Vitruvius is a *primary source*. This is Vitruvius on how to site a well.

> The following test should be applied. Before sunrise, lie down flat in the place where the search is to be made, and placing the chin on the earth and supporting it there, take a look out over the country. In this way the

CHAPTER FOURTEEN
Evaluating Information

sight will not range higher than it ought, the chin being immovable, but will range over a definitely limited height on the same level through the country. Then, dig in places where vapors are seen curling and rising up into the air. This sign cannot show itself in a dry spot.

Now let's look at a modern writer reporting Vitruvius. This extract is from J. G. Landels' book, *Engineering in the Ancient World*.

His account of water supplies begins at the basic and practical level, with some procedures for locating underground sources of water. The first and simplest method is to search for water vapor rising from the ground. This is best done at sunrise, when the moisture has risen to the surface (by capillary attraction) during the night, and evaporates as soon as the soil surface is warmed. The best way to observe it, says Vitruvius, is to lie face down on the ground and look along the surface, where the refraction (he calls it 'moisture forming curls and rising into the air') can be most easily seen. This is a sure sign of the presence of water, and justifies a test dig in the area.

As you can see, four kinds of changes have occurred. First, the rerun skips some of Vitruvius' original detail. Then Landels adds his own ideas, despite the implication that he is simply reporting Vitruvius. Third, the "flavour" of the piece has changed—Vitruvius simply tells the reader what to do, while Landels fills in the scientific background. Finally, the facts are not the same: Vitruvius (in this translation) says "before sunrise" while Landels says "at sunrise." In general, Landels is a careful writer: the problems arise because a secondary source always uses the original for some new purpose; the only *exact* account of the original is the original itself.

The general principle: *to avoid being misled, consult the primary source whenever you can. If you use secondary sources, as you often must, stay suspicious.*

Concept Review

Primary or Secondary Source?

Let's stay with Landels' fascinating book, *Engineering in the Ancient World*. Landels' material runs on two tracks: (a) a digest of what he found in the ancient writings and (b) his own experimental work. Where he is reporting, he is a *secondary source*; where he is experimenting, he is a *primary source*. Look at these extracts and decide in each case: *primary source* or *secondary source*?

a. When making a working reconstruction of this device [Hero's ancient Egyptian steam turbine], I had the greatest difficulty reaching a compromise between a loose joint which leaks steam and lowers the pressure, and a tight one which wastes energy in friction.

Primary source ☐ Secondary source ☐

b. In his introductory chapter, Hero speaks of his various devices as providing "some of them useful everyday applications, others quite remarkable effects."

Primary source ☐ Secondary source ☐

c. It is widely held that the Greeks and Romans were unable to get their furnaces much above 1150°C, and that this hindered the development of their iron technology.

Primary source ☐ Secondary source ☐

d. My own working model has achieved speeds of the order of 1,500 rpm, and, with the possible exception of a spinning top, the ball on Hero's machine may well have been the most rapidly rotating object in the world of his time.

Primary source ☐ Secondary source ☐

e. There is no evidence for deep mining; all the coal used was outcrop, and probably of rather poor quality. It was not normally used in smelting furnaces, though Pliny (*Nat. Hist.* 34,8,96) does apparently mention its use in copper casting.

Primary source ☐ Secondary source ☐

3 •

Does Your Source Make Plain Sense?

If your source is up-to-date and primary, the next question is this: Does it make sense? This question must be approached at two levels: some material is so blatantly out of line that it can be rejected without further ado; a deeper level of scrutiny will uncover more subtle tricks and blunders.

• Blatant Absurdity

You are entitled to reject anything that is plainly nonsensical. Two examples have already been cited: *Time* magazine on the factory that provides 250 pounds a day of canned meat for every Czech and Robert Whiteside's crass stereotyping of people on the basis of their facial features. Let's glance at one more case of this type:

> Motorcycle markets worldwide have shrunk, with Britain's among the worst hit. In 1980, nearly 316m powered two-wheelers were registered, close to the peak in 1959 before the British took to buying cars. The total slipped to 275m in 1981 and 232m in 1982. It looks, from sales so far this year, as if a mere 180m–185m two-wheelers will be registered in 1983—a drop of 20%.
>
> *Economist,* August 13, 1983

The Economist corrected the all too-apparent error here in its next issue.

Concept Review

Blatant Absurdity

A few years ago, a group of students from the University of Maryland visited Moscow. A report of their trip, reprinted below, appeared in a high-circulation newspaper. Read it critically and then answer the questions. (The names of the students and so on have been changed; otherwise the article is reproduced in its original form.)

The Russian proletariat may be picking up some capitalist habits.

"According to our tourist guide, the Soviet Union is being forced to build a chewing gum factory because of American tourists who trade their packages of chewing gum for Russian belt buckles or party badges and medals," Claire Dickinson said here.

Dickinson and 21 other Americans recently spent four days in Moscow after taking a University of Maryland course on the history of the Soviet Union.   5

"You can use chewing gum to tip or bribe your way into a restaurant," she said.

"The Russian bread tasted pretty good because it is made from American wheat," said Bob Jobbins. "Moscow is a nice place to visit but I wouldn't want to live there," he said.

Several of those interviewed said that Moscow is quiet and austere, especially at night   10
when even the cars do not make any noise.

"The people seemed like they wanted to be friendly. One man attempted to talk to some of us on the street but a policeman told him to move on," said Moses Jones. Terry di Capua said he was approached near his hotel by a man who wanted to buy western clothing.

"He also wanted to exchange his rubles for dollars. Almost everywhere we went, people   15
wanted foreign money," said di Capua.

Jobbins said he saw very few women who weighed less than 200 lbs.

"Night life," he said, "is restricted to hotels that are run by the state and that cater only to foreign guests."

Mrs. Rosina Leone, the trip coordinator, said the hotels have signs stating that the bars   20
and restaurants are for foreign tourists only.

"The thing that bothered me the most about Moscow was the silence," she said.

Members of the group said they saw a large number of drunks staggering and falling down on the streets. "Alcoholism seems to be a big problem," Leone said.

a. The article asserts (lines 2–4) that American tourists are taking so much chewing gum into the Soviet Union that the central planners have decided to build a chewing-gum factory to stop the flow. Roughly 20,000 U.S. tourists a year visited the Soviet Union in this period. Where is the blatant absurdity?

b. Hearsay evidence is inadmissible in common law. How long is the chain of hearsay evidence between the reporter and the original source of the chewing gum story?

c. Do you believe that party members, a small elite in the Soviet Union, would exchange party badges for gum (line 4)?

d. Soviet bread is not made of American wheat. Is a journalist behaving responsibly in reporting such ill-informed ideas as news?

e. Do you see any self-contradiction between lines 12–13 (the police breaking off all contact) and lines 15–16 (the endless potential trades)?

f. Is there any way of reconciling the idea of silence (line 22) with the picture of the drunks (lines 23–24)?

g. Find at least two further examples of self-contradiction in the piece.

h. What sort of reader might fail to notice the blatant absurdity of this piece?

• The Question of Proof

Where a source is obvious nonsense or is self-contradictory, no time need be wasted on further evaluation. In Chapter 8, *Making a Case*, a number of logic traps were discussed. Obviously you should scan your sources for such problems. If you spot one of these traps, then it's fair to assume that the writer either is incapable of straight thinking or is a crook. Either way, you should treat the source with extreme caution.

Where no blemishes show on the surface, it is necessary to go deeper. The essential research question is always the same: Does this source make sense? The answer is a matter of "proof." To understand what constitutes proof, it will help to examine two situations where the word *proof* is commonly used: a courtroom trial and a mathematics classroom. First the courtroom.

A sad story: a little old lady was knocked down and robbed of $170 just after evening class let out. She described her assailant closely, especially his sneakers. The police picked up Ed Green next night, identifying him by his sneakers. Next, the little old lady identified Ed in a lineup of ten men. Ed was discovered to have $150 on him, even though he was known to be broke: Ed said he'd found the money in a trash can. Then the little old lady died of her injuries. Under pressure Ed confessed to the murder. He was tried and executed. The prosecution had all the proof it needed: opportunity, motive, identification, confession. Nevertheless, *Ed didn't do it*. A classmate of Ed's finally confessed, producing as evidence the old lady's purse with the money still in it. (Stranger things have happened.) Ed was executed because a jury of twelve felt his guilt had been *proved beyond all reasonable doubt*. But his guilt had not been *proved in an absolute sense*.

Mathematical proof is more certain:

> If A is greater than B
> And if B is greater than C
> Then A is greater than C

If words mean anything, then that conclusion is inescapable—the conclusion is *proved in an absolute sense*.

These two kinds of proof have ancient labels: the courtroom proof is called *inductive proof* and mathematical proof is called *deductive proof*. As researcher, you are looking for proven facts, so it is essential to understand the strengths and weaknesses of the only two kinds of proof available to us. Since the researcher encounters mathematical proof only occasionally, let's get it out of the way first.

• Deductive Proof: The Problem of Validity

A *deductive proof* is a chain of reasoning that begins with two "givens," two premises that are unquestioningly accepted. If a conclusion can be drawn from these two facts, then this conclusion has been *deduced* from the premises. Let's look at our mathematical example again. It begins:

> If *A* is greater than *B*
> And if *B* is greater than *C*

These are premises, sublimely beyond argument or dispute. Deduction swings into play with the conclusion:

> Then *A* is greater than *C*

This conclusion, as we have said, is perfectly valid. The single concern of deductive proof is this validity: given the premises, is the conclusion *valid*?

The strength of the deductive method is the clarity of its answers: an argument is *valid* or *invalid*—and 100 percent provable either way. The weakness of the method emerges if we replace the symbols *A*, *B*, and *C* with words:

> If mice are bigger than zebras
> And if zebras are bigger than elephants
> Then mice are bigger than elephants

Is the reasoning still valid? Yes, it is absolutely valid. Is the conclusion true? No, it is perfect gibberish. As you can see, a test of valid reasoning is *not* the same thing as a test of truth. This is the essential problem with deductive logic: it does not—it cannot—test the truth of the premises; it seeks only to test the validity of a conclusion drawn from them.

A chapter on evaluating research materials is not the place for an in-depth study of deductive logic: there are more than 200 forms that a three-line deductive statement can take, some of them still debated by logicians. For our present purposes, a general understanding is enough.

Let's look first at the exact shape of a three-line argument. The first question: why *three* lines? Are chains of argument always so short? The answer is that, however long a chain of argument might be, it must be tested link by link, and each link contains the classic three parts. This cluster of three lines is called a *syllogism*. The first of the three parts is a general statement; logicians call it the *major premise*:

> It always rains on my birthday

Then comes a particular, local statement: the *minor premise*. Let's take two examples:

a. Yesterday was my birthday
b. Yesterday it rained

From these two premises is deduced the *conclusion*:

a. Therefore yesterday it rained
b. Therefore yesterday was my birthday

Look carefully at the two conclusions. Conclusion (a) is based on the chain of reasoning:

> It always rains on my birthday
> Yesterday was my birthday
> Therefore yesterday it rained

This conclusion is *valid*. Conclusion (*b*) is based on a different chain:

> It always rains on my birthday
> Yesterday it rained
> Therefore yesterday was my birthday

This conclusion is *invalid*. Why? To make the deductive process "visible," logicians often use diagrams. Let's go back to the mathematical syllogism used earlier:

> *Major premise:* If *A* is greater than *B*
> *Minor premise:* And if *B* is greater than *C*
> *Conclusion:* Then *A* is greater than *C*

In algebra this syllogism could be simplified to:

> If $a > b$, and if and $b > c$, then $a > c$

Visually, the same idea could be rendered by three circles:

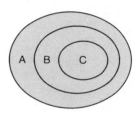

If circle *A* encloses circle *B*, and if circle *B* encloses circle *C*, it follows that circle *A* also encloses circle *C*. Now let's return to the rain on my birthday:

> *Major premise:* It always rains on my birthday
> *Minor premise:* Yesterday was my birthday
> *Conclusion:* Yesterday it rained

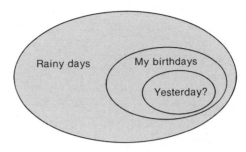

The major premise forces us to draw the circle for *My birthdays* wholly within the circle for *Days on which it rains*. The minor premise forces us to draw *Yesterday* wholly within the circle for *My birthdays*. It is therefore valid to conclude that it must have rained yesterday. And the invalid conclusion?

Major premise: It always rains on my birthday
Minor premise: Yesterday it rained
Conclusion: Yesterday was my birthday

The major premise, as before, forces us to draw the circle for *My birthdays* wholly within the circle for *Days on which it rains*. The minor premise forces us to draw the circle for *Yesterday* within the circle for *Days on which it rains*, but not necessarily within the circle of *My Birthdays*. This means that the conclusion *might* be true (the odds are 365 to 1), but the reasoning is invalid.

This is how logical testing always works, although with more than 200 forms of the syllogism to deal with, things often become hectic. The next question is: what practical value is there in such tests?

Concept Review

Testing the Syllogism

Using the three circles, depict each of these syllogisms and decide on the validity of the conclusion. Remember, a valid conclusion may be ridiculous if it is based on ridiculous premises. Similarly a conclusion you know to be *true* might be based on *invalid* reasoning.

1. All ranchers marry fat wives
   Grady was a rancher
   Therefore Grady married a fat wife

2. All ranchers marry fat wives
   Grady married a fat wife
   Therefore Grady was a rancher

3. To be elected president, a candidate must be a born American
   Ronald Reagan was elected president
   Therefore Ronald Reagan was a born American

4. To be elected president, a candidate must be a born American
   Ronald Reagan was a born American
   Therefore Ronald Reagan was elected president

5. Winged horses can fly higher than robins
   Pegasus was a winged horse
   Therefore Pegasus could fly higher than a robin

Many of your sources will make a great show of reasoning. If you can *test* this reasoning, you'll know whether or not the conclusion reached by the source is valid. If it is not valid, you'll know the grounds for setting up a rebuttal. (The technique of rebuttal will be discussed in Chapter 16.) The main obstacle to testing is that the reasoning in your sources is seldom, if ever, set up as a formal syllogism. To apply the logic test, you must recast the argument as a syllogism and then test it. For example:

To do a good job a mother must spend plenty of time with her children. A mother who doesn't have a job and is home all day spends many hours with her children; that means she must be doing a good job.

How does that look as a formal syllogism?

Major premise: All effective mothers spend plenty of time with their children
Minor premise: Mother X spends plenty of time with her children
Conclusion: Therefore Mother X is an effective mother

This line of argument is clearly *invalid.* (If you don't see why, draw the circles.)
Sometimes it's necessary to add back a "missing line" to complete the three-line set. A syllogism with a missing line is called an *enthymeme.* For example:

My father never drank anything but water, so water is good enough for me.

Major premise: (Missing) Anything that was good enough for my father is good enough for me
Minor premise: My father never drank anything but water
Conclusion: Water is good enough for me

The conclusion here is obviously *valid*. Here is another example of an enthymeme that can be seen as logically *valid* once it is fully reconstructed:

Heroin addicts don't live long; I don't think Lizzie will make old bones.

Major premise: Heroin addicts don't live long
Minor premise: (Missing) Lizzie is a heroin addict
Conclusion: Lizzie will not make old bones

What does this mean to you as a writer and a researcher? It means that you must distinguish carefully between logical validity and truth. The fact that reasoning is *valid* never means that a conclusion is *true*. Many valid conclusions are based on false premises, as we saw with the animal example earlier:

If mice are bigger than zebras
And if zebras are bigger than elephants
Then mice are bigger than elephants

The two premises here are not illogical, they are simply *false*. To establish what is true and what is false, the researcher must leave the abstract kingdom of logic (having seen only a tiny corner of it) and return to the uncertainties of inductive observation that generally reign on Earth.

Concept Review

Text into Syllogism

In the following examples, reduce (or expand) the text into a syllogism, and then comment on the *validity of its logic*. Comment on the major premises: do you believe they are *true* or *false*?

1. To do a good job, a mother must spend a great deal of time each day with her children. Mary Smith did an excellent job as a mother. It follows that she spent a great deal of time with her children.

2. The cigarette industry says that cigarette smoking has not been shown to cause lung cancer. You should view this statement with suspicion. (Enthymeme with major premise missing.)

3. War involves violence, and pacifists are opposed to violence, or so they tell us. But are they really? Let's take Jim Jones as our typical pacifist, and let's say someone attacks his sister in the street. Does Jim stand there and say: "My beliefs forbid me to use violence. If you wish to beat up my sister, just go ahead." I doubt it. Probably he'd swallow his so-called principles and protect his sister just as any man would. Inside, he's as ready to go to war as the generals. (The major premise in this case is the first three words.)

4. Because Japanese cars are a good bargain, they sell well in the United States. (Enthymeme with the major premise missing.)

5. Have you ever wondered why people with an artistic temperament are so touchy about criticism? The answer is simple: only people who are extremely sensitive can have a true artistic temperament, and resenting criticism means that one is extremely sensitive. (The conclusion in this case is given first.)

• Inductive Evidence: The Problem of Truth

The jury who convicted Ed Green of murdering the little old lady for her $150 *believed* that he had committed this crime. They had evidence for their belief —opportunity, motive, identification, and confession. They were deciding not about the validity of arguments but about the *truth* of the matter. The "proof" offered in a courtroom is not logical proof based on given premises; it is an inductive judgment based on observed facts.

Much of the business of a courtroom is concerned with establishing facts beyond reasonable doubt. Let's take Ed's sneakers as an example. The court will hear exactly how the little old lady described Ed's sneakers. It will check that Ed's sneakers exactly fit this description. It will want evidence that the sneakers produced in court really belong to Ed, and that he was wearing them on the night of the murder. It will ensure that the little old lady's description has not been falsified since she gave it. In other words, facts must be established *as* facts. Once the jury accepts the facts, a simple syllogism sends Ed to death row:

> The killer was wearing these sneakers at 10:29 p.m.
> Ed was wearing these sneakers at 10:29 p.m.
> Therefore Ed is the killer

The jury *accepts* the facts—but does this mean that the facts are proven? Unfortunately not. There is no way of proving with mathematical certainty that the killer was wearing those sneakers or that Ed was wearing them. What is true of Ed's sneakers is true of everything we can observe about our world: facts can be established with a greater or a lesser degree of probability, but they can never be "proved."

For the researcher this is a headache. If facts are beyond proof, what should one believe? What establishes a fact or a theory *beyond reasonable doubt*? The experimental scientist faces exactly this question at all times; to cope with the uncertainty, a kind of "inductive logic" has evolved, a set of principles known collectively as *scientific method*. Four principles are important to you as writer and researcher: (a) it is reasonable to accept a self-evident fact; (b) it is reasonable to accept a fact stated on sufficient authority; (c) it is reasonable to accept facts known personally to you from experience; (d) it is reasonable to accept facts based on "adequate" evidence. Let's look at these principles one by one.

a. Self-evidence. Water flows downhill; buildings in Toronto are shady on their north side—without sturdy evidence to the contrary, these beliefs can be accepted without comment. In your research, you would not expect (or find) evidence for what is self-evident. But the danger is obvious: it is self-evident that the sun moves round the earth, that the stars are "up in the sky," and that two straight lines cannot enclose an area—but none of these ideas happens to be true. Worse, although some things are self-evident, there is little agreement as to what these things are. As researcher, whenever you read such words as "It is self-evident that . . ." or "It goes without saying that . . ." or "Obviously . . .," make sure that the point is as obvious to *you* as it is to the writer.

b. Authority. It is reasonable to believe something on the grounds of "sufficient" authority. (Life would be impossible if it were not.) You can believe what the Bureau of Census says about the population; you can believe what senior politicians say on oath before congressional hearings; you can believe what Darwin says he observed during his famous voyage (although not necessarily his interpretations). As soon as the authority might have a reason to shade the facts, belief is less justified: it is wise to be wary about a fireside chat from the Oval Office or a newspaper editorial. At the opposite extreme, the courtroom arguments of a corporation lawyer, a speech by a senator seeking re-election, or the memoirs of a movie star should be read for their entertainment value only.

c. Experience. What you have seen with your own eyes and felt on your own hide can be trusted. The celebrated logician Max Black in his book *Critical Thinking* cites a good example: my dentist tells me on the authority of his excellent training and years of practice that my tooth does not hurt—yet it does, and I *know* that it does. Or perhaps the government assures me that there are plenty of jobs if I'll only get off my armchair and look for one—but I *know* differently. If a "fact" you come across in your reading reflects your first-hand experience, that is fair grounds for belief; if it contradicts your experience, that is fair grounds for suspicion.

d. Evidence. Finally, evidence provides grounds for belief, inconclusive as all evidence must ultimately be. Let's study an example of the way scientific method handles evidence.

Many "scientific facts" start life as casual observations. Let's say that in a group of twelve convicts serving sentences for armed robbery, I happen to notice quite a few have a mole behind the left ear. I form a hypothesis: *those who commit armed robbery tend to have a mole behind the left ear.* Am I justified in believing this hypothesis? Certainly not. What kind of evidence, then, could turn my hypothesis into a "scientific fact"?

First I would have to study the convicts carefully. In casually glancing at them, I may have been deceived by one or two dramatic cases of prominent moles. Let's say study shows that more than half these convicts do have the crucial mole. Does that "prove" anything? The answer is still no: but I do have a hypothesis that is, on the face of it, worth testing.

In setting up a test, I have to ask two questions: (a) how can I devise an experiment that would show whether my hypothesis was *true*? and (b) would this experiment also expose the fact that my hypothesis was *false*? Both questions are equally important. As an example of a hypothesis that cannot be disproved, take the idea that God created the universe six thousand years ago, including all the layers of rock with their fossils, all the destroyed buildings and so on. You can believe that hypothesis or not as you choose, but it is not a scientific hypothesis because no conceivable experiment could show it to be false.

As to my theory about the moles, a simple experiment would quickly show its truth or falsehood. Like nearly all scientific experiments, my experiment would work positively and negatively. Positively I would have to show that, across the nation, armed robbery convicts generally have such moles—a simple task of counting. Then, since I'm linking moles to armed robbery, I would have to work negatively, excluding other possible causes of the moles. Let's say, for example, that those convicted of armed robbery are mostly sentenced to hard labor. Might the hard labor, not the tendency to commit armed robbery, produce the moles? If the experiment produced the necessary positive and negative evidence, the result would still need confirmation.

Confirmation of experimental results takes two forms: the use of a control group, and the repetition of my results by other researchers. In my case, the control group would be a sample of the population at large: how many of them have moles behind their left ears? If most of them had such moles, my findings would collapse on the spot. Then, observations by other experimenters, probably in other countries, should confirm my results. If Russian, English, Chinese and Australian armed robbers all have the mole, then my hypothesis becomes a "scientific fact."

Let's look at the steps again:

1. The experimenter formulates a hypothesis based on systematic, objective observations.

2. An experiment is set up that would show the truth or falsehood of the theory. This experiment works positively (it confirms the theory), and it works negatively (it excludes the possibility that some external factor produced the observed result).

3. The results are confirmed by comparison with results for a control group and by the results achieved by other experimenters.

As a researcher, you should trust only material that is based on this kind of method. As we have stressed, however, today's "fact" becomes tomorrow's "outdated opinion" if new evidence emerges; this is the only way that science can progress.

Concept Review

Examining Sources

The research reported in professional journals is normally conducted to the highest standard the other hand, the quality of observation, demonstration and argument in less prestigious so can be shoddy. The questions below move from simple problems of argumentation to co questions of evaluation. You should use the checklist of questions given at the end of the chap tackling problems *D* and *E*.

A. Special Effects

What arguments would you use against someone who believes that the whole space program is a hoax, and that the photographs and films of so-called "space exploration" are manufactured by the special effects department of one of the Hollywood studios?

B. Letters to the Editor

Many magazines publish "Letters to the Editor" as a public forum. After the bombing of Libya in April 1986, *Time* published on May 12, 1986, the letters given below (among others). The letters are quoted in full. In each case, what do you think of the reasoning? Is the deductive reasoning valid? Are the premises, whether stated or implied, true? Do you find any of the inductive errors listed in Chapter 8?

a. Colonel Muammar Gaddafi got a taste of his own medicine in the U.S. air strike on Libya. I respect President Reagan's decision to use military force. This may not be the solution to terrorism, but it may act as a deterrent to attacks on Americans.

b. I am one of the minority who are shaken, scared and embarrassed by our country's bombing of Libya. This is intolerable behavior for an educated people.

c. The West European countries can be held largely responsible for the escalation of the conflict between the U.S. and Libya. These governments refused to go along with economic sanctions after the Rome and Vienna airport attacks. Apparently European nations are more concerned about Libya's oil and their trade with that country than about protecting their citizens.

d. The U.S. should have sent in the Marines to infiltrate and destroy Libyan redoubts on the ground. Attacking Libya was a task for the stealthy, not the cavalry. I tremble to think that Reagan's hand is on the nuclear trigger.

e. The recurring theme in the condemnation of the U.S. for the Libya raid appears to be that innocent civilians were killed. I deeply regret the loss of life. But why is there not similar worldwide condemnation of the terrorists who kill innocent victims because they hold American passports?

f. As a European, I am shocked by the American raid on Libya. Reagan's policy will not make Gaddafi change his mind but will lead to a long series of increasingly dangerous attacks and retaliatory strikes, injuring and killing many innocent civilians.

C. "We hold these truths to be self-evident . . . "

This passage is taken from a speech made by the Vice President of the Confederation, Alexander Stephens, at the beginning of the Civil War. It still carries an emotional charge nearly 130 years later. Read it critically. Study the arguments. Do you think Stephens' argument is logically *valid*? Can you see possible grounds for refusing to believe that it is *true*? Be careful to separate these two questions.

The prevailing ideas entertained by him [Jefferson] and most of the leading statesmen at the time of the formation of the old Constitution, were that the enslavement of the African was in violation of the laws of nature; that it was wrong in *principle*, socially, morally, and politically. . . . Our new government is founded upon exactly the opposite idea; its foundations are laid, its corner-stone rests upon the great truth, that the negro is not equal to the white man; that slavery—subordination to the superior race—is his natural and normal condition. This, our new government, is the first, in the history of the world, based upon this great physical, philosophical, and moral truth. . . . The substratum of our society is made of the material fitted by nature for it, and by experience we know that it is best, not only for the superior, but for the inferior race, that it should be so. It is, indeed, in conformity with the ordinance of the Creator. It is not for us to inquire into the wisdom of his ordinances, or to question them. For his own purposes he has made one race to differ from another, as he has made "one star to differ from another star in glory." The great objects of humanity are best attained when there is conformity to his laws and decrees, in the formation of governments as well as in all things else. Our Confederacy is founded upon principles in strict conformity with these laws.

D. Visitors from Outer Space

The theories of Erich von Däniken are well known. In essence, von Däniken argues that Earth was visited at some stage by beings from another planet. These beings interbred with certain apes to produce the human race. When they moved on, the space people also left behind a store of technological knowledge; without this other-worldly knowledge, the construction of such ancient monuments as the pyramids would have been impossible. Evaluate the evidence in these extracts from *Chariots of the Gods?*

a. "There were giants in the earth in those days; and also after that, when the sons of God came in unto the daughters of men, and they bare children to them, the same became mighty men which were of old, men of renown" (Genesis 6:4).

Once again we have the sons of God, who interbreed with human beings. Here, too, we have the first mention of giants. "Giants" keep on cropping up in all parts of the globe: in the mythology of East and West, in the sagas of Tiahuanaco and the epics of the Eskimos. "Giants" haunt the pages of almost all ancient books. So they must have existed.

b. Where did the narrators of *The Thousand and One Nights* get their staggering wealth of ideas? How did anyone come to describe a lamp from which a magician spoke when the owner wished?

What daring imagination invented the "Open, Sesame!" incident in the tale of Ali Baba and the forty thieves?

Of course, such ideas no longer astonish us today, for the television set shows us talking pictures at the turn of a switch. And as the doors of most large department stores open by photocells, even the "Open, Sesame!" incident no longer conceals any special mystery. Nevertheless the imaginative power of the old storytellers was so incredible that the books of contemporary writers of science fiction seem banal in comparison. So it must be that the ancient storytellers had a store of things already seen, known, and experienced ready at hand to spark off their imagination!

E. Homeopathy and Hayfever

Homeopathic medicine has been around for 150 years. Its main principle is this: a medical complaint can be cured by giving the patient a tiny dose of an agent that would, in a normal dose, produce the symptoms of the disease. An experiment reported in *The Lancet* in October 1986 (*The Lancet* is a highly prestigious British medical journal) examines this theory. The experiment took 144 people who suffered from acute hayfever. They were divided into two equal groups. One group was given a homeopathic pill said to cure hayfever; the other was given a sugar and alcohol pill. The pills looked and tasted the same. The patients did not know which group they were in. Similarly the doctors administering the pills were not told which pills they were prescribing. The group given the remedy showed some improvement in their condition; the control group showed no improvement.

Does this experiment, as reported so far, give reasonable grounds for believing in a homeopathic cure for hayfever? Does it give grounds for believing in homeopathic cures in general?

To continue: homeopathic cures are prepared by dilution. First, the pure agent is prepared. To this agent is added 99 parts of a neutral solution. The medicine is now a 1 percent dilution. This process of dilution is repeated 30 or more times. In the hayfever experiment, a mixture of 12 grass pollens was the starting point. After dilution, the pollen was finally in a "concentration" of 1 part of

en to 10^{60} parts of neutral solution (10 and fifty-nine zeros!). The mathematics of dilution says
 in a dilution of 10^{24} (10 and twenty-three zeros) not a single molecule of the original sample
bably remains. Adding another thirty-six zeros makes it utterly unlikely that even one molecule of
en came through the dilution process.

This mathematical principle and the result of the experiment are in direct contradiction. How do
 assess the evidence now? Do you have reasonable grounds for belief in a homeopathic cure for
fever? If not, what would give you such grounds?

Summary: A Checklist

Evaluating research material depends on close, critical reading. There should be an
ever-present query in your mind: Does this material make sense? This umbrella
question comprises a number of smaller questions:

1. **The Pre-checks**

    a. Is the source up-to-date?

    b. Is the source primary or secondary?

2. **The Surface Checks**

    a. Do any of the errors in logic discussed in Chapter 8 occur? (See p. 239.)

    b. Is anything absurdly out of line?

    c. Is there blatant self-contradiction?

3. **The Check for Validity of Argument**
Do the conclusions follow logically from the premises?

4. **The Checks for Credibility**

    a. Are the facts *self-evident* and thus in need of no further evidence of any kind?

    b. Are the facts advanced by an authority that I can respect?

    c. Are the facts supported by my own experience and observation?

    d. If evidence is offered, what kind of observation supports this evidence?

        i. Is the observation systematic or casual?

        ii. Is the observation objective or subjective?

        iii. Was the observer trained and qualified or an amateur?

    e. Observed facts are used to support a theory (or hypothesis). Has the theory
    been tested by an experiment? If yes:

        i. Would a negative result from the experiment have shown the theory to be
        false?

        ii. Did the test exclude any extraneous factors that might have influenced
        the result?

        iii. Did the experiment use a control group to show that the same result does
        not occur outside the test group?

  f. Have the experimental results been successfully duplicated by other researchers?

  g. Are there any further objections to the observations, to the experimental technique, or to the conclusions drawn from the results?

Note: These questions all concern experimental method. In evaluating other kinds of sources, historical sources for example, the questions would have to be slightly reworded.

Evaluating Figures: A Special Case

In our society everything from the performance of a company to the physique of a beauty queen is reduced to statistics. Innumeracy—the inability to cope with figures—is almost as great a social handicap as illiteracy—the inability to cope with written words. For the researcher, especially in such fields as business, psychology or sociology, a sound grasp of statistics is essential. This chapter is not a mini-course in statistical evaluation: it is simply a layman's overview of some of the basics. The goal is to make you cautious about figures, both as producer and as consumer.

les and Populations

Imagine that a food laboratory produces a startling new product: strawberry flavored butter. To find out if the product will sell, the manufacturer will test the reactions of several hundred people to the new butter. The test group should obviously represent a cross-section of the potential market. A representative cross-section like this is called a *sample*; the total group (in this case all the potential purchasers of strawberry butter) is called a *population*. Sampling is a reasonable enough idea: when I cook rice, I test that it's ready by eating a sample of one grain—if that is cooked, I assume the rest is cooked too. (It wouldn't make much sense to test all the grains—that is, the whole *population*.)

Sampling, easy as it sounds in theory, is tough in practice. This is because the sample has to be truly *representative* of the population. With a pan of rice, a one-grain sample is usually representative; with a sample of people, problems occur. To see why, let's look at some *sampling techniques* our butter company might use; its goal is to find out if the idea of strawberry butter appeals to the public.

SAMPLING TECHNIQUE A: A TELEPHONE SURVEY

To conduct a telephone survey, the company must call every tenth (every twentieth or every hundredth) name in the telephone book. Two sampling problems arise with this technique: (a) it automatically misses all those in the population who have no telephone, and (b) if the survey is conducted in the daytime, women who are home all day will be over-represented. The sample will not be representative.

SAMPLING TECHNIQUE B: A DOOR-TO-DOOR SURVEY

A pollster conducting a door-to-door survey rings doorbells in different neighborhoods and asks the survey questions on the doorstep. Again there are sampling problems: the pollster won't gain access to the houses of the wealthy and will probably steer clear of "tough" areas. A daytime survey, once more, will be unduly slanted toward housewives. A sample that excludes the rich, the poor, and working women will not be representative.

SAMPLING TECHNIQUE C: A STREET SURVEY

In a street survey, the pollster simply approaches people in the street, trying to work "at random." The sampling problem here is that street surveys are *never* random; they miss people in a hurry (working mothers, for example), people who hate people (but who might love strawberry butter), people that the pollster feels intimidated by (workmen in greasy overalls, for example) and many others. Little old ladies with time on their hands are usually over-represented.

There are other sampling techniques, but these three are enough to show the essential problem: the unrepresentative or *skewed* sample. This *Broom Hilda* cartoon highlights the problem exactly.

"Broom Hilda" cartoon by Russell Myers. Reprinted by permission: Tribune Media Services.

CHAPTER FIFTEEN
Evaluating Figures: A Special Case

These three sampling techniques are open to another objection: the answers to the survey questions may simply be lies. Let's say a charming young student (earning a little money by working with a survey team) approaches a respondent and says: "I represent Big Cow Dairies, and we need to know if you like the sound of strawberry butter." Many people will say *yes* just to be nice. This is not strictly speaking a problem of sampling, but a problem of asking the right questions —something we discussed in Chapter 11. For you as researcher the moral is this: in evaluating a survey, make sure you carefully study the exact wording of the questions. The answers to loaded questions should be ignored.

Sampling is a science in its own right. Typically a well constructed sample of the public at large balances all the major divisions of the population: race, sex, region, age, and so on. Professional survey firms tend to poll a minimum of 800 respondents; at about 1,300, a well-selected sample can be truly representative. A survey should take place in the shortest possible time, especially if it is collecting opinions on current affairs; if a startling and related news story breaks in mid-survey, it can change opinions and thus make the survey meaningless.

CHECKLIST: WHAT TO ASK ABOUT A SAMPLE

A. Choosing the Sample
Does the source explain how the sample was chosen?
If no, be suspicious.
If yes: Did the sampling technique create a representative sample—that is, a sample that was not skewed to favor or exclude some particular group?

B. The Wording of the Questions
Does the source give the exact wording of the questions?
If no, be suspicious.
If yes: Was the wording "loaded" in any way?

C. **The Size of the Sample**
Does the source mention the size of the sample?
If no, be suspicious.
If yes: Was the sample big enough to be representative?

D. **The Time Period of the Survey** (Important Only for *Opinion* Surveys)
Does the source mention the period over which the survey was held?
If no, be suspicious.
If yes: Was the time period short enough to escape swings of opinion triggered
by events in the news?

oncept Review

Samples

Use the Checklist above in arriving at your answers.

1. After the Italian government released the terrorist, Abul Abbas, the prime minister, Craxi, was
forced to resign. How would you evaluate this comment in *Time*, (November 11, 1985) on the
attitude of the Italians to the resignation?

> [Craxi] sought to appear as a wounded but loyal ally standing up for his nation's
> independence. Italians responded positively to the Prime Minister's posture. Indeed, a poll in
> the newsweekly *L'Espresso* showed 61% approval for Craxi's show of independence from
> the U.S., while only 19% disapproved.

2. After the failure of Ronald Reagan and Mikhail Gorbachev to reach agreement at Reykjavik in
1986, *Time* commissioned a survey of public opinion. The published survey stated that the firm
Yankelovich Clancy Shulman had surveyed 806 Americans by telephone on the evening of
Wednesday, October 22. Of the respondents, 62 percent said they had been "following the issue
in the news." Only the answers of this 62 percent were included in the results. The questions
asked in the survey were all given verbatim in *Time*; the question below is typical. How would
you rate this survey?

Who do you think is more to blame for the failure to reach an agreement?	
Reagan	14%
Gorbachev	45%
Both equally	25%

3. A report published in March, 1986, in the *New England Journal of Medicine* tracked the health and
the lifestyles of 16,936 men who entered Harvard between 1916 and 1950. Statistics were kept
until 1978, by which time 1,413 had died. The study homed in on the amount of exercise the men
performed and the length of their lives. There were two findings: (a) men who walked nine or
more miles a week had a 21 percent lower risk of early death than those who walked less than three
miles; (b) burning off up to 3,500 calories a week increased the chances of longevity, but burning
off more decreased the chances again. *Question:* The results concern a sample: How relevant are
these results to the population at large?

es and Norms

What Kind of Average?

Once the figures are in, something has to be done with them. Very often the figures are lumped together and presented to the reader as an *average*, or a *central tendency* as statisticians call it. An *average* is a single figure (or value) that represents the mid-point of a string of different figures (or values). In fact, everyone is familiar with averages from sports—a baseball player's batting average, for example. Your familiarity with sporting averages and the way they are calculated may lull you into a false sense of security when you come across "averages" during your research. Unfortunately, there are *three* ways of calculating averages; unless you know which has been used, an "average" figure is, strictly speaking, meaningless. Let's look at a case.

Grobucket Industries makes buckets. Its factory is close to the Mexican border, and many of its employees earn poor wages. This is the wage structure of the company:

Owner (John Grobucket)	140,000	
Marketing manager (Amos Grobucket)	60,000	
Bookkeeper	14,000	
Secretary to the owner	12,000	
Secretary to marketing manager	11,000	
Secretary to the bookkeeper	10,000	
Factory worker 1	7,000	
Factory worker 2	7,000	Salaries Paid
Factory worker 3	7,000	to Grobucket
Factory worker 4	7,000	Employees
Factory worker 5	7,000	(in $ per year)

Under these circumstances, it is not surprising that there is a strike for more pay at the Grobucket factory. A journalist on a radical newspaper becomes interested. He requests and receives a statement from the owner: "Since the average wage at the factory is $25,636 a year, I can't imagine what everyone is complaining about." The strike leader is the bookkeeper's secretary; she also makes a statement: "The average wage for Grobucket employees is $10,000 a year." She leaks the wage structure at Grobucket to the journalist who runs the dramatic headline: GROBUCKET PAYS AVERAGE WAGE OF $7,000 A YEAR. These three conflicting figures are all correct: $25,636, $10,000, $7,000. What is different is the way the average has been calculated.

A. THE MEAN AVERAGE OR ARITHMETIC MEAN

As an old baseball player, the owner has simply added all the wages and divided by the number of wage-earners: $282,000 split 11 ways gives each person $25,636.

This creates a *mean average*. The figure is clearly misleading, since only two people earn more than that, and nobody earns within $10,000 of that actual figure.

B. THE MEDIAN AVERAGE

The bookkeeper's secretary has discovered what Ms. Middle-of-the-road earns: five people earn more than $10,000, five people earn less. The middle-of-the-road figure is the *median average*. In fact $10,000 is also a somewhat misleading figure: those above this figure earn a total of $237,000 a year, while those below earn only $35,000. The median average does not reveal this disproportion.

C. THE MODAL AVERAGE

It is often useful to locate the most numerous group within a population, the *modal average*. For example, a question such as "Does the average American smoke?" can only be answered by using a modal average: dividing Americans into smokers and nonsmokers, the larger group does not smoke. The journalist sees that five workers all earn $7,000 a year; they constitute a modal average. Is $7,000 a fair figure? Not really.

Which of these averages is the *true* figure? In fact, none of them shows what is really happening at Grobucket.

For the researcher, the lessons are clear: ignore all "average" figures unless it is clear how the average was calculated. If the calculation is clear, try to imagine how the average figure would differ if the other calculation methods had been used.

Concept Review

Three kinds of Average

1. Newspapers often report earnings. This example is from the Associated Press.

   > Medical doctors in the United States earned an average of $86,210 last year, the consumer advocate group Public Citizen reported . . . . The survey found neurosurgeons to be top earners with average yearly salaries of $135,690, followed by orthopedic surgeons at $134,670. At the other end of the scale, general practitioners averaged $63,950 and pediatricians $65,380.

   Do the figures mean *anything* as they stand? If you assume that the figures are *mean* averages precise figures often are), what patterns of earnings could be hidden in the figure of $86,21 year?

2. *Time* magazine is reporting here the cost of weddings in Japan:

   > The families of both bride and groom [in Japan] share the cost of weddings and they pay dearly. They will lay out $17 billion this year for knot-tying festivities, an astonishing $22,000 per couple, six times the price of the average U.S. ceremony.

   Do you think that *festivities* in Japan and a *ceremony* in the U.S. refer to exactly the same thin they do not, is there any point in the comparison? How do you think the two average calculated? If they are not calculated in the same way, how will that affect the value o comparison?

CHAPTER FIFTEEN
Evaluating Figures: A Special Case

• Comparing Averages

Another game with averages is played by comparing them. At the end of every year, countless agencies and institutions perform this trick. The question is typically: did the company do better this year than last year? Let's say that in the first month of 1986, Grobucket International earned 10 million in profits. Profits increased steadily each month until, in November 1986, Grobucket was earning 11 million—a 10 percent increase in profits over the previous year. Then what happened? Grobucket stuck at 11 million for the next thirteen months: the year 1987 was absolutely flat, stagnant, and depressing. This is the picture:

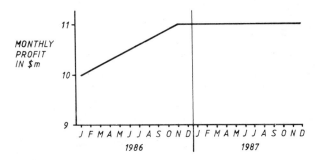

Every cloud can be spray-painted with a silver lining. In this case, averaging will do the trick. What was the (mean) *average* profit in dynamic 1986? Roughly, 10.5 million per month. And in stagnant 1987? In fact 1987 showed 11 million a month—an increase of a half-million. So there was growth after all!! From 10.5 million up to 11 million is roughly 5 per cent, so the company can announce that profits in 1987 increased by a healthy 5 percent as compared with 1986; the shareholders—at least the innumerate among them—will be happy.

Responsible organizations always make it clear how they calculate their figures, even when they are apple polishing. Unfortunately, when the media report the more sensational figures, the method of calculation is often omitted; then the figures become perfectly meaningless. As researcher, it is your task to decide what, if anything, the figures show.

Concept Review

Comparing Averages

Below are the quarterly unemployment figures for 1986 and 1987 for the Republic of Ruritania. How could an unscrupulous commentator show that unemployment had fallen in 1987?

1986	1st quarter	4 million
	2nd quarter	3.66 million
	3rd quarter	3.33 million
	4th quarter	3 million

1987	1st quarter	3 million
	2nd quarter	3 million
	3rd quarter	3 million
	4th quarter	3 million

• Variation, Averages and the Normal Curve

Averages can, and probably should, be made "visible" by means of a graph. Figures, let's say the shoe sizes of adult males, are plotted on a graph to show the *distribution* (or spread). Roughly:

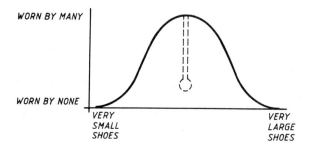

The line of this graph looks like a bell, the famous "bell curve." As you can see, the mean, median and modal averages all lie in the same place, about where the clapper of the bell would hang. A symmetrical spread like this is called a *normal distribution*: this means that the figures create an exactly balanced pattern on either side of a *norm* (or average). Thus, it is possible to say that the *normal* (or average) man takes size 9 shoes. Naturally, anyone who does not take size 9 shoes is up in arms: "Are you trying to tell me I'm not normal?" If the *norm* is specified as the figure occupying the central position in a balanced distribution, then anyone who does not take size nines is definitely not "normal."

The danger of misunderstanding the statistical norm becomes serious in such fields as the assessment of child development. The Denver Child Development Study, for example, found that the "normal" child (in the statistical sense) can say three words other than *mommy* and *daddy* at 15½ months or can drink out of a cup at 10½ months. Does this mean that children who perform later are retarded and that children who perform earlier are gifted? Not at all, according to the Denver specialists. The range of satisfactory development is huge: only the slowest 2½ percent and the fastest 2½ percent are in any way "abnormal" in the non-statistical sense of the word. *Variation*, as you can see, is a problem in evaluating "norms" or averages.

Variation, informally defined, is the amount of spread that figures show on either side of a norm. To see why variation is so important, let's take a classic example, average weather. The (mean) average annual temperature in San

Francisco is 56.8°; Kansas City, Missouri, has the identical average annual temperature: 56.8°. Do they therefore have the same climate? Hardly. San Francisco has no recorded temperature hotter than 106° or colder than 20°, while Kansas City has a record high of 113° and a record low of −22°. Record temperatures can be freakish, but the monthly figures (mean monthly averages) are very differently distributed; a graph shows the difference clearly:

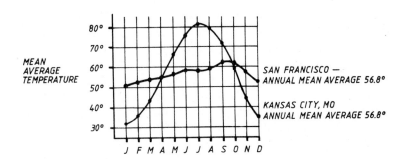

As you can see, an average or normal figure (56.8° in both cases) tells you nothing about the climate until you know the amount of variation.

Statisticians have created ways of calculating the variability of scores; unfortunately these calculations of what is called *standard deviation* are complicated and would soon take us out of our depth.

The point for you as researcher is this: you can avoid being misled by an average figure if you ask what lies *behind* it: a wide variation or a narrow variation. In the best kind of reporting, a table or a graph gives you the detailed figures as well as the "average."

CHECKLIST: WHAT TO ASK ABOUT AN AVERAGE

A. Method of Calculation
Does the source say (or is it obvious) how the average was calculated?
If no, the figure is meaningless.
If yes: What quirks or anomalies may lie hidden in the figures? How might the average come out if it were calculated in a different way?

B. Comparison of Averages
If averages for two time periods are compared to show a trend, is the trend a real one or a "statistical" one?

C. Variation
Does the source indicate how much the figures vary on either side of the norm?
Is there perhaps a table or a graph that shows this variation?
If no, be suspicious of the average.

ncept Review

Variations around a Norm

1. The statistically normal baby first takes off some of its clothes at 15 months. In deciding whether the development of an individual child is satisfactory, what must you know in addition to this fact?

2. Mean elevation is the average height of land above sea level. Both North Dakota and Alaska have a mean elevation of 1,900 feet. Does this figure tell you anything about the appearance of the land?

3. After the Second World War, the mean average size of the American family was 3.6 members. (Naturally, no family actually had 3.6 members!) The building industry assumed, therefore, that most families would have either three or four members. Accordingly, millions of two-bedroom dwellings were built—fine for the three-member family, and acceptable to a four-member family with children of the same sex. But the building industry got it wrong. In fact, only 45 percent of American families had three or four members. What went wrong with the calculation?

centages

If you earn $1,000 a month and you are offered a 10 percent pay raise, your new salary will be $100 more than your old one: $1,100. The figure of $1,000 is called a *base*. A *base* is the starting figure on which a percentage is calculated. The figure *10 percent* means, literally "10 per 100." In other words, for every 100 parts of the base, 10 are to be "set aside", in this case as a salary raise. A percentage without a base is meaningless. Nevertheless, in your reading you may well come across sentences such as:

> The Grobucket company makes a 500 percent profit on every plastic bucket it sells to the U.S. Air Force.

What does this mean? As it stands, it means nothing whatsoever; it is a percentage without a base. Grobucket might well offer an alternative figure: an 83 percent profit. Since this figure is also unattached, it is also meaningless. A little math will show you that the two figures, 500 percent and 83 percent, are, oddly enough, consistent with each other. Let's say Grobucket makes a bucket for $1 and sells it to the Air Force for $6; it is true to say that profit ($5) is 500 percent of the *cost price*. On the other hand, $5 is only 83 percent of the *selling price*.

As a researcher, watch like a hawk for meaningless percentages.

A variation of the percentage trick is to use a *shifting base*. This is common in certain kinds of advertising:

CHAPTER FIFTEEN
Evaluating Figures: A Special Case

> Save up to 70%! We are slashing prices by 50% and offering an extra
> 20% discount to anyone born under the sign of Pisces!

For an item costing $100, those born under the sign of Pisces might expect to pay $30, but they will probably be asked to pay $40. The reason is that the base will shift. The 50 percent discount will take the original price of $100 as its base. The selling price is now $50. The second discount of 20 percent will take $50 as its base, producing a final price of $40. (Pisces people weren't offered a 70 percent saving, but a saving *up to* 70 percent.)

A more sophisticated example: in 1986, the United States had a trade gap—we imported goods that cost about twice as much as those we exported. When you read the following sentence about our 1987 performance, does it suggest that the trade gap is improving or that it is getting worse?

> While exports have roared ahead by a full 10 percent, imports have
> slowed right back, growing at a sluggish 5½ percent.

Getting better or getting worse? At a glance, 10 percent looks bigger than 5½ percent—but it isn't. The trick is that the figures are attached to different bases. Let's rework the percentages into actual figures. We know that imports were twice exports, so let's call imports 200 and exports 100. In 1987, exports increased from 100 to 110. Imports, however, increased from 200 to 211. The old trade gap was 100, the new trade gap is 101, so things are getting worse, not better!

A researcher cannot be too careful about percentages, especially when two percentages are compared.

A third and final trick shows how changing the base can throw a very different light on a situation. A big-city company with 100 employees is accused by a newspaper of showing racial bias: only 3 employees are from racial minorities, while the figure for minorities in the local community is 25 percent. When 3 old hands retire, the company replaces them with members of minorities. A year after the accusation, the company has a total of 6 non-white workers. Now look at the way in which a skillful choice of percentage shades this situation:

a. Our figure for employment of minorities now stands at 200 percent of what it was a year ago. Anyone can see the company's overwhelming commitment to achieving a balanced workforce.

b. We have increased minority employment by no less that 100 percent during the last year—a fine record.

c. The number of minority employees a year ago was some 50 percent of the figure today.

d. Minority employment stands at 6 percent of the work force, up only slightly from the disgraceful 3 percent figure of a year ago; this shows how little the company cares about this issue.

e. Employment of minorities has increased at a snail's pace: a mere 3 percentage points as compared with a year ago.

The numbers 200 percent, 100 percent, 50 percent, 6 percent, 3 percentage points—are all true figures, but they create very different impressions. Seeing this difference should make you cautious in your reading: always try to separate the figures from the rhetoric.

CHECKLIST: WHAT TO ASK ABOUT PERCENTAGES

A. **The Percentage and its Base**
   Is the percentage attached to a base?
   Is the base constant, or does it shift?
   If two percentages are compared, are they attached to the same base?
   If not, how would the comparison turn out if expressed in actual terms?

B. **The Truth behind the Percentage**
   Cutting through the rhetoric, what is the real situation behind the percentages?

Concept Review

On a Percentage Basis

1. In a certain year at Johns Hopkins University, 33⅓ percent of the female students mar faculty member. (Fact.) Can you reasonably conclude that marriages between female stu and faculty members are fairly common?

2. Today electric power from the grid is available to 98.7 percent of American farms. (Fact.) this fact permit the conclusion that the United States has now achieved almost cor electrification of the countryside?

3. During the Shah's last years in Iran, he applied a great deal of pressure for education. reported this drive enthusiastically. Does this sentence, in fact, establish that educa opportunities for women have increased?

   > As recently as 1960, only 2% of Iran's women had attended a university; today women make up 38% of the university population. (*Time*, September 18, 1978)

4. In November 1980, the UPI reported on a survey conducted by the National Center for F Studies. The survey covered 110,000 persons living in 41,000 households. Evaluate extracts from the UPI report.

   > One in four Americans above the age of 20 no longer eats breakfast, but 38 percent of the population snacks at least once a day, a government survey shows.
   >
   > The breakfast eating habits also differ with age. A total of 86 percent of those aged 65 or more report eating breakfast, while more than 35 percent in the 20 to 43 age category start the day on an empty stomach . . . .
   >
   > Blacks are more likely to go without breakfast than whites or Hispanics. But there are almost no differences in breakfast eating habits between men and women, regardless of race.
   >
   > About 38 percent of all Americans eat between meals every day; 27 percent do it sometimes and 35 percent say they never snack.

4 •

What Figures Mean

We've already seen that missing information (the type of an average, the base of a percentage) can make a figure meaningless. We've also seen some of the problems of poor technique (using a badly chosen sample, for instance). Let us say, though, that the figures are collected and presented in perfect good faith and with unimpeachable numeracy. It is still fair to ask: what do they signify? The first concern is *accuracy*, the margin of error.

• The Margin of Error

Figures have to be collected, and no collection procedure is perfect. An IQ test does not produce consistent results even from the same testee; a census never counts *everyone*. Statisticians call this unreliability *error*, and they have accurate ways of assessing it.

The classic example for calculating "error" is field pacing. Your task is to measure fields by pacing them. How accurate is this procedure? You find out in this way. Measure out an exact hundred yards. Then pace it quite a number of times. Let's say your (mean) average number of paces for 100 yards is 120 paces (with a variation between 118 and 122). Now try taking 120 paces and measuring how far you actually traveled, repeating this exercise a number of times. You will seldom hit exactly 100 yards: in fact, half the time you finish up within two yards of the target; half the time you do not. This figure of 2 yards, your margin of error half the time, is a key figure for statisticians; they would say you have a *probable error* of two yards. Any counting procedure has a *probable error*: it is defined as the margin within which you are certain to fall *half the time*. (Another calculation is *standard error*; this is the margin within which you are certain to fall two-thirds of the time.) Let's look at a practical case.

IQ testing is common in schools. Usually a child is tested once and given an IQ rating. Let's say John scores 111 and Mary scores 116. Mary "wins" by 5 points. What do these figures really mean? First, one would have to know the *probable error* or the *standard error* on the intelligence test. If the Stanford-Binet test is used, the *standard error* is 3 points for a single test. In other words, the test will get within 3 points of the *true* score two-thirds of the time. For John this means that there is a 2 to 1 chance that his IQ falls between 108 and 114; for Mary there is a 2 to 1 chance that her IQ falls between 113 and 116. The conclusion that Mary is more intelligent than John is absolutely inadmissible: the margin of error on the test makes the matter "too close to call." Thus, quite apart from the debate as to what IQ tests actually test, the testing procedure itself makes no claim to super-accuracy.

A figure without a margin of error is always suspect, but unfortunately it's impossible for a non-specialist to evaluate whether the margin of error on a figure has been properly calculated. For you as researcher, the problem is at a lower level:

scrutinize statistics in the knowledge that they always have some "play" in them. If a strong conclusion is drawn from numbers that are really very close together, remain suspicious.

• Correlation

If two fingerprints show a perfect match, it is strong evidence that the same finger made them. The same is *not* true of figures. When two sets of figures are, broadly speaking, comparable, statisticians can measure the relationship between them. Monthly totals, for instance, can be compared, whatever they happen to measure: let's take as an example the monthly figure for live births in New York and the monthly figure for average military pay. A statistician could search for a *correlation* between these figures. A correlation can be defined as a correspondence between two sets of variables. In fact, the birth figures go up and down rapidly, but hover around a (slightly falling) trend; military pay stays level for long periods and then shoots up. The statistician would say there is *no correlation* between these figures.

Let's turn things around. What figures *do* show a correlation? In fact, perfect correlation produces some odd matchups. Notoriously, there is a close correlation between the salaries of Presbyterian ministers in Massachusetts and the price of rum in Havana. The increase in the number of television channels available in France correlates nicely with the silting up of the River Ganges. The offerings collected in church on Sunday mornings have increased at much the same rate as the fees charged by prostitutes. There is strong correlation here, but does the correlation have any *meaning*? Clearly not; these cases are all pure coincidence, or spurious correlation, as it is called. The general rule: a correlation is significant only when a cause-and-effect relationship can be established.

In your reading, you'll find many studies based on techniques of correlation. You might decide, for example, to write on the question: Does diet increase vulnerability to certain types of cancer? Everything you read will present patterns of correlation: high milk consumption seems to accompany one type of cancer; high consumption of eggs seems to accompany another type; and so on. These correlations give the scientist a pointer—but in themselves they prove nothing. Laboratory research is required to establish a chain of cause-and-effect between the foodstuff and the medical condition. Making this connection can be difficult: for example, the link between cigarette smoking and lung cancer is still "only" a statistical correlation: a biological mechanism by which cigarettes actually *cause* cancer has not yet been described. In writing up your sources, be careful to avoid taking correlation as proof: it isn't.

Statisticians use different kinds of correlation to tackle different problems; for the beginner, some of the calculations look terrifying. Even so, as we have said several times in this chapter, understanding the basic concept may keep you out of trouble in your own researches.

CHECKLIST: WHAT TO ASK ABOUT THE MEANING OF A FIGURE

A. The Margin of Error

Does the source give the margin of error on this figure?

If no, be suspicious.

If yes, are conclusions being drawn from figures that fall within the margin of error? Is the matter really too close to call?

B. Correlation

If the source claims that two figures are closely correlated, is further evidence provided to show that this correlation is not *spurious*?

---

pt Review

at does the Figure Mean?

During the Reagan/Carter election campaign, Congressman Wyche Fowler of Georgia suggested that the baseball World Series reliably predicts election results. If the American League champion wins, the Republican candidate goes to the White House; if the National League champion takes the series, then it's the Democrat. Between 1916 and 1976, only three elections bucked this trend; from 1952 to 1976, all seven elections ran true to form. *Question:* What is the *name* given to this type of statistical error? (P.S. Fowler's joke backfired. In 1980, the Philadelphia Phillies won, but Reagan was elected anyway.)

On the subject of the Reagan/Carter election, what do you think the opinion pollsters meant when they said it was "too close to call"?

The cover story in the March 15, 1982 issue of *Time* was headlined *Salt: A New Villain?* It was by Claudia Wallis. Wallis is writing about technical matters for a non-technical audience, so her language is free of statistical jargon; nevertheless, the article depends entirely on statistics. Read the following extracts from the story, and then answer the questions below.

> The case against salt (or rather, the sodium that is in salt) has been accumulating steadily. . . . For decades, cutting down on salt has been a primary medical treatment for the control of hypertension. More important, an extraordinary statistical connection has been found between the amount of salt that a population consumes and the incidence of hypertension [high blood pressure].
>
> Since World War II, mainly because of the growing popularity of presalted, processed and frozen foods as well as a penchant for eating out, Americans have been taking megadoses of salt. In the United States today, the average adult consumes 2½ teaspoons a day, more than 20 times what the body needs. An estimated 35 million people suffer from hypertension, 60 million if mild cases are included . . . .
>
> Statistically the link is clear. In countries where sodium intake is high, so is the frequency of hypertension. Japan is the most striking example. With a diet based largely on fish, pickled vegetables and soy sauce (1,029 mg sodium per tablespoon), the average Japanese citizen consumes nearly three teaspoons of salt a day. In the northern agricultural provinces, where salt is still widely used as a preservative, six teaspoons or more a day is not uncommon. And what is probably the highest sodium diet in the world coincides with what seems to be the world's highest rate of hypertension; in some villages fully 40% of the residents have high blood pressure . . . .

PART THREE
The Research Paper

In a classic study, Dr. Lot Page headed up a Harvard team that from 1966 to 1972 studied six tribes in the Solomon Islands. Three were totally unaffected by Western culture and three otherwise very primitive (no roads, no telephones, no pollution), got to eat salt-heavy canned ham and beef jerky supplied them by Chinese traders. Only in the second group did blood pressure increase with age. It was highest in the tribe that traditionally cooked its fish and vegetables in sea water . . . .

Lowering salt intake seems to reduce hypertension too. Beginning in 1972, Dr. John Farquhar of Stanford University conducted a three-year study of 1,500 men and women selected at random in three California towns. In two of the towns, subjects cut salt intake by 30%. In the third, no dietary change was made. The result: blood pressure was 6.4% lower among low-salt people than in the control town.

At the heart of the salt debate is a medical mystery. Salt may contribute directly to hypertension, but nobody knows exactly how.

Questions:

a. The article depends heavily on correlations, although this word is not used. Can you pinp[oint] statements that are, in fact, correlations?

b. Comment on the way Farquhar's experiment is reported. Do the facts as reported here g[ive] reasonable grounds for believing the statement: "Lowering salt intake seems to reduce hy[perten-] sion too"?

c. Comment on the relationship between the last sentence quoted and the rest of the mater[ial].

d. Overall, do you think Wallis has done a good job in reporting highly technical material so [the] general public can understand it? Can you suggest anywhere she could have made improve[ments]

Presenting Information

In the Biblical account of the Creation, chaos preceded order. Toward the end of your research, you may begin to grasp what primeval chaos was like. The final step in the research process is to *present* what you have discovered, to reduce a chaos of ideas to the orderly structure of an essay.

After your reading is finished, the next step is to give your game plan a tough going-over. Writing up the "final" version of your game plan follows much the same path whether the piece is a paragraph of static description or a professional monograph. The question now must be: are there are *new* problems of presentation when the paper has a heavy research component? There are, in fact four new problems, each of which is handled in a separate section below.

1. **The Integrated Style.** If an essay is based on library research, you'll have two kinds of writing to deal with: yours and that of your sources. Working the mixture into a smooth blend takes practice.

2. **Documentation.** Your sources must be documented. This involves a simple mechanical trick, but it's a trick you must learn.

3. **Working with Statistics.** Original research or research based heavily on statistics requires special presentation skills.

4. Working with a Sparring Partner. Sometimes your sources are a fountain of pure information; sometimes they are a log jam that must be blasted apart. The art of destructive rebuttal must be practiced.

When you've tried your hand at these techniques and brought your own research paper to a successful conclusion, you'll have traveled a long way toward becoming a writer.

1 •

You and Your Sources: Developing an Integrated Style

Finding information generates a well-sorted card index. Evaluation helps you decide what makes sense and what does not. This heap of scraps must now be assembled into a coherent whole; it must be *presented*. It is now that your research finally bears fruit, or fails to bear it. Let's make the problems concrete by studying an example of presentation.

Stalin's years as leader of the Soviet Union saw what Robert Conquest called The Great Terror. Million of victims, many of them members of Stalin's own Bolshevik party, were rounded up, interrogated and sent to labor camps. Many never returned. Some of those arrested, especially Stalin's party rivals, were publicly tried. During the notorious "show trials," most confessed to extraordinary crimes. In a research paper on this period, surely one of the most interesting in history, one might well ask the question *why?*—why did so many top people publicly and openly confess to crimes against the country they had built? There is an avalanche of information on this subject: the seven notecards that follow have been chosen to show the problems of writing, not to illustrate the results of in-depth research.

Confessions at Public Trials   The hope of ultimate pardon

A few of them, Radek and Rakovsky, were not indeed brought before the firing squad; and one man's escape from death would induce ten or twenty to hope that they, too, might escape. They certainly believed that their self-accusations were so absurd and so obviously made under duress as not to blot their reputations.

Deutscher, *Stalin*, p. 371

Confessions at Public Trials   Use of relatives as hostages

Bukharin and Krestinskii :

It is said that Bukharin began to "testify" only after the investigators threatened to kill his wife and newborn son, while Krestinskii signed the record of the investigation when his wife and daughter were similarly threatened. The defendants were warned that the tortures would be continued even after the trial if they did not give the necessary testimony.

Medvedev, *Let History Judge*, p. 187

CHAPTER SIXTEEN
Presenting Information

Confessions at Public Trials   Use of torture

Yet, in spite of Khrushchev's remarks, torture is not an adequate explanation of all the confessions of the oppositionists. We should record its extent, and its overwhelmingly powerful effects throughout the period. But critics were right in saying that torture alone could probably not have produced the public self-humiliation of a whole series of Stalin's enemies, when returned to health and given a platform.

Conquest, The Great Terror, p. 197

Confessions at Public Trials   Use of torture
Iakubovich (Deposition sent in 1967 to the Procurator General of the USSR about his trial in 1930)

I was beside myself. How should I behave at the trial? Deny the depositions I had made during the investigation? Try to disrupt the trial? Create a worldwide scandal? Whom would that help?

I won't hide the fact that I had something else in mind. If I repudiated my earlier depositions at the trial, what would the investigators, the torturers, do to me? It was terrible just to think of it. If it were only death. I wanted death. I sought it, I tried to die. But they wouldn't let me die; they would slowly torture me, torture for an infinitely long time. They wouldn't let me sleep until death came. And if it came from lack of sleep? Probably madness would come first. How could I bring myself to that? In the name of what?

Medvedev, Let History Judge, p. 129

Confessions at Public Trials   Use of drugs and hypnosis

People have speculated about a Tibetan potion that deprives a man of his will, and about the use of hypnosis. Such explanations must by no means be rejected: if the NKVD possessed such methods, clearly *there were no moral rules* to prevent resorting to them. Why not weaken or muddle the will? And it is a known fact that in the twenties some leading hypnotists gave up their careers and entered the service of the GPU. It is also reliably known that in the thirties a school for hypnotists existed in the NKVD.

Solzhenitsyn, Gulag Archipelago I, p. 409

Confessions at Public Trials   Use of drugs and hypnosis

The stories that they were hypnotized or given mysterious drugs may be safely dismissed. But it cannot be doubted that they were subjected to physical and moral torture of the sort that is used in third-degree interrogation in Russia – and elsewhere.

Deutscher, Stalin, p. 371

Confessions at Public Trials   Psychological reasons
Arthur Koestler's Interpretation in Darkness at Noon

Rubashov in Darkness at Noon is not tortured, pp. 178-9. After a long interrogation he voluntarily confesses because (a) he was a loyal party man, and the party needed his confession, pp. 156-7; (b) he did hate Stalin and so he was, in a sense, guilty, p. 167; (c) as a communist, he believed that, where conflict exists, the collective is right and the individual is wrong — the collective says he is guilty, p. 79 and p. 121.

Writing up this kind material is a challenge. The reader expects a smooth and coherent argument; what often emerges is a patchwork quilt of poorly matched snippets. Let's look at a patchwork example:

> Why did so many people confess during the Soviet show trials? Torture was used to extract some confessions, as the deposition of Iakubovich confirms. Relatives were held hostage to force confessions; according to Medvedev, this occurred in the cases of Bukharin and Krestinskii. Deutscher says some of those who confessed believed they would be freed, as happened to Radek and Rakovsky. Deutscher comments: "They certainly believed that their self-accusations were so absurd and so obviously made under duress as not to blot their reputations." Solzhenitsyn says that drugs and hypnosis may have been used; Deutscher says: "The stories that they were hypnotized or given mysterious drugs may be safely dismissed." Koestler suggests that the confessions were the result of the intellectual confusion and a sense of loyalty to the communist party. He believes the confessions were sometimes voluntary.

This is dreadful stuff. It suffers from the four weaknesses typical of a poor research style: (a) the writer has vanished under a shower of notecards; (b) six sources are named, but not one is *identified*: the reader is left to guess who the sources are and what weight to attach to their opinions; (c) there is no continuity: the text zips like an irresponsible grasshopper from one source to the next; and (d) there is no sense of *direction*, no sign of a thesis statement anywhere on the horizon. Let's take these problems one by one and see how to put things right.

• Correction 1: Bringing the Writer to the Fore

Students often complain that a research paper is simply other people's ideas warmed over; they feel left out of their own work. This effect can arise when a student sticks to *facts* and forgets about *evaluation*. The research fragment above states the facts—Solzhenitsyn says this, Deutscher says the opposite, and so on—but there is no attempt at evaluation. The writer's task is to sift and discuss the information, arriving at a balanced conclusion. In the reworking of this material given below, you'll see how a writer can take center stage in a research paper without seeming opinionated or pushy.

• Correction 2: Identification of Names

When you quote a source for the first time, it's usually helpful to give this source some kind of "credentials." The name *Iakubovich*, for example, is not widely known even among professional historians. To fill in his background, you might write:

> Mikhail Iakubovich was an early and active member of the Bolshevik Party. Nevertheless, he was tried as a "saboteur" in the first of the show trials in 1930. In 1967, he explained in a deposition to the Procurator General of the USSR <u>why</u> he had confessed.

After this identification, the reader knows what Iakubovich's evidence is worth. Often these "credentials" can be handled more briefly:

> The respected historian Isaac Deutscher in his biography of Stalin, says that . . . .

These identifications are not mere facts—they are a key part of your argument. They establish that a source is trustworthy and that the ideas form part of your overall case. Or an identification might repudiate a source:

Nikolai Krylenko, the infamous prosecutor in the 1930 sabotage trial, argued in this way about the truth of the confessions: "If we should admit even for one second that these people were telling untruths, then why were they arrested . . . ?" To a prosecutor, it seems, arrest is the ultimate proof of guilt.

Some names are so well known that they need no identification. For example, if you wanted to quote Stalin's speech to the Communist Party in 1939 when the Great Terror was all but finished, which of these two versions would you use?

Version 1: Joseph Stalin (real name Yossif Vissarionovich Djugashvili), the General Secretary of the Communist Party from 1922 until his death in 1953, said: "Our party is now somewhat smaller in membership, but on the other hand it is better in quality. That is a big achievement."

Version 2: Stalin's epitaph for his victims was this: "Our party is now somewhat smaller in membership, but on the other hand it is better in quality. That is a big achievement."

• Correction 3: Continuity

With material that relies heavily on sources, it can be difficult to keep the relationships among your "contributors" clear. Look, for example, at the note-cards on *Use of Drugs and Hypnosis*. Deutscher says that stories about drugs and hypnosis "may be safely dismissed." Solzhenitsyn says such explanations "must by no means be rejected." How will you handle this flat contradiction? You have two choices: you can refuse to take sides, or you can resolve the conflict in some way. If you refuse to take sides, then you might write:

The use of drugs and hypnosis to obtain confessions is an open question. Deutscher dismisses the subject without discussion; presumably, he found no convincing evidence. Solzhenitsyn, on the other hand, believes that such techniques may have been used, citing reports that hypnotists had been recruited by the secret police. Whatever the truth of the matter, no one claims that drugs nor hypnotism played a major role in obtaining confessions.

If you try to resolve the conflict, you'll have to sift the evidence carefully. In the present case, it may strike you that Solzhenitsyn does not claim that drugs or hypnosis were actually used: he says that both were available, and that no moral rules *prevented* their use. A diplomatic solution is now at hand:

Did the secret police use drugs and hypnosis to obtain confessions? Solzhenitsyn is certainly right in saying that such techniques were available to the interrogators, and that, given the widespread use of physical torture, no moral rules prevented their use. Since, however, he produces no direct evidence, it is probably fair to conclude with Isaac Deutscher that stories of drugs and hypnosis "may be safely dismissed."

With the material set up in this way, the reader knows exactly how your sources relate to each other. Your own thoughts are also to the fore: this is *your* paper, not a patchwork of citations.

Another continuity problem lies in fitting direct quotations into your own sentences. Always ensure that the grammar of your sentence and the grammar of your quotation form a perfect match. For example:

> **Awkward splice:** The respected historian Isaac Deutscher in his biography of Stalin says that "they were hypnotized or given mysterious drugs may be safely dismissed."

> **Clean splice:** The respected historian Isaac Deutscher in his biography of Stalin says that stories of drugs and hypnosis "may be safely dismissed."

• Correction 4: Thesis Orientation

We've already said that an *evaluative* approach highlights the researcher's ideas and feelings. Evaluation should constantly point the paper toward the thesis statement; this gives the whole presentation coherence and "readability." The following research fragment shows how the facts on the seven notecards can be brought into line with a thesis. (In the following text, sourcenotes have been used to document the information. The use of sourcenotes is explained in the next section. An assumption should be made that Medvedev, Solzhenitsyn and Deutscher were identified earlier in the essay.)

A mystery is posed and the problem is set up.	A mystery still hangs over the Moscow show trials of the 1930's. Why did so many ardent revolutionaries eagerly confess appalling crimes, weeping sometimes with gratitude when they were sentenced to be shot? To what extent were these extraordinary confessions voluntary? And if they were not voluntary, how were they obtained?

First aspect: physical torture	The routine use of torture to obtain confessions is well documented—the case of Iakubovich is typical. Mikhail Iakubovich was an early and active member of the Bolshevik Party. Nevertheless, he was tried as a "saboteur" in the first of the show trials in 1930. In 1967, he explained in a deposition to the Procurator General of the USSR why he had confessed at his trial. Iakubovich had been tortured to the point of attempting suicide; at the trial he knew his confession was lies, but:	*Iakubovich identified*
Long quotation is indented and clearly set off from the main text.	If I repudiated my earlier depositions at the trial, what would the investigators, the torturers, do to me? It was terrible just to think of it. If it were only death. I wanted death. I sought it, I tried to die. But they wouldn't let me die; they would slowly torture me, torture me for an infinitely long time. They wouldn't let me sleep until death came. And if it came from lack of sleep? Probably madness would come first. How could I bring myself to that? In the name of what? (Medvedev 129) The vividness of Iakubovich's fear rings true after nearly sixty years.	*Comment shows that the quote is taken positively.*
Second aspect: mental torture	Mental torture was used too, particularly threats against family hostages. Bukharin, the leading intellectual of the Bolshevik party, began to confess only when his wife and newborn son were threatened (Medvedev 187). Cunningly, the secret police spared the lives of some who confessed; this tactic of creating hope certainly broke the resistance of some victims (Deutscher 371).	*Bukharin is identified.*

CHAPTER SIXTEEN
Presenting Information

Third aspect: drugs and hypnosis	Did the secret police use drugs and hypnosis to obtain confessions? Solzhenitsyn is certainly right in saying that such techniques were available to the interrogators, and that, given the widespread use of physical torture, no moral rules prevented their use (409). However, since he produces no direct evidence, it is probably fair to conclude with Isaac Deutscher that stories of drugs and hypnosis "may be safely dismissed" (371).	Solzhenitsyn and Deutscher are evaluated: contradiction is resolved.
Summing up: Transition to psychological reasons Shorter quote is included within the main text.	Fear of torture, the desire to protect one's family, and the hope of pardon—these factors undoubtedly produced some confessions. Nevertheless, most commentators look for deeper, psychological reasons. Robert Conquest's authoritative book The Great Terror reviews the sources available up to 1970; he remarks: ". . . critics were right in saying that torture alone could probably not have produced the public self-humiliation of a whole series of Stalin's enemies . . . ." (197). It is the enthusiastic groveling of Stalin's victims that makes the confessions so mysterious.	Conquest is identified.
Fourth aspect: psychology Summary	Oddly, it is a novel that is generally accepted as getting the psychology right. Arthur Koestler's novel Darkness at Noon is set in a jail where N. S. Rubashov, a composite of several show trial victims known to Koestler personally (Dedication), is being prepared for confession. Rubashov is not physically tortured; his confession must be voluntary (178–179). During interrogation, he sees that the future of the communist party—the party to which he has devoted his life—depends on his confession. Everything he has lived for will be at risk if he betrays the party at his trial (156–157). As to the lies he must tell, he begins to doubt that they are lies: he did hate Stalin, so confessing a plot to kill him is in a sense the truth (167). At the deepest level, as a communist Rubashov believes that the collective knows better than the individual—and in this case the collective says Rubashov is guilty (79 and 121). These psychological pressures within the "party mind" were perhaps more compelling than any physical torture.	Koestler is identified. Koestler's ideas are summarized. There is no direct quotation; even so, each idea is sourcenoted.
Thesis statement	The workings of the "party mind" make it likely that at least some of the public confessions were, in a sense, voluntary.	

Works Cited

The list of *Works Cited* is in alphabetical order and uses *MLA* form as given in Chapter 13.	Conquest, Robert. The Great Terror. Harmondsworth: Penguin, 1971. Deutscher, Isaac. Stalin. Harmondsworth: Penguin, 1966. Koestler, Arthur. Darkness at Noon. Trans. Daphne Hardy. 1941. New York: Bantam, 1968. Medvedev, Roy A. Let History Judge. Trans. Colleen Taylor. New York: Knopf, 1972. Solzhenitsyn, Alexander. The Gulag Archipelago. Trans. Thomas Whitney. 3 vols. London: Collins, 1974. Vol. 1.

This research fragment is now readable: the names are all clearly identified (some here, some earlier in the essay), there is good continuity, and there is a coherent argument leading to a conclusion. Above all, the sources and the essay work fluently together—the style is *integrated*.

Review Assignment

The Integrated Style

The death of Marilyn Monroe is surrounded by mystery. The notecards below represent a tiny splinter of all that is known on this subject. Your assignment is to write a "research fragment" based on these cards, avoiding the problems discussed above. (To help with the identifications, a critical bibliography appears after the notecards.)

Summers' Position

Summers' book _Goddess_ (1985) is the fullest and best investigation. He examines all the theories about Monroe's death. He concludes that she had a love affair with John Kennedy (217), that John had passed her on to brother Robert (225). That Monroe, half-crazed with drugs, believed that Robert would divorce his wife, Ethel, and marry her (281). That Robert visited her on the afternoon of August 4 to break off with her (354). That this blow, coupled with the cancellation of her current film, caused Monroe to kill herself (355).

Evaluation of Summers' Evidence

"Despite the fact that Summers' _Goddess_ is a heartless, graceless book..., he is a relentless investigative journalist with good credentials, and the bulk of the material he has gathered — no matter how sleazy — appears to be sound."

Bryan. _Rolling Stone_ 5 Dec. 1985: 41.

Evaluation of Summers' Evidence

"Summers relies on gossip and speculation, presenting no compelling evidence linking Bobby [Kennedy] and Monroe."

Conant. _Newsweek_ 14 Oct. 1985: 37.

Evidence for Suicide : The Huge Overdose

The autopsy showed that Monroe had 13 milligrams percent of pentobarbital (a sleeping drug) in the liver; this implies taking ten times the normal dose. She had 8 milligrams percent chloral hydrate (a sedative) in the blood — twenty times the normal dose. "Either of the drugs, taken in such quantities, could individually have proved fatal. Taken together, they were even more likely to kill."

Summers. _Goddess_ 319.

Evidence for Suicide: Rejection of the Suicide Theory
Monroe's maid did not believe in the suicide theory:

> Marilyn knew exactly what her body could take. Within those limits, she was extremely careful. To this day, her death has remained a mystery to me.

Pepitone. *Marilyn Monroe Confidential* 249

Theories about Monroe's death as Murder
1. The Mafia killed Monroe to cause a scandal around Robert Kennedy who was investigating organized crime.
2. Extreme conservatives killed Monroe to create a scandal around the too-liberal Kennedys.
3. Extreme conservatives say that pro-Kennedy communists killed Monroe to get her out of the Kennedys' hair and to <u>prevent</u> a scandal.
4. The Kennedys killed her because she was threatening them with a sex scandal.

Steinem. *Marilyn* 133.

The Murder Theories: Triggered by Poor Investigation
"Had Pat Newcomb [Monroe's Press Secretary] or anyone else been permitted to answer questions and deal with the press in a sane fashion, the death of Marilyn Monroe might have been explained. As it was, reporters left the scene feeling that more had been concealed about Marilyn's passing than had been revealed.... In the evil way that gossip spreads, some of the newspapermen began to embroider a story which would fill in the holes."

Hoyt. *Marilyn: The Tragic Venus* 15-16

The Murder Theories: Triggered by the Cover-Up
There was a "cover-up": Monroe's telephone records disappeared — now recovered, they show many calls to Robert Kennedy; the Kennedys denied that Robert was in California the day Monroe died — he was. Overall, the cover-up was poorly conducted. Comment:
"It is ironic that, assuming the death was just the simple and tragic suicide everyone tried to make it appear to be, it was precisely the ham-handed nature of the cover-up that has allowed a hundred conspiracy theories to blossom."

"The Misfit." *Saturday Review* Nov.-Dec. 1985: 68.

Works Cited: A Critical Bibliography

Bryan, C. D. B. "Say Goodbye to the Kennedys." <u>Rolling Stone</u> 5 Dec. 1985: 36+.

Bryan is basically disgusted by Summers' muckraking book, but he admits that Summers' research is probably sound. He sees the whole episode as a moral comment on our times.

Conant, Jennet. "The Star-Crossed Kennedys." <u>Newsweek</u> 14 Oct. 1985: 37.

> A defence of the Kennedys, rejecting all Summers' "evidence." Conant admits, however, that the Kennedys may have "a case to answer."

Hoyt, Edwin P. <u>Marilyn: The Tragic Venus</u>. New York: Duell, 1965.

> A middle-of-the-road study. Hoyt is pro-Kennedy and anti-Hollywood. He lays responsibility for Monroe's death at the door of the Hollywood star system. He had access to none of Summers' new information.

"The Misfit." Rev. of <u>Goddess</u> by Anthony Summers. <u>Saturday Review</u> Nov.–Dec. 1985: 66–70.

> A favorable review of Summers, stressing that Summers wisely leaves many issues open. The murder theories are broadly rejected.

Pepitone, Lena. <u>Marilyn Monroe Confidential</u>. New York: Simon, 1979.

> Pepitone was Monroe's maid in New York for many years. Her book is notable chiefly for its assertion that Monroe *did* have a child.

Steinem, Gloria. <u>Marilyn</u>. New York: Holt, 1986.

> Steinem is more concerned with Monroe as a victim than with a murder hunt. Broadly, she follows Summers' account of the facts.

Summers, Anthony. <u>Goddess</u>. New York: Macmillan, 1985.

> The book that caused all the trouble. Summers is very thorough, very objective, and probably reliable. He implicates the Kennedys in the "coverup" that surrounded Monroe's death, but he accuses them of no wrongdoing apart from a brutal callousness towards a forlorn woman.

2 •

Documenting Your Sources

• Sourcenotes: How to Use Them

The purpose behind the documentation of sources was discussed in Chapter 13: academic advance is impossible unless later researchers can trace earlier findings back to their origins. We must now discuss exactly how each reference to a source is documented. Some years ago, every reference was separately and fully documented. Sometimes the documentation was given at the foot of the page (footnotes); sometimes the documentation was clustered at the end of the essay (endnotes). Since 1984, the *MLA* (Modern Language Association) standard has used what are called *in-text citations*. Less clumsily, they can be called *sourcenotes*. A *sourcenote* is an indication in a text of where a source can be tracked down. If you look again at the research fragment on the show trials, you'll see how these notes work. The first sourcenote occurs at the end of the long quotation from Iakubovich:

CHAPTER SIXTEEN
Presenting Information

> (Medvedev 129)

The next two sourcenotes are similar in form:

> (Medvedev 187)   (Deutscher 371)

A glance at the list of *Works Cited* makes the sources clear: the Medvedev notes refer to the book *Let History Judge* cited in that list, pages 129 and 187; similarly the Deutscher note refers to page 371 of his book *Stalin*. The next sourcenote is even shorter:

> Solzhenitsyn is certainly right in saying that such techniques were available to the interrogators, and that, given the widespread use of physical torture, no moral rules prevented their use (409).

The page is 409, but in what book? The context makes it clear that this is the work by Solzhenitsyn listed in the *Works Cited*, Volume 1 of *The Gulag Archipelago*.

As you can see, the *MLA* system is *minimalist*. The sourcenotes offer the smallest amount of information that identifies the exact source. Anyone who has used the older system will see immediately how much work this saves. The key to the sourcenotes is the Bibliography or list of *Works Cited*. (See Chapter 13 to review how a bibliography is set up.) The examples of sourcenotes given so far cover most references; a handful of refinements covers the rest. Let's now spell out the *MLA* system in detail.

• The *MLA* System for Sourcenotes

A. THE GOLDEN RULE

If the context contains a clear reference to a single title on the list of *Works Cited*, then a page number and nothing more is used as a sourcenote. If the sourcework is not clear from the context, then the sourcenote adds a minimal title. The way in which each sourcenote works in immediate conjunction with the list of *Works Cited* is shown in this example:

> Solzhenitsyn mentions no actual cases (409).

> There seems to be no direct evidence (Solzhenitsyn 409).

> Works Cited
> Solzhenitsyn, Alexander. The Gulag Archipelago. Trans. Thomas Whitney. 3 vols. London: Collins, 1974. Vol. 1.

B. A SOURCE BY AN AUTHOR OF SEVERAL WORKS CITED

The list of *Works Cited* might contain two (or more) works by one author (or by a group of authors)—for example, Solzhenitsyn:

> Solzhenitsyn, Alexander. The Gulag Archipelago. Trans. Thomas Whitney. 3 vols. London:
> Collins, 1974. Vol. 1.
> ---. The Oak and the Calf. Trans. Harry Willets. New York: Harper, 1980.

In this case, a sourcenote such as "(Solzhenitsyn 409)" could refer to either book. Unless the title is absolutely clear from the context, the sourcenote adds a mini-title to the page number:

> Solzhenitsyn discusses the subject in The Gulag Archipelago but offers no direct evidence (409).

> Solzhenitsyn mentions no actual cases (Gulag 409).

> There seems to be no direct evidence (Solzhenitsyn, Gulag 409).

C. A SOURCEWORK BY MORE THAN ONE AUTHOR

A sourcenote referencing a work by two or three authors should name them all (despite the obvious redundancy). In the list of *Works Cited*, for example, this title might occur:

> Burg, David, and George Feifer. Solzhenitsyn. London: Hodder, 1972.

A sourcenote referring to this work might read:

> Solzhenitsyn himself was interrogated by the secret police for four months (Burg and Feifer 78).

If more than three authors are involved, the sourcenote uses the name of the first writer and *et al.* (*and others*), for example:

> Stalin discussed the matter at length with Beria (Jonas et al. 33).

D. A SOURCEWORK IN SEVERAL VOLUMES

A work in several volumes often starts with a new page 1 in each volume. In this case, the volume must be identified by adding a number and a colon to the sourcepage:

> George Orwell's attitude to the show trials was one of honest disgust (1:334).

The list of *Works Cited* shows:

> Orwell, George. The Collected Essays, Journalism and Letters of George Orwell. Ed. Sonia
> Orwell and Ian Angus. 4 vols. London: Secker, 1968.

E. AN ANONYMOUS SOURCEWORK

Many magazine articles have no byline. In the list of *Works Cited*, they are alphabetized under their title, ignoring *A* and *The*.

> "The Politics of Soviet Culture." Economist 2 July 1983: 53.

Unless the title of the article is clear from the context, the sourcenote simply uses a short title, usually the word under which the article is alphabetized:

> An article in The Economist, "The Politics of Soviet Culture," makes it clear that plays about
> the Stalin years are sometimes staged in Moscow.

> Despite official policy, Moscow theaters occasionally present plays on the Stalin years ("Politics").

A sourcenote referring to an anonymous *book* would similarly use a short title.

F. A CLUSTER OF REFERENCES TO SEVERAL SOURCEWORKS

When the same point is made by several writers, references can be clustered into a single sourcenote:

> Most commentators agree that torture alone would not have secured the necessary
> confessions (Conquest 197; Deutscher 371–372; Medvedev 187).

G. MATERIAL FROM A SECONDARY SOURCE

If one of your writers quotes from a source inaccessible to you, the list of *Works Cited* simply gives the work where you found the quotation. The reference to the primary source occurs in the essay itself. For example, Medvedev in *Let History Judge* makes frequent reference to the published transcripts of the show trials. If you cannot find a copy of the transcripts but wish to quote them "secondhand" from Medvedev, the procedure is simple. The list of *Works Cited* shows where *you* found the material, the book by Medvedev. The essay itself contains a sourcenote referring to Medvedev, *not* to the original source. The abbreviation *qtd* means *quoted*:

> Bukharin did, in fact, try to defend himself at his trial. The transcripts show him defiantly
> calling other witnesses liars (qtd. in Medvedev: 177).

H. OTHER SYSTEMS

Other systems for sourcenoting exist. The *APA* (American Psychological Association) standard, for example, uses the name of the author and the *year* of the publication, adding page numbers only when they are of special importance. Using this system, two specimen sentences from the research fragment on the show trials would run:

> Bukharin, the leading intellectual of the Bolshevik party, apparently began to confess only when his wife and newborn son were threatened (Medvedev 1972).

> Isaac Deutscher (1966: 371) in his biography of Stalin says that stories of drugs and hypnosis "may be safely dismissed."

The list of *Works Cited* is again the key to identifying the source. Unfortunately, space prohibits a detailed description of the alternative systems. As with the bibliography, you should consult the manual issued by the appropriate body for your discipline. There is a list of manuals in Chapter 13.

Concept Review

Documenting Sources

Look again at your research fragment on the death of Marilyn Monroe. Add to it the necessary sourcenotes.

• Sourcenotes: When to Use Them

An essay based on library research inevitably contains many direct quotations. It also contains facts and figures that you gleaned from your sources and arguments that appealed to you during your reading. All three kinds of material should be documented with sourcenotes. As a rule of thumb, *if you use material from a notecard, you should add a sourcenote.*

The only kinds of "borrowed" materials that require no sourcenotes are the dates of public events or facts and figures that are in the "public domain." It is usually obvious what these are.

A word of caution. If you turn in an essay in which the sources are poorly documented, you may be accused of *plagiarism. Plagiarism* is simply stealing other people's ideas and passing them off as your own. The penalties vary—in some institutions, expulsion is the rule. What is called "plagiarism" is usually just laziness: the student can't be bothered with the intricacies of sourcenoting. Deliberate plagiarism also occurs. For the reader, it is impossible to tell the two types apart, so the lazy suffer the same fate as the wicked. The sad thing about deliberate plagiarism is that it is *pointless*—nobody expects the student researcher to come up with new information or brilliant new theories. Your task as writer is to think through the material and to reach a personal conclusion about it; there is no reason to disguise your sources or to pretend that you knew it all from the start.

Concept Review

Sourcenote or no Sourcenote?

Read the eight facts below. They all came from (or were verified in) reference books, but not all of them require a sourcenote. Which do and which don't?

1. In Sweden the currency is the krona; there are 100 öre to one krona.

2. It is predicted that the krona will rise sharply against the dollar.

3. John Pierpoint Morgan died in 1913.

4. In his spare time, J. P. Morgan used to go into empty churches and sing hymns in solitude.

5. Stalin's real name was Yossif Vissarionovich Djugashvili.

6. Stalin's language betrays an astonishing barrenness of imagination, one that is rare even among politicians.

7. The Dead Sea is 1,286 feet below sea level.

8. The salts in the Dead Sea, including magnesium chloride, calcium chloride and magnesium bromide, are Israel's most important mineral resources.

• The Informative Endnote

Some writers keep up a running commentary on their own work in the form of endnotes (or footnotes). In some cases the endnotes are longer than the main text. The effect for the reader is somewhat fidgety. As a general rule, it's better to include in the essay what is important and to leave out the rest. Sometimes, however, you may wish to avoid cluttering your main line of argument with counterarguments, yet you feel the counterarguments should be heard. In this case, or when anything similar occurs, an endnote is appropriate. For the convenience of the typist, it is easier to cluster all the notes as *endnotes* at the end of the essay, just before the list of *Works Cited*. For the convenience of the reader, notes are more accessible as *footnotes* at the bottom of each page. If in doubt, find out what your instructor prefers. In a research paper, endnotes are numbered consecutively, starting with 1. The comment on Koestler in the research fragment above, for example, might be annotated in this way:

> Oddly enough, it is a novel rather than a history book that is generally accepted as getting the psychology right.[1] Arthur Koestler, author of Darkness at Noon, was himself twice imprisoned by the Fascists.[2]

Endnotes

[1] Conquest, while accepting Koestler's explanation, points out that Koestler himself does not claim any general significance for Rubashov's case (189).

[2] Koestler's personal experiences are fictionalized in his novel Arrival and Departure.

3 •
Writing About Figures

• Presenting Figures

If field research was part of your research project, then you will have compiled some statistics of your own. Presenting these statistics to the reader is no easy task. Most readers hate figures, probably because human memories have such a tiny space allocated for short-term storage of figures: some people have to look twice at a telephone number while dialing it! For that reason, a wise writer avoids using figures in a text wherever possible. A case in point: this short discussion of how to choose a cheap printer is the result of simple but careful research. The presentation is a disaster.

CHOOSING A CHEAP LETTER-QUALITY PRINTER

Many cheap letter-quality printers are available today for under $1,000. It is sometimes possible to find one costing only $600, or even $500. In purchasing such a printer, many factors must be considered. Let's compare four printers in the hope that one will be suitable for you.

Speed is an important factor in choosing a printer. The Messenger III from Smith-Corona prints at only 10 characters per second (cps), the Transtar 130 or a Star Powertype at 18 cps, while the Brother HR 25 hits 23 cps. Faster speeds are out of our price range.

Another factor is pitch. All machines today have 10, 12, or 15 pitch capability. As to proportional spacing, all four printers except the Smith-Corona offer this facility. (Pitch is the ability of a printer to print letters of large, medium or small width.)

Will you want to print on paper 16.5 inches wide? If so, the HR 25 or the 130 may be your choice. The Messenger III allows only 12 inches, while the Powertype is restricted to a measly 8.5 inches.

What about cost? Cheapest is the Powertype at $499; most expensive, the Brother at $995. In between lie the Transtar at $699 and the Memory III at $769.

All you have to do now is decide what features you want, and find the machine that suits your pocket.

What went wrong? Four common problems have spoiled this piece.

A. FAILURE OF READERSHIP ANALYSIS

Every piece is written with a target reader in mind: in this case the target was, presumably, a novice who has never owned a printer before. Readership analysis (see Chapter 9 for a review) would show that the novice needs a *definition* of the technical terms. What is "pitch," for example? Further, the novice cannot assess the *significance* of the concepts. Is 10 characters per second adequate for typing a letter or a term paper? How often and for what purposes does one need a printer that takes paper wider than 8½ inches? Insensitivity to the needs of the reader is fatal.

B. LACK OF DISCUSSION OF THE STUDY DESIGN

Whenever figures are presented, the reader needs to know where the figures came from and why these figures in particular are being discussed—in a word, the *study design*. In the present case, are the figures manufacturer's claims, or has the writer verified them? Are the prices those of a discount warehouse or a swank specialist? Another problem: Why have *these* four printers been chosen for discussion? Are the chosen criteria specially significant for a *cheap* printer? And so on. Without this kind of background information, the figures themselves are close to useless.

C. INCONSISTENT NAMING

Consistent naming is important in any study: if the names change, the reader may fail to realize that the object itself has stayed the same. This is particularly important in discussing figures; figures are easily forgotten—to keep them in mind, they must be securely attached to an unforgettable label. One example from our case: the Smith-Corona Messenger III is sometimes called the *Smith-Corona* and sometimes the *Messenger III*. This is not "reader-friendly."

D. EXCESSIVE USE OF FIGURES IN THE TEXT

A text sprinkled with figures quickly becomes unreadable. In general, figures should be consolidated in a table. The text itself should cite only the figures that have some special significance. The golden rule: "If you don't want a reader to remember a figure, don't use it." In the case above, a simple table would solve the problem. Such a table would list choices against criteria. In this case:

The four machines: Brother HR II, Messenger III, Star Powertype, Transtar 130
The five criteria: Speed, pitch, proportional spacing, width, price

The key criterion (price in this case) generally goes on the right; the favored alternative (the Transtar 130) at the bottom. The table might look like this:

	SPEED	PITCH	PROPORTIONAL SPACING	WIDTH	PRICE
Brother HR 25	23 cps	10,12,15	Yes	16.5	$995
Messenger III	10 cps	10,12,15	No	12	$769
Star Powertype	18 cps	10,12,15	Yes	8.5	$499
Transtar 130	18 cps	10,12,15	Yes	16.5	$699

The writer can now concentrate on the matter in hand: explaining to a novice how to choose a suitable printer.

Review Assignment

The Text and the Table

Provide a short text to accompany the table. Your text should avoid the four problems discussed above.

• Arguing from Figures

Statistics can be massaged to show virtually anything. In fact, the *same* figures can be used to make exactly *opposite* cases. The devil's advocate will show us how this is done. Two dirty tricks are necessary: *omission* and *selection*. What must be omitted? The complete set of figures: never allow the reader to see a table of the figures, or your interpretation may be challenged. What must be selected? Anything that favors your case. Once you grasp these two principles of unfair argument, becoming a clever manipulator of the truth is simply a matter of practice.

Review Assignment

What the Figures Show

In the two cases below, you are provided with a complete set of figures. Your assignment is to use the figures to argue two exactly opposite cases. The *real* purpose behind this is not to corrupt your standards of statistical demonstration but to alert you to the twists and turns that statistical argument can take. The honest commentator always presents the full table; that excludes any possible accusation of fraud.

Case 1: Seat-Belt Usage

At your place of work, you are in charge of a program to encourage seat-belt use by employees. This program has been running for a year. Each day you have monitored seat-belt use in vehicles leaving the parking lot between 4:00 p.m. and 5:00 p.m. The following quarterly figures show the mean average seat-belt use per day.

	ONE PERSON IN CAR		MORE THAN ONE PERSON IN CAR			
	Buckled	*Unbuckled*	*Only Driver Buckled*	*Only Others Buckled*	*All Buckled*	*None Buckled*
Jan.–Mar. 87	60	40	15	10	45	30
Apr.–Jun. 87	65	35	17	13	45	25
Jul.–Sep. 87	70	30	20	15	45	20
Oct.–Dec. 87	60	40	20	20	45	15

Conclusion 1: You are heartily sick of counting seat-belt users, and you wish to prove that the program is no longer needed. Write a short report recommending that the program be discontinued on the grounds of its success.

Conclusion 2: You rather enjoy conducting this program: it's interesting and gets you out of the office. Write a short report recommending the continuance of the program on the grounds that it has not yet achieved its goals.

Case 2: Quality Control

Grobucket Coolers Incorporated makes large air-conditioning units. The management has believed for some years that drug use by factory workers causes a high rate of rejects on the production line. On January 1, 1987, a strict policy forbidding the use of drugs or alcohol during the working day was introduced. Production line figures for rejects for 1986 and 1987 have been collected, as well as figures for the month of June in each year:

	TOTAL UNITS PRODUCED	PASSED	FAILED FOR ONE DEFECT	FAILED FOR MORE THAN ONE DEFECT
Total 1986	80,000	40%	50%	10%
Total 1987	100,000	50%	15%	35%
June 1986	8,000	50%	14%	36%
June 1987	9,000	45%	40%	15%

Conclusion 1: You have long been a crusader for a "drug-free workplace." Write a short report establishing that the management's anti-drug campaign has definitely paid off.

Conclusion 2: You feel that low-key, undemanding work on a production line is not really influenced by drug use. Write a short report establishing that the management's anti-drug campaign has achieved nothing.

4 •

The Use of a Sparring Partner

In evaluating your sources, you may come across material that is evident nonsense. Don't automatically discard such material; it may help you make your point negatively—that is, by means of a destructive rebuttal. In some cases, the bulk of a research paper is in this negative mode: for example, if you're researching the authorship of "Shakespeare's" plays, it's difficult to establish that Shakespeare actually wrote them; a better technique is to show that the case for any other candidate is blatantly ridiculous. Mounting a destructive attack depends in part on your having a "killer instinct." There are, however, certain guidelines that may help when you need to "fix" an opponent.

Health Warning.   Although the three following texts are taken from historical writings (the most recent is nearly a half-century old), you may find parts of them offensive. It must be stressed that the passages are offered as targets for attack. Regrettably such things are still published in our society. One instinctive reaction is to turn away in disgust. Another is to avoid all comment because comment, however rejective, simply gains publicity for fanatical viewpoints. A third reaction is to write a counterblast. If you decide on this latter course, how do you set to work?

• A Case: The Civilian Atomic Energy Control Commission

Anti-Semitic writing was not uncommon in America before the Second World War. In Hemingway's novels, for example, his denigratory references to Jews make readers today wince and wonder how they "got through." More systematic was Henry Ford's violently anti-Semitic newspaper, the *Dearborn Independent*, with its 700,000 circulation. The headlines give the flavor: "Jewish Gamblers Corrupt American Baseball," "Jewish Jazz Becomes Our National Music," and so on. Since the Second World War and the exposure of the holocaust, social attitudes to bigotry and prejudice have changed. Nevertheless, in 1946, when the facts of the holocaust were known, M. R. Allen published this piece in Salt Lake City. The situation that triggered Allen's piece was the formation just after the war of the *Civilian Atomic Energy Control Commission*. Henry Wallace, President Truman's ultra-liberal Secretary of Commerce, recommended David Lilienthal to head this commission.

> The first choice of pro-Russian liberal, Henry A. Wallace, for head of our Civilian Atomic Energy Control Commission was the Jew, David Lilienthal, and he so recommended to Mr. Truman; who very obligingly appointed Mr. Lilienthal together with two other Jews, and two non-Jews. Now isn't that just dandy? Especially since it was Jews, both in the U.S. and otherwise, who financed the Bolshevik Revolution in Russia, and whose first love is Russia.
>
> Russia's German stooge-scientists in Germany are now turning out about 300 rocket planes per month (as fast or faster than anything we have): there is a city of 400,000 in Russia (well blocked off and top-drawer secret), probably somewhere in the vast stretches of Siberia-Asia, called Atomgrad, where atom bombs are being manufactured. In the meantime, Russia's Bolshevik leaders stall around in the U.N. until they have had time to manufacture a sufficient stockpile of these bombs to blot out American cities.
>
> Jews continually scream that they are being persecuted and abused: yet here on what is said to be the most important commission in the world, the Jews are three to two, in what is supposed to be a Christian non-Jew nation. This same sort of thing prevails throughout our government.
>
> One grants that there are some noble, fearless, unselfish Jews . . .

but too many of the Jews work hand-in-glove with Communism: inciting the Negroes against the Whites: fomenting trouble and strikes among the labor unions. They work for the Sanhedrin; for the Kehillah: for a foreign state: for their own selfish interests: for aid in smuggling 60,000 illegal refugees, mostly Russian-Communist-Jews, into this country every month: this in addition to the number already coming in under quota. This situation is appallingly serious, and threatens the jobs, security, rights, liberty, homes, and lives of every genuine American. Already we have reaped a vicious crop of paralyzing strikes, due largely to this foreign element in labor unions. Fortunately, some of the unions are beginning to wake up, and rid themselves of this menace.

The people's safety and security is fast disappearing in the United States! If we keep on importing more revolutionists from Europe and Asia, and placing our welfare and security at home in the hands of these people, the honest, decent, native Christian American will have no rights in his own country. If you think this is just propaganda, you had better wake up and get hep to what is going on in America, not abroad. Write your Congressmen and Senators against importing any more foreigners until we have made this country safe for Americans: also write them objecting to the personnel of the Atomic Energy Commission.

M. R. Allen
From *Judaic-Communism Versus Christian Americanism: A
Pro-American Publication*

The first task is to find out in detail what is *wrong* with Allen's piece. This means going through his text and raising objections. These objections will draw heavily on the analysis of logical errors presented in Chapter 8, Making a Case, and in Chapter 14, Evaluating Sources.

A list of objections does not constitute a rebuttal. If you simply write your way through the list, your piece will be incoherent. "I object to this . . . and this . . . and this . . . and . . . ." A stronger technique is to classify your objections according to the type of error Allen makes. If you study the list of error labels, you'll see that Allen specializes in four types:

(a) Argument based on ignorance (that is, on unverifiable information)—Allen presents facts and figures we have no way of disproving.

(b) Argument based on fear—he tries to frighten the reader into believing what he says.

(c) Argument based on prejudice—he trades on our (supposed) prejudices against Jews and Russians.

(d) The invalid syllogism—one syllogistic argument is invalid; one is based on a false premise.

Clustering your objections under the four types of error involved, gives your rebuttal a fair degree of coherence. A simple game plan, then, is as follows:

1. Rebuttal of arguments based on uncheckable facts

2. Rebuttal of bent syllogisms

3. Rebuttal of arguments based on fear

4. Rebuttal of arguments based on prejudice

The order of the four sections is not arbitrary, of course. Allen's attempt to whip up prejudice is his worst offense, so prejudice is kept until last. His unscrupulous use of fears is little better; it takes Slot 3. At the other end of the scale, the uncheckable facts are the most glaring, but the least offensive, of the errors; they can go first. The bent syllogisms drop neatly into the second slot.

REMARK	WHY I DON'T LIKE IT	ERROR LABEL
Truman has made three Jewish appointments to the Commission.	The word *Jew* denotes a person's religion. It is not a put-down word.	Argument based on prejudice
Jews financed the Bolshevik Revolution.	Untrue. Classic use of the scare-word Bolshevik.	Argument based on prejudice
The first love of the Jews is Russia.	Nonsense. Use of the scare-word *Russia* to discredit all Jews.	Prejudice and false syllogism
Russia's stooge-Germans are making 300 rocket planes a month.	What are rocket planes? And how does he know?	Argument based on ignorance
Atomgrad's bombs will blot out American cities.	How does he know? He is trying to scare us.	Arguments based on fear and ignorance.
Jews scream about persecution.	He wrote this in 1946!!	Argument based on prejudice
America is a Christian, non-Jew nation, so Jews cannot be good Americans.	Constitutionally, it is *not*. The syllogism is based on false premises.	Syllogism based on false premises
Jews incite Negroes against whites, cause strikes, and so on.	Fear. Blame the Jews for everything the reader fears.	Argument based on fear
60,000 illegal refugees enter each month.	How does he know?	Argument based on ignorance
Jobs, security, rights, homes, lives are threatened.	Fear. He's trying for mob hysteria.	Argument based on fear
The honest, decent, native, Christian American is threatened.	Native Americans are Indians. Fear.	Argument based on fear

The writing style for a rebuttal depends on the readership. To simplify matters, this rebuttal simply addresses Allen's original readers, using his own sleeve-tugging style.

Unselfish love of one's country is a great virtue. M. R. Allen's Pro-American Publication tells us that his patriotic heart is in the right place. Whether the same can be said for his intellect is another question. Mr. Allen offers us some remarkable information. He has discovered a city of 400,000 inhabitants in Siberia named Atomgrad ("top-drawer secret," he says) where atom bombs are stockpiled for use against America. Mr. Allen also has access to Soviet production figures for "rocket planes," whatever these fearful weapons are: 300 a month. In his zeal for the public good, the intrepid Mr. Allen has also penetrated the illegal immigration racket; the exactness of his figures suggests he has got close to the gangsters who run it. A dangerous business—but not as dangerous as betraying the plans of the "Sanhedrin" and the "Kehillah" to the world. We should be grateful to Mr. Allen for so fearlessly exposing these dreadful facts. Or are they facts? My question to Mr. Allen is this: how did you discover all this "information"? Or are you just making it up? What sources of information are open to you that are not open to the U.S. government?

But let's grant Mr. Allen his "facts"; let's pretend to believe him. What follows? Mr. Allen uses some pretty strange arguments. He tells us that some Jews
are known to have supported the Bolsheviks. True enough. From that he deduces that all Jews
are communists. Think about it. We also know that some non-Jews
are communists—Lenin, Stalin and Mao Tse-tung, to name only three. If we apply Mr. Allen's logic, we must deduce that all non-Jews
are communists. In that case, even Mr. Allen himself must be a Red. Or another example. America, he says, is a Christian nation, so non-Christians cannot be true Americans. Oddly for such a patriot, Mr. Allen has forgotten that the First Amendment to the Constitution separates church and state. Go back to school, Mr. Allen, and learn to think straight.

Let's allow that Mr. Allen is a patriotic (if misguided) American; his right to be called a Christian, however, is more doubtful. In his article he plays mercilessly on our fears, threatening our jobs, our homes, and our lives; he believes he can terrorize us into losing all sense of justice. Can Mr. Allen, so well-informed as he claims to be on secret matters, have overlooked the extermination of millions of people of Christ's own race? Can he have looked at the pictures of the death camps and still accuse the victims of "continually screaming that they are being persecuted"? Such murderous spite is not the act of a Christian.

Mr. Allen uses lies to inflame us with hatred and terror. He urges us to persecute a minority to the point of extermination. In fact, he is seeking to turn America into a carbon copy of Hitler's Germany. Mr. Allen: in a free country where people speak out against your kind of perverted bigotry, you will not succeed.

Review Assignment

Writing a Rebuttal

The two passages below are both objectionable in different ways. Using the technique illustrated above, try writing a destructive rebuttal of one of them. In choosing a style, either address the same audience as the original writer, or write the rebuttal within the framework of an academic essay.

A. Women

These paragraphs are from a much longer essay. Schopenhauer's views are so extreme that they may cause laughter or bewilderment rather than anger. His opinions stand, however, in a long tradition to which even saints have contributed. Schopenhauer was a German philosopher, the most important of the so-called pessimistic school.

> One need only look at a woman's shape to discover that she is not intended for either too
> much mental or too much physical work. She pays the debt of life not by what she does but by

what she suffers—by the pains of child-bearing, care for the child, and by subjection to man, to whom she should be a patient and cheerful companion. The greatest sorrows and joys or great exhibition of strength are not assigned to her; her life should flow more quietly, more gently, and less obtrusively than man's, without her being essentially happier or unhappier.

Women are directly adapted to act as the nurses and educators of our early childhood, for the simple reason that they themselves are childish, foolish, and short-sighted—in a word, are big children all their lives, something intermediate between the child and the man, who is a man in the strict sense of the word. Consider how a young girl will toy day after day with a child, dance with it and sing to it; and then consider what a man, with the very best intentions in the world, could do in her place.

With girls, Nature has had in view what is called in a dramatic sense a "striking effect," for she endows them for a few years with a richness of beauty and a fulness of charm at the expense of the rest of their lives; so that they may during these years ensnare the fantasy of a man to such a degree as to make him rush into taking the honorable care of them, in some kind of form, for a lifetime—a step which would not seem sufficiently justified if he only considered the matter. Accordingly, Nature has furnished woman, as she has the rest of her creatures, with the weapons and implements necessary for the protection of her existence and for just the length of time that they will be of service to her; so that Nature has proceeded here with her usual economy. Just as the female ant after coition loses her wings, which then become superfluous, nay, dangerous for breeding purposes, so for the most part does a woman lose her beauty after giving birth to one or two children; and probably for the same reasons. . . . Moreover, she is intellectually short-sighted, for although her intuitive understanding quickly perceives what is near to her, on the other hand her circle of vision is limited and does not embrace anything that is remote; hence everything that is absent or past, or in the future, affects women in a less degree than men. This is why they have greater inclination for extravagance, which sometimes borders on madness. Women in their hearts think that men are intended to earn money so that they may spend it, if possible during their husband's lifetime, but at any rate after his death.

As soon as he has given them his earnings on which to keep house they are strengthened in this belief. Although all this entails many disadvantages, yet it has this advantage—that a woman lives more in the present than a man, and that she enjoys it more keenly if it is at all bearable. This is the origin of that cheerfulness which is peculiar to woman and makes her fit to divert man, and in case of need, to console him when he is weighed down by cares.

It is only the man whose intellect is clouded by his sexual instinct that could give that stunted, narrow-shouldered, broad-hipped, and short-legged race the name of *the fair sex*; for the entire beauty of the sex is based on this instinct. One would be more justified in calling them the *unaesthetic sex* than the beautiful. Neither for music, nor for poetry, nor for fine art have they any real or true sense and susceptibility, and it is mere mockery on their part, in their desire to please, if they affect any such thing.

Nothing different can be expected of women if it is borne in mind that the most eminent of the whole sex have never accomplished anything in the fine arts that is really great, genuine, and original, or given to the world any kind of work of permanent value. This is most striking in regard to painting, the technique of which is as much within their reach as within ours; this is why they pursue it so industriously. Still, they have not a single great painting to show, for the simple reason that they lack that objectivity of mind which is precisely what is so directly necessary in painting. They always stick to what is subjective. They are the *sexus sequior*, the second sex in every respect.

Artur Schopenhauer
From *On Women*

2. Non-Nordics

In many German universities during the Hitler era, there was a Department of Race Research. These departments originally studied the tribal migrations of early history. Later they swung over to propaganda, "proving" the superiority of the Nordic/Aryan race. The passage offered here is from a book by Professor Hermann Gauch, *New Principles for the Study of Race*.

> In non-Nordics, the teeth, corresponding to the snout-like narrowness of the upper jaw, stand at a more oblique angle than in animals. The grinding motion of chewing in Nordics allows mastication to take place with the mouth closed, whereas men of other races are inclined to make the same smacking noise as animals. . . .
>
> The Nordic mouth has further superiorities. Just as the color red has a stirring effect, the bright red mouth of Nordics attracts and provokes kisses and courtship. The Nordic mouth is kiss-capable. On the other hand, the non-Nordic's broad, thick-lipped mouth together with his wide-dilated nostrils displays sensual eagerness, a false and malicious sneering expression and a dipping movement indicative of voluptuous self-indulgence.
>
> Talking with the aid of hands and feet is characteristic of non-Nordics, whereas the Nordic man stands calmly, often enough with his hands in his pockets.
>
> Generally speaking, the Nordic race alone can emit sounds of untroubled clearness, whereas among non-Nordics the pronunciation is impure, the individual sounds are more confused and like the noises made by animals, such as barking, sniffing, snoring, squeaking. . . . That birds can learn to talk better than other animals is explained by the fact that their mouths are Nordic in structure—that is to say, high, narrow, and short-tongued. The shape of the Nordic gum allows a superior movement of the tongue, which is the reason why Nordic talking and singing are fuller. . . . .
>
> If non-Nordics are more closely allied to monkeys and apes than to Nordics, why is it possible for them to mate with Nordics and not with apes? The answer is this: it has not been proved that non-Nordics cannot mate with apes.
>
> Hermann Gauch
> From *New Principles for the Study of Race*

• Summary

This chapter has dealt with four special techniques that you should add to your repertoire before writing up the results of your researches.

1. **Achieving an Integrated Style.** Quotations and references must be worked into a coherent whole: the writer must be "visible" at all times, steering the paper in the direction of its thesis statement.

2. **Documenting Sources.** Every direct quotation or indirect reference to a source must be documented. This last-minute chore has been greatly simplified by the new *MLA* system.

3. **Writing from Figures.** Two skills are needed when figures are an important component of your research: you must present the figures clearly, and you must know how to use them in developing your argument.

4. **Using a Sparring Partner.** If a point is best made negatively (or if it can be made only by refuting a wrong-headed view), then a rebuttal is in order. A rebuttal demands a close logical analysis of the target piece; classifying the logical errors you discover often provides a coherent structure for your attack.

Conclusion—A Research Paper

The cover story in the November 1986 issue of *Writer's Digest* was entitled *How to Write Fast*. The magazine made high claims for the article: "Double—or even triple—your writing speed and productivity by following these easy steps . . . ." In her article, Lisa Collier Cool briefed her readers on some tactics that are also suggested in this book: don't get hung up on the opening paragraph; write fast while the ideas are flowing, and correct details later; leave the first draft for a while before reviewing; and so on. The January issue of *Writer's Digest* printed a letter by Isaac Asimov, the incredibly prolific writer of, among other things, science fiction. The letter offers a valuable caution:

FAST TALK

I'm afraid that almost everything Lisa Collier Cool advises ("How to Write Fast," Nov.), I don't do—but that's all right. I have the feeling that there are as many systems for fast writing as there are fast writers. I would advise all people who want to be fast writers to work out a system of their own. What works very successfully for someone else may not work for them at all.

Isaac Asimov
New York City

Asimov is right—and not just about *fast* writing. For this reason, a "model paper" may be more helpful to some students that good advice. The "model paper" is a goal: shoot for it in your own way. In that spirit, the following essay is presented to you. Commentary in the margin does not concern writing technique so much as it does the mechanics of presentation.

The essay itself is straightforward and businesslike, perhaps even hard-nosed in places. It lacks the graces of fine writing and the thoughtful quality that might be appropriate in a more philosophical context. These are not weaknesses; the information and the way it is presented are well targeted for the context: a freshman business course. In fact, two business professors who graded the essay both gave it a solid *A*. But remember: other contexts, other styles.

There is no generally agreed-upon format for presenting a research paper. Rather than review the suggestions in countless reference books, a standard format has been chosen for Robert Di Michiel's paper: the format suggested in the *MLA Handbook for Writers of Research Papers*. Like the *MLA* standard for bibliographies and sourcenotes, this format is minimalist: it requires no title page and no outline or abstract; it specifies a narrow one-inch margin on all sides. The title is not underlined. Typing is not a must. If the paper is typed, hand-entered corrections (neat and occasional) are allowed. The paper is not submitted in a folder of any kind but is simply held together with a single paper clip. The format is functional but by no means glamorous, and it ignores the embellishments possible with a word processor and printer. Naturally you should confirm with your instructor the format your own paper should use.

1

Robert Di Michiel

Dr. Agnes Cornello

BMGT 110

February 3, 1988.

The Productive Office:
A Controlled Environment

Competitiveness depends on productivity: the output generated for every dollar invested. With a factory, productivity is easy to measure. If a factory produces 9 million widgets instead of 6 million for the same investment, then productivity has obviously risen. Office work is not so easy to quantify. If 200 office workers produce 1,000 reports per year, are they necessarily more productive if they write 1,500 reports? Is a manager who makes 50 decisions a week more productive than one who makes 40? Obviously 40 right decisions are worth far more than 50 wrong ones. With office work, quality is usually more important than quantity.

Quality is the problem this paper addresses: what makes an office more efficient? What makes it a pleasant and motivating place to work? Researchers into office design have four main concerns: office layout, color and lighting, noise, and the design of equipment. As an office worker myself, I have a personal interest in each of these subjects. Accordingly I have examined each of them in theory and - - by means of an informal office survey - - in practice.

The formal study of ergonomics was launched in 1947 at Johns Hopkins University (Stockton 16). What is "ergonomics"? In an article in World Health in 1974, Martti Karvonen explained ergonomics as:

> . . . applied science that combines biomedical and engineering expertise. It helps define methods of work, tools and the environment to fit man's structure, function and ability. Its purpose is to reduce fatigue and wear and tear of the worker (30).

Ergonomics has applications wherever workers and machines come into contact: a lathe, the controls of an automobile, even high-legibility street signs should all be designed to "reduce fatigue and wear and tear of the worker." Richard Stockton, in an important article on office ergonomics, stresses that investment in good design pays off handsomely in increased productivity (33–34). This increased productivity arises from lower stress levels, lower absenteeism, and lower employee turnover, as Judy Linscott points out in an article in the New York Daily News (25).

Offices are laid out in two ways: the traditional pattern with dozens of small rooms where most workers enjoy a degree of privacy, and the modern, so-called "landscape" office. This is the single, open office where perhaps 100 people work in one room. In 1980, some 30% of office space in the United States was landscaped; by 1990, estimates put the figure between 60% and 80% (Kallaus and Keeling 305). Because it is the wave of the future, this paper will concentrate exclusively on the landscape office.

Left margin annotations:

The name of the writer, instructor, and course, and the date of submission are widely spaced at the left margin.

There is *no outline*.

Introduction (The problem of assessing productivity in the office is stated.)

The opening section of six paragraphs indicates the design of the paper; key terms such as *ergonomics* and *landscape* are defined; the problems addressed by the paper are spelled out.

A long quotation is indented

Stockton is identified.

This reference runs from p. 33 onto p. 34.

Figures over 10 are given as figures. Percentages use the symbol %.

Right margin annotations:

The first page is simply numbered top right.

The title is centered and followed by three empty lines.

All paragraphs, even those that follow a heading, are indented five spaces.

The work is double spaced.

The sourcenote uses the writer's name and page number.

The sourcenote gives only the page, since the work is easy to identify from the name *Karvonen*.

A book by two authors uses both names.

R. Di Michiel 2

A comment can be made "marginal" by use of parentheses.	The landscape office has problems. (Calling 20,000 square feet of steel and concrete a "landscape" already suggests what they might be.) The first problem is overcrowding. Let us say an office is designed to hold 80 people. When management wishes to take on more employees, it often seems cheaper to cram another 15 into a landscape environment than to rent more office space. In fact, it is not cheaper: productivity inevitably sags in overcrowded conditions, a point stressed by Judy Klein in her authoritative The Office Book (40). Nevertheless, many landscape offices are	The second and later pages have the writer's name and the page number top right.

A comment is shifted right out of the main text via an "endnote." The number 1 is raised half a line.

The introduction summarized.

seriously overcrowded.[1]

The second problem of the landscape office is its tendency to become impersonal. Franklin Becker and James Riggs in two book-length studies of office environments agree that productive employees always identify themselves with their place of work; they decorate it with plants, photographs and works of art (Becker 201, Riggs 276). The landscape office, especially when it is overcrowded, can be disastrously lacking in these personal touches: there is nowhere to stand a plant and nowhere to hang a picture.

Where two sourcenotes are clustered, they are separated by a comma.

This is the crux of the problem: humanizing the landscape office. How can it be done?

A section heading is not underlined or capitalized.

Office Layout

Laufer is identified.

An office is most productive when the workers see themselves as a team - - yet deprivation of human contact and a sense of alienation are extremely common in the modern office (Riggs 299). In theory, the landscape office should offer more personal contact than the old honeycomb of personal offices. What has gone wrong? Arthur Laufer in his extremely practical book, Operations Management, stresses that the designer of a landscape office should search out small groups of workers who "belong together." Their desks should be clustered together to give them a sense of group identity. Free space should then open up around the group to give them a sense of territory (252). Further, the work-flow should be analyzed. It should be possible for each group to pass on completed work to the group "just across the gangway" (249,255). Planning a rational work-flow from small group to small group can be difficult - - even moving the furniture into trial positions involves backbreaking labor. On the other hand, as James Riggs points out in the latest update of his book, Production Systems, computers are ideally suited to this kind of planning (289). The computer can create alternative plans without the need to move heavy furniture around a crowded space. If the plan allows any spare space, this can be creatively used as a rest area. Rest areas give the workers two places within the office where they can "feel at home."

Riggs is more closely identified.

This is a double sourcenote to two pages of the same book.

The discussion so far is summarized (pointed).

The layout of an office deserves the same intensity of thought that is devoted to a production line - - even though the end product of an office is ideas and not merchandise. In the best designed landscape offices, there is human contact and a sense of belonging: there is also high productivity.

The shift from library research to field research is strongly labeled. (The field research enlivens the paper considerably.)

During my reading, I became curious as to how many offices put the ideas of such theoreticians as Riggs into practice. I work in an office block of ten floors, all of them landscaped. On each floor, I asked workers about the small-group concept and about the pattern of work-flow. In only two offices (both recently redesigned) did the workers even understand the question. The others, my own office included, seem to have grown at random. If my office block is typical, then the business world is not much concerned with office design.

The switch from third person to first person is acceptable for making personal comment. If you mean I, say I.

R. Di Michiel 3

Color and the Office

Color creates mood, and mood directly influences productivity. Kallaus and Keeling in a book based on extensive research devote a whole section to the do's and don't's of color. The most obvious colors to avoid are "institutional" grays and greens: these colors are seldom used in the home, and they should be avoided in the office, too. White, on the other hand, is a popular color domestically: even so, it is inappropriate in the office. White contributes to glare, a serious problem in the automated office where there are many VDT's (visual display terminals). White in the office also creates a sterile, even a harsh atmosphere, especially in conjunction with the cold lines of modern office equipment (322). Violently stimulating colors such as brilliant red or orange seem to create higher stress levels and should therefore be avoided. The ideal colors are subdued. Sunlight is the major factor in deciding the right shades. In a sunny office, cooler shades, such as green, blue, or a combination of green and yellow, are recommended. If there is no sunshine, golden yellow, peach, or tan generate a feeling of warmth (332). It is important that the colors chosen for the walls, the ceiling, the carpet, even for the furniture, are coordinated. Poorly matched colors create a fidgety, tense, unproductive atmosphere.

There is some evidence that large, decorative paintings boost morale and decrease boredom. If the style or the subject matter of the paintings is too stimulating, however, it can induce stress ("Paintings" 48).

None of these recommendations goes beyond common sense and the rudiments of interior decoration. My observations "in the field" showed serious deficiencies, however. Two of the ten offices I surveyed were decorated in prison green and one in asylum gray. Two were glaring white - - even the floor-tiles were white. In three offices I could detect no color scheme of any sort: every niche, every column, every wall was "doing its own thing." Unfortunately my office was one of these. The two recently designed offices were different: they created an immediate impression of harmony and relaxation. The importance of color had never struck me before; nor apparently had it occurred to the managers of eight of the companies in our building.

Office Lighting

Adequate lighting is essential to a feeling of well-being. This point is heavily stressed in Joel Makower's authoritative study, Office Hazards (77). Eyestrain results from insufficient lighting or from glare, and eyestrain leads quickly to fatigue or even depression (Becker 107). What characterizes good lighting?

Not surprisingly, the best light for office needs is natural daylight. In daylight conditions, perception is sharpest and eye fatigue is minimal (Makower 77). Workers invariably prefer daylight when they have the option (Riggs 294). For south-facing windows, tinted glass or a sunshade is obviously essential in summer months (Riggs 294). Daylight is uncontroversial. Problems arise when artificial light must be introduced.

The most common source of artificial light is the fluorescent tube. Many tubes flicker, an effect that can be irritating. Makower's study finds that harsh white or yellow tubes are perceived as more "glaring" than pink or orange ones. Red and blue fluorescent tubes have been linked to depression and should be avoided (81).

Margin notes:

Kallaus and Keeling are identified (an earlier mention of their work merely picked up a statistic).

A whole chain of comments occurs in a single paragraph; they can be sourcenoted as a single cluster.

The first time an abbreviation occurs, it is spelled out in full in parentheses.

An anonymous article is sourcenoted by the short title (normally, the word under which it is alphabetized).

Makower is identified.

A quick succession of separate points is sourcenoted one by one.

R. Di Michiel 4

In this paragraph, only the documented sentences are attributed to a source; the first part of the paragraph contains the writer's own remarks.

A recent development is the extensive use of VDT's in the office. There is little published research on the lighting best suited to these screens. Screens reflect strongly any light that shines directly on them, so indirect lighting is essential, though difficult to achieve in a landscape office: indirect lighting for one screen may cause glare on another. Certainly light levels must be reduced for the automated office (Makower 80, Pollack 38). There is no authoritative research, but Makower suggests cutting the normal office light level of 70 candlepower to between 15 and 20 candlepower in an automated office, a very steep reduction (80).

Once again, my informal survey found several offices in which commonsense rules are not followed, especially with regard to VDT's. Many screens had direct sunlight falling on them, making them illegible unless the shadow of the operator shielded the screen. In some offices, secretaries were using typewriters while word processors stood idly on a shelf: the reason was that the screen "caused eyestrain." In this case, a simple problem of incorrect lighting was wasting a costly investment in electronic equipment. Presumably redesigning the office around the new equipment was felt to be too time-consuming.

The full form of this abbreviation was given earlier.

Noise

Next to improper lighting, intolerable levels of noise are the main office hazard. In the landscape office, hundreds of people work together, and the level of noise can become frightening. The efffect on productivity is disastrous. Top executives at the Omega watch company found that the very early morning or late evening were the only periods quiet enough for serious work (Makower 138). No noise standard exists for office workers, although the 90 decibel limit fixed for factory workers by the Occupational Safety and Health Administration also applies in offices. Kallaus and Keeling report office workers suffering from stress fatigue at a mere 70 decibels (342). They recommend the use of sound-absorbent materials wherever possible: in particular, carpets, ceiling tiles, and partitions should be used to reduce noise. The traditional ringing telephone, they say, has no place in the landscape office (342).

Music should perhaps be mentioned here as "positive noise." Makower reports that some large firms claim success with office music, although the subject is controversial. What seems to work best is a range of musical styles, though with nothing too exciting. Rock'n'roll, for example, produces a high level of stress. The best time to play music appears to be before the morning break, before lunch, and before quitting time (139). It is easy to imagine that a tactful use of music in this way could make an office seem more pleasant.

This page reference is quite widely separated from its author. Such separation cannot cross the boundaries of a paragraph.

Personal comment and comment from a source are blended here.

Of the ten offices I visited, only two had the simplest noise-control device, carpet. (These were the recently designed offices, once more.) The carpet gave them a more comfortable, quieter atmosphere. In both offices, the noise of the telephone had also been subdued. I have no evidence that this makes the workers in these offices more productive, but the research suggests that it might (Kallaus and Keeling 341).

Equipment

For many workers, their workplace consists of a computer terminal and a chair in which they spend ever greater amounts of time (Minicucci, "Designing" 42). Rick Minicucci, a well-published

Minicucci contributed two articles. The note makes it clear which article is referred to.

R. Di Michiel 5

Minicucci is
identified.

writer on such down-to-earth subjects, points out that in one important respect, the chair and the terminal are representative of hundreds of items of equipment: despite years of research, neither has been ergonomically perfected. I will discuss the chair first, since it has been around the longer.

A chair must be stable, and it must be comfortable. A typical work-station chair runs on wheels. If it has four wheels, it is unstable; it needs five. As to comfort, research is continuing (Stockton 16). A chair should have a fully adjustable seat height and back rest; it should have no hard front edge, because this cuts off the blood supply to the legs. A poorly-designed chair leads to discomfort and medical problems, but no one chair design is right for every worker. For this reason, Thomas Sinopoli, writing in Today's Office, suggests that each worker should be allowed to test a range of chairs and to select the most comfortable (49). Selection should not take the appearance of the chair into account - - the best-looking office furniture is seldom the most practical (Minicucci, "Chairs" 21). Backache and neckache - - after a hundred years of typing chairs, these things are still with us.

Sinopoli is
identified.

This is the
second
article by
Minicucci.

The computer terminal is also a potential source of physical problems. Long-term use of the VDT may produce depression, eye irritation or even cataracts (Makower 90). Slightly more sinister are the low levels of radiation emitted by cathode-ray tubes: again the long-term effects are uncertain, as Mary Cooper concluded in a well-researched report (535). Psychological problems are better documented: alienation, loneliness, and isolation are often reported. Stress is also common because a supervisor can so easily monitor and compare the output of employees ("Painting" 48, Makower 85).

Cooper is
identified.

Double
reference to
an author
and an
anonymous
source.

In my own survey, I naturally made no long-term observations about radiation from computers. I did, however, find out some startling facts about chairs. Chairs with four wheels are still common, although they are dangerous. In none of the ten offices surveyed were employees (below the rank of senior manager or executive secretary) consulted about their chairs, even though they spent up to seven hours a day sitting in them. I saw many chairs with cushions attached to them in various ways, a sure sign that something is wrong. Even the well-designed offices had apparently made no attempt to consult the worker about this most basic of day-to-day concerns.

Conclusion

This is a
second
informative
endnote, this
time in
mid-
sentence. It
is
consecutively
numbered as
Note 2.

In a survey conducted in 1981,[2] Working Women found that 72% of those interviewed rated their offices as "stressful" (41). Stress can obviously arise from factors other than the office environment, but, as we have seen, the environment often contributes significantly to stress. Researchers now know enough to minimize environmental stress: color, light, noise, physical comfort - - such things can be brought under control. Can be. As shown in Table 1, my untrained eye and casual observation spotted many deficiencies in ten probably typical offices.

R. Di Michiel 6

A table is given two labels: the word *Table* and a number, and a title. In the title only main words are capitalized.

The appearance of the table is rather unsophisticated. No one will complain if you make improvements.

Table 1

Deficiencies Occurring in Ten Landscape Offices Surveyed by the Writer

	Follow Recommendations	Do Not Follow Recommendations	Partly Follow Recommendations
Desks clustered in small groups	1	8	1
Workflow moving from group to group	1	8	1
Color coordinated	2	8	0
Color appropriate to sunshine	2	8	0
Use of large pictures	3	5	2
VDT's placed to cut glare	3	6	1
Noise-absorbent surfaces used	2	8	0
Chairs selected by workers	0	10	0

The thesis statement.

The conclusion is inescapable: if these figures are typical, then office managers are paying little heed to what researchers have learned about office productivity. This could be an expensive mistake.

CONCLUSION—A RESEARCH PAPER

The *Notes*
begin a new
page. The
number of
the note is
raised half a
line and it is
not followed
by a period.
Each note is
indented 5
spaces, like a
normal
paragraph.

R. Di Michiel 7

The *Notes*
page is
numbered.

Notes

[1] Since overcrowding can create a health hazard, especially in an office where smoking is allowed, employers may well face law suits on these grounds (Hubbard 21).

[2] This survey was difficult to evaluate, because it mentioned neither the number of respondents nor the sampling technique used.

R. Di Michiel 8 | The *Works Cited* page is numbered.

The heading *Works Cited* is centered, but it is not underlined or capitalized.

Bibliography items are in alphabetical order. If an item runs onto a second line, the second line is indented five spaces.

The form of the bibliography entries follows *MLA* guidelines exactly. See Chapter 13.

Works Cited

Becker, Franklin. The Successful Office. Reading: Addison, 1982.

Cooper, Mary H. "Technology and Employment." Editorial Research Reports 22 July 1983: 535–539.

Hubbard, William S. "Smoking at Work: An Emerging Office Issue." Administrative Management
    Feb. 1986: 21–24.

Kallaus, Norman F., and Lewis B. Keeling. Administrative Office Management. Cincinnati:
    Southwestern, 1983.

Karvonen, Martti J. "Ergonomics: A Young Technology." World Health July–Aug. 1974: 30–35.

Klein, Judy G. The Office Book. New York: Facts on File, 1982.

Laufer, Arthur C. Operations Management. Cincinnati: Southwestern, 1975.

Linscott, Judy. "The Workplace is Changing . . . but not Fast." Daily News 10 Mar. 1981,
    New York City ed.: 25+.

Makower, Joel. Office Hazards. Washington: Tilden, 1981.

Minicucci, Rick. "Designing the Masterpiece Office." Today's Office Nov. 1985: 41–43.

- - -. "Office Chairs: Sitting down on the Job." Today's Office Mar. 1986: 18–21.

"Painting Cures the Hi-tech 'Blah's.'" Administrative Management Mar. 1986: 48–49.

Pollack, Randel. "Where Automation is Taking Office Design." Office Administration and Automation
    Jan. 1983: 36–39.

Riggs, James L. Production Systems. 3rd ed. New York: Wiley, 1981.

Sinopoli, Thomas R. "Overcoming User Resistance to O.A.: Part Two." Today's Office Mar. 1982:
    49–50.

Stockton, Richard F. "Ergonomics: Science or Art?" The Lamp Spring 1984: 16+.

"Warning: Health Hazards for Office Workers." Working Women Apr. 1981: 31+.

• Afterword

When your research paper is finally returned to you and when you've digested your instructor's comments, a long path of study will have come to an end. In pursuing that path, you'll have mastered the principles that underlie good academic writing. This doesn't mean there are no more challenges; every paper you write will be a new mountain to climb. But, like the skillful mountaineer, you'll know how to think through the climb ahead, you'll know the right tools for the job, and you'll know how to use them. Good luck on the way up.

A

Abstract:
    as overview of essay 114–115
Abstraction:
    see also Hot air; distinguished from
    concreteness 3–6, 267–268; degrees of 3–6;
    degeneration into "hot air" 5; as reduction in
    cost-effectiveness 35
Abstracts:
    use of in a search for sources in periodicals
    328–329
Absurdity in sources:
    see Evaluating information
Accepted authority, argument using an:
    see Argument
Accessibility:
    of material and message to a reader 272–273,
    277
Adjectives:
    coordinate 38; in a series 38; compound 38
Adverbial clauses:
    see Subordinate clauses
Agreement:
    see Subject-verb agreement
All-or-nothing choice, argument based on:
    see Argument
Alternative:
    as a form of the thesis statement 105, 106
Ambiguity:
    check for 165
Analysis:
    in hierarchy of learning skills xv–xvi
"And":
    plain-and vs. comma-and 38
Anecdote:
    see Narrative
"Anglo-Saxon" vs. "Norman-French" words:
    see Style

APA standard:
    for bibliographies 338, 348–349; for
    sourcenotes 408
Apostrophe:
    correctness check for 37
Application:
    in hierarchy of learning skills xv–xvi
Argument:
    use of argument in making a case 233–241; fair
    vs. unfair argument 233–234; logical vs. illogical
    argument 233–234; solutio ad hominem
    (making a case that satisfies the audience but is
    untrue) 234–236; solutio ad hominem
    distinguished from solutio recta (making a true
    case) 233–234; examples of ad hominem
    arguments – argument using an accepted
    authority 234, argument based on prejudice
    234–235, argument based on a concession
    235, arguments based on fear, pity or greed
    235–236, 247, argument based on unverifiable
    information 236; examples of non sequiturs –
    confusion of chronology with causality 236–237,
    the pure non sequitur 237, 248, false analogy
    237–238; examples of misleading options –
    all-or-nothing choice 238, 248, false dilemma
    238; summary of types 239–240; exercise on
    the types 240–241; syllogistic argument
    366–371; inductive evidence and scientific
    method 372–377; checklist for evaluating
    arguments 377–378; rebuttal of false arguments
    414–419
Argumentum ad . . . :
    see Argument (under English translation)
Arithmetic mean:
    see Statistics
"As":
    see Comparison clauses
Author card:
    in library catalog 321–322